THE COMPLETE RESULTS AND LINE-UPS OF THE UEFA EUROPA LEAGUE 2021-2024

Dirk Karsdorp

British Library Cataloguing in Publication Data
A catalogue record for this book is available from the British Library

ISBN: 978-1-86223-528-1

Copyright © 2024, SOCCER BOOKS LIMITED (01472 696226)
72 St. Peter's Avenue, Cleethorpes, DN35 8HU, United Kingdom

Website   www.soccer-books.co.uk
e-mail   info@soccer-books.co.uk

All rights are reserved. No part of this publication may be reproduced, stored in a retrieval system or transmitted, in any form or by any means, electronic, mechanical, photocopying, recording, or otherwise, without the prior written permission of Soccer Books Limited.

Printed in the UK by 4edge Ltd

FOREWORD

Between the years of 1971 and 2009, the UEFA Cup was the second most important European Club competition, having itself superseded both the Fairs Cup and the European Cup-Winners' Cup competitions in this regard. From 1995 onwards, the Intertoto Cup also became an official UEFA competition and was, effectively, the third-ranked European club competition until it ended in 2008.

From 2009, in an attempt to streamline their club tournaments, UEFA decided to end both the UEFA Cup and the Intertoto Cup competitions and instead replaced them with a single highly-ranked competition named the UEFA Europa League. This proved to be a great success but, in 2021, UEFA's desire to further-increase the number of clubs playing in Europe led to the introduction a new third-tier competition, the UEFA Europa Conference League. This new competition was intended as a means of giving clubs from the lower-ranked UEFA member countries a chance of progressing beyond their customary elimination in the qualifiers for the group stages of the Champions League and Europa League. It also, of course, allowed UEFA the opportunity to sell TV broadcasting and media rights for another competition!

The introduction of this new competition meant that the scope of the UEFA Europa League was greatly reduced as the many clubs from low-ranked UEFA countries who had previously entered a lengthy qualification process, instead entered the Europa Conference League directly. This meant that the rather bloated Europa League was slimmed down as many fewer qualification matches were played before the group stage which itself was reduced to 8 groups instead of 12 groups.

This publication provides a comprehensive statistical record of the UEFA Europa League competition from the first game played in the qualifying stages of the 2021/2022 competition through to the 2024 Final itself. Similar publications covering the Europa League from 2009-2012, 2012-2015, 2015-2018 and 2018-2021 are also available from Soccer Books Limited as is a book covering the first two seasons of the UEFA Europa Conference League, 2021-2023. We also publish a selection of books containing statistics for other European competitions including the Champions League, the earlier European Cup and the European Cup-Winners Cup. Please check the back page of this book for a listing of these and many other of our publications.

Although the contents of this book are, we believe, as accurate as possible, it is not always easy to obtain reliable statistics for such a pan-European competition. On occasions, different sources can provide different information for the same match, particularly in relation to attendances. In such cases as this the most trustworthy information which could be discovered was used in this book.

Throughout this book, rather than use English spellings, we have used the correct spelling of Club names and places as used in the country of origin. For example, Rome is Roma, Copenhagen is København etc.

UEFA EUROPA LEAGUE
2021-2022

THIRD QUALIFYING ROUND

(Champions Path)

03.08.21 Bakcell Arena, Baku: Neftçi PFK – HJK Helsinki 2-2 (0-0)
Neftçi PFK: Aqil Mammadov (18' Kamran Ibrahimov), Vojislav Stankovic, Mamadou Mbodj, Emin Makhmudov, Romain Basque, Khayal Najafov (71' Fahmin Muradbayli), Sabir Bougrine, Mamadou Kané, Yusuf Lawal, César Meza Colli (76' Mirabdulla Abbasov), Harramiz. Coach: Samir Abbasov.
HJK Helsinki: Jakob Tånnander, Valtteri Moren, Janne Saksela (75' Matti Peltola), Daniel O'Shaughnessy, Luis Murillo, Miro Tenho, Filip Valencic (90' Anthony Olusanya), Lucas Lingman, Jair, Roope Riski, David Browne (55' Riku Riski). Coach: Toni Koskela.
Goals: 59' Sabir Bougrine 1-0, 61' Roope Riski 1-1, 65' Jair 1-2, 80' Emin Makhmudov 2-2.
Referee: William Collum (SCO) Attendance: 3,500

05.08.21 Otaliq Stadion, Almaty: FK Kairat – FC Alashkert 0-0
FK Kairat: Stas Pokatilov, Denis Polyakov, Yan Vorogovskiy, Rade Dugalic, Nuraly Alip, Kamo Hovhannisyan, Aybol Abiken, Gulzhygit Alykulov (72' Daniyar Usenov), Arsen Buranchiev (63' Ricardo Alves), Vágner Love, Artur Shushenachev (84' Andrey Ulshin). Coach: Kirill Keker.
FC Alashkert: Ognjen Cancarevic, Dejan Boljevic, Didier Kadio, Taron Voskanyan, Tiago Cametá, James (62' Aghvan Papikyan), Artak Grigoryan, Rumyan Hovsepyan (75' Vincent Bezecourt), Branko Mihajlovic (81' Artak Yedigaryan), David Khurtsidze, Aleksandar Glisic (62' Nikita Tankov). Coach: Aleksandr Grigoryan.
Referee: Aleksei Kulbakov (BLS) Attendance: played behind closed doors.

Aleksandar Glisic missed a penalty kick (36').

05.08.21 Neo GSP Stadium, Strovolos: Omonia Nicosia – FC Flora Tallinn 1-0 (1-0)
Omonia Nicosia: Fabiano, Jan Lecjaks, Tomás Hubocan (46' Nikolas Panagiotou), Ádám Lang, Jordi Gómez, Éric Bauthéac, Mikkel Diskerud, Abdullahi Shehu, Marinos Tzionis (80' Kiko), Marko Scepovic (80' Andronikos Kakoullis), Loizos Loizou (64' Fotis Papoulis). Coach: Henning Berg.
FC Flora Tallinn: Matvei Igonen, Märten Kuusk, Henrik Pürg, Marco Lukka (80' Ken Kallaste), Michael Lilander, Konstantin Vassiljev, Henrik Ojamaa, Martin Miller, Markus Soomets (62' Markus Poom), Sergei Zenjov (75' Rauno Alliku), Rauno Sappinen. Coach: Jürgen Henn.
Goal: 12' Marinos Tzionis 1-0.
Referee: Radu Petrescu (ROM) Attendance: 8,033

05.08.21 Victoria Stadium, Gibraltar: Lincoln Red Imps – Slovan Bratislava 1-3 (0-1)
Lincoln Red Imps: Lolo Soler, Scott Wiseman, Bernardo Lopes, Jesús Toscano, Roy Chipolina (39' John Sergeant), Fernando Carralero (46' Braian Gómez), Liam Walker, Mustapha Yahaya, Marco Rosa (82' Kian Ronan), Lee Casciaro (82' Alan Araiza), Kike Gómez (69' Emmanuel Ocran). Coach: Michael McElwee.
Slovan Bratislava: Adrián Chovan, Guram Kashia, Vasil Bozhikov, Lukás Pauschek, Myenty Abena (46' Vernon De Marco), Jaba Kankava, Vladimír Weiss (86' Dejan Drazic), Ibrahim Rabiu, Jaromír Zmrhal (73' Dávid Hrncár), Ezekiel Henty (82' Joeri de Kamps), Dávid Strelec (73' Rafael Ratão). Coach: Vladimír Weiss.
Goals: 16' Guram Kashia 0-1, 48' Jarolím Zmrhal 0-2, 69' Ezekiel Henty 0-3, 73' Liam Walker 1-3 (p).
Referee: Athanasios Tzilos (GRE)   Attendance: 637

05.08.21 Mestni Stadion Fazanerija, Murska Sobota: NS Mura – FK Zalgiris 0-0
NS Mura: Matko Obradovic, Ziga Kous, Klemen Sturm (87' Klemen Pucko), Jan Gorenc, Zan Karnicnik, Matic Marusko, Alen Kozar (67' Mitja Lotric), Luka Bobicanec (87' Amadej Marosa), Tomi Horvat, Mihael Klepac (67' Ziga Skoflek), Kai Cipot (67' Nik Lorbek). Coach: Ante Simundza.
FK Zalgiris: Edvinas Gertmonas, Joël Bopesu, Elhadji Pape Diaw, Nemanja Ljubisavljevic, Ogenyi Onazi (74' Mantas Kuklys), Hugo Vidémont (87' Gustas Jarusevicius), Ovidijus Verbickas, Francis Kyeremeh (74' Josip Tadic), Karolis Uzéla, Jakub Sylvestr (54' Tomislav Kis), Saulius Mikoliūnas. Coach: Vladimir Cheburin.
Referee: Andreas Ekberg (SWE)   Attendance: 2,500

10.08.21 A. Le Coq Arena, Tallinn: FC Flora Tallinn – Omonia Nicosia 2-1 (0-1,2-1) (AET)
FC Flora Tallinn: Matvei Igonen, Ken Kallaste (83' Marco Lukka), Märten Kuusk, Henrik Pürg, Michael Lilander, Konstantin Vassiljev (112' Rocco Shein), Henrik Ojamaa, Martin Miller (77' Rauno Alliku), Markus Poom (78' Markus Soomets), Sergei Zenjov, Rauno Sappinen (109' Sten Reinkort). Coach: Jürgen Henn.
Omonia Nicosia: Fabiano, Ádám Lang, Kiko (81' Héctor Yuste), Jordi Gómez, Éric Bauthéac (52' Fotis Papoulis), Mikkel Diskerud (105' Andreas Asimenos), Abdullahi Shehu (105' Iyayi Atiemwen), Marinos Tzionis, Nikolas Panagiotou, Andronikos Kakoullis (90' Angelos Zefki), Loizos Loizou (85' Paris Psaltis). Coach: Henning Berg.
Goals: 43' Andronikos Kakoullis 0-1, 48', 88' Rauno Sappinen 1-1, 2-1.
Referee: Ivan Kruzliak (SVK)   Attendance: 1,560
Sent off: 120+1' Märten Kuusk.

Omonia Nicosia won on penalties (5:4).

Penalties: Jordi Gómez 1-0, Ojamaa 1-1, Papoulis 2-1, Zenjov 2-2, Atiemwen 3-2,
  Lilander 3-3, Psaltis 4-3, Lukka missed, Lang missed, Alliku 4-4,
  Héctor Yuste 5-4, Reinkort missed.

10.08.21   Stadión Tehelné pole, Bratislava: Slovan Bratislava – Lincoln Red Imps 1-1 (1-0)
Slovan Bratislava: Michal Sulla, Guram Kashia, Vasil Bozhikov, Lukás Pauschek (90+1'
Richard Krizan), Vernon De Marco, Jaba Kankava, Vladimír Weiss (90+1' Filip Lichý), Joeri
de Kamps, Jaromír Zmrhal, Ezekiel Henty (70' Rafael Ratão), Dávid Strelec (80' Aleksandar
Cavric). Coach: Vladimír Weiss.
Lincoln Red Imps: Lolo Soler, Scott Wiseman, Bernardo Lopes, Ethan Britto, Fernando
Carralero (66' Braian Gómez), Liam Walker, John Sergeant (86' Julian Valarino), Marco Rosa
(86' Kian Ronan), Graeme Torrilla, Lee Casciaro (79' Alan Araiza), Emmanuel Ocran (66'
Kike Gómez). Coach: Michael McElwee.
Goals: 38' Jaromír Zmrhal 1-0, 90' Kike Gómez 1-1.
Referee: Mykola Balakin (UKR)   Attendance: 4,688
Sent off: 54' Vernon De Marco.

12.08.21   Vazgen Sargsyan anvan Hanrapetakan Marzadasht, Yerevan:
           FC Alashkert – FK Kairat 3-2 (1-1,2-2) (AET)
FC Alashkert: Ognjen Cancarevic, Dejan Boljevic (97' Grigor Aghekyan), Didier Kadio, Taron
Voskanyan, Tiago Cametá, James (70' Wangu Gome), Artak Grigoryan, Rumyan Hovsepyan
(75' Vincent Bezecourt), Aghvan Papikyan (70' Artak Yedigaryan), David Khurtsidze, José
Embaló (82' Aleksandar Glisic). Coach: Aleksandr Grigoryan.
FK Kairat: Stas Pokatilov, Denis Polyakov, Macky Bagnack (65' Ricardo Alves), Dino
Mikanovic (112' Gulzhygit Alykulov), Yan Vorogovskiy (55' Artur Shushenachev), Rade
Dugalic, Nuraly Alip, Kamo Hovhannisyan, Aybol Abiken, Vágner Love, José Kanté (102'
Arsen Buranchiev). Coach: Kirill Keker.
Goals: 43' José Embaló 1-0, 45+1' Aybol Abiken 1-1, 50' José Embaló 2-1,
61' Artur Shushenachev 2-2, 103' Aleksandar Glisic 3-2.
Referee: Lawrence Visser (BEL)   Attendance: 7,000
Sent off: 62' Denis Polyakov, 91' Aybol Abiken.

FC Alashkert won after extra time.

*FC Alashkert played their home match at Vazgen Sargsyan anvan Hanrapetakan Marzadasht,
Yerevan, instead of their regular stadium Alashkert Stadium Yerevan, which did not meet
UEFA requirements.*

12.08.21   Bolt Arena, Helsinki: HJK Helsinki – Neftçi Baku 3-0 (0-0)
HJK Helsinki: Jakob Tånnander, Valtteri Moren, Janne Saksela (76' Kevin Kouassivi-
Benissan), Daniel O'Shaughnessy, Luis Murillo, Miro Tenho, Filip Valencic (82' Tim Sparv),
Lucas Lingman (89' Matti Peltola), Jair, Roope Riski, David Browne (46' Riku Riski).
Coach: Toni Koskela.
Neftçi PFK: Aqil Mammadov, Vojislav Stankovic, Mamadou Mbodj (72' Mert Çelik), Emin
Makhmudov, Romain Basque, Sabir Bougrine, Mamadou Kané, Yusuf Lawal, César Meza
Colli (72' Khayal Najafov), Harramiz, Mirabdulla Abbasov (63' Fahmin Muradbayli).
Coach: Samir Abbasov.
Goals: 46' Riku Riski 1-0, 60', 89' Roope Riski 2-0 (p), 3-0.
Referee: Deniz Aytekin (GER)   Attendance: 4,068

12.08.21   Vilniaus LFF stadionas, Vilnius: FK Zalgiris – NS Mura 0-1 (0-1)
FK Zalgiris: Edvinas Gertmonas, Joël Bopesu, Elhadji Pape Diaw, Nemanja Ljubisavljevic, Ogenyi Onazi, Hugo Vidémont, Francis Kyeremeh (59' Jakub Sylvestr), Karolis Uzéla (84' Milen Gamakov), Josip Tadic, Tomislav Kis, Saulius Mikoliūnas. Coach: Vladimir Cheburin.
NS Mura: Matko Obradovic, Ziga Kous, Klemen Sturm, Jan Gorenc, Zan Karnicnik, Matic Marusko, Alen Kozar, Luka Bobicanec, Tomi Horvat (71' Nik Lorbek), Mitja Lotric (71' Mihael Klepac), Kai Cipot (64' Ziga Skoflek). Coach: Ante Simundza.
Goal: 12' Ziga Kous 0-1.
Referee: Bartosz Frankowski (POL)   Attendance: 2,921

(Main Path)

05.08.21   Stadion Strelnice, Jablonec nad Nisou: FK Jablonec – Celtic FC 2-4 (1-2)
FK Jablonec: Jan Hanus, Jan Krob, Jaroslav Zelený, Michal Surzyn, Jakub Martinec, Václav Pilar (78' Libor Holík), Jakub Povazanec (86' Tomás Hübschman), Vojtech Kubista (85' Tomás Cvancara), Milos Kratochvíl (74' David Houska), Dominik Plestil (73' Tomás Malínský), Martin Dolezal. Coach: Petr Rada.
Celtic FC: Joe Hart, Carl Starfelt, Anthony Ralston, Greg Taylor, Nir Bitton, James Forrest, Callum McGregor, David Turnbull (65' Ryan Christie), Ismaila Soro, Kyogo Furuhashi (66' Odsonne Édouard), Liel Abada (65' Tom Rogic). Coach: Ange Postecoglou.
Goals: 12' Liel Abada 0-1, 16' Kyogo Furuhashi 0-2, 17' Václav Pilar 1-2, 64' James Forrest 1-3, 85' Nir Bitton 2-3 (og), 90' Ryan Christie 2-4.
Referee: Halil Umut Meler (TUR)   Attendance: 4,805

05.08.21   Basaksehir Fatih Terim Stadyumu, Istanbul:
              Galatasaray – St Johnstone FC 1-1 (0-0)
Galatasaray: Fernando Muslera, Patrick van Aanholt (46' Ömer Bayram), Marcão Teixeira, Christian Luyindama, Sacha Boey, Aytaç Kara (57' Berk Balaban *goalkeeper*), Taylan Antalyali, Kerem Aktürkoglu, Berkan Kutlu (86' Jesse Sekidika), Ryan Babel (46' Arda Turan), Mostafa Mohamed (46' Mbaye Diagne). Coach: Fatih Terim.
St Johnstone FC: Zander Clark, Shaun Rooney (87' James Brown), Liam Gordon, Jamie McCart, Jason Kerr, Reece Devine (88' Callum Booth), Murray Davidson, David Wotherspoon, Alistair McCann, Michael O'Halloran (76' Callum Hendry), Christopher Kane (62' Stevie May). Coach: Callum Davidson.
Goals: 58' Jason Kerr 0-1 (p), 60' Sacha Boey 1-1.
Referee: Sandro Schärer (SUI)   Attendance: 6,216
Sent off: 55' Fernando Muslera.

Galatasaray played their home match at Basaksehir Fatih Terim Stadyumu, Istanbul, instead of their regular stadium Türk Telekom Stadium, Istanbul, due to renovation.

05.08.21 Allianz Stadion, Vienna: Rapid Wien – Anorthosis Famagusta 3-0 (1-0)
Rapid Wien: Richard Strebinger, Maximilian Hofmann, Maximilian Ullmann, Leo Greiml, Christoph Knasmüllner (71' Lion Schuster), Thorsten Schick, Srdjan Grahovac, Taxiarchis Fountas (78' Oliver Strunz), Ercan Kara, Marco Grüll (87' Lukas Sulzbacher), Kelvin Arase (78' Jonas Auer). Coach: Dietmar Kühbauer.
Anorthosis Famagusta: Assaf Tzur (59' Giorgi Loria), Paulus Arajuuri, Marios Antoniades, Anderson Correia, Pavlos Korrea (59' Hovhannes Hambardzumyan), Lazaros Christodoulopoulos (72' Dimitris Christofi), Josef Husbauer, Kostakis Artymatas, Michalis Ioannou (46' Denis Popovic), Kyle Lafferty, Nikolaos Kaltsas (46' Milo Deletic).
Coach: Temuri Ketsbaia.
Goals: 35' Ercan Kara 1-0, 64' Taxiarchis Fountas 2-0, 83' Marco Grüll 3-0.
Referee: Maurizio Mariani (ITA)   Attendance: 11,400

Christoph Knasmüllner missed a penalty kick (62').

12.08.21 Stadio Antonis Papadopoulos, Larnaca:
Anorthosis Famagusta – Rapid Wien 2-1 (1-0)
Anorthosis Famagusta: Giorgi Loria, Paulus Arajuuri, Hovhannes Hambardzumyan, Anderson Correia, Spiros Risvanis, Lazaros Christodoulopoulos (76' Michalis Ioannou), Josef Husbauer (71' Charles Eloundou), Denis Popovic (76' Andreas Chrysostomou), Kostakis Artymatas, Kyle Lafferty (65' Onisiforos Roushias), Milo Deletic (65' Dimitris Christofi). Coach: Temuri Ketsbaia.
Rapid Wien: Richard Strebinger, Maximilian Hofmann, Maximilian Ullmann, Leo Greiml, Thorsten Schick (61' Kevin Wimmer), Srdjan Grahovac, Robert Ljubicic (60' Lion Schuster), Taxiarchis Fountas, Ercan Kara (79' Koya Kitagawa), Marco Grüll (68' Christoph Knasmüllner), Kelvin Arase (79' Lukas Sulzbacher). Coach: Dietmar Kühbauer.
Goals: 45+1' Kyle Lafferty 1-0, 64' Ercan Kara 1-1, 88' Onisiforos Roushias 2-1.
Referee: Aleksandar Stavrev (MKD)   Attendance: 3,574

12.08.21 McDiarmid Park, Perth: St Johnstone FC – Galatasaray 2-4 (1-1)
St Johnstone FC: Zander Clark, Callum Booth (82' Reece Devine), Liam Gordon, Jamie McCart, Jason Kerr, James Brown (67' Shaun Rooney), Liam Craig (71' Callum Hendry), Murray Davidson, Alistair McCann, Michael O'Halloran, Christopher Kane (66' Stevie May). Coach: Callum Davidson.
Galatasaray: Ismail Çipe, Patrick van Aanholt, Marcão Teixeira, Christian Luyindama, Sacha Boey, Arda Turan (73' Ryan Babel), Sofiane Féghouli (88' Emre Kilinç), Taylan Antalyali (89' Alpaslan Öztürk), Kerem Aktürkoglu (82' Mostafa Mohamed), Berkan Kutlu, Mbaye Diagne (83' Aytaç Kara). Coach: Fatih Terim.
Goals: 29' Mbaye Diagne 0-1, 36' Jason Kerr 1-1, 64' Kerem Aktürkoglu 1-2, 70' Sofiane Féghouli 1-3, 90+2' Emre Kilinç 1-4, 90+3' Michael O'Halloran 2-4.
Referee: Andris Treimanis (LAT)   Attendance: 9,106

12.08.21   Celtic Park, Glasgow: Celtic FC – FK Jablonec 3-0 (1-0)
Celtic FC: Joe Hart, Carl Starfelt, Anthony Ralston, Greg Taylor, Stephen Welsh, James Forrest, Callum McGregor (84' Nir Bitton), Tom Rogic (73' Ismaila Soro), Ryan Christie (74' Adam Montgomery), David Turnbull (74' Albian Ajeti), Kyogo Furuhashi (66' Odsonne Édouard). Coach: Ange Postecoglou.
FK Jablonec: Jan Hanus, Jan Krob, Jaroslav Zelený, Libor Holík, Václav Pilar (87' Tomás Smejkal), Jakub Povazanec (87' Jakub Martinec), David Houska, Vojtech Kubista, Milos Kratochvíl, Dominik Plestil (70' Tomás Malínský), Martin Dolezal (70' Tomás Cvancara). Coach: Petr Rada.
Goals: 26', 62' David Turnbull 1-0, 2-0, 70' James Forrest 3-0.
Referee: Daniel Siebert (GER)   Attendance: 50,076

PLAY-OFF ROUND

17.08.21   Stadion Rajko Mitic, Beograd: Crvena Zvezda Beograd – CFR Cluj 4-0 (2-0)
Crvena Zvezda Beograd: Milan Borjan, Aleksandar Dragovic, Milan Rodic, Milos Degenek (45+3' Radovan Pankov), Marko Gobeljic, Aleksandar Katai, Sékou Sanogo, Guélor Kanga (73' Nenad Krsticic), Mirko Ivanic (80' Slavoljub Srnic), El Fardou Ben Nabouhane, Milan Pavkov (80' Nikola Krstovic). Coach: Dejan Stankovic.
CFR Cluj: Griedius Arlauskis, Camora, Mike Cestor, Cristian Manea, Denis Ciobotariu, Ciprian Deac (71' Catalin Itu), Rúnar Sigurjónsson, Jonathan Rodríguez, Claudiu Petrila, Billel Omrani (62' Denis Alibec), Gabriel Debeljuh (62' Valentin Ionut Costache). Coach: Marius Sumudica.
Goals: 5' Milan Pavkov 1-0, 38' Aleksandar Katai 2-0, 68' El Fardou Ben Nabouhane 3-0, 77' Mirko Ivanic 4-0.
Referee: Georgi Kabakov (BUL)   Attendance: 22,482

18.08.21   Celtic Park, Glasgow: Celtic FC – AZ Alkmaar 2-0 (1-0)
Celtic FC: Joe Hart, Carl Starfelt, Anthony Ralston, Greg Taylor, Stephen Welsh, James Forrest, Callum McGregor, Tom Rogic (75' James McCarthy), David Turnbull (88' Ismaila Soro), Kyogo Furuhashi (74' Adam Montgomery), Liel Abada (58' Odsonne Édouard). Coach: Ange Postecoglou.
AZ Alkmaar: Hobie Verhulst, Bruno Martins Indi, Timo Letschert, Thijs Oosting, Yukinari Sugawara, Fredrik Midtsjø (72' Jordy Clasie), Albert Gudmundsson (72' Håkon Evjen), Dani de Wit, Teun Koopmeiners, Vangelis Pavlidis (80' Ernest Poku), Zakaria Aboukhlal. Coach: Pascal Jansen.
Goals: 11' Kyogo Furuhashi 1-0, 61' Timo Letschert 2-0 (og).
Referee: Ovidiu Hategan (ROM)   Attendance: 52,916

19.08.21   Neo GSP Stadium, Nicosia: Omonia Nicosia – Royal Antwerp FC 4-2 (1-1)
Omonia Nicosia: Fabiano, Jan Lecjaks, Ádám Lang, Jordi Gómez, Mikkel Diskerud (76' Panayiotis Zachariou), Fouad Bachirou (81' Paris Psaltis), Abdullahi Shehu, Nikolas Panagiotou, Fotis Papoulis (81' Michal Duris), Andronikos Kakoullis (73' Iyayi Atiemwen), Loizos Loizou (73' Marinos Tzionis). Coach: Henning Berg.
Royal Antwerp FC: Jean Butez, Ritchie De Laet, Björn Engels (77' Abdoulaye Seck), Samuel Vines, Jelle Bataille (77' Aurélio Buta), Pieter Gerkens (60' Koji Miyoshi), Birger Verstraete, Alhassan Yusuf, Benson Manuel (60' Radja Nainggolan), Johannes Eggestein (89' Faris Haroun), Michel Balikwisha. Coach: Brian Priske.
Goals: 26' Benson Manuel 0-1, 43' Loizos Loizou 1-1, 48' Andronikos Kakoullis 2-1, 55' Loizos Loizou 3-1, 62' Koji Miyoshi 3-2, 84' Iyayi Atiemwen 4-2 (p).
Referee: Andreas Ekberg (SWE)   Attendance: 7,585

19.08.21   Cepheus Park Randers, Randers: Randers FC – Galatasaray 1-1 (0-1)
Randers FC: Patrik Carlgren, Björn Kopplin, Erik Marxen, Simon Piesinger, Mikkel Kallesøe (76' Oliver Bundgaard Kristensen), Simon Tibbing (64' Jakob Andersen), Vito Hammershøy-Mistrati (76' Filip Bundgaard Kristensen), Frederik Lauenborg, Lasse Berg Johnsen, Tobias Klysner (64' Tosin Kehinde), Marvin Egho (87' Nicolai Brock-Madsen).
Coach: Thomas Thomasberg.
Galatasaray: Fernando Muslera, Patrick van Aanholt, Alpaslan Öztürk, DeAndre Yedlin, Christian Luyindama, Taylan Antalyali (84' Aytaç Kara), Emre Kılınç (61' Arda Turan), Emre Akbaba (61' Sofiane Féghouli), Kerem Aktürkoglu (61' Ryan Babel), Berkan Kutlu, Mostafa Mohamed (76' Radamel Falcao). Coach: Fatih Terim.
Goals: 26' Kerem Aktürkoglu 0-1, 54' Frederik Lauenborg 1-1.
Referee: Jesús Gil Manzano (ESP)   Attendance: 7,064

19.08.21   Sinobo Stadium, Prague: Slavia Praha – Legia Warszawa 2-2 (2-2)
Slavia Praha: Ondrej Kolár, Alexander Bah, David Zima, Nicolae Stanciu (82' Stanislav Tecl), Tomás Holes, Lukás Masopust (67' Daniel Samek), Jakub Hromada (46' Jan Kuchta), Ibrahim Traoré, Oscar Dorley, Ivan Schranz (61' Ondrej Lingr), Abdallah Sima (61' Ubong Ekpai).
Coach: Jindich Trpisovský.
Legia Warszawa: Artur Boruc, Lindsay Rose (46' Mateusz Holownia), Filip Mladenovic, Mateusz Wieteska, Josip Juranovic, Maik Nawrocki, André Martins, Luquinhas, Kacper Skibicki (46' Maciej Rosolek), Rafael Lopes (46' Josué), Mahir Emreli.
Coach: Czeslaw Michniewicz.
Goals: 20' Mahir Emreli 0-1, 33' Alexander Bah 1-1, 37' Josip Juranovic 1-2, 45+3' Lukás Masopust 2-2.
Referee: Felix Zwayer (GER)   Attendance: 14,543

19.08.21   Mestni Stadion Fazanerija, Murska Sobota: NS Mura – Sturm Graz 1-3 (1-1)
NS Mura: Matko Obradovic, Ziga Kous, Klemen Sturm, Jan Gorenc, Zan Karnicnik (71' Amadej Marosa), Matic Marusko, Ziga Skoflek (71' Klemen Pucko), Alen Kozar, Luka Bobicanec (62' Stanisa Mandic), Tomi Horvat, Mitja Lotric (79' Mihael Klepac).
Coach: Ante Simundza.
Sturm Graz: Jörg Siebenhandl, Gregory Wüthrich, Jusuf Gazibegovic (81' Lukas Jäger), David Affengruber, Amadou Dante, Stefan Hierländer, Jon Stankovic, Ivan Ljubic (80' Niklas Geyrhofer), Otar Kiteishvili (76' Andreas Kuen), Jakob Jantscher (66' Manprit Sarkaria), Kelvin Yeboah (75' Anderson Niangbo). Coach: Christian Ilzer.
Goals: 3' Ziga Skoflek 1-0, 18' Jakob Jantscher 1-1 (p), 60' Otar Kiteishvili 1-2, 63' Kelvin Yeboah 1-3.
Referee: Michael Oliver (ENG)   Attendance: 4,000

19.08.21   Ülker Stadyumu Fenerbahçe Sükrü Saracoglu Sport Kompleksi, Istanbul:
Fenerbahçe – HJK Helsinki 1-0 (0-0)
Fenerbahçe: Altay Bayindir, Serdar Aziz, Filip Novák (67' Arda Güler), Marcel Tisserand, Attila Szalai, Mesut Özil (62' Muhammed Gümüskaya), Luiz Gustavo, José Sosa, Miha Zajc, Irfan Kahveci (55' Ferdi Kadioglu), Bright Osayi-Samuel (62' Nazim Sangaré).
Coach: Vítor Pereira.
HJK Helsinki: Jakob Tånnander, Valtteri Moren, Janne Saksela, Daniel O'Shaughnessy, Luis Murillo (86' Matti Peltola), Tim Sparv (81' Santeri Väänänen), Filip Valencic (87' Anthony Olusanya), Santeri Hostikka (81' Kevin Kouassivi-Benissan), Jair, Riku Riski (64' David Browne), Roope Riski. Coach: Toni Koskela.
Goal: 65' Muhammed Gümüskaya 1-0.
Referee: Benoît Bastien (FRA)   Attendance: 6,769

19.08.21   Allianz Stadion, Vienna: Rapid Wien – Zorya Lugansk 3-0 (1-0)
Rapid Wien: Richard Strebinger, Filip Stojkovic (71' Thorsten Schick), Maximilian Hofmann, Maximilian Ullmann, Leo Greiml, Srdjan Grahovac (79' Lion Schuster), Robert Ljubicic (80' Dejan Petrovic), Taxiarchis Fountas (60' Christoph Knasmüllner), Ercan Kara, Marco Grüll, Kelvin Arase (79' Koya Kitagawa). Coach: Dietmar Kühbauer.
Zorya Lugansk: Mykyta Shevchenko, Vitaliy Vernydub, Maksym Imerekov (85' Lovro Cvek), Denys Favorov, Juninho, Artem Gromov (64' Shahab Zahedi Tabar), Vladyslav Kochergin, Sergiy Buletsa (84' Cristian), Yegor Nazaryna, Vladyslav Kabaev (76' Dmytro Khomchenovskyi), Allahyar Sayyadmanesh (84' Raymond Owusu). Coach: Viktor Skrypnyk.
Goals: 29' Taxiarchis Fountas 1-0, 78' Ercan Kara 2-0, 85' Marco Grüll 3-0.
Referee: Sandro Schärer (SUI)   Attendance: 13,900

19.08.21   Stadio Georgios Karaiskáki, Piraeus:
Olympiakos Piraeus – Slovan Bratislava 3-0 (1-0)
Olympiakos Piraeus: Tomás Vaclík, Sokratis Papastathopoulos, Kenny Lala, Pape Cissé (75' Svetozar Markovic), Oleg Reabciuc, Mathieu Valbuena (74' Henry Onyekuru), Yann M'Vila, Giorgis Masouras (87' Marios Vrousai), Mohamed Camara (81' Pierre Malong), Youssef El-Arabi, Aguibou Camara (80' Andreas Bouchalakis). Coach: Pedro Martins.
Slovan Bratislava: Adrián Chovan, Guram Kashia, Vasil Bozhikov, Lukás Pauschek (67' Dávid Strelec), Myenty Abena, Jaba Kankava, Vladimír Weiss, Ibrahim Rabiu (67' Ezekiel Henty), Joeri de Kamps, Jaromír Zmrhal, Aleksandar Cavric. Coach: Vladimír Weiss.
Goals: 37' Mohamed Camara 1-0, 52' Pape Cissé 2-0, 68' Vasil Bozhikov 3-0 (og).
Referee: Marco Guida (ITA)   Attendance: 9,823

19.08.21   Ibrox Stadium, Glasgow: Glasgow Rangers FC – FC Alashkert 1-0 (0-0)
Glasgow Rangers FC: Allan McGregor, James Tavernier, Connor Goldson, Filip Helander, Calvin Bassey, Steven Davis, John Lundstram, Joe Ayodele-Aribo (81' Scott Arfield), Ianis Hagi (90+5' Stephen Kelly), Alfredo Morelos (83' Cedric Itten), Ryan Kent (46' Scott Wright). Coach: Steven Gerrard.
FC Alashkert: Ognjen Cancarevic, Dejan Boljevic, Didier Kadio, Taron Voskanyan, Tiago Cametá, James (75' Artak Yedigaryan), Artak Grigoryan, Rumyan Hovsepyan, Aghvan Papikyan (9' Wangu Gome, 75' Vincent Bezecourt), David Khurtsidze (80' Aleksandar Glisic), José Embaló. Coach: Aleksandr Grigoryan.
Goal: 67' Alfredo Morelos 1-0.
Referee: Anastasios Sidiropoulos (GRE)   Attendance: 42,649
Sent off: 43' John Lundstram.

26.08.21   Vazgen Sargsyan anvan Hanrapetakan Marzadasht, Yerevan:
FC Alashkert – Glasgow Rangers FC 0-0
FC Alashkert: Ognjen Cancarevic, Dejan Boljevic, Vladislav Kryuchkov, Taron Voskanyan, Tiago Cametá, James, Artak Grigoryan (75' Wangu Gome), Rumyan Hovsepyan (46' Vincent Bezecourt), David Khurtsidze (88' Ismaël Fofana), José Embaló (88' Grigor Aghekyan), Aleksandar Glisic (61' Nikita Tankov). Coach: Aleksandr Grigoryan.
Glasgow Rangers FC: Robby McCrorie, Connor Goldson, Filip Helander, Borna Barisic, Nathan Patterson, Steven Davis, Scott Arfield, Glen Kamara, Joe Ayodele-Aribo, Ianis Hagi (64' Cedric Itten), Alfredo Morelos. Coach: Steven Gerrard.
Referee: Tobias Stieler (GER)   Attendance: 6,800
Sent off: 39' James.

FC Alashkert played their home match at Vazgen Sargsyan anvan Hanrapetakan Marzadasht, Yerevan, instead of their regular stadium Alashkert Stadium Yerevan, which did not meet UEFA requirements.

26.08.21   Bolt Arena, Helsinki: HJK Helsinki – Fenerbahçe 2-5 (1-2)
HJK Helsinki: Jakob Tånnander, Valtteri Moren, Janne Saksela (61' Casper Terho), Daniel O'Shaughnessy, Luis Murillo (46' Matti Peltola), Tim Sparv (41' Santeri Väänänen), Filip Valencic (61' Sebastian Dahlström), Santeri Hostikka (61' David Browne), Jair, Riku Riski, Roope Riski. Coach: Toni Koskela.
Fenerbahçe: Altay Bayindir, Marcel Tisserand, Nazim Sangaré, Attila Szalai, Mesut Özil (73' Arda Güler), Luiz Gustavo, José Sosa (62' Mert Hakan Yandas), Miha Zajc, Bright Osayi-Samuel (62' Muhammed Gümüskaya), Ferdi Kadioglu, Enner Valencia (81' Fatih Sanlitürk). Coach: Vítor Pereira.
Goals: 11', 14' Enner Valencia 0-1, 0-2, 27' Roope Riski 1-2, 52' Enner Valencia 1-3, 88' Riku Riski 2-3, 90+1' Fatih Sanlitürk 2-4, 90+4' Matti Peltola 2-5 (og).
Referee: Ivan Kruzliak (SVK)   Attendance: 3,785

26.08.21   Slavutych-Arena, Zaporizhzhia: Zorya Lugansk – Rapid Wien 2-3 (1-2)
Zorya Lugansk: Mykyta Shevchenko (48' Dmytro Matsapura), Vitaliy Vernydub, Juninho (83' Denys Favorov), Artem Gromov, Dmytro Khomchenovskyi, Lovro Cvek, Vladyslav Kochergin, Sergiy Buletsa (64' Vladyslav Kabaev), Yegor Nazaryna, Oleksandr Gladkyi (83' Cristian), Allahyar Sayyadmanesh (64' Shahab Zahedi Tabar). Coach: Viktor Skrypnyk.
Rapid Wien: Paul Gartler, Filip Stojkovic, Maximilian Hofmann (67' Kevin Wimmer), Maximilian Ullmann, Leo Greiml, Srdjan Grahovac (67' Lion Schuster), Robert Ljubicic (67' Dejan Petrovic), Taxiarchis Fountas, Ercan Kara (67' Christoph Knasmüllner), Marco Grüll, Kelvin Arase (30' Thorsten Schick). Coach: Dietmar Kühbauer.
Goals: 10' Marco Grüll 0-1, 15' Leo Greiml 0-2, 40' Oleksandr Gladkyi 1-2, 68' Taxiarchis Fountas 1-3, 86' Shahab Zahedi Tabar 2-3 (p).
Referee: István Kovács (ROM)   Attendance: 2,563

Shahab Zahedi Tabar missed a penalty kick (89').

Zorya Lugansk played their home match at Slavutych-Arena, Zaporizhzhia, instead of their regular stadium Avanhard Stadium, Lugansk, due to the war in Eastern Ukraine.

26.08.21   Recep Tayyip Erdogan Stadyumu, Istanbul: Galatasaray – Randers FC 2-1 (0-1)
Galatasaray: Fernando Muslera, Patrick van Aanholt, Alpaslan Öztürk, Christian Luyindama, Sacha Boey, Sofiane Féghouli (88' Emre Akbaba), Taylan Antalyali (80' Aytaç Kara), Kerem Aktürkoglu (46' Baris Yilmaz), Berkan Kutlu, Ryan Babel (73' Emre Kilinç), Mbaye Diagne (88' Mostafa Mohamed). Coach: Fatih Terim.
Randers FC: Patrik Carlgren, Björn Kopplin (62' Oliver Bundgaard Kristensen), Erik Marxen, Simon Piesinger, Mikkel Kallesøe, Simon Tibbing (62' Jakob Ankersen), Vito Hammershøy-Mistrati (62' Tobias Klysner), Frederik Lauenborg, Tosin Kehinde (83' Filip Bundgaard Kristensen), Lasse Berg Johnsen, Marvin Egho (70' Alhaji Kamara).
Coach: Thomas Thomasberg.
Goals: 11' Marvin Egho 0-1, 48' Patrick van Aanholt 1-1, 59' Frederik Lauenborg 2-1 (og).
Referee: Aleksei Kulbakov (BLS)   Attendance: 3,947

Galatasaray played their home match at Recep Tayyip Erdogan Stadyumu, Istanbul, instead of their regular stadium Türk Telekom Stadium, Istanbul, due to renovation.

26.08.21   AFAS Stadion, Alkmaar: AZ – Celtic FC 2-1 (2-1)
AZ Alkmaar: Hobie Verhulst, Bruno Martins Indi, Timo Letschert, Aslak Witry, Yukinari Sugawara, Fredrik Midtsjø (75' Sam Beukema), Dani de Wit, Teun Koopmeiners, Vangelis Pavlidis (71' Albert Gudmundsson), Jesper Karlsson, Zakaria Aboukhlal (71' Ernest Poku). Coach: Pascal Jansen.
Celtic FC: Joe Hart, Carl Starfelt, Anthony Ralston, Greg Taylor (24' Adam Montgomery), Stephen Welsh, Callum McGregor, Tom Rogic (60' Odsonne Édouard), Ryan Christie, David Turnbull, Kyogo Furuhashi (86' Ismaila Soro), Liel Abada. Coach: Ange Postecoglou.
Goals: 3' Kyogo Furuhashi 0-1, 6' Zakaria Aboukhlal 1-1, 26' Carl Starfelt 2-1 (og).
Referee: Tiago Martins (POR)   Attendance: 10,041

26.08.21   Stadionul Dr. Constantin Radulescu, Cluj-Napoca:
           CFR Cluj – Crvena Zvezda Beograd 1-2 (1-1)
CFR Cluj: Griedius Arlauskis (46' Cristian Balgradean), Camora, Danijel Graovac, Cristian Manea, Denis Ciobotariu, Ciprian Deac (66' Alexandru Chipciu), Rúnar Sigurjónsson, Adrian Paun (46' Claudiu Petrila), Jonathan Rodríguez, Valentin Ionut Costache (73' Billel Omrani), Gabriel Debeljuh (73' Denis Alibec). Coach: Marius Sumudica.
Crvena Zvezda Beograd: Milan Borjan, Aleksandar Dragovic (66' Radovan Pankov), Milan Rodic, Milos Degenek, Marko Gobeljic, Aleksandar Katai (73' Veljko Nikolic), Sékou Sanogo (77' Njegos Petrovic), Guélor Kanga, Mirko Ivanic (67' Nenad Krsticic), El Fardou Ben Nabouhane, Milan Pavkov (73' Loïs Diony). Coach: Dejan Stankovic.
Goals: 4' Aleksandar Katai 0-1 (p), 34' Gabriel Debeljuh 1-1, 53' Milan Pavkov 1-2.
Referee: Michael Oliver (ENG)   Attendance: 4,200
Sent off: 78' Jonathan Rodríguez.

Ciprian Deac missed a penalty kick (63').

26.08.21   Stadión Tehelné pole, Bratislava: Slovan Bratislava – Olympiakos Piraeus 2-2 (1-1)
Slovan Bratislava: Adrián Chovan, Guram Kashia, Vasil Bozhikov, Lukás Pauschek (85'
Richard Krizan), Vernon De Marco, Jaba Kankava, Vladimír Weiss (79' Dávid Strelec),
Jaromír Zmrhal, Aleksandar Cavric (67' Joeri de Kamps), Ezekiel Henty (79' Dejan Drazic),
Andre Green (85' Dávid Hrncár). Coach: Vladimír Weiss.
Olympiakos Piraeus: Tomás Vaclík, Sokratis Papastathopoulos, Kenny Lala, Pape Cissé, Oleg
Reabciuk, Mathieu Valbuena (60' Rony Lopes), Yann M'Vila (72' Pierre Malong), Mohamed
Camara (36' Andreas Bouchalakis), Youssef El-Arabi (72' Marios Vrousai), Henry Onyekuru
(72' Ahmed Hassan "Koka"), Aguibou Camara. Coach: Pedro Martins.
Goals: 33' Youssef El-Arabi 0-1, 41' Ezekiel Henty 1-1, 54' Henry Onyekuru 1-2,
62' Andre Green 2-2.
Referee: Deniz Aytekin (GER)   Attendance: 7,201
Sent off: 26' Vernon De Marco.

26.08.21   Merkur Arena, Graz: Sturm Graz – NS Mura 2-0 (1-0)
Sturm Graz: Jörg Siebenhandl, Gregory Wüthrich, Jusuf Gazibegovic, David Affengruber (81'
Niklas Geyrhofer), Amadou Dante, Stefan Hierländer (81' Anderson Niangbo), Jon Stankovic
(74' Andreas Kuen), Ivan Ljubic, Otar Kiteishvili (74' Alexander Prass), Jakob Jantscher,
Kelvin Yeboah (67' Manprit Sarkaria). Coach: Christian Ilzer.
NS Mura: Matko Obradovic, Ziga Kous (63' Amadej Marosa), Klemen Sturm, Klemen Pucko,
Jan Gorenc, Zan Karnicnik, Matic Marusko, Ziga Skoflek (46' Mihael Klepac), Stanisa Mandic
(56' Alen Kozar), Tomi Horvat (77' Tio Cipot), Mitja Lotric (46' Kai Cipot).
Coach: Ante Simundza.
Goals: 39' Otar Kiteishvili 1-0, 66' Jakob Jantscher 2-0.
Referee: José María Sánchez Martínez (ESP)   Attendance: 8,237
Sent off: 54' Matic Marusko.

26.08.21   Bosuilstadion, Deurne: Royal Antwerp FC – Omonia Nicosia 2-0 (1-0,2-0) (AET)
Royal Antwerp FC: Jean Butez, Ritchie De Laet, Björn Engels (90' Alhassan Yusuf), Aurélio
Buta, Jelle Bataille (78' Samuel Vines), Radja Nainggolan (78' Abdoulaye Seck), Birger
Verstraete, Koji Miyoshi, Benson Manuel (71' Pieter Gerkens), Johannes Eggestein, Michel
Balikwisha. Coach: Brian Priske.
Omonia Nicosia: Fabiano, Jan Lecjaks, Ádám Lang, Jordi Gómez, Mikkel Diskerud (86'
Panayiotis Zachariou), Fouad Bachirou, Abdullahi Shehu (111' Paris Psaltis), Nikolas
Panagiotou, Fotis Papoulis (57' Marinos Tzionis), Andronikos Kakoullis (46' Iyayi
Atiemwen), Loizos Loizou (81' Héctor Yuste). Coach: Henning Berg.
Goals: 28' Koji Miyoshi 1-0, 84' Pieter Gerkens 2-0.
Referee: Andris Treimanis (LAT)   Attendance: 10,470

Royal Antwerp FC won after extra time on penalties (3:2)

Penalties: Jordi Gómez missed, Verstraete 0-1, Atiemwen 1-1, Gerkens missed,
Lecjaks missed, Eggestein 1-2, Héctor Yuste 2-2, Miyoshi 2-3, Zachariou missed.

26.08.21 Stadion Miejski Legii Warszawa im. Marszalka Józefa Pilsudskiego, Warszawa:
Legia Warszawa – Slavia Praha 2-1 (0-1)
Legia Warszawa: Artur Boruc, Artur Jedrzejczyk, Filip Mladenovic, Mateusz Wieteska, Mateusz Holownia (56' Tomás Pekhart), Maik Nawrocki, Josué, André Martins (25' Rafael Lopes), Bartosz Slisz, Luquinhas, Mahir Emreli (80' Ernest Muçi).
Coach: Czeslaw Michniewicz.
Slavia Praha: Ondrej Kolár, Ondrej Kúdela, Jan Boril, Alexander Bah (70' Abdallah Sima), David Zima, Nicolae Stanciu (81' Peter Olayinka), Tomás Holes, Jakub Hromada (70' Ibrahim Traoré), Ubong Ekpai, Stanislav Tecl (65' Ondrej Lingr), Ivan Schranz (81' Michal Krmencík). Coach: Jindich Trpisovský.
Goals: 45' Ubong Ekpai 0-1, 59', 70' Mahir Emreli 1-1, 2-1.
Referee: Artur Soares Dias (POR)   Attendance: 20,641
Sent off: 3' Tomás Holes, 90+5' Jakub Hromada.

GROUP STAGE

The group winners advance to Round of 16

The numbers second in the group advance to Knockout Round Play-offs

The numbers three in the group transfer to Europa Conference League

GROUP A

Olympique Lyonnais	6	5	1	0	16 - 5	16
Glasgow Rangers FC	6	2	2	2	6 - 5	8
Sparta Praha	6	2	1	3	6 - 9	7
Brøndby IF	6	0	2	4	2 - 11	2

GROUP B

AS Monaco	6	3	3	0	7 - 4	12
Real Sociedad	6	2	3	1	9 - 6	9
PSV Eindhoven	6	2	2	2	8 - 8	8
Sturm Graz	6	0	2	4	3 - 10	2

GROUP C

Spartak Moskva	6	3	1	2	10 - 9	10
SSC Napoli	6	3	1	2	15 - 10	10
Leicester City	6	2	2	2	12 - 11	8
Legia Warszawa	6	2	0	4	11 - 7	6

GROUP D

Eintracht Frankfurt	6	3	3	0	10 - 4	12
Olympiakos Piraeus	6	3	0	3	8 - 7	9
Fenerbahçe	6	1	3	2	7 - 8	6
Royal Antwerp FC	6	1	2	3	6 - 10	5

GROUP E

Galatasaray	6	3	3	0	7	-	3	12
Lazio Roma	6	2	3	1	7	-	3	9
Olympique Marseille	6	1	4	1	6	-	7	7
Lokomotiv Moskva	6	0	2	4	2	-	9	2

GROUP F

Crvena Zvezda Beograd	6	3	2	1	6	-	4	11
Sporting Braga	6	3	1	2	12	-	9	10
FC Midtjylland	6	2	3	1	7	-	17	9
PFC Ludogorets Razgrad	6	0	2	4	3	-	8	2

GROUP G

Bayer Leverkusen	6	4	1	1	14	-	5	13
Real Betis	6	3	1	2	12	-	12	10
Celtic FC	6	3	0	3	13	-	15	9
Ferencvárosi TC	6	1	0	5	5	-	12	3

GROUP H

West Ham United	6	4	1	1	11	-	3	13
Dinamo Zagreb	6	3	1	2	9	-	6	10
Rapid Wien	6	2	0	4	4	-	9	6
KRC Genk	6	1	2	3	4	-	10	5

GROUP A

16.09.21   Ibrox Stadium, Glasgow: Glasgow Rangers FC – Olympique Lyonnais 0-2 (0-1)
Glasgow Rangers FC: Allan McGregor, Leon Balogun, James Tavernier, Connor Goldson, Borna Barisic, Steven Davis (59' Scott Wright), John Lundstram, Glen Kamara, Joe Ayodele-Aribo (76' Fashion Sakala), Alfredo Morelos, Ryan Kent (70' Kemar Roofe).
Coach: Steven Gerrard.
Olympique Lyonnais: Anthony Lopes, Jérôme Boateng (65' Sinaly Diomandé), Emerson, Jason Denayer, Malo Gusto, Bruno Guimarães, Houssem Aouar, Lucas Paquetá, Maxence Caqueret, Islam Slimani, Karl Toko Ekambi (71' Xherdan Shaqiri). Coach: Peter Bosz.
Goals: 23' Karl Toko Ekambi 0-1, 55' James Tavernier 0-2 (og).
Referee: Andreas Ekberg (SWE)   Attendance: 44,906

16.09.21   Brøndby Stadion, Brøndbyvester: Brøndby IF – Sparta Praha 0-0
Brøndby IF: Mads Hermansen, Kevin Mensah (85' Jens Martin Gammelby), Sigurd Rosted (75' Tobias Borchgrevink Børkeeiet), Andreas Maxsø, Andreas Bruus, Kevin Tshiembe, Josip Radosevic, Morten Frendrup, Anis Ben Slimane (69' Christian Cappis), Simon Hedlund (75' Andrija Pavlovic), Mikkel Uhre (69' Marko Divkovic). Coach: Niels Frederiksen.
Sparta Praha: Florin Nita, Ondrej Celustka, Dávid Hancko, Tomás Wiesner, David Pavelka, Lukás Haraslín (64' David Moberg-Karlsson), Jakub Pesek, Matej Polidar (38' Andreas Vindheim), Michal Sácek (90' Václav Drchal), Filip Soucek, Adam Hlozek.
Coach: Pavel Vrba.
Referee: Aleksandar Stavrev (MKD)   Attendance: 18,867

30.09.21 Groupama Stadium, Décines-Charpieu:
           Olympique Lyonnais – Brøndby IF 3-0 (0-0)
Olympique Lyonnais: Anthony Lopes, Damien Da Silva, Emerson, Léo Dubois (83' Malo Gusto), Sinaly Diomandé, Xherdan Shaqiri (65' Rayan Cherki), Thiago Mendes, Houssem Aouar, Lucas Paquetá (83' Habib Keita), Maxence Caqueret (83' Tino Kadewere), Karl Toko Ekambi. Coach: Peter Bosz.
Brøndby IF: Mads Hermansen, Sigurd Rosted, Andreas Maxsø, Jens Martin Gammelby (62' Kevin Mensah), Andreas Bruus, Henrik Heggheim (62' Kevin Tshiembe), Josip Radosevic (84' Tobias Borchgrevink Børkeeiet), Mathias Greve (63' Anis Ben Slimane), Morten Frendrup, Andrija Pavlovic, Simon Hedlund (73' Christian Cappis). Coach: Niels Frederiksen.
Goals: 64', 71' Karl Toko Ekambi 1-0, 2-0, 86' Houssem Aouar 3-0.
Referee: Harald Lechner (AUT)   Attendance: 25,466

30.09.21 Generali Ceská pojistovna Arena, Prague:
           Sparta Praha – Glasgow Rangers FC 1-0 (1-0)
Sparta Praha: Florin Nita, Ondrej Celustka, Filip Panák, Dávid Hancko, Tomás Wiesner, David Pavelka, Lukás Haraslín (75' David Moberg-Karlsson), Jakub Pesek, Michal Sácek, Martin Minchev (69' Václav Drchal), Adam Hlozek (90' Borek Dockal). Coach: Pavel Vrba.
Glasgow Rangers FC: Allan McGregor, Leon Balogun, James Tavernier, Borna Barisic, Calvin Bassey, Steven Davis, Glen Kamara, Joe Ayodele-Aribo (77' John Lundstram), Juninho Bacuna (38' Ianis Hagi), Kemar Roofe (66' Alfredo Morelos), Fashion Sakala.
Coach: Steven Gerrard.
Goal: 29' Dávid Hancko 1-0.
Referee: Ali Palabiyik (TUR)   Attendance: 10,879
Sent-off: 74' Glen Kamara.

21.10.21 Generali Ceská pojistovna Arena, Prague:
           Sparta Praha – Olympique Lyonnais 3-4 (2-1)
Sparta Praha: Florin Nita, Ondrej Celustka, Filip Panák, Dávid Hancko, Tomás Wiesner, David Pavelka (84' Adam Karabec), Lukás Haraslín, Jakub Pesek (84' Matej Polidar), Michal Sácek (73' Ladislav Krejci (II)), Martin Minchev (63' Borek Dockal), Adam Hlozek.
Coach: Pavel Vrba.
Olympique Lyonnais: Anthony Lopes, Jérôme Boateng (69' Sinaly Diomandé), Henrique (46' Emerson), Jason Denayer, Malo Gusto, Xherdan Shaqiri (75' Léo Dubois), Thiago Mendes, Bruno Guimarães, Houssem Aouar (90+5' Maxence Caqueret), Karl Toko Ekambi, Tino Kadewere (46' Lucas Paquetá). Coach: Peter Bosz.
Goals: 4', 19' Lukás Haraslín 1-0, 2-0, 42' Karl Toko Ekambi 2-1, 53' Houssem Aouar 2-2, 67' Lucas Paquetá 2-3, 88' Karl Toko Ekambi 2-4, 90+6' Ladislav Krejci (II) 3-4.
Referee: Matej Jug (SVN)   Attendance: 12,427
Sent-off: 74' Malo Gusto.

21.10.21 Ibrox Stadium, Glasgow: Glasgow Rangers FC – Brøndby IF 2-0 (2-0)
Glasgow Rangers FC: Allan McGregor, Leon Balogun (64' Calvin Bassey), James Tavernier, Connor Goldson, Borna Barisic, Steven Davis, John Lundstram (78' Scott Arfield), Joe Ayodele-Aribo, Ianis Hagi (78' Scott Wright), Kemar Roofe (78' Juninho Bacuna), Alfredo Morelos (71' Fashion Sakala). Coach: Steven Gerrard.
Brøndby IF: Thomas Mikkelsen, Kevin Mensah (62' Blas Riveros), Sigurd Rosted, Andreas Maxsø, Jens Martin Gammelby, Henrik Heggheim, Christian Cappis (81' Mathias Greve), Morten Frendrup (73' Tobias Borchgrevink Børkeeiet), Anis Ben Slimane (46' Josip Radosevic), Andrija Pavlovic, Mikkel Uhre (63' Simon Hedlund). Coach: Niels Frederiksen.
Goals: 18' Leon Balogun 1-0, 30' Kemar Roofe 2-0.
Referee: Fran Jovic (CRO)   Attendance: 46,842

04.11.21   Groupama Stadium, Décines-Charpieu:
Olympique Lyonnais – Sparta Praha 3-0 (0-0)
Olympique Lyonnais: Anthony Lopes, Damien Da Silva, Henrique, Jason Denayer, Sinaly Diomandé, Xherdan Shaqiri, Thiago Mendes, Houssem Aouar (69' Karl Toko Ekambi), Maxence Caqueret (68' Bruno Guimarães), Islam Slimani (69' Lucas Paquetá), Rayan Cherki (82' Bradley Barcola). Coach: Peter Bosz.
Sparta Praha: Florin Nita, Ondrej Celustka (7' Andreas Vindheim), Filip Panák, Dávid Hancko, Tomás Wiesner, David Pavelka, Lukás Haraslín (82' Adam Karabec), Jakub Pesek (68' Matej Pulkrab), Michal Sácek (68' Borek Dockal), Ladislav Krejci (II), Martin Minchev. Coach: Pavel Vrba.
Goals: 61', 63' Islam Slimani 1-0, 2-0, 90+2' Karl Toko Ekambi 3-0.
Referee: Maurizio Mariani (ITA)   Attendance: 33,934

04.11.21   Brøndby Stadion, Brøndbyvester: Brøndby IF – Glasgow Rangers FC 1-1 (1-0)
Brøndby IF: Mads Hermansen, Kevin Mensah, Sigurd Rosted, Andreas Maxsø, Andreas Bruus (64' Blas Riveros), Kevin Tshiembe, Josip Radosevic, Christian Cappis (63' Anis Ben Slimane), Morten Frendrup, Simon Hedlund (86' Andrija Pavlovic), Mikkel Uhre (75' Mathias Greve). Coach: Niels Frederiksen.
Glasgow Rangers FC: Allan McGregor, Leon Balogun, James Tavernier, Connor Goldson, Borna Barisic (81' Calvin Bassey), Steven Davis (72' Juninho Bacuna), Scott Arfield (56' Ianis Hagi), Glen Kamara, Joe Ayodele-Aribo, Alfredo Morelos (56' Kemar Roofe), Fashion Sakala (56' Ryan Kent). Coach: Steven Gerrard.
Goals: 45' Leon Balogun 1-0 (og), 77' Ianis Hagi 1-1.
Referee: Nikola Dabanovic (MNE)   Attendance: 20,462

25.11.21   Ibrox Stadium, Glasgow: Glasgow Rangers FC – Sparta Praha 2-0 (1-0)
Glasgow Rangers FC: Allan McGregor, James Tavernier, Connor Goldson, Borna Barisic, Calvin Bassey, Steven Davis (89' John Lundstram), Glen Kamara, Joe Ayodele-Aribo (81' Scott Arfield), Ianis Hagi (66' Nathan Patterson), Alfredo Morelos, Ryan Kent (81' Fashion Sakala). Coach: Giovanni van Bronckhorst.
Sparta Praha: Dominik Holec, Filip Panák, Dávid Hancko, Tomás Wiesner, David Pavelka, Ladislav Krejci (I) (59' Adam Karabec), Lukás Haraslín (59' David Moberg-Karlsson), Michal Sácek, Ladislav Krejci (II), Martin Minchev (58' Borek Dockal), Adam Hlozek (85' Matej Pulkrab). Coach: Pavel Vrba.
Goals: 15', 49' Alfredo Morelos 1-0, 2-0.
Referee: Danny Makkelie (HOL)   Attendance: 48,370

25.11.21   Brøndby Stadion, Brøndbyvester: Brøndby IF – Olympique Lyonnais 1-3 (0-0)
Brøndby IF: Mads Hermansen, Andreas Maxsø, Blas Riveros (63' Kevin Mensah), Andreas Bruus, Kevin Tshiembe, Henrik Heggheim (81' Sigurd Rosted), Josip Radosevic (75' Christian Cappis), Mathias Greve (63' Anis Ben Slimane), Morten Frendrup, Simon Hedlund, Mikkel Uhre (75' Marko Divkovic). Coach: Niels Frederiksen.
Olympique Lyonnais: Anthony Lopes, Damien Da Silva, Henrique, Castello Lukeba, Malo Gusto (87' Hugo Vogel), Thiago Mendes (75' Bruno Guimarães), Habib Keita (75' Maxence Caqueret), Islam Slimani, Moussa Dembélé (75' Lucas Paquetá), Tino Kadewere (75' Karl Toko Ekambi), Rayan Cherki. Coach: Peter Bosz.
Goals: 51' Mikkel Uhre 1-0, 57', 66' Rayan Cherki 1-1, 1-2, 76' Islam Slimani 1-3.
Referee: Georgi Kabakov (BUL)   Attendance: 16,645

09.12.21 Groupama Stadium, Décines-Charpieu:
Olympique Lyonnais – Glasgow Rangers FC 1-1 (0-1)
Olympique Lyonnais: Julian Pollersbeck, Damien Da Silva, Henrique, Castello Lukeba, Hugo Vogel (62' Léo Dubois), Xherdan Shaqiri (62' Houssem Aouar), Maxence Caqueret (76' Bruno Guimarães), Habib Keita, Karl Toko Ekambi (44' Tino Kadewere), Moussa Dembélé (76' Islam Slimani), Rayan Cherki. Coach: Peter Bosz.
Glasgow Rangers FC: Jon McLaughlin, Connor Goldson, Borna Barisic, Calvin Bassey, Nathan Patterson, John Lundstram, Glen Kamara (46' Steven Davis), Scott Wright (61' Scott Arfield), Ianis Hagi (61' Juninho Bacuna), Kemar Roofe (73' Joe Ayodele-Aribo), Ryan Kent. Coach: Giovanni van Bronckhorst.
Goals: 42' Scott Wright 0-1, 49' Calvin Bassey 1-1 (og).
Referee: Radu Petrescu (ROM)   Attendance: 26,842

09.12.21 Generali Ceská pojistovna Arena, Prague: Sparta Praha – Brøndby IF 2-0 (1-0)
Sparta Praha: Dominik Holec, Filip Panák, Dávid Hancko, Tomás Wiesner, David Pavelka, Lukás Haraslín (86' Martin Minchev), Jakub Pesek (69' Ladislav Krejci (I)), Ladislav Krejci (II), Filip Soucek, Matej Pulkrab (60' Andreas Vindheim), Adam Hlozek. Coach: Pavel Vrba.
Brøndby IF: Mads Hermansen, Kevin Mensah, Sigurd Rosted, Andreas Maxsø, Blas Riveros (61' Andreas Bruus), Henrik Heggheim (46' Mathias Greve), Josip Radosevic (61' Christian Cappis), Morten Frendrup, Anis Ben Slimane, Simon Hedlund (72' Jagvir Singh Sidhu), Mikkel Uhre (80' Mathias Kvistgaarden). Coach: Niels Frederiksen.
Goals: 43' Dávid Hancko 1-0, 49' Adam Hlozek 2-0.
Referee: Craig Pawson (ENG)   Attendance: 976
Sent-off: 57' Tomás Wiesner, 75' Anis Ben Slimane.

GROUP B

16.09.21 Philips Stadion, Eindhoven: PSV Eindhoven – Real Sociedad 2-2 (1-2)
PSV Eindhoven: Joël Drommel, Phillipp Mwene (68' Jordan Teze), André Ramalho, Philipp Max, Olivier Boscagli, Armando Obispo, Mario Götze, Marco van Ginkel (63' Ryan Thomas), Eran Zahavi (63' Carlos Vinícius), Cody Gakpo (89' Bruma), Noni Madueke (63' Yorbe Vertessen). Coach: Roger Schmidt.
Real Sociedad: Álex Remiro, Joseba Zaldúa (79' Cristo), Aritz Elustondo, Robin Le Normand (61' Zubeldía), Aihen Muñoz (61' Jon Pacheco), Adnan Januzaj (79' Andoni Gorosabel), Mikel Merino, Guevara, Martín Zubimendi, Mikel Oyarzabal, Alexander Isak (83' Alexander Sørloth). Coach: Imanol Alguacil.
Goals: 31' Mario Götze 1-0, 34' Adnan Januzaj 1-1, 39' Alexander Isak 1-2, 54' Cody Gakpo 2-2.
Referee: William Collum (SCO)   Attendance: 23,135

16.09.21 Stade Louis II, Monaco: AS Monaco – Sturm Graz 1-0 (0-0)
AS Monaco: Alexander Nübel, Ruben Aguilar, Guillermo Maripán, Strahinja Pavlovic, Gelson Martins (46' Aleksandr Golovin), Aurélien Tchouaméni, Eliot Matazo (73' Youssouf Fofana), Kevin Volland (61' Wissam Ben Yedder), Ismail Jakobs (46' Caio Henrique), Krépin Diatta, Wilson Isidor (46' Cesc Fàbregas). Coach: Niko Kovac.
Sturm Graz: Jörg Siebenhandl, Jon Stankovic, Gregory Wüthrich (78' Niklas Geyrhofer), Jusuf Gazibegovic (71' Lukas Jäger), David Affengruber, Amadou Dante, Stefan Hierländer, Ivan Ljubic, Otar Kiteishvili (71' Alexander Prass), Jakob Jantscher (61' Manprit Sarkaria), Kelvin Yeboah (71' Anderson Niangbo). Coach: Christian Ilzer.
Goal: 66' Krépin Diatta 1-0.
Referee: Donatas Rumsas (LTU)   Attendance: 2,941

30.09.21   Reale Arena, San Sebastián: Real Sociedad – AS Monaco 1-1 (0-1)
Real Sociedad: Álex Remiro, Joseba Zaldúa (71' Andoni Gorosabel), Aritz Elustondo, Aihen Muñoz, Adnan Januzaj, Mikel Merino, Zubeldía, Guevara (61' Beñat Turrientes), Martín Zubimendi, Portu (71' Ander Barrenetxea), Mikel Oyarzabal (90' Jon Karrikaburu). Coach: Imanol Alguacil.
AS Monaco: Alexander Nübel, Djibril Sidibé (46' Ruben Aguilar), Axel Disasi, Caio Henrique (90' Strahinja Pavlovic), Benoît Badiashile, Aurélien Tchouaméni, Jean Lucas, Youssouf Fofana (65' Aleksandr Golovin), Sofiane Diop (74' Guillermo Maripán), Myron Boadu (65' Kevin Volland), Krépin Diatta. Coach: Niko Kovac.
Goals: 16' Axel Disasi 0-1, 53' Mikel Merino 1-1.
Referee: Sergey Ivanov (RUS)   Attendance: 23,765

30.09.21   Merkur Arena, Graz: Sturm Graz – PSV Eindhoven 1-4 (0-1)
Sturm Graz: Jörg Siebenhandl, Jon Stankovic, Gregory Wüthrich, Jusuf Gazibegovic, David Affengruber, Amadou Dante, Stefan Hierländer (82' Christoph Lang), Ivan Ljubic (46' Andreas Kuen), Otar Kiteishvili (82' Alexander Prass), Jakob Jantscher (68' Manprit Sarkaria), Kelvin Yeboah (78' Anderson Niangbo). Coach: Christian Ilzer.
PSV Eindhoven: Joël Drommel, Phillipp Mwene, André Ramalho, Philipp Max, Olivier Boscagli, Mario Götze (81' Érick Gutiérrez), Marco van Ginkel (81' Armando Obispo), Ibrahim Sangaré, Eran Zahavi (65' Carlos Vinícius), Ritsu Doan (65' Yorbe Vertessen), Cody Gakpo (90' Mauro Júnior). Coach: Roger Schmidt.
Goals: 32' Ibrahim Sangaré 0-1, 51' Eran Zahavi 0-2, 55' Jon Stankovic 1-2, 74' Philipp Max 1-3, 78' Yorbe Vertessen 1-4.
Referee: Yevhen Aranovskiy (UKR)   Attendance: 15,026
Sent-off: 89' Ibrahim Sangaré.

21.10.21   Merkur Arena, Graz: Sturm Graz – Real Sociedad 0-1 (0-0)
Sturm Graz: Jörg Siebenhandl, Jon Stankovic, Gregory Wüthrich, Jusuf Gazibegovic (73' Lukas Jäger), David Affengruber, Amadou Dante, Andreas Kuen (66' Niklas Geyrhofer), Alexander Prass (38' Stefan Hierländer), Jakob Jantscher, Anderson Niangbo (66' Ivan Ljubic), Kelvin Yeboah (73' Manprit Sarkaria). Coach: Christian Ilzer.
Real Sociedad: Álex Remiro, Andoni Gorosabel (62' Joseba Zaldúa), Robin Le Normand, Aihen Muñoz, David Silva (62' Alexander Sørloth), Adnan Januzaj (77' Beñat Turrientes), Mikel Merino, Zubeldía, Martín Zubimendi (19' Guevara), Portu, Alexander Isak (77' Julen Lobete). Coach: Imanol Alguacil.
Goal: 69' Alexander Isak 0-1.
Referee: Tobias Stieler (GER)   Attendance: 14,809
Sent-off: 87' Jon Stankovic.

21.10.21   Philips Stadion, Eindhoven: PSV Eindhoven – AS Monaco 1-2 (0-1)
PSV Eindhoven: Joël Drommel, Phillipp Mwene, André Ramalho, Philipp Max, Olivier Boscagli, Armando Obispo, Mario Götze, Marco van Ginkel, Cody Gakpo (64' Bruma), Carlos Vinícius (87' Eran Zahavi), Noni Madueke (56' Yorbe Vertessen). Coach: Roger Schmidt.
AS Monaco: Alexander Nübel, Ruben Aguilar, Guillermo Maripán, Axel Disasi (74' Gelson Martins), Caio Henrique, Benoît Badiashile, Aurélien Tchouaméni, Jean Lucas (75' Sofiane Diop), Youssouf Fofana (70' Eliot Matazo), Kevin Volland, Myron Boadu (70' Wissam Ben Yedder). Coach: Niko Kovac.
Goals: 19' Myron Boadu 0-1, 59' Cody Gakpo 1-1, 89' Sofiane Diop 1-2.
Referee: Davide Massa (ITA)   Attendance: 33,000

04.11.21 Stade Louis II, Monaco: AS Monaco – PSV Eindhoven 0-0
AS Monaco: Alexander Nübel, Ruben Aguilar (46' Aleksandr Golovin), Guillermo Maripán, Axel Disasi (46' Djibril Sidibé), Caio Henrique, Benoît Badiashile, Aurélien Tchouaméni, Jean Lucas (46' Sofiane Diop), Youssouf Fofana, Kevin Volland (75' Krépin Diatta), Myron Boadu (66' Wissam Ben Yedder). Coach: Niko Kovac.
PSV Eindhoven: Joël Drommel, Phillipp Mwene, André Ramalho, Philipp Max, Olivier Boscagli, Jordan Teze, Érick Gutiérrez, Ibrahim Sangaré, Eran Zahavi (89' Maxi Romero), Carlos Vinícius (58' Ritsu Doan), Yorbe Vertessen (45' Bruma). Coach: Roger Schmidt.
Referee: Cüneyt Çakir (TUR)   Attendance: 5,840

04.11.21 Reale Arena, San Sebastián: Real Sociedad – Sturm Graz 1-1 (0-1)
Real Sociedad: Álex Remiro, Andoni Gorosabel, Robin Le Normand, Aihen Muñoz (83' Diego Rico), David Silva, Adnan Januzaj, Mikel Merino, Zubeldía, Martín Zubimendi, Portu (65' Ander Barrenetxea), Alexander Sørloth (83' Alexander Isak). Coach: Imanol Alguacil.
Sturm Graz: Jörg Siebenhandl, Gregory Wüthrich, David Affengruber, Niklas Geyrhofer, Amadou Dante, Lukas Jäger, Ivan Ljubic, Alexander Prass, Jakob Jantscher (72' Andreas Kuen), Anderson Niangbo (83' Moritz Wels), Manprit Sarkaria. Coach: Christian Ilzer.
Goals: 38' Jakob Jantscher 0-1, 53' Alexander Sørloth 1-1.
Referee: Andris Treimanis (LAT)   Attendance: 25,010

25.11.21 Stade Louis II, Monaco: AS Monaco – Real Sociedad 2-1 (2-1)
AS Monaco: Alexander Nübel, Djibril Sidibé, Guillermo Maripán, Caio Henrique, Benoît Badiashile (68' Axel Disasi), Aleksandr Golovin (90+1' Eliot Matazo), Jean Lucas, Youssouf Fofana, Sofiane Diop (76' Gelson Martins), Kevin Volland (90+2' Chrislain Matsima), Wissam Ben Yedder (77' Myron Boadu). Coach: Niko Kovac.
Real Sociedad: Mathew Ryan, Joseba Zaldúa (46' Andoni Gorosabel), Aritz Elustondo, Robin Le Normand, Aihen Muñoz, David Silva (46' Ander Barrenetxea), Adnan Januzaj (75' Portu), Mikel Merino (66' Beñat Turrientes), Martín Zubimendi, Mikel Oyarzabal, Alexander Isak (73' Alexander Sørloth). Coach: Imanol Alguacil.
Goals: 28' Kevin Volland 1-0, 35' Alexander Isak 1-1, 38' Youssouf Fofana 2-1.
Referee: Ivan Kruzliak (SVK)   Attendance: 3,834
Sent-off: 89' Youssouf Fofana.

25.11.21 Philips Stadion, Eindhoven: PSV Eindhoven – Sturm Graz 2-0 (1-0)
PSV Eindhoven: Joël Drommel, Phillipp Mwene, André Ramalho, Olivier Boscagli (58' Armando Obispo), Mario Götze (70' Marco van Ginkel), Érick Gutiérrez (70' Davy Pröpper), Mauro Júnior, Ibrahim Sangaré, Bruma, Ritsu Doan (87' Jeremy Antonisse), Carlos Vinícius (58' Yorbe Vertessen). Coach: Roger Schmidt.
Sturm Graz: Jörg Siebenhandl, Jon Stankovic (62' Aleksandar Borkovic), Gregory Wüthrich (75' Niklas Geyrhofer), David Affengruber, Amadou Dante (46' Jusuf Gazibegovic), Lukas Jäger, Andreas Kuen (62' Alexander Prass), Ivan Ljubic, Jakob Jantscher, Manprit Sarkaria, Kelvin Yeboah (62' Anderson Niangbo). Coach: Christian Ilzer.
Goals: 45' Carlos Vinícius 1-0 (p), 56' Bruma 2-0.
Referee: Pawel Raczkowski (POL)   Attendance: 0

09.12.21   Reale Arena, San Sebastián: Real Sociedad – PSV Eindhoven 3-0 (1-0)
Real Sociedad: Álex Remiro, Joseba Zaldúa, Aritz Elustondo, Robin Le Normand, Aihen
Muñoz, Adnan Januzaj (70' Beñat Turrientes), Zubeldía, Martín Zubimendi (86' Andoni
Gorosabel), Portu (70' Ander Barrenetxea), Mikel Oyarzabal (85' Jon Pacheco), Alexander
Isak (81' Alexander Sørloth). Coach: Imanol Alguacil.
PSV Eindhoven: Joël Drommel, Phillipp Mwene (68' Jordan Teze), André Ramalho, Olivier
Boscagli, Mario Götze, Érick Gutiérrez, Mauro Júnior (86' Philipp Max), Ibrahim Sangaré,
Bruma, Ritsu Doan (62' Noni Madueke, 68' Yorbe Vertessen), Cody Gakpo (62' Carlos
Vinícius). Coach: Roger Schmidt.
Goals: 43', 62' Mikel Oyarzabal 1-0 (p), 2-0, 90+3' Alexander Sørloth 3-0.
Referee: Felix Zwayer (GER)   Attendance: 24,940
Sent-off: 74' Ibrahim Sangaré.

09.12.21   Merkur Arena, Graz: Sturm Graz – AS Monaco 1-1 (1-1)
Sturm Graz: Jörg Siebenhandl, Jon Stankovic, Gregory Wüthrich, Jusuf Gazibegovic (81'
Lukas Jäger), David Affengruber, Amadou Dante, Ivan Ljubic (87' Samuel Stückler),
Alexander Prass, Jakob Jantscher (46' Kelvin Yeboah), Anderson Niangbo (73' Philipp
Huspek), Manprit Sarkaria (82' Moritz Wels). Coach: Christian Ilzer.
AS Monaco: Radoslaw Majecki, Ruben Aguilar, Caio Henrique (46' Ismail Jakobs), Strahinja
Pavlovic, Chrislain Matsima, Aleksandr Golovin (57' Sofiane Diop), Aurélien Tchouaméni
(46' Jean Lucas), Eliot Matazo, Kevin Volland, Wissam Ben Yedder (46' Myron Boadu),
Wilson Isidor (80' Gelson Martins). Coach: Niko Kovac.
Goals: 7' Jakob Jantscher 1-0 (p), 30' Kevin Volland 1-1.
Referee: Mohammed Al-Hakim (SWE)   Attendance: 0

GROUP C

15.09.21   Otkrytiye Arena, Moskva: Spartak Moskva – Legia Warszawa 0-1 (0-0)
Spartak Moskva: Aleksandr Maksimenko, Georgi Dzhikiya, Samuel Gigot, Ayrton (69'
Aleksandr Lomovitskiy), Nikolai Rasskazov, Victor Moses (82' Zelimkhan Bakaev), Roman
Zobnin (23' Jorrit Hendrix), Quincy Promes, Nail Umyarov, Ezequiel Ponce, Jordan Larsson
(82' Aleksandr Sobolev). Coach: Rui Vitória.
Legia Warszawa: Artur Boruc, Artur Jedrzejczyk, Mattias Johansson, Filip Mladenovic,
Mateusz Wieteska, Maik Nawrocki, Josué (90+3' Rafael Lopes), Igor Kharatin (59' Lirim M.
Kastrati), Bartosz Slisz, Luquinhas (83' Ernest Muçi), Mahir Emreli (83' Tomás Pekhart).
Coach: Czeslaw Michniewicz.
Goal: 90+1' Lirim M.Kastrati 0-1.
Referee: Nikola Dabanovic (MNE)   Attendance: 6,832

16.09.21   King Power Stadium, Leicester: Leicester City – SSC Napoli 2-2 (1-0)
Leicester City: Kasper Schmeichel, Jonny Evans (46' Çaglar Söyüncü), Ryan Bertrand, Jannik
Vestergaard, Timothy Castagne, Wilfred Ndidi, Boubakary Soumaré (78' James Maddison),
Harvey Barnes, Ayoze Pérez (46' Youri Tielemans), Kelechi Iheanacho (88' Jamie Vardy),
Patson Daka (71' Ademola Lookman). Coach: Brendan Rodgers.
SSC Napoli: David Ospina, Kalidou Koulibaly, Kévin Malcuit (84' Juan Jesus), Giovanni Di
Lorenzo, Amir Rrahmani, Piotr Zielinski (64' Eljif Elmas), Fabián Ruiz, André Zambo
Anguissa (84' Andrea Petagna), Lorenzo Insigne (74' Adam Ounas), Hirving Lozano (63'
Matteo Politano), Victor Osimhen. Coach: Luciano Spalletti.
Goals: 9' Ayoze Pérez 1-0, 64' Harvey Barnes 2-0, 69', 87' Victor Osimhen 2-1, 2-2.
Referee: Tiago Martins (POR)   Attendance: 29,579
Sent-off: 90+3' Wilfred Ndidi.

30.09.21 Stadio Diego Armando Maradona, Napoli: SSC Napoli – Spartak Moskva 2-3 (1-0)
SSC Napoli: Alex Meret, Kostas Manolas, Mário Rui, Kalidou Koulibaly, Giovanni Di Lorenzo, Piotr Zielinski (46' André Zambo Anguissa), Fabián Ruiz, Eljif Elmas (82' Adam Ounas), Lorenzo Insigne (41' Kévin Malcuit), Matteo Politano (73' Hirving Lozano), Andrea Petagna (46' Victor Osimhen). Coach: Luciano Spalletti.
Spartak Moskva: Aleksandr Maksimenko, Georgi Dzhikiya, Samuel Gigot, Ayrton, Maximiliano Caufriez, Ruslan Litvinov (73' Mikhail Ignatov), Victor Moses, Quincy Promes, Zelimkhan Bakaev (89' Aleksandr Lomovitskiy), Nail Umyarov, Ezequiel Ponce (45+1' Aleksandr Sobolev). Coach: Rui Vitória.
Goals: 1' Eljif Elmas 1-0, 55' Quincy Promes 1-1, 80' Mikhail Ignatov 1-2, 90' Quincy Promes 1-3, 90+4' Victor Osimhen 2-3.
Referee: Ivan Kruzliak (SVK)   Attendance: 13,373
Sent-off: 29' Mário Rui, 82' Maximiliano Caufriez.

30.09.21 Stadion Miejski Legii Warszawa im. Marszalka Józefa Pilsudskiego, Warszawa:
Legia Warszawa – Leicester City 1-0 (1-0)
Legia Warszawa: Cezary Miszta, Artur Jedrzejczyk, Mattias Johansson (78' Joel Abu Hanna), Filip Mladenovic, Mateusz Wieteska, Maik Nawrocki, Josué (82' Rafael Lopes), André Martins (70' Lirim M. Kastrati), Igor Kharatin, Bartosz Slisz, Mahir Emreli (84' Tomás Pekhart). Coach: Czeslaw Michniewicz.
Leicester City: Kasper Schmeichel, Jannik Vestergaard, Daniel Amartey (78' Ademola Lookman), Timothy Castagne, Çaglar Söyüncü, Luke Thomas, Youri Tielemans, Boubakary Soumaré, Kiernan Dewsbury-Hall (67' James Maddison), Ayoze Pérez (67' Harvey Barnes), Patson Daka (82' Jamie Vardy). Coach: Brendan Rodgers.
Goal: 31' Mahir Emreli 1-0.
Referee: Ivan Bebek (CRO)   Attendance: 27,087

20.10.21 Otkrytiye Arena, Moskva: Spartak Moskva – Leicester City 3-4 (2-1)
Spartak Moskva: Aleksandr Maksimenko, Georgi Dzhikiya, Samuel Gigot, Ayrton, Nikolai Rasskazov, Ruslan Litvinov, Victor Moses, Roman Zobnin (68' Mikhail Ignatov), Zelimkhan Bakaev (68' Quincy Promes), Jordan Larsson (90' Aleksandr Lomovitskiy), Aleksandr Sobolev. Coach: Rui Vitória.
Leicester City: Kasper Schmeichel, Jonny Evans (82' Jannik Vestergaard), Ricardo Pereira (59' Marc Albrighton), Daniel Amartey, Çaglar Söyüncü, Luke Thomas (82' Ryan Bertrand), Youri Tielemans (65' Hamza Choudhury), James Maddison, Boubakary Soumaré, Kelechi Iheanacho, Patson Daka. Coach: Brendan Rodgers.
Goals: 11' Aleksandr Sobolev 1-0, 44' Jordan Larsson 2-0, 45', 48', 54', 79' Patson Daka 2-1, 2-2, 2-3, 2-4, 86' Aleksandr Sobolev 3-4.
Referee: Anastasios Sidiropoulos (GRE)   Attendance: 11,366

21.10.21 Stadio Diego Armando Maradona, Napoli: SSC Napoli – Legia Warszawa 3-0 (0-0)
SSC Napoli: Alex Meret, Kostas Manolas (72' Matteo Politano), Juan Jesus, Kalidou Koulibaly, Giovanni Di Lorenzo, Diego Demme, André Zambo Anguissa (57' Fabián Ruiz), Eljif Elmas, Dries Mertens (72' Andrea Petagna), Lorenzo Insigne (81' Amir Rrahmani), Hirving Lozano (57' Victor Osimhen). Coach: Luciano Spalletti.
Legia Warszawa: Cezary Miszta, Artur Jedrzejczyk, Mattias Johansson, Filip Mladenovic, Mateusz Wieteska, Maik Nawrocki, Josué, André Martins (77' Igor Kharatin), Luquinhas (71' Lirim M. Kastrati), Rafael Lopes (59' Bartosz Slisz), Ernest Muçi (71' Mahir Emreli). Coach: Czeslaw Michniewicz.
Goals: 76' Lorenzo Insigne 1-0, 80' Victor Osimhen 2-0, 90+5' Matteo Politano 3-0.
Referee: Carlos del Cerro Grande (ESP)   Attendance: 10,346

04.11.21 Stadion Miejski Legii Warszawa im. Marszalka Józefa Pilsudskiego, Warszawa: Legia Warszawa – SSC Napoli 1-4 (1-0)
Legia Warszawa: Cezary Miszta, Artur Jedrzejczyk, Mattias Johansson, Filip Mladenovic, Mateusz Wieteska, Yuri Ribeiro, Josué, Bartosz Slisz (70' André Martins), Luquinhas, Mahir Emreli (80' Rafael Lopes), Lirim M. Kastrati (67' Ernest Muçi). Coach: Marek Golebiewski.
SSC Napoli: Alex Meret, Juan Jesus, Kalidou Koulibaly, Giovanni Di Lorenzo, Amir Rrahmani, Diego Demme (65' Stanislav Lobotka), Piotr Zielinski (73' Dries Mertens), André Zambo Anguissa, Eljif Elmas (65' Matteo Politano), Andrea Petagna (83' Alessandro Zanoli), Hirving Lozano (83' Adam Ounas). Coach: Luciano Spalletti.
Goals: 10' Mahir Emreli 1-0, 51' Piotr Zielinski 1-1 (p), 75' Dries Mertens 1-2 (p), 78' Hirving Lozano 1-3, 90' Adam Ounas 1-4.
Referee: Lawrence Visser (BEL)   Attendance: 25,706

04.11.21 King Power Stadium, Leicester: Leicester City – Spartak Moskva 1-1 (0-0)
Leicester City: Kasper Schmeichel, Jonny Evans, Ryan Bertrand (58' Ademola Lookman), Daniel Amartey, Timothy Castagne, Çaglar Söyüncü, Youri Tielemans, Boubakary Soumaré (83' Kiernan Dewsbury-Hall), Ayoze Pérez (58' Wilfred Ndidi), Kelechi Iheanacho, Patson Daka (71' Jamie Vardy). Coach: Brendan Rodgers.
Spartak Moskva: Aleksandr Selikhov, Georgi Dzhikiya, Samuel Gigot, Ayrton, Maximiliano Caufriez, Ruslan Litvinov (90+3' Ilya Kutepov), Victor Moses, Roman Zobnin, Quincy Promes (77' Nail Umyarov), Mikhail Ignatov (87' Aleksandr Lomovitskiy), Aleksandr Sobolev (77' Zelimkhan Bakaev). Coach: Rui Vitória.
Goals: 51' Victor Moses 0-1, 58' Daniel Amartey 1-1.
Referee: Halil Umut Meler (TUR)   Attendance: 30,222

Jamie Vardy missed a penalty kick (75').

24.11.21 Otkrytiye Arena, Moskva: Spartak Moskva – SSC Napoli 2-1 (2-0)
Spartak Moskva: Aleksandr Selikhov, Georgi Dzhikiya, Samuel Gigot, Ayrton, Maximiliano Caufriez, Ruslan Litvinov, Victor Moses (83' Nikolai Rasskazov), Quincy Promes (90+2' Jordan Larsson), Nail Umyarov, Mikhail Ignatov (72' Aleksandr Lomovitskiy), Aleksandr Sobolev. Coach: Rui Vitória.
SSC Napoli: Alex Meret, Juan Jesus, Mário Rui, Kalidou Koulibaly, Giovanni Di Lorenzo, Piotr Zielinski, Stanislav Lobotka (79' Amir Rrahmani), Eljif Elmas, Dries Mertens, Andrea Petagna, Hirving Lozano. Coach: Luciano Spalletti.
Goals: 3', 28' Aleksandr Sobolev 1-0 (p), 2-0, 64' Eljif Elmas 2-1.
Referee: Clément Turpin (FRA)   Attendance: 10,852

25.11.21 King Power Stadium, Leicester: Leicester City – Legia Warszawa 3-1 (3-1)
Leicester City: Kasper Schmeichel, Daniel Amartey, Timothy Castagne, Çaglar Söyüncü, Luke Thomas, Wilfred Ndidi, James Maddison (63' Ayoze Pérez), Boubakary Soumaré (62' Kiernan Dewsbury-Hall), Harvey Barnes, Patson Daka (85' Kelechi Iheanacho), Ademola Lookman (84' Marc Albrighton). Coach: Brendan Rodgers.
Legia Warszawa: Cezary Miszta, Artur Jedrzejczyk, Mattias Johansson (46' Mateusz Holownia), Filip Mladenovic (71' Kacper Skibicki), Mateusz Wieteska, Yuri Ribeiro, André Martins (71' Jurgen Çelhaka), Bartosz Slisz, Luquinhas (78' Tomás Pekhart), Mahir Emreli (78' Szymon Wlodarczyk), Ernest Muçi. Coach: Marek Golebiewski.
Goals: 11' Patson Daka 1-0, 21' James Maddison 2-0, 26' Filip Mladenovic 2-1, 33' Wilfred Ndidi 3-1.
Referee: Deniz Aytekin (GER)   Attendance: 30,658

Mahir Emreli missed a penalty kick (26').

09.12.21   Stadio Diego Armando Maradona, Napoli: SSC Napoli – Leicester City 3-2 (2-2)
SSC Napoli: Alex Meret, Juan Jesus, Mário Rui, Giovanni Di Lorenzo, Amir Rrahmani, Diego Demme (78' Kostas Manolas), Piotr Zielinski, Adam Ounas (63' Dries Mertens), Eljif Elmas, Andrea Petagna, Hirving Lozano (45' Kévin Malcuit). Coach: Luciano Spalletti.
Leicester City: Kasper Schmeichel, Jonny Evans, Ryan Bertrand, Timothy Castagne, Çaglar Söyüncü, Youri Tielemans (77' Boubakary Soumaré), Wilfred Ndidi, James Maddison, Kiernan Dewsbury-Hall (89' Marc Albrighton), Harvey Barnes (72' Patson Daka), Jamie Vardy. Coach: Brendan Rodgers.
Goals: 4' Adam Ounas 1-0, 24' Eljif Elmas 2-0, 27' Jonny Evans 2-1, 33' Kiernan Dewsbury-Hall 2-2, 53' Eljif Elmas 3-2.
Referee: Antonio Mateu Lahoz (ESP)   Attendance: 14,646

09.12.21   Stadion Miejski Legii Warszawa im. Marszalka Józefa Pilsudskiego, Warszawa:
            Legia Warszawa – Spartak Moskva 0-1 (0-1)
Legia Warszawa: Artur Boruc, Mattias Johansson, Mateusz Wieteska, Yuri Ribeiro, Maik Nawrocki, Josué (65' Rafael Lopes), André Martins (72' Szymon Wlodarczyk), Bartosz Slisz (65' Igor Kharatin), Luquinhas, Mahir Emreli (72' Tomás Pekhart), Lirim M. Kastrati (90' Kacper Skwierczynski). Coach: Marek Golebiewski.
Spartak Moskva: Aleksandr Selikhov, Georgi Dzhikiya, Samuel Gigot, Ayrton, Maximiliano Caufriez, Victor Moses, Roman Zobnin (76' Jorrit Hendrix), Quincy Promes, Zelimkhan Bakaev (88' Aleksandr Lomovitskiy), Nail Umyarov, Mikhail Ignatov (77' Georgi Melkadze). Coach: Rui Vitória.
Goal: 17' Zelimkhan Bakaev 0-1.
Referee: Matej Jug (SVN)   Attendance: 21,629

Tomás Pekhart missed a penalty kick (90+8').

GROUP D

16.09.21   Deutsche Bank Park, Frankfurt am Main:
            Eintracht Frankfurt – Fenerbahçe 1-1 (1-1)
Eintracht Frankfurt: Kevin Trapp, Martin Hinteregger, Erik Durm, Danny da Costa, Evan N'Dicka, Filip Kostic, Djibril Sow, Daichi Kamada, Kristijan Jakic, Rafael Borré (72' Jens Hauge), Sam Lammers. Coach: Oliver Glasner.
Fenerbahçe: Altay Bayindir, Serdar Aziz, Attila Szalai, Kim Min-Jae, Mesut Özil (77' Dimitrios Pelkas), Luiz Gustavo, Mert Hakan Yandas (77' Max Meyer), Bright Osayi-Samuel, Ferdi Kadioglu (77' Muhammed Gümüskaya), Enner Valencia (76' Mërgim Berisha), Diego Rossi. Coach: Vítor Pereira.
Goals: 10' Mesut Özil 0-1, 41' Sam Lammers 1-1.
Referee: Maurizio Mariani (ITA)   Attendance: 25,000

Dimitrios Pelkas missed a penalty kick (90+2').

16.09.21 Stadio Georgios Karaiskáki, Piraeus:
Olympiakos Piraeus – Royal Antwerp FC 2-1 (0-0)
Olympiakos Piraeus: Tomás Vaclík, Sokratis Papastathopoulos, Pape Cissé, Oleg Reabciuk, Michal Karbownik, Yann M'Vila (76' Mathieu Valbuena), Andreas Bouchalakis, Mohamed Mady Camara (81' Pierre Malong), Youssef El-Arabi (88' Ousseynou Ba), Henry Onyekuru (81' Tiquinho Soares), Aguibou Camara (81' Marios Vrousai). Coach: Pedro Martins.
Royal Antwerp FC: Jean Butez, Ritchie De Laet, Dinis Almeida, Aurélio Buta, Jelle Bataille, Radja Nainggolan (67' Pieter Gerkens), Birger Verstraete, Michael Frey (80' Johannes Eggestein), Viktor Fischer, Mbwana Samatta, Koji Miyoshi (67' Benson Manuel).
Coach: Brian Priske.
Goals: 52' Youssef El-Arabi 1-0, 74' Mbwana Samatta 1-1, 87' Oleg Reabciuk 2-1.
Referee: Tamás Bognár (HUN)   Attendance: 15,615
Sent-off: 90' Jelle Bataille.

30.09.21 Bosuilstadion, Deurne: Royal Antwerp FC – Eintracht Frankfurt 0-1 (0-0)
Royal Antwerp FC: Jean Butez, Ritchie De Laet, Dorian Dessoleil, Dinis Almeida, Aurélio Buta, Radja Nainggolan, Birger Verstraete, Viktor Fischer, Mbwana Samatta (67' Pieter Gerkens), Benson Manuel (77' Koji Miyoshi), Johannes Eggestein (46' Michael Frey).
Coach: Brian Priske.
Eintracht Frankfurt: Kevin Trapp, Makoto Hasebe (72' Stefan Ilsanker), Timothy Chandler, Martin Hinteregger, Almamy Touré, Filip Kostic, Ajdin Hrustic (46' Daichi Kamada), Djibril Sow (90+3' Tuta), Kristijan Jakic, Rafael Borré (86' Gonçalo Paciência), Sam Lammers (72' Jesper Lindstrøm). Coach: Oliver Glasner.
Goal: 90+1' Gonçalo Paciência 0-1 (p).
Referee: Jakob Kehlet (DEN)   Attendance: 13,193

30.09.21 Ülker Stadyumu Fenerbahçe Sükrü Saracoglu Spor Kompleksi, Istanbul:
Fenerbahçe – Olympiakos Piraeus 0-3 (0-1)
Fenerbahçe: Altay Bayindir, Filip Novák, Attila Szalai, Kim Min-Jae, Luiz Gustavo (70' Miha Zajc), Dimitrios Pelkas, Mert Hakan Yandas (75' Max Meyer), Bright Osayi-Samuel, Ferdi Kadioglu (84' Fatih Sanlitürk), Enner Valencia (75' Muhammed Gümüskaya), Diego Rossi (70' Mërgim Berisha). Coach: Vítor Pereira.
Olympiakos Piraeus: Tomás Vaclík, Sokratis Papastathopoulos, Pape Cissé, Oleg Reabciuk, Ousseynou Ba (46' Kenny Lala), Andreas Bouchalakis, Georgios Masouras (89' Mathieu Valbuena), Mohamed Mady Camara (89' Marios Vrousai), Tiquinho Soares (86' Youssef El-Arabi), Henry Onyekuru (64' Pierre Malong), Aguibou Camara. Coach: Pedro Martins.
Goals: 6' Tiquinho Soares 0-1, 63', 68' Georgios Masouras 0-2, 0-3.
Referee: Alejandro Hernández Hernández (ESP)   Attendance: 22,160

21.10.21   Ülker Stadyumu Fenerbahçe Şükrü Saracoglu Spor Kompleksi, Istanbul:
Fenerbahçe – Royal Antwerp FC 2-2 (2-1)
Fenerbahçe: Altay Bayindir, Marcel Tisserand, Attila Szalai (87' Filip Novák), Kim Min-Jae, Mesut Özil (66' Dimitrios Pelkas), Luiz Gustavo, José Sosa (67' Miha Zajc), Bright Osayi-Samuel, Ferdi Kadioglu (67' Nazim Sangaré), Enner Valencia, Mërgim Berisha (66' Diego Rossi). Coach: Vítor Pereira.
Royal Antwerp FC: Jean Butez, Ritchie De Laet, Dinis Almeida, Sam Vines, Jelle Bataille, Pieter Gerkens, Birger Verstraete, Alhassan Yusuf (63' Pierre Dwomoh), Michael Frey (70' Benson Manuel), Viktor Fischer (46' Michel Balikwisha), Mbwana Samatta.
Coach: Brian Priske.
Goals: 2' Mbwana Samatta 0-1, 20', 45' Enner Valencia 1-1, 2-1 (p), 62' Pieter Gerkens 2-2.
Referee: Sergey Ivanov (RUS)   Attendance: 16,629

Enner Valencia missed a penalty kick (36').

21.10.21   Deutsche Bank Park, Frankfurt am Main:
Eintracht Frankfurt – Olympiakos Piraeus 3-1 (2-1)
Eintracht Frankfurt: Kevin Trapp, Makoto Hasebe, Martin Hinteregger, Almamy Touré (82' Erik Durm), Tuta (60' Evan N'Dicka), Filip Kostic, Djibril Sow (88' Jens Hauge), Daichi Kamada, Kristijan Jakic, Gonçalo Paciência (82' Sebastian Rode), Rafael Borré.
Coach: Oliver Glasner.
Olympiakos Piraeus: Tomás Vaclík, Sokratis Papastathopoulos, Kenny Lala (77' Athanasios Androutsos), Pape Cissé, Oleg Reabciuk, Yann M'Vila (61' Henry Onyekuru), Andreas Bouchalakis, Georgios Masouras (77' Rony Lopes), Mohamed Mady Camara (65' Pierre Malong), Youssef El-Arabi (65' Tiquinho Soares), Aguibou Camara. Coach: Pedro Martins.
Goals: 26' Rafael Borré 1-0 (p), 30' Youssef El-Arabi 1-1 (p), 45+3' Almamy Touré 2-1, 59' Daichi Kamada 3-1.
Referee: Tiago Martins (POR)   Attendance: 35,000

04.11.21   Stadio Georgios Karaiskáki, Piraeus:
Olympiakos Piraeus – Eintracht Frankfurt 1-2 (1-1)
Olympiakos Piraeus: Tomás Vaclík, Sokratis Papastathopoulos, Kenny Lala, Oleg Reabciuk, Ousseynou Ba, Yann M'Vila, Georgios Masouras (83' Rony Lopes), Mohamed Mady Camara (89' Pierre Malong), Youssef El-Arabi (83' Tiquinho Soares), Henry Onyekuru (71' Mathieu Valbuena), Aguibou Camara. Coach: Pedro Martins.
Eintracht Frankfurt: Kevin Trapp, Makoto Hasebe, Timothy Chandler, Evan N'Dicka, Tuta, Djibril Sow (82' Stefan Ilsanker), Daichi Kamada, Kristijan Jakic (78' Sebastian Rode), Aymane Barkok (58' Almamy Touré), Rafael Borré (78' Jens Hauge), Sam Lammers (58' Jesper Lindstrøm). Coach: Oliver Glasner.
Goals: 12' Youssef El-Arabi 1-0, 17' Daichi Kamada 1-1, 90+2' Jens Hauge 1-2.
Referee: Aleksei Kulbakov (BLS)   Attendance: 23,050

04.11.21   Bosuilstadion, Deurne: Royal Antwerp FC – Fenerbahçe 0-3 (0-3)
Royal Antwerp FC: Jean Butez, Ritchie De Laet, Dinis Almeida, Sam Vines, Jelle Bataille (77'
Michel Balikwisha), Pieter Gerkens (68' Pierre Dwomoh), Birger Verstraete, Alhassan Yusuf
(46' Dorian Dessoleil), Michael Frey, Viktor Fischer (61' Mbwana Samatta), Benson Manuel
(62' Koji Miyoshi). Coach: Brian Priske.
Fenerbahçe: Berke Özer, Filip Novák, Marcel Tisserand (73' Attila Szalai), Kim Min-Jae, José
Sosa (80' Dimitrios Pelkas), Max Meyer, Irfan Kahveci (64' Diego Rossi), Mert Hakan Yandas
(65' Miha Zajc), Bright Osayi-Samuel, Ferdi Kadioglu (73' Nazim Sangaré), Mërgim Berisha.
Coach: Vítor Pereira.
Goals: 8' Mert Hakan Yandas 0-1, 16' Max Meyer 0-2, 29' Mërgim Berisha 0-3.
Referee: Irfan Peljto (BIH)   Attendance: 0

25.11.21   Deutsche Bank Park, Frankfurt am Main:
           Eintracht Frankfurt – Royal Antwerp FC 2-2 (1-1)
Eintracht Frankfurt: Kevin Trapp, Makoto Hasebe, Timothy Chandler, Evan N'Dicka, Tuta,
Filip Kostic, Djibril Sow, Daichi Kamada (90' Gonçalo Paciência), Kristijan Jakic (90'
Sebastian Rode), Jesper Lindstrøm (78' Jens Hauge), Rafael Borré (69' Sam Lammers).
Coach: Oliver Glasner.
Royal Antwerp FC: Jean Butez, Ritchie De Laet, Dorian Dessoleil, Dinis Almeida, Sam Vines,
Radja Nainggolan, Birger Verstraete, Pierre Dwomoh (66' Alhassan Yusuf), Michael Frey,
Viktor Fischer (76' Johannes Eggestein), Mbwana Samatta. Coach: Brian Priske.
Goals: 13' Daichi Kamada 1-0, 33' Radja Nainggolan 1-1, 88' Mbwana Samatta 1-2,
90+4' Gonçalo Paciência 2-2.
Referee: Paul Tierney (ENG)   Attendance: 30,000

25.11.21   Stadio Georgios Karaiskáki, Piraeus: Olympiakos Piraeus – Fenerbahçe 1-0 (0-0)
Olympiakos Piraeus: Tomás Vaclík, Sokratis Papastathopoulos (25' Ousseynou Ba), Kenny
Lala, Pape Cissé, Oleg Reabciuk, Yann M'Vila, Georgios Masouras (68' Mathieu Valbuena),
Mohamed Mady Camara (46' Andreas Bouchalakis), Youssef El-Arabi (81' Tiquinho Soares),
Henry Onyekuru (46' Rony Lopes), Aguibou Camara. Coach: Pedro Martins.
Fenerbahçe: Berke Özer, Filip Novák (78' Attila Szalai), Marcel Tisserand, Kim Min-Jae, José
Sosa, Miha Zajc (65' Max Meyer), Irfan Kahveci (65' Dimitrios Pelkas), Mert Hakan Yandas
(90+1' Muhammed Gümüskaya), Bright Osayi-Samuel, Mërgim Berisha, Diego Rossi (78'
Ferdi Kadioglu). Coach: Vítor Pereira.
Goal: 89' Tiquinho Soares 1-0.
Referee: Antonio Mateu Lahoz (ESP)   Attendance: 22,405

09.12.21   Ülker Stadyumu Fenerbahçe Sükrü Saracoglu Spor Kompleksi, Istanbul:
           Fenerbahçe – Eintracht Frankfurt 1-1 (1-1)
Fenerbahçe: Berke Özer, Serdar Aziz, Filip Novák (72' Bright Osayi-Samuel), Nazim Sangaré,
Attila Szalai, Kim Min-Jae, José Sosa (72' Luiz Gustavo), Miha Zajc (76' Max Meyer), Irfan
Kahveci (76' Diego Rossi), Dimitrios Pelkas (81' Muhammed Gümüskaya), Mërgim Berisha.
Coach: Vítor Pereira.
Eintracht Frankfurt: Kevin Trapp, Makoto Hasebe, Timothy Chandler (69' Danny da Costa),
Evan N'Dicka, Tuta, Filip Kostic, Djibril Sow (78' Ajdin Hrustic), Daichi Kamada, Kristijan
Jakic (69' Sebastian Rode), Jens Hauge (69' Sam Lammers), Rafael Borré (60' Gonçalo
Paciência). Coach: Oliver Glasner.
Goals: 29' Djibril Sow 0-1, 42' Mërgim Berisha 1-1.
Referee: Srdjan Jovanovic (SRB)   Attendance: 8,932

09.12.21 Bosuilstadion, Deurne: Royal Antwerp FC – Olympiakos Piraeus 1-0 (1-0)
Royal Antwerp FC: Jean Butez, Ritchie De Laet (57' Robbe Quirynen), Dorian Dessoleil (57' Björn Engels), Dinis Almeida, Jelle Bataille, Pieter Gerkens, Birger Verstraete, Pierre Dwomoh, Benson Manuel (73' Mbwana Samatta), Johannes Eggestein (73' Michael Frey), Michel Balikwisha (87' Alhassan Yusuf). Coach: Brian Priske.
Olympiakos Piraeus: Tomás Vaclík, Sokratis Papastathopoulos, Kenny Lala (66' Athanasios Androutsos), Pape Cissé, Oleg Reabciuk, Yann M'Vila, Andreas Bouchalakis (46' Aguibou Camara), Mohamed Mady Camara, Tiquinho Soares (46' Youssef El-Arabi), Rony Lopes (46' Georgios Masouras), Henry Onyekuru (60' Marios Vrousai). Coach: Pedro Martins.
Goal: 7' Michel Balikwisha 1-0.
Referee: Marco Di Bello (ITA) Attendance: 7,992

GROUP E

16.09.21 RZD Arena, Moskva: Lokomotiv Moskva – Olympique Marseille 1-1 (0-0)
Lokomotiv Moskva: Guilherme, Tin Jedvaj, Murilo Cerqueira, Dmitry Barinov, Rifat Zhemaletdinov (63' Tino Anjorin), Nayair Tiknizyan, Daniil Kulikov (56' Konstantin Maradishvili), Stanislav Magkeev, Alexis Beka Beka (64' Aleksandr Silyanov), Fedor Smolov (75' Vitaliy Lisakovich), François Kamano (75' Gyrano Kerk). Coach: Marko Nikolic.
Olympique Marseille: Pau López, Álvaro González, Luan Peres, Boubacar Kamara, William Saliba, Valentin Rongier, Gerson (83' Pape Gueye), Cengiz Ünder, Amine Harit (56' Konrad de la Fuente), Mattéo Guendouzi (83' Pol Lirola), Cheikh Bamba Dieng (82' Luis Henrique). Coach: Jorge Sampaoli.
Goals: 59' Cengiz Ünder 0-1 (p), 89' Tino Anjorin 1-1.
Referee: Irfan Peljto (BIH) Attendance: 8,100
Sent-off: 57' Nayair Tiknizyan.

16.09.21 NEF Stadyumu, Istanbul: Galatasaray – Lazio Roma 1-0 (0-0)
Galatasaray: Fernando Muslera, Patrick van Aanholt, DeAndre Yedlin, Marcão, Victor Nelsson, Taylan Antalyali (78' Emre Kilinç), Alexandru Cicâldau (90' Christian Luyindama), Olimpiu Morutan (85' Sofiane Féghouli), Kerem Aktürkoglu (79' Ryan Babel), Berkan Kutlu, Halil Dervisoglu (90' Mostafa Mohamed). Coach: Fatih Terim.
Lazio Roma: Thomas Strakosha, Francesco Acerbi, Elseid Hysaj, Luiz Felipe, Lucas Leiva (83' Danilo Cataldi), Luis Alberto (65' Toma Basic), Jean-Daniel Akpa-Akpro (56' Sergej Milinkovic-Savic), Manuel Lazzari, Mattia Zaccagni, Ciro Immobile (56' Vedat Muriqi), Felipe Anderson (66' Pedro). Coach: Maurizio Sarri.
Goal: 67' Thomas Strakosha 1-0 (og).
Referee: Matej Jug (SVN) Attendance: 15,353

30.09.21 Stadio Olimpico, Roma: Lazio Roma – Lokomotiv Moskva 2-0 (2-0)
Lazio Roma: Thomas Strakosha, Francesco Acerbi, Elseid Hysaj, Patric, Luis Alberto (60' Sergej Milinkovic-Savic), Manuel Lazzari (74' Adam Marusic), Danilo Cataldi (60' Lucas Leiva), Toma Basic, Pedro (74' Raúl Moro), Ciro Immobile (41' Vedat Muriqi), Felipe Anderson. Coach: Maurizio Sarri.
Lokomotiv Moskva: Guilherme, Pablo Castro, Dmitri Zhivoglyadov, Dmitry Barinov, Rifat Zhemaletdinov (82' Vitaliy Lisakovich), Dmitry Rybchinsky, Daniil Kulikov, Tino Anjorin (82' Maksim Petrov), Konstantin Maradishvili (72' Gyrano Kerk), Alexis Beka Beka, Fedor Smolov. Coach: Marko Nikolic.
Goals: 13' Toma Basic 1-0, 38' Patric 2-0.
Referee: Craig Pawson (ENG) Attendance: 6,767

30.09.21 Stade Orange Vélodrome, Marseille: Olympique Marseille – Galatasaray 0-0
Olympique Marseille: Pau López, Álvaro González, Luan Peres, Pol Lirola, William Saliba, Dimitri Payet, Cengiz Ünder, Amine Harit (79' Konrad de la Fuente), Mattéo Guendouzi, Pape Gueye, Cheikh Bamba Dieng (61' Arkadiusz Milik). Coach: Jorge Sampaoli.
Galatasaray: Fernando Muslera, Patrick van Aanholt, Marcão, Victor Nelsson, Sacha Boey (65' DeAndre Yedlin), Taylan Antalyali, Alexandru Cicâldau, Olimpiu Morutan (72' Emre Kilinç), Kerem Aktürkoglu (87' Ryan Babel), Berkan Kutlu (87' Christian Luyindama), Halil Dervisoglu (72' Mbaye Diagne). Coach: Fatih Terim.
Referee: Pawel Raczkowski (POL) Attendance: 49,870

21.10.21 Stadio Olimpico, Roma: Lazio Roma – Olympique Marseille 0-0
Lazio Roma: Thomas Strakosha, Francesco Acerbi, Adam Marusic, Luiz Felipe, Manuel Lazzari, Mattia Zaccagni (77' Raúl Moro), Danilo Cataldi (77' Lucas Leiva), Sergej Milinkovic-Savic (56' Jean-Daniel Akpa-Akpro), Toma Basic (57' Luis Alberto), Ciro Immobile, Felipe Anderson (56' Pedro). Coach: Maurizio Sarri.
Olympique Marseille: Pau López, Duje Caleta-Car, Luan Peres, Pol Lirola (61' Cheikh Bamba Dieng), Boubacar Kamara, William Saliba, Dimitri Payet, Valentin Rongier (85' Leonardo Balerdi), Cengiz Ünder, Mattéo Guendouzi (73' Pape Gueye), Arkadiusz Milik (73' Gerson). Coach: Jorge Sampaoli.
Referee: Deniz Aytekin (GER) Attendance: 8,329

21.10.21 RZD Arena, Moskva: Lokomotiv Moskva – Galatasaray 0-1 (0-0)
Lokomotiv Moskva: Guilherme, Maciej Rybus (89' Dmitri Zhivoglyadov), Pablo Castro, Tin Jedvaj, Dmitry Barinov, Rifat Zhemaletdinov, Gyrano Kerk, Nayair Tiknizyan, Konstantin Maradishvili, Alexis Beka Beka, Fedor Smolov. Coach: Markus Gisdol.
Galatasaray: Fernando Muslera, Patrick van Aanholt (90' Ömer Bayram), DeAndre Yedlin, Marcão, Victor Nelsson, Taylan Antalyali, Alexandru Cicâldau (90' Christian Luyindama), Berkan Kutlu, Ryan Babel (76' Olimpiu Morutan), Mostafa Mohamed (76' Mbaye Diagne), Baris Yilmaz (67' Kerem Aktürkoglu). Coach: Fatih Terim.
Goal: 82' Kerem Aktürkoglu 0-1.
Referee: Harald Lechner (AUT) Attendance: 8,100

04.11.21 NEF Stadyumu, Istanbul: Galatasaray – Lokomotiv Moskva 1-1 (1-0)
Galatasaray: Fernando Muslera, Patrick van Aanholt (76' Ömer Bayram), DeAndre Yedlin, Marcão, Victor Nelsson, Sofiane Féghouli (71' Baris Yilmaz), Alexandru Cicâldau, Olimpiu Morutan (76' Mostafa Mohamed), Kerem Aktürkoglu, Berkan Kutlu, Halil Dervisoglu (89' Mbaye Diagne). Coach: Fatih Terim.
Lokomotiv Moskva: Guilherme, Maciej Rybus, Tin Jedvaj, Maksim Nenakhov (46' Dmitri Zhivoglyadov), Dmitry Barinov, Rifat Zhemaletdinov, Gyrano Kerk, Dmitry Rybchinsky (65' François Kamano), Konstantin Maradishvili, Alexis Beka Beka (85' Murilo Cerqueira), Vitaliy Lisakovich (46' Fedor Smolov). Coach: Markus Gisdol.
Goals: 43' Sofiane Féghouli 1-0, 72' François Kamano 1-1.
Referee: Sandro Schärer (SUI) Attendance: 27,776

04.11.21   Stade Orange Vélodrome, Marseille: Olympique Marseille – Lazio Roma 2-2 (1-1)
Olympique Marseille: Pau López, Duje Caleta-Car, Luan Peres, Pol Lirola (85' Pape Gueye), Boubacar Kamara (55' Amine Harit), William Saliba, Dimitri Payet, Valentin Rongier, Cengiz Ünder, Mattéo Guendouzi, Arkadiusz Milik. Coach: Jorge Sampaoli.
Lazio Roma: Thomas Strakosha, Francesco Acerbi, Elseid Hysaj, Luiz Felipe, Lucas Leiva (52' Danilo Cataldi), Luis Alberto (75' Jean-Daniel Akpa-Akpro), Manuel Lazzari (26' Adam Marusic), Toma Basic (52' Sergej Milinkovic-Savic), Pedro, Ciro Immobile, Felipe Anderson (75' Raúl Moro). Coach: Maurizio Sarri.
Goals: 33' Arkadiusz Milik 1-0 (p), 45+7' Felipe Anderson 1-1, 49' Ciro Immobile 1-2, 82' Dimitri Payet 2-2.
Referee: José María Sánchez Martínez (ESP)   Attendance: 59,163

25.11.21   NEF Stadyumu, Istanbul: Galatasaray – Olympique Marseille 4-2 (2-0)
Galatasaray: Fernando Muslera, Patrick van Aanholt, DeAndre Yedlin, Marcão, Victor Nelsson, Sofiane Féghouli (82' Christian Luyindama), Taylan Antalyali, Alexandru Cicâldau (51' Olimpiu Morutan), Kerem Aktürkoglu (82' Ryan Babel), Berkan Kutlu (90+3' Bartug Elmaz), Mbaye Diagne (90+3' Mostafa Mohamed). Coach: Fatih Terim.
Olympique Marseille: Pau López, Duje Caleta-Car, Luan Peres, Pol Lirola, Boubacar Kamara, William Saliba, Gerson, Mattéo Guendouzi, Pape Gueye (63' Konrad de la Fuente), Arkadiusz Milik, Cheikh Bamba Dieng. Coach: Jorge Sampaoli.
Goals: 12' Alexandru Cicâldau 1-0, 30' Duje Caleta-Car 2-0 (og), 64' Sofiane Féghouli 3-0, 68' Arkadiusz Milik 3-1, 83' Ryan Babel 4-1, 85' Arkadiusz Milik 4-2.
Referee: Tobias Stieler (GER)   Attendance: 39,758

Arkadiusz Milik missed a penalty kick (68').

25.11.21   RZD Arena, Moskva: Lokomotiv Moskva – Lazio Roma 0-3 (0-0)
Lokomotiv Moskva: Daniil Khudyakov, Maciej Rybus, Tin Jedvaj, Maksim Nenakhov (28' Aleksandr Silyanov), Murilo Cerqueira, Dmitry Barinov, Dmitry Rybchinsky (59' Fedor Smolov), Konstantin Maradishvili (77' Kirill Zinovich), Alexis Beka Beka, François Kamano (77' Grigoriy Borisenko), Vitaliy Lisakovich. Coach: Markus Gisdol.
Lazio Roma: Thomas Strakosha, Francesco Acerbi, Elseid Hysaj, Patric, Luiz Felipe, Lucas Leiva (59' Danilo Cataldi), Luis Alberto (59' Sergej Milinkovic-Savic), Mattia Zaccagni (82' Manuel Lazzari), Toma Basic, Ciro Immobile (66' Vedat Muriqi), Felipe Anderson (46' Pedro). Coach: Maurizio Sarri.
Goals: 56', 63' Ciro Immobile 0-1 (p), 0-2 (p), 87' Pedro 0-3.
Referee: Artur Soares Dias (POR)   Attendance: 8,100

09.12.21   Stadio Olimpico, Roma: Lazio Roma – Galatasaray 0-0
Lazio Roma: Thomas Strakosha, Francesco Acerbi, Elseid Hysaj (63' Manuel Lazzari), Adam Marusic, Luiz Felipe, Lucas Leiva (73' Danilo Cataldi), Mattia Zaccagni, Sergej Milinkovic-Savic, Toma Basic (73' Luis Alberto), Pedro (63' Felipe Anderson), Ciro Immobile. Coach: Maurizio Sarri.
Galatasaray: Fernando Muslera, Patrick van Aanholt, DeAndre Yedlin, Marcão, Victor Nelsson, Sofiane Féghouli (63' Olimpiu Morutan), Taylan Antalyali, Kerem Aktürkoglu (88' Mostafa Mohamed), Berkan Kutlu (88' Christian Luyindama), Ryan Babel (63' Emre Kilinç), Mbaye Diagne (69' Ömer Bayram). Coach: Fatih Terim.
Referee: Carlos del Cerro Grande (ESP)   Attendance: 13,178

09.12.21 Stade Orange Vélodrome, Marseille:
Olympique Marseille – Lokomotiv Moskva 1-0 (1-0)
Olympique Marseille: Steve Mandanda, Luan Peres, Leonardo Balerdi, William Saliba, Valentin Rongier, Gerson, Cengiz Ünder (86' Luis Henrique), Mattéo Guendouzi (69' Pol Lirola), Pape Gueye (68' Boubacar Kamara), Arkadiusz Milik (68' Dimitri Payet), Konrad de la Fuente (82' Cheikh Bamba Dieng). Coach: Jorge Sampaoli.
Lokomotiv Moskva: Daniil Khudyakov, Maciej Rybus, Pablo Castro (84' Vitaliy Lisakovich), Tin Jedvaj, Maksim Nenakhov, Konstantin Maradishvili (56' Nayair Tiknizyan), Maksim Petrov, Alexis Beka Beka, Sergey Babkin, Fedor Smolov, François Kamano (32' Dmitry Rybchinsky). Coach: Markus Gisdol.
Goal: 35' Arkadiusz Milik 1-0.
Referee: William Collum (SCO)   Attendance: 42,614
Sent-off: 80' Valentin Rongier.

GROUP F

16.09.21   MCH Arena, Herning: FC Midtjylland – PFC Ludogorets Razgrad 1-1 (1-1)
FC Midtjylland: Elías Ólafsson, Erik Sviatchenko, Henrik Dalsgaard, Joel Andersson, Paulinho (85' Dion Cools), Juninho, Pione Sisto (86' Charles), Evander, Gustav Isaksen (75' Victor Lind), Raphael Onyedika, Júnior Brumado (75' Awer Mabil). Coach: Bo Henriksen.
PFC Ludogorets Razgrad: Kristijan Kahlina, Cicinho, Igor Plastun, Josué Sá, Anton Nedyalkov (54' Shaquille Pinas), Stéphane Badji, Claude Gonçalves, Alex Santana (74' Dominik Yankov), Elvis Manu (54' Pieros Sotiriou), Kiril Despodov (60' Mavis Tchibota), Bernard Tekpetey (74' Olivier Verdon). Coach: Valdas Dambrauskas.
Goals: 3' Gustav Isaksen 1-0, 32' Kiril Despodov 1-1.
Referee: Aliyar Aghayev (AZE)   Attendance: 6,568

16.09.21   Stadion Rajko Mitic, Beograd: Crvena Zvezda Beograd – Sporting Braga 2-1 (0-0)
Crvena Zvezda Beograd: Milan Borjan, Aleksandar Dragovic, Milan Rodic, Milos Degenek, Marko Gobeljic, Aleksandar Katai (87' Slavoljub Srnic), Sékou Sanogo (87' Radovan Pankov), Guélor Kanga, Mirko Ivanic, El Fardou Ben Nabouhane (39' Loïs Diony), Richairo Zivkovic (65' Nenad Krsticic). Coach: Dejan Stankovic.
Sporting Braga: Matheus Magalhães, Paulo Oliveira (87' Nuno Sequeira), Diogo Leite, Vítor Tormena, Fabiano (86' Yan Couto), Ali Musrati, Lucas Mineiro (78' André Horta), Lucas Piazón (78' Fábio Martins), Ricardo Horta, Galeno, Abel Ruiz (70' Mario González).
Coach: Carlos Carvalhal.
Goals: 74' Milan Rodic 1-0, 76' Galeno 1-1, 85' Aleksandar Katai 2-1 (p).
Referee: John Beaton (SCO)   Attendance: 24,671

30.09.21   Huvepharma Arena, Razgrad:
PFC Ludogorets Razgrad – Crvena Zvezda Beograd 0-1 (0-0)
PFC Ludogorets Razgrad: Kristijan Kahlina, Cicinho, Igor Plastun, Josué Sá (71' Kiril Despodov), Olivier Verdon, Shaquille Pinas (71' Jordan Ikoko), Stéphane Badji (88' Show), Claude Gonçalves, Alex Santana (78' Mavis Tchibota), Pieros Sotiriou, Bernard Tekpetey.
Coach: Valdas Dambrauskas.
Crvena Zvezda Beograd: Zoran Popovic, Milan Rodic, Marko Gobeljic, Radovan Pankov, Strahinja Erakovic, Slavoljub Srnic, Sékou Sanogo, Guélor Kanga (71' Petar Stanic, 86' Nenad Krsticic), Mirko Ivanic, El Fardou Ben Nabouhane (86' Richairo Zivkovic), Loïs Diony (57' Milan Pavkov). Coach: Dejan Stankovic.
Goal: 64' Guélor Kanga 0-1.
Referee: Jérôme Brisard (FRA)   Attendance: 3,078
Sent-off: 77' Cicinho.

30.09.21 Estádio Municipal de Braga, Braga: Sporting Braga – FC Midtjylland 3-1 (0-1)
Sporting Braga: Matheus Magalhães, Paulo Oliveira, Nuno Sequeira (46' Francisco Moura), Diogo Leite, Yan Couto, André Castro (46' Mario González), Ali Musrati (72' Lucas Mineiro), Chiquinho, Lucas Piazón (61' Iuri Medeiros), Ricardo Horta (82' André Horta), Galeno.
Coach: Carlos Carvalhal.
FC Midtjylland: Elías Ólafsson, Erik Sviatchenko, Henrik Dalsgaard, Joel Andersson, Paulinho, Juninho, Pione Sisto (79' Victor Lind), Evander, Gustav Isaksen (71' Marrony), Raphael Onyedika (70' Jens-Lys Cajuste), Júnior Brumado. Coach: Bo Henriksen.
Goals: 19' Evander 0-1 (p), 55' Galeno 1-1 (p), 62' Ricardo Horta 2-1, 90+5' Galeno 3-1.
Referee: Stéphanie Frappart (FRA)   Attendance: 5,449
Sent-off: 84' Juninho.

Ricardo Horta missed a penalty kick (35').

21.10.21 Huvepharma Arena, Razgrad: PFC Ludogorets Razgrad – Sporting Braga 0-1 (0-1)
PFC Ludogorets Razgrad: Kristijan Kahlina, Josué Sá, Jordan Ikoko, Olivier Verdon (46' Igor Plastun), Shaquille Pinas, Stéphane Badji (87' Dimitar Mitkov), Claude Gonçalves (70' Alex Santana), Dominik Yankov (59' Elvis Manu), Pieros Sotiriou, Kiril Despodov, Bernard Tekpetey (59' Mavis Tchibota). Coach: Stanislav Genchev.
Sporting Braga: Matheus Magalhães, Paulo Oliveira, Nuno Sequeira, Diogo Leite, Fabiano, André Castro (77' Chiquinho, Ali Musrati, Iuri Medeiros (60' Lucas Piazón), Ricardo Horta (77' Lucas Mineiro), Galeno (90+1' Francisco Moura), Abel Ruiz (60' Mario González).
Coach: Carlos Carvalhal.
Goal: 7' Ricardo Horta 0-1.
Referee: Kristo Tohver (EST)   Attendance: 2,280

21.10.21 MCH Arena, Herning: FC Midtjylland – Crvena Zvezda Beograd 1-1 (0-0)
FC Midtjylland: Elías Ólafsson, Erik Sviatchenko, Henrik Dalsgaard, Joel Andersson, Paulinho, Nikolas Dyhr (90+2' Awer Mabil), Pione Sisto, Evander, Gustav Isaksen (73' Marrony), Jens-Lys Cajuste (62' Victor Lind), Raphael Onyedika. Coach: Bo Henriksen.
Crvena Zvezda Beograd: Milan Borjan, Aleksandar Dragovic, Milan Rodic, Milos Degenek, Marko Gobeljic, Slavoljub Srnic (46' Nenad Krsticic), Filippo Falco (56' Loïs Diony), Sékou Sanogo, Guélor Kanga (81' Radovan Pankov), Mirko Ivanic, El Fardou Ben Nabouhane (90+5' Milan Gajic). Coach: Dejan Stankovic.
Goals: 58' Mirko Ivanic 0-1, 78' Nikolas Dyhr 1-1.
Referee: Roi Reinshreiber (ISR)   Attendance: 8,438

04.11.21 Estádio Municipal de Braga, Braga: Sporting Braga – Ludogorets Razgrad 4-2 (3-1)
Sporting Braga: Matheus Magalhães, Paulo Oliveira, Nuno Sequeira (74' Bruno Rodrigues), Diogo Leite, Yan Couto, André Castro (70' André Horta), Ali Musrati (62' Lucas Mineiro), Iuri Medeiros, Ricardo Horta, Galeno (70' Francisco Moura), Vítor Oliveira (61' Mario González). Coach: Carlos Carvalhal.
PFC Ludogorets Razgrad: Kristijan Kahlina, Cicinho, Igor Plastun, Jordan Ikoko, Olivier Verdon, Mavis Tchibota (65' Bernard Tekpetey), Claude Gonçalves, Show (65' Stéphane Badji), Dominik Yankov, Pieros Sotiriou (74' Elvis Manu), Kiril Despodov.
Coach: Stanislav Genchev.
Goals: 25' Ali Musrati 1-0, 33' Pieros Sotiriou 1-1, 37' Iuri Medeiros 2-1, 40' Galeno 3-1, 73' Mario González 4-1, 79' Igor Plastun 4-2.
Referee: Glenn Nyberg (SWE)   Attendance: 6,221

04.11.21   Stadion Rajko Mitic, Beograd: Crvena Zvezda Beograd – FC Midtjylland 0-1 (0-0)
Crvena Zvezda Beograd: Milan Borjan, Aleksandar Dragovic, Milan Rodic (83' Strahinja Erakovic), Milos Degenek, Marko Gobeljic, Aleksandar Katai (63' Radovan Pankov), Sékou Sanogo, Guélor Kanga (74' Richairo Zivkovic), Mirko Ivanic, El Fardou Ben Nabouhane (83' Loïs Diony), Milan Pavkov. Coach: Dejan Stankovic.
FC Midtjylland: Jonas Lössl, Erik Sviatchenko, Henrik Dalsgaard, Joel Andersson (74' Dion Cools), Paulinho, Nikolas Dyhr (84' Juninho), Pione Sisto (74' Victor Lind), Evander, Charles (66' Jens-Lys Cajuste), Gustav Isaksen (84' Mads Hansen), Raphael Onyedika.
Coach: Bo Henriksen.
Goal: 56' Guélor Kanga 0-1 (og).
Referee: Tamás Bognár (HUN)   Attendance: 23,070
Sent-off: 11' Milos Degenek, 90+4' Marko Gobeljic.

25.11.21   MCH Arena, Herning: FC Midtjylland – Sporting Braga 3-2 (1-1)
FC Midtjylland: Jonas Lössl, Erik Sviatchenko, Henrik Dalsgaard, Joel Andersson, Paulinho (72' Nikolas Dyhr), Juninho, Pione Sisto (88' Victor Lind), Evander, Gustav Isaksen, Raphael Onyedika (88' Jens-Lys Cajuste), Júnior Brumado (72' Charles). Coach: Bo Henriksen.
Sporting Braga: Tiago Sá, Paulo Oliveira, Diogo Leite, Yan Couto, Bruno Rodrigues (72' Francisco Moura), André Castro (58' Chiquinho), Lucas Mineiro, Iuri Medeiros (71' Abel Ruiz), Ricardo Horta, Galeno, Vítor Oliveira (72' Mario González). Coach: Carlos Carvalhal.
Goals: 2' Erik Sviatchenko 1-0, 43' Ricardo Horta 1-1, 48' Gustav Isaksen 2-1, 85' Galeno 2-2, 90+3' Evander 3-2 (p).
Referee: Matej Jug (SVN)   Attendance: 7,189

25.11.21   Stadion Rajko Mitic, Beograd:
Crvena Zvezda Beograd – PFC Ludogorets Razgrad 1-0 (0-0)
Crvena Zvezda Beograd: Milan Borjan, Aleksandar Dragovic, Milan Gajic, Radovan Pankov, Strahinja Erakovic, Aleksandar Katai (46' El Fardou Ben Nabouhane), Slavoljub Srnic, Guélor Kanga (82' Sékou Sanogo), Mirko Ivanic, Njegos Petrovic (67' Nenad Krsticic), Milan Pavkov (81' Marko Lazetic). Coach: Dejan Stankovic.
PFC Ludogorets Razgrad: Sergio Padt, Igor Plastun, Georgi Terziev, Jordan Ikoko, Shaquille Pinas, Mavis Tchibota (77' Dorin Rotariu), Stéphane Badji (88' Dimitar Mitkov), Claude Gonçalves (65' Show), Dominik Yankov, Pieros Sotiriou, Kiril Despodov (65' Elvis Manu). Coach: Stanislav Genchev.
Goal: 57' Mirko Ivanic 1-0.
Referee: José María Sánchez Martínez (ESP)   Attendance: 11,252

09.12.21   Huvepharma Arena, Razgrad: PFC Ludogorets Razgrad – FC Midtjylland 0-0
PFC Ludogorets Razgrad: Sergio Padt, Cicinho, Igor Plastun, Jordan Ikoko, Olivier Verdon, Stéphane Badji, Claude Gonçalves, Show (90+5' Shaquille Pinas), Dominik Yankov (76' Dorin Rotariu), Pieros Sotiriou (63' Elvis Manu), Kiril Despodov. Coach: Stanislav Genchev.
FC Midtjylland: Jonas Lössl, Henrik Dalsgaard, Joel Andersson, Paulinho (88' Erik Sviatchenko), Juninho, Nikolas Dyhr (78' Dion Cools), Pione Sisto (78' Victor Lind), Evander, Charles, Gustav Isaksen, Júnior Brumado (68' Oliver Sørensen). Coach: Bo Henriksen.
Referee: Tobias Stieler (GER)   Attendance: 556

09.12.21   Estádio Municipal de Braga, Braga:
Sporting Braga – Crvena Zvezda Beograd 1-1 (0-0)
Sporting Braga: Matheus Magalhães, Raúl Silva, Paulo Oliveira, Diogo Leite (83' Lucas Piazón), Yan Couto, Ali Musrati, André Horta (71' Abel Ruiz), Iuri Medeiros (71' Lucas Mineiro), Ricardo Horta, Galeno (65' Francisco Moura), Vítor Oliveira (83' Mario González).
Coach: Carlos Carvalhal.
Crvena Zvezda Beograd: Milan Borjan, Aleksandar Dragovic, Milan Rodic, Marko Gobeljic (62' Milan Gajic), Radovan Pankov (77' Milos Degenek), Strahinja Erakovic, Aleksandar Katai (77' Nenad Krsticic), Slavoljub Srnic (62' El Fardou Ben Nabouhane), Guélor Kanga, Mirko Ivanic, Richairo Zivkovic (62' Milan Pavkov). Coach: Dejan Stankovic.
Goals: 52' Galeno 1-0 (p), 70' Aleksandar Katai 1-1 (p).
Referee: Marco Guida (ITA)   Attendance: 5,344

GROUP G

16.09.21   BayArena, Leverkusen: Bayer Leverkusen – Ferencvárosi TC 2-1 (1-1)
Bayer Leverkusen: Lukás Hrádecký, Jonathan Tah, Daley Sinkgraven (67' Piero Hincapié), Jeremie Frimpong, Odilon Kossounou, Kerem Demirbay, Exequiel Palacios (50' Charles Aránguiz), Amine Adli (67' Karim Bellarabi), Lucas Alario (66' Patrik Schick), Moussa Diaby, Florian Wirtz (81' Nadiem Amiri). Coach: Gerardo Seoane.
Ferencvárosi TC: Dénes Dibusz, Miha Blazic, Eldar Civic, Henry Wingo, Samy Mmaee, Bálint Vécsei (66' Myrto Uzuni), Kristoffer Zachariassen, Stjepan Loncár (76' Zeljko Gavric), Tokmac Nguen, Oleksandr Zubkov (86' Marijan Cabraja), Ryan Mmaee. Coach: Peter Stöger.
Goals: 8' Ryan Mmaee 0-1, 37' Exequiel Palacios 1-1, 69' Florian Wirtz 2-1.
Referee: Andris Treimanis (LAT)   Attendance: 11,013

16.09.21   Estadio Benito Villamarín, Sevilla: Real Betis – Celtic FC 4-3 (2-2)
Real Betis: Claudio Bravo, Víctor Ruíz, Martín Montoya, Édgar González, Juan Miranda (69' Álex Moreno), Joaquín (54' Aitor Ruibal), Andrés Guardado (69' William Carvalho), Sergio Canales (82' Rober), Juanmi, Nabil Fekir (68' Guido Rodríguez), Borja Iglesias.
Coach: Manuel Pellegrini.
Celtic FC: Joe Hart, Carl Starfelt, Cameron Carter-Vickers, Josip Juranovic, Anthony Ralston, Adam Montgomery, Tom Rogic, David Turnbull, Ismaila Soro (56' James McCarthy), Albian Ajeti, Jota. Coach: Ange Postecoglou.
Goals: 15' Albian Ajeti 0-1, 27' Josip Juranovic 0-2 (p), 32' Juan Miranda 1-2, 34' Juanmi 2-2, 51' Borja Iglesias 3-2, 53' Juanmi 4-2, 87' Anthony Ralston 4-3.
Referee: Fran Jovic (CRO)   Attendance: 30,893

30.09.21   Celtic Park, Glasgow: Celtic FC – Bayer Leverkusen 0-4 (0-2)
Celtic FC: Joe Hart, Carl Starfelt, Cameron Carter-Vickers, Anthony Ralston, Adam Montgomery, Callum McGregor (66' James McCarthy), Tom Rogic (66' Nir Bitton), David Turnbull (74' Georgios Giakoumakis), Jota, Kyogo Furuhashi (74' Albian Ajeti), Liel Abada.
Coach: Ange Postecoglou.
Bayer Leverkusen: Lukás Hrádecký, Jonathan Tah, Jeremie Frimpong, Mitchel Bakker, Piero Hincapié, Charles Aránguiz (65' Nadiem Amiri), Kerem Demirbay, Lucas Alario (74' Patrik Schick), Moussa Diaby (65' Karim Bellarabi), Paulinho (79' Panagiotis Retsos), Florian Wirtz (74' Amine Adli). Coach: Gerardo Seoane.
Goals: 25' Piero Hincapié 0-1, 35' Florian Wirtz 0-2, 58' Lucas Alario 0-3 (p), 90+4' Amine Adli 0-4.
Referee: Marco Di Bello (ITA)   Attendance: 55,436

30.09.21   Groupama Aréna, Budapest: Ferencvárosi TC – Real Betis 1-3 (1-1)
Ferencvárosi TC: Dénes Dibusz, Endre Botka (81' Oleksandr Zubkov), Miha Blazic, Eldar Civic, Henry Wingo, Samy Mmaee, Bálint Vécsei, Kristoffer Zachariassen (61' Tokmac Nguen), Aïssa Laïdouni (89' Stjepan Loncár), Myrto Uzuni, Ryan Mmaee.
Coach: Peter Stöger.
Real Betis: Rui Silva, Marc Bartra, Martín Montoya, Germán Pezzella, Álex Moreno, Joaquín (57' Cristian Tello), Andrés Guardado, Paul Akouokou (57' Guido Rodríguez), Rodri (81' Rober), Nabil Fekir, Borja Iglesias (57' Willian José). Coach: Manuel Pellegrini.
Goals: 17' Nabil Fekir 0-1, 44' Myrto Uzuni 1-1, 76' Henry Wingo 1-2 (og), 90+5' Cristian Tello 1-3.
Referee: Roi Reinshreiber (ISR)   Attendance: 16,759

19.10.21   Celtic Park, Glasgow: Celtic FC – Ferencvárosi TC 2-0 (0-0)
Celtic FC: Joe Hart, Carl Starfelt, Cameron Carter-Vickers, Anthony Ralston, Adam Montgomery (75' Liam Scales), Callum McGregor, Tom Rogic (71' Nir Bitton), David Turnbull, Jota, Kyogo Furuhashi (86' Mikey Johnston), Liel Abada (71' Georgios Giakoumakis). Coach: Ange Postecoglou.
Ferencvárosi TC: Dénes Dibusz, Miha Blazic, Eldar Civic, Henry Wingo, Samy Mmaee, Bálint Vécsei, Kristoffer Zachariassen (66' Stjepan Loncár), Aïssa Laïdouni (67' Somália), Tokmac Nguen (83' Róbert Mak), Myrto Uzuni, Ryan Mmaee. Coach: Peter Stöger.
Goals: 57' Kyogo Furuhashi 1-0, 81' Bálint Vécsei 2-0 (og).
Referee: Jakob Kehlet (DEN)   Attendance: 50,427

Callum McGregor missed a penalty kick (62').

21.10.21   Estadio Benito Villamarín, Sevilla: Real Betis – Bayer Leverkusen 1-1 (0-0)
Real Betis: Claudio Bravo, Martín Montoya, Germán Pezzella, Édgar González, Juan Miranda (46' Álex Moreno), Joaquín (46' Diego Lainez), William Carvalho, Guido Rodríguez, Nabil Fekir (64' Sergio Canales), Borja Iglesias (85' Willian José), Aitor Ruibal (71' Juanmi).
Coach: Manuel Pellegrini.
Bayer Leverkusen: Lukás Hrádecký, Jonathan Tah, Jeremie Frimpong, Edmond Tapsoba, Piero Hincapié (76' Mitchel Bakker), Kerem Demirbay, Robert Andrich, Amine Adli (69' Florian Wirtz), Karim Bellarabi (76' Paulinho), Lucas Alario (69' Patrik Schick), Moussa Diaby (90+1' Exequiel Palacios). Coach: Gerardo Seoane.
Goals: 75' Borja Iglesias 1-0 (p), 82' Robert Andrich 1-1.
Referee: Bartosz Frankowski (POL)   Attendance: 39,230

04.11.21   BayArena, Leverkusen: Bayer Leverkusen – Real Betis 4-0 (1-0)
Bayer Leverkusen: Lukás Hrádecký, Jonathan Tah, Jeremie Frimpong (88' Panagiotis Retsos), Edmond Tapsoba, Piero Hincapié (77' Daley Sinkgraven), Kerem Demirbay, Robert Andrich, Amine Adli (77' Nadiem Amiri), Moussa Diaby, Paulinho (69' Exequiel Palacios), Florian Wirtz (88' Odilon Kossounou). Coach: Gerardo Seoane.
Real Betis: Rui Silva, Víctor Ruíz, Marc Bartra, Héctor Bellerín, Juan Miranda (46' Álex Moreno), Joaquín (79' Juanmi), William Carvalho (46' Sergio Canales), Guido Rodríguez, Nabil Fekir, Borja Iglesias (72' Willian José), Aitor Ruibal (59' Rodri).
Coach: Manuel Pellegrini.
Goals: 42', 52' Moussa Diaby 1-0, 2-0, 86' Florian Wirtz 3-0, 90' Nadiem Amiri 4-0.
Referee: Anthony Taylor (ENG)   Attendance: 15,208
Sent-off: 90+3' Kerem Demirbay, 90+3' Nabil Fekir.

04.11.21   Groupama Aréna, Budapest: Ferencvárosi TC – Celtic FC 2-3 (1-2)
Ferencvárosi TC: Ádám Bogdán, Miha Blazic, Eldar Civic (73' Marijan Cabraja), Samy Mmaee, Somália, Bálint Vécsei (73' Stjepan Loncár), Kristoffer Zachariassen (67' Róbert Mak), Aïssa Laïdouni, Tokmac Nguen (67' Ryan Mmaee), Oleksandr Zubkov (81' Regö Szánthó), Myrto Uzuni. Coach: Peter Stöger.
Celtic FC: Joe Hart, Cameron Carter-Vickers, Josip Juranovic, Anthony Ralston, Stephen Welsh (89' Liam Scales), Nir Bitton (78' James McCarthy), Callum McGregor, David Turnbull, Jota (70' Mikey Johnston), Kyogo Furuhashi (70' Georgios Giakoumakis), Liel Abada (70' James Forrest). Coach: Ange Postecoglou.
Goals: 3' Kyogo Furuhashi 0-1, 11' Josip Juranovic 1-1 (og), 23' Jota 1-2, 60' Liel Abada 1-3, 86' Myrto Uzuni 2-3.
Referee: Fábio Veríssimo (POR)   Attendance: 16,501

25.11.21   BayArena, Leverkusen: Bayer Leverkusen – Celtic FC 3-2 (1-1)
Bayer Leverkusen: Lukás Hrádecký, Jonathan Tah, Jeremie Frimpong, Odilon Kossounou, Piero Hincapié (75' Daley Sinkgraven), Robert Andrich, Exequiel Palacios, Amine Adli, Moussa Diaby, Paulinho (75' Nadiem Amiri), Florian Wirtz (89' Edmond Tapsoba). Coach: Gerardo Seoane.
Celtic FC: Joe Hart, Cameron Carter-Vickers, Josip Juranovic, Anthony Ralston, Stephen Welsh, Nir Bitton (76' James McCarthy), James Forrest (72' Liel Abada), Callum McGregor, David Turnbull, Jota (72' Mikey Johnston), Kyogo Furuhashi (76' Albian Ajeti). Coach: Ange Postecoglou.
Goals: 16' Robert Andrich 1-0, 40' Josip Juranovic 1-1 (p), 56' Jota 1-2, 82' Robert Andrich 2-2, 87' Moussa Diaby 3-2.
Referee: Anastasios Sidiropoulos (GRE)   Attendance: 19,830

25.11.21   Estadio Benito Villamarín, Sevilla: Real Betis – Ferencvárosi TC 2-0 (1-0)
Real Betis: Claudio Bravo (71' Rui Silva), Marc Bartra, Héctor Bellerín, Édgar González, Juan Miranda, Joaquín (72' Diego Lainez), Sergio Canales, Guido Rodríguez, Cristian Tello, Borja Iglesias, Rober (67' Andrés Guardado). Coach: Manuel Pellegrini.
Ferencvárosi TC: Dénes Dibusz, Endre Botka (79' Henry Wingo), Miha Blazic, Adnan Kovacevic, Samy Mmaee, Marijan Cabraja, Bálint Vécsei (71' Aïssa Laïdouni), Kristoffer Zachariassen (88' Zeljko Gavric), Stjepan Loncár, Tokmac Nguen (88' Regö Szánthó), Ryan Mmaee (71' Róbert Mak). Coach: Peter Stöger.
Goals: 5' Cristian Tello 1-0, 52' Sergio Canales 2-0.
Referee: Ruddy Buquet (FRA)   Attendance: 30,137

09.12.21   Celtic Park, Glasgow: Celtic FC – Real Betis 3-2 (1-0)
Celtic FC: Scott Bain, Liam Scales, Stephen Welsh, Osaze Urhoghide, Adam Montgomery (65' Mikey Johnston), James McCarthy, Nir Bitton, Ismaila Soro (65' David Turnbull), Liam Shaw (65' Callum McGregor), Albian Ajeti (28' Kyogo Furuhashi, 71' Ewan Henderson), Liel Abada. Coach: Ange Postecoglou.
Real Betis: Rui Silva, Germán Pezzella, Édgar González, Juan Miranda (75' Álex Moreno), Joaquín, William Carvalho (79' Willian José), Paul Akouokou, Diego Lainez (63' Sergio Canales), Cristian Tello (79' Juanmi), Borja Iglesias, Aitor Ruibal (75' Martín Montoya). Coach: Manuel Pellegrini.
Goals: 3' Stephen Welsh 1-0, 69' Scott Bain 1-1 (og), 72' Ewan Henderson 2-1, 74' Borja Iglesias 2-2, 78' David Turnbull 3-2 (p).
Referee: Daniel Stefanski (POL)   Attendance: 54,548

09.12.21   Groupama Aréna, Budapest: Ferencvárosi TC – Bayer Leverkusen 1-0 (0-0)
Ferencvárosi TC: Dénes Dibusz, Endre Botka, Miha Blazic, Adnan Kovacevic, Samy Mmaee, Kristoffer Zachariassen (71' Somália), Aïssa Laïdouni, Stjepan Loncár (81' Bálint Vécsei), Tokmac Nguen (46' Ryan Mmaee), Oleksandr Zubkov (88' Marijan Cabraja), Myrto Uzuni. Coach: Peter Stöger.
Bayer Leverkusen: Andrey Lunev, Daley Sinkgraven, Panagiotis Retsos, Edmond Tapsoba (46' Jonathan Tah), Odilon Kossounou, Charles Aránguiz (71' Jeremie Frimpong), Nadiem Amiri, Exequiel Palacios (64' Robert Andrich), Karim Bellarabi (71' Moussa Diaby), Lucas Alario (81' Amine Adli), Paulinho. Coach: Gerardo Seoane.
Goal: 82' Aïssa Laïdouni 1-0.
Referee: Kirill Levnikov (RUS)   Attendance: 12,127

GROUP H

16.09.21   Stadion Maksimir, Zagreb: Dinamo Zagreb – West Ham United 0-2 (0-1)
Dinamo Zagreb: Dominik Livakovic, Kévin Théophile-Catherine (46' Deni Juric), Stefan Ristovski (63' Sadegh Moharrami), Rasmus Lauritsen, Josip Sutalo, Arijan Ademi, Josip Misic (75' Marko Tolic), Luka Ivanusec (84' Amer Gojak), Bartol Franjic, Mislav Orsic (83' Luka Menalo), Bruno Petkovic. Coach: Damir Krznar.
West Ham United: Lukasz Fabianski, Aaron Cresswell, Kurt Zouma, Ryan Fredericks, Issa Diop, Michail Antonio (83' Andrey Yarmolenko), Manuel Lanzini (52' Saïd Benrahma), Nikola Vlasic (69' Jarrod Bowen), Tomás Soucek, Declan Rice (82' Mark Noble), Pablo Fornals (83' Arthur Masuaku). Coach: David Moyes.
Goals: 22' Michail Antonio 0-1, 50' Declan Rice 0-2.
Referee: Ruddy Buquet (FRA)   Attendance: 12,344

16.09.21   Allianz Stadion, Vienna: Rapid Wien – KRC Genk 0-1 (0-0)
Rapid Wien: Paul Gartler, Filip Stojkovic, Maximilian Hofmann, Maximilian Ullmann (74' Jonas Auer), Emanuel Aiwu, Leo Greiml (83' Kevin Wimmer), Srdjan Grahovac (58' Dejan Petrovic), Taxiarchis Fountas (74' Christoph Knasmüllner), Ercan Kara, Marco Grüll, Kelvin Arase (58' Thorsten Schick). Coach: Dietmar Kühbauer.
KRC Genk: Maarten Vandevoordt, Jhon Lucumí, Carlos Cuesta, Gerardo Arteaga, Daniel Muñoz, Carel Eiting (90+3' Mark McKenzie), Bryan Heynen, Kristian Thorstvedt, Paul Onuachu, Théo Bongonda (46' Mike Trésor), Junya Ito. Coach: John van den Brom.
Goal: 90+2' Paul Onuachu 0-1.
Referee: Kristo Tohver (EST)   Attendance: 18,400

30.09.21   Cegeka Arena, Genk: KRC Genk – Dinamo Zagreb 0-3 (0-2)
KRC Genk: Maarten Vandevoordt, Jhon Lucumí, Carlos Cuesta, Gerardo Arteaga, Daniel Muñoz, Bryan Heynen, Bastien Toma (70' Ángelo Preciado), Kristian Thorstvedt (64' Théo Bongonda), Paul Onuachu (76' Iké Ugbo), Junya Ito (70' Carel Eiting), Joseph Paintsil (64' Mike Trésor). Coach: John van den Brom.
Dinamo Zagreb: Dominik Livakovic, Kévin Théophile-Catherine, Stefan Ristovski, Rasmus Lauritsen, Arijan Ademi (64' Amer Gojak), Josip Misic, Luka Ivanusec (83' Martin Baturina), Bartol Franjic (70' Marin Leovac), Duje Cop (70' Luka Menalo), Mislav Orsic, Bruno Petkovic (83' Komnen Andric). Coach: Damir Krznar.
Goals: 10' Luka Ivanusec 0-1, 45+3', 67' Bruno Petkovic 0-2 (p), 0-3 (p).
Referee: Mattias Gestranius (FIN)   Attendance: 11,262
Sent-off: 65' Daniel Muñoz.

30.09.21 London Stadium, London: West Ham United – Rapid Wien 2-0 (1-0)
West Ham United: Alphonse Aréola, Aaron Cresswell, Craig Dawson, Issa Diop, Ben Johnson, Mark Noble (62' Tomás Soucek), Andrey Yarmolenko (76' Pablo Fornals), Michail Antonio (62' Jarrod Bowen), Nikola Vlasic (62' Manuel Lanzini), Declan Rice, Saïd Benrahma. Coach: David Moyes.
Rapid Wien: Paul Gartler, Kevin Wimmer, Maximilian Ullmann (74' Jonas Auer), Emanuel Aiwu, Leo Greiml (62' Filip Stojkovic), Christoph Knasmüllner, Srdjan Grahovac, Dejan Petrovic (81' Robert Ljubicic), Taxiarchis Fountas (62' Koya Kitagawa), Ercan Kara (62' Marco Grüll), Kelvin Arase. Coach: Dietmar Kühbauer.
Goals: 29' Declan Rice 1-0, 90+4' Saïd Benrahma 2-0.
Referee: Tobias Stieler (GER) Attendance: 50,004

21.10.21 Allianz Stadion, Vienna: Rapid Wien – Dinamo Zagreb 2-1 (2-1)
Rapid Wien: Paul Gartler, Filip Stojkovic, Maximilian Hofmann (90+2' Kevin Wimmer), Maximilian Ullmann, Emanuel Aiwu, Leo Greiml, Robert Ljubicic, Taxiarchis Fountas (70' Thierno Ballo), Ercan Kara (89' Koya Kitagawa), Marco Grüll, Kelvin Arase (89' Thorsten Schick). Coach: Dietmar Kühbauer.
Dinamo Zagreb: Dominik Livakovic, Kévin Théophile-Catherine, Stefan Ristovski (78' Sadegh Moharrami), Rasmus Lauritsen (46' Josip Sutalo), Josip Misic, Amer Gojak (46' Martin Baturina), Luka Ivanusec (78' Marko Tolic), Bartol Franjic, Mislav Orsic, Bruno Petkovic (39' Komnen Andric), Luka Menalo. Coach: Damir Krznar.
Goals: 9' Marco Grüll 1-0, 24' Mislav Orsic 1-1, 34' Maximilian Hofmann 2-1.
Referee: Kateryna Monzul (UKR) Attendance: 22,300

21.10.21 London Stadium, London: West Ham United – KRC Genk 3-0 (1-0)
West Ham United: Alphonse Aréola, Aaron Cresswell (67' Ryan Fredericks), Craig Dawson, Issa Diop, Ben Johnson, Andrey Yarmolenko, Manuel Lanzini (89' Daniel Chesters), Nikola Vlasic (83' Pablo Fornals), Tomás Soucek, Declan Rice (67' Mark Noble), Jarrod Bowen (83' Saïd Benrahma). Coach: David Moyes.
KRC Genk: Maarten Vandevoordt, Jhon Lucumí, Carlos Cuesta (46' Mujaid Sadick), Ángelo Preciado, Gerardo Arteaga, Patrik Hrosovský, Bryan Heynen, Kristian Thorstvedt (83' Bastien Toma), Paul Onuachu (73' Iké Ugbo), Théo Bongonda (73' Mike Trésor), Junya Ito (83' Luca Oyen). Coach: John van den Brom.
Goals: 45+1' Craig Dawson 1-0, 57' Issa Diop 2-0, 59' Jarrod Bowen 3-0.
Referee: Donatas Rumsas (LTU) Attendance: 45,980

04.11.21 Cegeka Arena, Genk: KRC Genk – West Ham United 2-2 (1-0)
KRC Genk: Maarten Vandevoordt, Jhon Lucumí, Gerardo Arteaga, Daniel Muñoz (87' Ángelo Preciado), Mujaid Sadick, Patrik Hrosovský, Bryan Heynen, Kristian Thorstvedt (87' Iké Ugbo), Paul Onuachu, Junya Ito, Joseph Paintsil (90+4' Luca Oyen).
Coach: John van den Brom.
West Ham United: Alphonse Aréola, Aaron Cresswell, Craig Dawson, Vladimír Coufal, Arthur Masuaku (58' Pablo Fornals), Issa Diop, Mark Noble (58' Tomás Soucek), Michail Antonio (58' Jarrod Bowen), Manuel Lanzini (85' Alex Král), Declan Rice, Saïd Benrahma.
Coach: David Moyes.
Goals: 4' Joseph Paintsil 1-0, 59', 82' Saïd Benrahma 1-1, 1-2, 88' Tomás Soucek 2-2 (og).
Referee: Aleksandar Stavrev (MKD) Attendance: 12,239

04.11.21 Stadion Maksimir, Zagreb: Dinamo Zagreb – Rapid Wien 2-1 (2-1)
Dinamo Zagreb: Dominik Livakovic, Kévin Théophile-Catherine, Sadegh Moharrami (89' Stefan Ristovski), Josip Sutalo, Josip Misic, Amer Gojak, Luka Ivanusec (73' Luka Menalo), Bartol Franjic, Mislav Orsic (89' Dario Spikic), Bruno Petkovic, Komnen Andric (79' Marko Bulat). Coach: Damir Krznar.
Rapid Wien: Paul Gartler, Maximilian Hofmann, Maximilian Ullmann, Emanuel Aiwu, Martin Moormann (21' Leopold Querfeld), Christoph Knasmüllner, Srdjan Grahovac (81' Denis Bosnjak), Robert Ljubicic, Ercan Kara (69' Koya Kitagawa), Marco Grüll (69' Thierno Ballo), Kelvin Arase (46' Thorsten Schick). Coach: Dietmar Kühbauer.
Goals: 8' Christoph Knasmüllner 0-1, 12' Bruno Petkovic 1-1, 34' Komnen Andric 2-1, 83' Josip Sutalo 3-1.
Referee: John Beaton (SCO)   Attendance: 7,835

25.11.21 Stadion Maksimir, Zagreb: Dinamo Zagreb – KRC Genk 1-1 (1-1)
Dinamo Zagreb: Dominik Livakovic, Kévin Théophile-Catherine, Sadegh Moharrami (86' Marko Bulat), Josip Sutalo, Arijan Ademi (76' Amer Gojak), Josip Misic, Luka Ivanusec, Bartol Franjic, Mislav Orsic (76' Komnen Andric), Bruno Petkovic (86' Duje Cop), Luka Menalo (69' Dario Spikic). Coach: Damir Krznar.
KRC Genk: Maarten Vandevoordt, Mark McKenzie, Ángelo Preciado, Gerardo Arteaga, Mujaid Sadick, Patrik Hrosovský, Carel Eiting (66' Kristian Thorstvedt), Bryan Heynen, Théo Bongonda, Iké Ugbo, Junya Ito (67' Joseph Paintsil). Coach: John van den Brom.
Goals: 35' Luka Menalo 1-0, 45' Iké Ugbo 1-1.
Referee: Glenn Nyberg (SWE)   Attendance: 6,892

25.11.21 Allianz Stadion, Vienna: Rapid Wien – West Ham United 0-2 (0-2)
Rapid Wien: Paul Gartler, Filip Stojkovic, Maximilian Hofmann, Emanuel Aiwu, Martin Moormann, Christoph Knasmüllner (59' Marco Grüll), Dejan Petrovic, Robert Ljubicic (90+1' Srdjan Grahovac), Taxiarchis Fountas (90+1' Oliver Strunz), Koya Kitagawa (59' Ercan Kara), Kelvin Arase (75' Thierno Ballo). Coach: Thomas Hickersberger.
West Ham United: Alphonse Aréola, Craig Dawson, Vladimír Coufal, Arthur Masuaku (77' Ryan Fredericks), Issa Diop, Mark Noble, Andrey Yarmolenko, Manuel Lanzini (65' Pablo Fornals), Nikola Vlasic (78' Sonny Perkins), Tomás Soucek (65' Alex Král), Jarrod Bowen (65' Saïd Benrahma). Coach: David Moyes.
Goals: 39' Andrey Yarmolenko 0-1, 45+2' Mark Noble 0-2 (p).
Referee: Sergey Ivanov (RUS)   Attendance: 0

09.12.21 Cegeka Arena, Genk: KRC Genk – Rapid Wien 0-1 (0-1)
KRC Genk: Maarten Vandevoordt, Mark McKenzie, Ángelo Preciado (78' Luka Oyen), Gerardo Arteaga (69' Simen Juklerød), Mujaid Sadick (46' Jhon Lucumí), Patrik Hrosovský, Kristian Thorstvedt, Théo Bongonda, Iké Ugbo (46' Paul Onuachu), Junya Ito (46' Carlos Cuesta), Joseph Paintsil. Coach: Bernd Storck.
Rapid Wien: Paul Gartler, Filip Stojkovic, Maximilian Ullmann (89' Marko Dijakovic), Emanuel Aiwu, Martin Moormann, Christoph Knasmüllner (46' Koya Kitagawa), Thorsten Schick, Dejan Petrovic, Robert Ljubicic (75' Srdjan Grahovac), Ercan Kara (40' Oliver Strunz), Marco Grüll (75' Jonas Auer). Coach: Ferdinand Feldhofer.
Goals: 29' Robert Ljubicic 0-1.
Referee: Tiago Martins (POR)   Attendance: 10,018

09.12.21   London Stadium, London: West Ham United – Dinamo Zagreb 0-1 (0-1)
West Ham United: Alphonse Aréola, Emmanuel Longelo Mbule, Aji Alese, Harrison Ashby, Jamal Baptiste, Mark Noble, Andrey Yarmolenko (87' Freddie Potts), Nikola Vlasic, Alex Král, Pablo Fornals (46' Saïd Benrahma), Sonny Perkins (87' Keenan Appiah-Forson).
Coach: David Moyes.
Dinamo Zagreb: Dominik Livakovic, Kévin Théophile-Catherine, Stefan Ristovski, Dino Peric, Josip Sutalo, Daniel Stefulj (80' Emir Dilaver), Arijan Ademi (71' Marko Bulat), Amer Gojak, Luka Ivanusec, Mislav Orsic (64' Josip Misic), Komnen Andric (64' Deni Juric).
Coach: Zeljko Kopic.
Goal: 4' Mislav Orsic 0-1.
Referee: Maurizio Mariani (ITA)   Attendance: 49,407

KNOCKOUT ROUND PLAY-OFFS

17.02.22   Camp Nou, Barcelona: FC Barcelona – SSC Napoli 1-1 (0-1)
FC Barcelona: Marc-André ter Stegen, Piqué, Jordi Alba, Óscar Mingueza (81' Sergiño Dest), Eric García, Frenkie de Jong (65' Sergio Busquets), Nico González (65' Gavi), Pedri, Pierre-Emerick Aubameyang (86' Luuk de Jong), Adama Traoré (65' Ousmane Dembélé), Ferrán Torres. Coach: Xavi.
SSC Napoli: Alex Meret, Juan Jesus, Kalidou Koulibaly, Giovanni Di Lorenzo, Amir Rrahmani, Piotr Zielinski (80' Diego Demme), Fabián Ruiz, André-Frank Zambo Anguissa (84' Kévin Malcuit), Eljif Elmas (84' Mário Rui), Lorenzo Insigne (72' Adam Ounas), Victor Osimhen (80' Dries Mertens). Coach: Luciano Spalletti.
Goals: 29' Piotr Zielinski 0-1, 59' Ferrán Torres 1-1 (p).
Referee: István Kovács (ROM)   Attendance: 73,525

17.02.22   Gazprom Arena, Saint Petersburg: Zenit Saint Petersburg – Real Betis 2-3 (2-3)
Zenit Saint Petersburg: Mikhail Kerzhakov, Yaroslav Rakitskiy (46' Danil Krugovoy), Vyacheslav Karavaev (46' Andrey Mostovoy), Douglas Santos, Dmitriy Chistyakov (88' Aleksandr Erokhin), Wilmar Barrios, Daler Kuzyaev, Claudinho (65' Yuri Alberto), Wendel, Artem Dzyuba (73' Ivan Sergeev), Malcom. Coach: Sergey Semak.
Real Betis: Rui Silva, Germán Pezzella, Youssouf Sabaly, Álex Moreno, Édgar González, Joaquín (58' William Carvalho), Andrés Guardado, Guido Rodríguez, Willian José (79' Borja Iglesias), Juanmi (58' Cristian Tello), Aitor Ruibal (86' Héctor Bellerín).
Coach: Manuel Pellegrini.
Goals: 8' Guido Rodríguez 0-1, 18' Willian José 0-2, 25' Artem Dzyuba 1-2, 28' Malcom 2-2, 41' Andrés Guardado 2-3.
Referee: Benoît Bastien (FRA)   Attendance: 28,936

17.02.22   Signal-Iduna-Park, Dortmund: Borussia Dortmund – Glasgow Rangers FC 2-4 (0-2)
Borussia Dortmund: Gregor Kobel, Mats Hummels, Raphaël Guerreiro, Manuel Akanji (55' Nico Schulz), Dan-Axel Zagadou, Axel Witsel (46' Gio Reyna), Julian Brandt (46' Youssoufa Moukoko), Mahmoud Dahoud, Jude Bellingham, Marco Reus (82' Reinier), Donyell Malen (68' Steffen Tigges). Coach: Marco Rose.
Glasgow Rangers FC: Allan McGregor, James Tavernier, Connor Goldson, Borna Barisic, Calvin Bassey, Scott Arfield (66' James Sands), Ryan Jack (86' Glen Kamara), John Lundstram, Joe Ayodele-Aribo (86' Aaron Ramsey), Alfredo Morelos (90+5' Scott Wright), Ryan Kent. Coach: Giovanni van Bronckhorst.
Goals: 38' James Tavernier 0-1 (p), 41' Alfredo Morelos 0-2, 49' John Lundstram 0-3, 51' Jude Bellingham 1-3, 54' Dan-Axel Zagadou 1-4 (og), 82' Raphaël Guerreiro 2-4.
Referee: Clément Turpin (FRA)   Attendance: 10,000

17.02.22   Bolshaya Sportivnaya Arena, Tiraspol: Sheriff Tiraspol – Sporting Braga 2-0 (1-0)
Sheriff Tiraspol: Georgios Athanasiadis, Stefanos Evangelou, Stjepan Radeljic, Keston Julien, Charles Petro, Sébastien Thill (90+5' Serafim Cojocari), Boban Nikolov (89' Moussa Kyabou), Jasurbek Yakhshiboev (89' Alexandr Belousov), Bruno Souza, Adama Traoré, Momo Yansane (78' Abdul Khalid Basit). Coach: Yuriy Vernydub.
Sporting Braga: Matheus Magalhães, Paulo Oliveira, Vítor Tormena, Yan Couto, Bruno Rodrigues, André Castro (64' André Horta), Ali Musrati, Iuri Medeiros (79' Roger Fernandes, 86' Miguel Falé), Ricardo Horta, Rodrigo Gomes (64' Francisco Moura), Vítor Oliveira "Vitinha" (64' Abel Ruiz). Coach: Carlos Carvalhal.
Goals: 43' Sébastien Thill 1-0 (p), 82' Adama Traoré 2-0.
Referee: Danny Makkelie (HOL)   Attendance: 3,062

17.02.22   Estadio Ramón Sánchez Pizjuán, Sevilla: Sevilla FC – Dinamo Zagreb 3-1 (3-1)
Sevilla FC: Yassine Bounou "Bono", Karim Rekik (50' Nemanja Gudelj), Marcos Acuña, Diego Carlos, Jules Koundé, Ivan Rakitic, Alejandro "Papu" Gómez, Fernando (61' Óliver Torres), Lucas Ocampos (84' Jesús Navas), Anthony Martial (61' Youssef En-Nesyri), Munir El-Haddadi (61' Thomas Delaney). Coach: Lopetegui.
Dinamo Zagreb: Dominik Livakovic, Kévin Théophile-Catherine (46' Rasmus Lauritsen), Stefan Ristovski (77' Sadegh Moharrami), Josip Sutalo, Arijan Ademi, Amer Gojak, Petar Bockaj (70' Daniel Stefulj), Bartol Franjic, Mislav Orsic, Bruno Petkovic (76' Dario Spikic), Deni Juric (58' Mahir Emreli). Coach: Zeljko Kopic.
Goals: 13' Ivan Rakitic 1-0 (p), 41' Mislav Orsic 1-1, 44' Lucas Ocampos 2-1, 45+1' Anthony Martial 3-1.
Referee: Marco Guida (ITA)   Attendance: 28,372

17.02.22   Gewiss Stadium, Bergamo: Atalanta Bergamo – Olympiakos Piraeus 2-1 (0-1)
Atalanta Bergamo: Juan Musso, Rafael Tolói, Berat Djimsiti, Merih Demiral, Giuseppe Pezzella, Joakim Mæhle (87' Hans Hateboer), Marten de Roon (72' Remo Freuler), Mario Pasalic, Ruslan Malinovskiy (66' Valentin Mihaila), Matteo Pessina (46' Teun Koopmeiners), Luis Muriel (46' Jérémie Boga). Coach: Gian Piero Gasperini.
Olympiakos Piraeus: Tomás Vaclík, Sokratis Papastathopoulos, Kostas Manolas, Kenny Lala, Pape Cissé, Oleg Reabciuk, Yann M'Vila (85' Andreas Bouchalakis), Georgios Masouras (64' Mohamed Mady Camara), Aguibou Camara, Tiquinho Soares (72' Youssef El-Arabi), Henry Onyekuru (85' Rony Lopes). Coach: Pedro Martins.
Goals: 16' Tiquinho Soares 0-1, 61', 63' Berat Djimsiti 1-1, 2-1.
Referee: Sandro Schärer (SUI)   Attendance: 9,448

17.02.22 Red Bull Arena, Leipzig: RB Leipzig – Real Sociedad 2-2 (1-1)
RB Leipzig: Péter Gulácsi, Lukas Klostermann, Angeliño, Mohamed Simakan, Josko Gvardiol, Kevin Kampl (86' Amadou Haïdara), Konrad Laimer (63' Emil Forsberg), Christopher Nkunku (80' Dominik Szoboszlai), Dani Olmo (79' Yussuf Poulsen), Tyler Adams (46' Benjamin Henrichs), André Silva. Coach: Domenico Tedesco.
Real Sociedad: Mathew Ryan, Joseba Zaldúa, Diego Rico (61' Aihen Muñoz), Aritz Elustondo, Robin Le Normand, Rafinha (78' Jon Pacheco), Mikel Merino (90+6' Illarramendi), Zubeldía, Portu, Alexander Sørloth, Mikel Oyarzabal (90+6' Ander Martín). Coach: Imanol Alguacil.
Goals: 8' Robin Le Normand 0-1, 30' Christopher Nkunku 1-1, 64' Mikel Oyarzabal 1-2 (p), 82' Emil Forsberg 2-2 (p).
Referee: Cüneyt Çakir (TUR) Attendance: 21,113

17.02.22 Estádio do Dragão, Porto: FC Porto – Lazio Roma 2-1 (1-1)
FC Porto: Diogo Costa, Pepe, Chancel Mbemba, Zaidu Sanusi, Mateus Uribe, Otávio, Marko Grujic (46' Galeno), Fábio Vieira (46' Vitinha), Toni Martínez (69' Evanilson), Pepê Aquino (88' Stephen Eustáquio), João Mário (88' Bruno Costa). Coach: Sérgio Conceição.
Lazio Roma: Thomas Strakosha, Stefan Radu (72' Elseid Hysaj), Patric, Adam Marusic, Luiz Felipe, Lucas Leiva (68' Danilo Cataldi), Luis Alberto (84' Toma Basic), Mattia Zaccagni (84' Raúl Moro), Sergej Milinkovic-Savic, Pedro (84' Jovane Cabral), Felipe Anderson.
Coach: Maurizio Sarri.
Goals: 23' Mattia Zaccagni 0-1, 37', 49' Toni Martínez 1-1, 2-1.
Referee: Serdar Gözübüyük (HOL) Attendance: 32,929

24.02.22 Stadion Maksimir, Zagreb: Dinamo Zagreb – Sevilla FC 1-0 (0-0)
Dinamo Zagreb: Dominik Livakovic, Kévin Théophile-Catherine, Stefan Ristovski (62' Dario Spikic), Josip Sutalo, Daniel Stefulj (62' Petar Bockaj), Josip Misic, Amer Gojak (75' Luka Menalo), Marko Tolic (53' Marko Bulat), Bartol Franjic, Mislav Orsic, Bruno Petkovic (62' Mahir Emreli). Coach: Zeljko Kopic.
Sevilla FC: Yassine Bounou "Bono", Marcos Acuña, Diego Carlos (46' Thomas Delaney), Gonzalo Montiel (46' Jesús Navas), Jules Koundé, Ivan Rakitic (71' Joan Jordán), Alejandro "Papu" Gómez, Fernando, Lucas Ocampos, Jesús Corona (71' Óliver Torres), Rafa Mir (81' Youssef En-Nesyri). Coach: Lopetegui.
Goal: 65' Mislav Orsic 1-0 (p).
Referee: François Letexier (FRA) Attendance: 9,788
Sent-off: 90+1' Thomas Delaney.

24.02.22 Stadio Georgios Karaiskáki, Piraeus:
Olympiakos Piraeus – Atalanta Bergamo 0-3 (0-1)
Olympiakos Piraeus: Tomás Vaclík, Sokratis Papastathopoulos, Kostas Manolas, Kenny Lala (67' Youssef El-Arabi), Pape Cissé (46' Georgios Masouras), Oleg Reabciuk, Yann M'Vila (67' Marios Vrousai), Mohamed Mady Camara, Aguibou Camara, Tiquinho Soares (74' Bandiougou Fadiga), Henry Onyekuru (60' Mathieu Valbuena). Coach: Pedro Martins.
Atalanta Bergamo: Juan Musso, Rafael Tolói, Berat Djimsiti, Hans Hateboer, Merih Demiral (90' Giorgio Cittadini), Joakim Mæhle (83' Giuseppe Pezzella), Marten de Roon, Remo Freuler, Mario Pasalic (56' Jérémie Boga), Ruslan Malinovskiy (84' Valentin Mihaila), Matteo Pessina (57' Teun Koopmeiners). Coach: Gian Piero Gasperini.
Goals: 40' Joakim Mæhle 0-1, 66', 69' Ruslan Malinovskiy 0-2, 0-3.
Referee: Carlos del Cerro Grande (ESP) Attendance: 15,835

24.02.22   Reale Arena, San Sebastián: Real Sociedad – RB Leipzig 1-3 (0-1)
Real Sociedad: Mathew Ryan, Joseba Zaldúa, Aritz Elustondo, Robin Le Normand (62' David Silva), Aihen Muñoz, Rafinha (84' Alexander Sørloth), Zubeldía, Martín Zubimendi, Portu (62' Adnan Januzaj), Mikel Oyarzabal, Alexander Isak (90' Naïs Djouahra).
Coach: Imanol Alguacil.
RB Leipzig: Péter Gulácsi, Willi Orban, Lukas Klostermann, Benjamin Henrichs (64' Angeliño), Mohamed Simakan, Josko Gvardiol, Kevin Kampl (90' Tyler Adams), Konrad Laimer (64' Amadou Haïdara), Christopher Nkunku, Dani Olmo (79' Yussuf Poulsen), André Silva (64' Emil Forsberg). Coach: Domenico Tedesco.
Goals: 39' Willi Orbán 0-1, 59' André Silva 0-2, 67' Martín Zubimendi 1-2, 89' Emil Forsberg 1-3 (p).
Referee: Anthony Taylor (ENG)   Attendance: 30,113

André Silva missed a penalty kick (39').

24.02.22   Stadio Olimpico, Roma: Lazio Roma – FC Porto 2-2 (1-1)
Lazio Roma: Thomas Strakosha, Stefan Radu (54' Elseid Hysaj), Patric, Adam Marusic, Luiz Felipe, Lucas Leiva (54' Danilo Cataldi), Luis Alberto, Sergej Milinkovic-Savic, Pedro (71' Raúl Moro), Ciro Immobile, Felipe Anderson. Coach: Maurizio Sarri.
FC Porto: Diogo Costa, Pepe, Chancel Mbemba, Zaidu Sanusi, Mateus Uribe, Otávio, Bruno Costa, Vitinha (78' Marko Grujic), Mehdi Taremi (79' Evanilson), Toni Martínez (56' Galeno), Pepê Aquino (69' João Mário). Coach: Sérgio Conceição.
Goals: 19' Ciro Immobile 1-0, 31' Mehdi Taremi 1-1 (p), 68' Mateus Uribe 1-2, 90+4' Danilo Cataldi 2-2.
Referee: Deniz Aytekin (GER)   Attendance: 24,948

24.02.22   Stadio Diego Armando Maradona, Napoli: SSC Napoli – FC Barcelona 2-4 (1-3)
SSC Napoli: Alex Meret, Mário Rui, Kalidou Koulibaly, Giovanni Di Lorenzo, Amir Rrahmani, Diego Demme (46' Matteo Politano), Piotr Zielinski (73' Dries Mertens), Fabián Ruiz (73' Adam Ounas), Eljif Elmas, Lorenzo Insigne (82' Andrea Petagna), Victor Osimhen (74' Faouzi Ghoulam). Coach: Luciano Spalletti.
FC Barcelona: Marc-André ter Stegen, Piqué, Jordi Alba, Ronald Araújo, Sergiño Dest, Sergio Busquets (62' Gavi), Frenkie de Jong, Pedri (75' Nico González), Pierre-Emerick Aubameyang (75' Luuk de Jong), Adama Traoré (74' Ousmane Dembélé), Ferrán Torres (82' Riqui Puig). Coach: Xavi.
Goals: 8' Jordi Alba 0-1, 13' Frenkie de Jong 0-2, 23' Lorenzo Insigne 1-2 (p), 45' Piqué 1-3, 59' Pierre-Emerick Aubameyang 1-4, 87' Matteo Politano 2-4.
Referee: Sergei Karasev (RUS)   Attendance: 37,858

24.02.22   Estadio Benito Villamarín, Sevilla: Real Betis – Zenit Saint Petersburg 0-0
Real Betis: Rui Silva, Germán Pezzella, Álex Moreno, Héctor Bellerín, Édgar González, Andrés Guardado (90' Cristian Tello), Sergio Canales (71' William Carvalho), Guido Rodríguez, Willian José (83' Borja Iglesias), Nabil Fekir (83' Joaquín), Aitor Ruibal.
Coach: Manuel Pellegrini.
Zenit Saint Petersburg: Daniil Odoevskiy, Douglas Santos, Dmitriy Chistyakov, Danil Krugovoy, Wilmar Barrios, Aleksey Sutormin (86' Andrey Mostovoy), Claudinho, Wendel, Artem Dzyuba (64' Ivan Sergeev), Malcom, Yuri Alberto (84' Aleksandr Erokhin).
Coach: Sergey Semak.
Referee: Halil Umut Meler (TUR)   Attendance: 44,236

24.02.22   Ibrox Stadium, Glasgow: Glasgow Rangers FC – Borussia Dortmund 2-2 (1-2)
Glasgow Rangers FC: Allan McGregor, James Tavernier, Connor Goldson, Borna Barisic (46'
Leon Balogun), Calvin Bassey, Scott Arfield (69' Glen Kamara), Ryan Jack, John Lundstram,
Joe Ayodele-Aribo, Alfredo Morelos, Ryan Kent. Coach: Giovanni van Bronckhorst.
Borussia Dortmund: Gregor Kobel, Mats Hummels, Thomas Meunier (46' Marius Wolf), Nico
Schulz, Thorgan Hazard (69' Reinier), Emre Can, Julian Brandt (69' Youssoufa Moukoko),
Mahmoud Dahoud, Jude Bellingham, Marco Reus (86' Axel Witsel), Donyell Malen (77'
Steffen Tigges). Coach: Marco Rose.
Goals: 22' James Tavernier 1-0 (p), 31' Jude Bellingham 1-1, 42' Donyell Malen 1-2,
57' James Tavernier 2-2.
Referee: Antonio Mateu Lahoz (ESP)   Attendance: 47,709

24.02.22   Estádio Municipal de Braga, Braga:
           Sporting Braga – Sheriff Tiraspol 2-0 (2-0,2-0) (AET)
Sporting Braga: Matheus Magalhães, Vítor Tormena, Fabiano Silva, David Carmo, Yan Couto
(89' Bruno Rodrigues), Ali Musrati, André Horta (90' André Castro), Iuri Medeiros (74' Abel
Ruiz), Ricardo Horta, Rodrigo Gomes (64' Francisco Moura), Vítor Oliveira "Vitinha" (109'
Miguel Falé). Coach: Carlos Carvalhal.
Sheriff Tiraspol: Georgios Athanasiadis, Gustavo Dulanto, Stjepan Radeljic, Keston Julien,
Charles Petro, Sébastien Thill, Jasurbek Yakhshiboev (111' Abdul Khalid Basit), Bruno Souza,
Edmund Addo, Adama Traoré, Momo Yansane (46' Boban Nikolov). Coach: Yuriy Vernydub.
Goals: 17' Iuri Medeiros 1-0, 43' Ricardo Horta 2-0.
Referee: José María Sánchez Martínez (ESP)   Attendance: 9,423

Braga won on penalties (3:2).

Penalties: Dulanto (missed), Ricardo Horta 0-1, Bruno Souza (missed), Musrati 0-2,
         Radeljic (missed), Abel Ruiz (missed), Khalid 1-2, David Carmo (missed), Thill 2-2,
         Francisco Moura 2-3.

ROUND OF 16

*RB Leizig won on walkover as UEFA suspended FK Spartak Moskva from European
competition following the Russian invasion of Ukraine.*

09.03.22   Estádio do Dragão, Porto: FC Porto – Olympique Lyonnais 0-1 (0-0)
FC Porto: Diogo Costa, Pepe (46' Rúben Semedo), Chancel Mbemba, Zaidu Sanusi, Mateus
Uribe, Otávio (88' Francisco Conceição), Vitinha, Mehdi Taremi (80' Fábio Vieira), Pepê
Aquino, João Mário (80' Galeno), Evanilson (72' Toni Martínez). Coach: Sérgio Conceição.
Olympique Lyonnais: Anthony Lopes, Emerson, Léo Dubois (83' Malo Gusto), Castello
Lukeba, Thiago Mendes, Tanguy NDombèlé, Romain Faivre (80' Houssem Aouar), Lucas
Paquetá, Maxence Caqueret, Karl Toko Ekambi, Moussa Dembélé. Coach: Peter Bosz.
Goal: 59' Lucas Paquetá 0-1.
Referee: José María Sánchez Martínez (ESP)   Attendance: 26,309

09.03.22   Estadio Benito Villamarín, Sevilla: Real Betis – Eintracht Frankfurt 1-2 (1-2)
Real Betis: Claudio Bravo, Germán Pezzella, Youssouf Sabaly, Édgar González, Sergio Canales, William Carvalho (61' Juan Miranda), Guido Rodríguez, Willian José (77' Borja Iglesias), Juanmi (61' Joaquín), Nabil Fekir, Aitor Ruibal (77' Cristian Tello).
Coach: Manuel Pellegrini.
Eintracht Frankfurt: Kevin Trapp, Martin Hinteregger, Evan N'Dicka, Tuta, Filip Kostic, Djibril Sow, Daichi Kamada (78' Christopher Lenz), Kristijan Jakic, Ansgar Knauff, Jesper Lindstrøm (73' Jens Hauge), Rafael Borré (86' Sam Lammers). Coach: Oliver Glasner.
Goals: 14' Filip Kostic 0-1, 30' Nabil Fekir 1-1, 32' Daichi Kamada 1-2.
Referee: Marco Guida (ITA)   Attendance: 36,574

Rafael Borré missed a penalty kick (52').

10.03.22   Estadio Ramón Sánchez Pizjuán, Sevilla: Sevilla FC – West Ham United 1-0 (0-0)
Sevilla FC: Yassine Bounou "Bono", Jesús Navas, Marcos Acuña, Jules Koundé, Nemanja Gudelj, Lucas Ocampos, Óliver Torres, Joan Jordán, Jesús Corona (87' Ludwig Augustinsson), Munir El-Haddadi (75' Anthony Martial), Youssef En-Nesyri (90+1' Rafa Mir).
Coach: Lopetegui.
West Ham United: Alphonse Aréola, Aaron Cresswell, Craig Dawson, Kurt Zouma, Ben Johnson, Manuel Lanzini (83' Mark Noble), Nikola Vlasic (67' Saïd Benrahma), Tomás Soucek, Declan Rice, Pablo Fornals (90+3' Arthur Masuaku), Michail Antonio.
Coach: David Moyes.
Goal: 60' Munir El-Haddadi 1-0.
Referee: Sandro Schärer (SUI)   Attendance: 34,728

10.03.22   Ibrox Stadium, Glasgow: Glasgow Rangers FC – Crvena Zvezda Beograd 3-0 2-0)
Glasgow Rangers FC: Allan McGregor, Leon Balogun, James Tavernier, Connor Goldson, Calvin Bassey, Ryan Jack (75' James Sands), John Lundstram, Glen Kamara, Joe Ayodele-Aribo (75' Fashion Sakala), Alfredo Morelos, Ryan Kent. Coach: Giovanni van Bronckhorst.
Crvena Zvezda Beograd: Milan Borjan, Aleksandar Dragovic, Milan Rodic, Cristiano Piccini (72' Milan Gajic), Strahinja Erakovic, Aleksandar Katai (84' Nemanja Motika), Slavoljub Srnic (61' El Fardou Ben Nabouhane), Sékou Sanogo, Guélor Kanga, Mirko Ivanic, Ohi Omoijuanfo (61' Milan Pavkov). Coach: Dejan Stankovic.
Goals: 11' James Tavernier 1-0 (p), 15' Alfredo Morelos 2-0, 51' Leon Balogun 3-0.
Referee: Serdar Gözübüyük (HOL)   Attendance: 48,589

Aleksandar Katai missed a penalty kick 24').

10.03.22   Estádio Municipal de Braga, Braga: Sporting Braga – AS Monaco 2-0 (1-0)
Sporting Braga: Matheus Magalhães, Vítor Tormena, Fabiano Silva, David Carmo, Yan Couto (65' Paulo Oliveira), Ali Musrati, André Horta (74' André Castro), Iuri Medeiros (65' Francisco Moura), Ricardo Horta, Abel Ruiz (65' Vítor Oliveira "Vitinha"), Rodrigo Gomes (80' Miguel Falé). Coach: Carlos Carvalhal.
AS Monaco: Alexander Nübel, Axel Disasi, Caio Henrique, Chrislain Matsima (46' Benoît Badiashile), Vanderson, Gelson Martins, Aurélien Tchouaméni, Jean Lucas, Eliot Matazo (58' Aleksandr Golovin), Kevin Volland (83' Sofiane Diop), Wissam Ben Yedder (77' Myron Boadu). Coach: Philippe Clement.
Goals: 3' Abel Ruiz 1-0, 89' Vítor Oliveira "Vitinha" (89').
Referee: Felix Zwayer (GER)   Attendance: 10,228

10.03.22   Gewiss Stadium, Bergamo: Atalanta Bergamo – Bayer Leverkusen 3-2 (2-1)
Atalanta Bergamo: Juan Musso, Rafael Tolói, Berat Djimsiti (69' José Palomino), Davide Zappacosta (77' Joakim Mæhle), Hans Hateboer, Merih Demiral, Marten de Roon, Remo Freuler, Ruslan Malinovskiy (69' Jérémie Boga), Teun Koopmeiners, Luis Muriel (77' Aleksey Miranchuk). Coach: Gian Piero Gasperini.
Bayer Leverkusen: Lukás Hrádecký, Jonathan Tah, Jeremie Frimpong (80' Timothy Fosu-Mensah), Mitchel Bakker, Edmond Tapsoba, Charles Aránguiz, Exequiel Palacios, Amine Adli (80' Paulinho), Lucas Alario (61' Odilon Kossounou), Moussa Diaby, Florian Wirtz (85' Sardar Azmoun). Coach: Gerardo Seoane.
Goals: 11' Charles Aránguiz 0-1, 23' Ruslan Malinovskiy 1-1, 25', 49' Luis Muriel 2-1, 3-1, 63' Moussa Diaby 3-2.
Referee: Srdjan Jovanovic (SRB)   Attendance: 13,134

10.03.22   Camp Nou, Barcelona: FC Barcelona – Galatasaray 0-0
FC Barcelona: Marc-André ter Stegen, Jordi Alba, Ronald Araújo (46' Piqué), Eric García, Sergiño Dest, Frenkie de Jong, Nico González (46' Sergio Busquets), Pedri, Memphis Depay (61' Pierre-Emerick Aubameyang), Adama Traoré (80' Luuk de Jong), Ferrán Torres (46' Ousmane Dembélé). Coach: Xavi.
Galatasaray: Iñaki Peña, Patrick van Aanholt, Marcão, Victor Nelsson, Sacha Boey, Sofiane Féghouli (79' Alexandru Cicâldau), Taylan Antalyali, Kerem Aktürkoglu (90+2' Baris Yilmaz), Berkan Kutlu, Ryan Babel (68' Emre Kilinç), Mostafa Mohamed (68' Bafétimbi Gomis). Coach: Domènec Torrent.
Referee: Benoît Bastien (FRA)   Attendance: 61,740

17.03.22   Stadion Rajko Mitic, Beograd:
            Crvena Zvezda Beograd – Glasgow Rangers FC 2-1 (1-0)
Crvena Zvezda Beograd: Milan Borjan, Aleksandar Dragovic, Milan Rodic (72' Filippo Falco), Cristiano Piccini (57' Milan Gajic), Strahinja Erakovic, Aleksandar Katai, Sékou Sanogo, Guélor Kanga, Mirko Ivanic (72' Nemanja Motika), Ohi Omoijuanfo (63' El Fardou Ben Nabouhane), Milan Pavkov. Coach: Dejan Stankovic.
Glasgow Rangers FC: Allan McGregor, Leon Balogun, James Tavernier, Connor Goldson, Calvin Bassey, Ryan Jack (69' James Sands), John Lundstram (81' Borna Barisic), Glen Kamara, Joe Ayodele-Aribo (68' Scott Arfield), Alfredo Morelos (80' Kemar Roofe), Ryan Kent (90' Scott Wright). Coach: Giovanni van Bronckhorst.
Goals: 10' Mirko Ivanic 1-0, 56' Ryan Kent 1-1, 90+3' El Fardou Ben Nabouhane 2-1 (p).
Referee: István Kovács (ROM)   Attendance: 47,024

17.03.22   Stade Louis II, Monaco: AS Monaco – Sporting Braga 1-1 (0-1)
AS Monaco: Alexander Nübel, Axel Disasi, Caio Henrique (62' Ismail Jakobs), Benoît Badiashile, Vanderson (84' Ruben Aguilar), Gelson Martins (52' Myron Boadu), Aurélien Tchouaméni, Jean Lucas (52' Guillermo Maripán), Sofiane Diop (52' Aleksandr Golovin), Kevin Volland, Wissam Ben Yedder. Coach: Philippe Clement.
Sporting Braga: Matheus Magalhães, Paulo Oliveira, Vítor Tormena, Fabiano Silva, David Carmo, André Castro (76' Iuri Medeiros), Ali Musrati, André Horta (69' Lucas Mineiro), Ricardo Horta, Abel Ruiz (76' Vítor Oliveira "Vitinha"), Rodrigo Gomes (62' Francisco Moura). Coach: Carlos Carvalhal.
Goals: 20' Abel Ruiz 0-1, 90' Axel Disasi 1-1.
Referee: Andreas Ekberg (SWE)   Attendance: 3,892

17.03.22   BayArena, Leverkusen: Bayer Leverkusen – Atalanta Bergamo 0-1 (0-0)
Bayer Leverkusen: Lukás Hrádecký, Jonathan Tah, Timothy Fosu-Mensah (61' Karim Bellarabi), Mitchel Bakker, Edmond Tapsoba, Piero Hincapié, Charles Aránguiz (82' Lucas Alario), Kerem Demirbay (61' Robert Andrich), Exequiel Palacios (61' Sardar Azmoun), Amine Adli, Moussa Diaby. Coach: Gerardo Seoane.
Atalanta Bergamo: Juan Musso, Rafael Tolói (10' Berat Djimsiti), José Palomino, Davide Zappacosta (78' Giuseppe Pezzella), Hans Hateboer, Merih Demiral, Marten de Roon, Remo Freuler, Ruslan Malinovskiy (65' Jérémie Boga), Teun Koopmeiners, Luis Muriel (79' Matteo Pessina). Coach: Gian Piero Gasperini.
Goal: 90+1' Jérémie Boga 0-1.
Referee: François Letexier (FRA)   Attendance: 19,871

17.03.22   NEF Stadyumu, Istanbul: Galatasaray – FC Barcelona 1-2 (1-1)
Galatasaray: Iñaki Peña, Patrick van Aanholt (85' Ömer Bayram), Marcão, Victor Nelsson, Sacha Boey, Taylan Antalyali, Alexandru Cicâldau (74' Olimpiu Morutan), Kerem Aktürkoglu, Berkan Kutlu, Ryan Babel (74' Halil Dervisoglu), Bafétimbi Gomis (63' Mostafa Mohamed). Coach: Domènec Torrent.
FC Barcelona: Marc-André ter Stegen, Piqué (81' Clément Lenglet), Jordi Alba, Eric García, Sergiño Dest (56' Ronald Araújo), Sergio Busquets, Frenkie de Jong (68' Gavi), Pedri, Pierre-Emerick Aubameyang (82' Memphis Depay), Adama Traoré (46' Ousmane Dembélé), Ferrán Torres. Coach: Xavi.
Goals: 29' Marcão 1-0, 37' Pedri 1-1, 49' Pierre-Emerick Aubameyang 1-2.
Referee: Daniele Orsato (ITA)   Attendance: 50,110

17.03.22   Groupama Stadium, Décines-Charpieu: Olympique Lyonnais – FC Porto 1-1 (1-1)
Olympique Lyonnais: Anthony Lopes, Emerson, Léo Dubois, Castello Lukeba, Thiago Mendes, Tanguy NDombèlé, Romain Faivre (65' Houssem Aouar), Lucas Paquetá, Maxence Caqueret, Karl Toko Ekambi, Moussa Dembélé (65' Tino Kadewere). Coach: Peter Bosz.
FC Porto: Diogo Costa, Pepe, Chancel Mbemba, Zaidu Sanusi, Marko Grujic (79' Vitinha), Bruno Costa (56' João Mário), Stephen Eustáquio (57' Mateus Uribe), Fábio Vieira, Toni Martínez (74' Mehdi Taremi), Galeno (74' Evanilson), Pepê Aquino. Coach: Sérgio Conceição.
Goals: 13' Moussa Dembélé 1-0, 27' Pepê Aquino 1-1.
Referee: Ovidiu Hategan (ROM)   Attendance: 54,551

17.03.22   London Stadium, London: West Ham United – Sevilla FC 2-0 (1-0,1-0) (AET)
West Ham United: Alphonse Aréola, Aaron Cresswell, Craig Dawson, Kurt Zouma, Ben Johnson, Manuel Lanzini (115' Mark Noble), Tomás Soucek, Declan Rice, Pablo Fornals (119' Issa Diop), Michail Antonio (120+1' Ryan Fredericks), Saïd Benrahma (87' Andrey Yarmolenko). Coach: David Moyes.
Sevilla FC: Yassine Bounou "Bono", Jesús Navas (106' Gonzalo Montiel), Ludwig Augustinsson, Jules Koundé, Ivan Rakitic (56' Óliver Torres), Thomas Delaney, Nemanja Gudelj (111' José Ángel Carmona), Joan Jordán, Jesús Corona (96' Munir El-Haddadi), Anthony Martial (102' Luismi Cruz), Youssef En-Nesyri (91' Rafa Mir). Coach: Lopetegui.
Goals: 39' Tomás Soucek 1-0, 112' Andrey Yarmolenko 2-0.
Referee: Clément Turpin (FRA)   Attendance: 59,981

West Ham United won after extra time.

17.03.22 Deutsche Bank Park, Frankfurt am Main:
Eintracht Frankfurt – Real Betis 1-1 (0-0,0-1) (AET)
Eintracht Frankfurt: Kevin Trapp, Martin Hinteregger, Evan N'Dicka, Tuta, Filip Kostic, Djibril Sow (104' Sebastian Rode), Daichi Kamada (66' Jens Hauge), Kristijan Jakic, Ansgar Knauff, Jesper Lindstrøm (104' Sam Lammers), Rafael Borré (83' Gonçalo Paciência).
Coach: Oliver Glasner.
Real Betis: Rui Silva, Marc Bartra, Germán Pezzella, Youssouf Sabaly, Juan Miranda (46' Juanmi), Joaquín (66' Diego Lainez), Sergio Canales (67' William Carvalho), Guido Rodríguez, Willian José (79' Borja Iglesias), Nabil Fekir (111' Rodri), Aitor Ruibal.
Coach: Manuel Pellegrini.
Goals: 90' Borja Iglesias 0-1, 120+1' Guido Rodríguez 1-1 (og).
Referee: Michael Oliver (ENG)   Attendance: 25,000

Eintracht Frankfurt won after extra time.

QUARTER-FINALS

07.04.22 Red Bull Arena, Leipzig: RB Leipzig – Atalanta Bergamo 1-1 (0-1)
RB Leipzig: Péter Gulácsi, Willi Orban, Lukas Klostermann, Benjamin Henrichs (87' Nordi Mukiele), Angeliño, Josko Gvardiol (73' Marcel Halstenberg), Kevin Kampl, Konrad Laimer, Christopher Nkunku (87' Hugo Novoa), Dani Olmo (73' Dominik Szoboszlai), André Silva (62' Emil Forsberg). Coach: Domenico Tedesco.
Atalanta Bergamo: Juan Musso, José Palomino, Davide Zappacosta (89' Giuseppe Pezzella), Hans Hateboer, Merih Demiral, Marten de Roon, Remo Freuler (67' Aleksey Miranchuk), Mario Pasalic (61' Jérémie Boga), Matteo Pessina (61' Giorgio Scalvini), Teun Koopmeiners, Luis Muriel (61' Duván Zapata). Coach: Gian Piero Gasperini.
Goals: 17' Luis Muriel 0-1, 58' Davide Zappacosta 1-1 (og).
Referee: Michael Oliver (ENG)   Attendance: 36,029

André Silva missed a penalty kick (58').

07.04.22 Deutsche Bank Park, Frankfurt am Main:
Eintracht Frankfurt – FC Barcelona 1-1 (0-0)
Eintracht Frankfurt: Kevin Trapp, Martin Hinteregger, Evan N'Dicka, Tuta, Filip Kostic, Djibril Sow, Daichi Kamada (81' Almany Touré), Kristijan Jakic (89' Sebastian Rode), Jesper Lindstrøm (73' Jens Hauge), Rafael Borré (89' Ragnar Ache), Ansgar Knauff.
Coach: Oliver Glasner.
FC Barcelona: Marc-André ter Stegen, Piqué (23' Clément Lenglet), Jordi Alba, Ronald Araújo, Eric García, Sergio Busquets, Pedri, Gavi (61' Frenkie de Jong), Pierre-Emerick Aubameyang, Adama Traoré (62' Ousmane Dembélé), Ferrán Torres. Coach: Xavi.
Goals: 48' Ansgar Knauff 1-0, 66' Ferrán Torres 1-1.
Referee: Srdjan Jovanovic (SRB)   Attendance: 48,000
Sent-off: Tuta (78').

07.04.22 London Stadium, London: West Ham United – Olympique Lyonnais 1-1 (0-0)
West Ham United: Alphonse Aréola, Aaron Cresswell, Craig Dawson, Kurt Zouma, Ryan Fredericks, Tomás Soucek, Declan Rice, Pablo Fornals, Michail Antonio, Saïd Benrahma (46' Ben Johnson), Jarrod Bowen. Coach: David Moyes.
Olympique Lyonnais: Anthony Lopes, Jérôme Boateng (64' Karl Toko Ekambi), Emerson, Castello Lukeba, Malo Gusto, Thiago Mendes (90' Jason Denayer), Tanguy NDombèlé, Romain Faivre (63' Tetê), Houssem Aouar, Lucas Paquetá, Moussa Dembélé.
Coach: Peter Bosz.
Goals: 52' Jarrod Bowen 1-0, 66' Tanguy NDombèlé 1-1.
Referee: Felix Zwayer (GER)   Attendance: 59,978
Sent-off: Aaron Cresswell (45+3').

07.04.22 Estádio Municipal de Braga, Braga:
Sporting Braga – Glasgow Rangers FC 1-0 (1-0)
Sporting Braga: Matheus Magalhães, Vítor Tormena, Fabiano Silva, David Carmo, Yan Couto (89' Paulo Oliveira), Ali Musrati (83' André Castro), André Horta (82' Lucas Mineiro), Iuri Medeiros (75' Miguel Falé), Ricardo Horta, Abel Ruiz (75' Vítor Oliveira "Vitinha"), Rodrigo Gomes. Coach: Carlos Carvalhal.
Glasgow Rangers FC: Allan McGregor, Leon Balogun (62' Borna Barisic), James Tavernier, Connor Goldson, Calvin Bassey, Scott Arfield, Ryan Jack (63' Joe Ayodele-Aribo), John Lundstram, Glen Kamara, Ryan Kent, Fashion Sakala (62' Kemar Roofe).
Coach: Giovanni van Bronckhorst.
Goal: 40' Abel Ruiz 1-0.
Referee: Davide Massa (ITA)   Attendance: 20,331

14.04.22 Gewiss Stadium, Bergamo: Atalanta Bergamo – RB Leipzig 0-2 (0-1)
Atalanta Bergamo: Juan Musso, José Palomino, Davide Zappacosta, Hans Hateboer, Merih Demiral (70' Giorgio Scalvini), Marten de Roon, Remo Freuler (88' Mario Pasalic), Ruslan Malinovskiy (58' Luis Muriel), Jérémie Boga (70' Aleksey Miranchuk), Teun Koopmeiners, Duván Zapata. Coach: Gian Piero Gasperini.
RB Leipzig: Péter Gulácsi, Willi Orban, Benjamin Henrichs (73' Lukas Klostermann), Angeliño, Mohamed Simakan, Josko Gvardiol (79' Yussuf Poulsen), Kevin Kampl (79' Marcel Halstenberg), Konrad Laimer (73' Tyler Adams), Christopher Nkunku, Dani Olmo, André Silva (63' Dominik Szoboszlai). Coach: Domenico Tedesco.
Goals: 18', 87' Christopher Nkunku 0-1, 0-2 (p).
Referee: Antonio Mateu Lahoz (ESP)   Attendance: 17,905

14.04.22 Camp Nou, Barcelona: FC Barcelona – Eintracht Frankfurt 2-3 (0-2)
FC Barcelona: Marc-André ter Stegen, Jordi Alba, Ronald Araújo, Óscar Mingueza (62' Sergiño Dest), Eric García (70' Luuk de Jong), Sergio Busquets, Pedri (46' Frenkie de Jong), Gavi, Pierre-Emerick Aubameyang (61' Adama Traoré), Ousmane Dembélé, Ferrán Torres (80' Memphis Depay). Coach: Xavi.
Eintracht Frankfurt: Kevin Trapp, Martin Hinteregger, Almany Touré (90+9' Makoto Hasebe), Evan N'Dicka, Sebastian Rode (80' Ajdin Hrustic), Filip Kostic, Daichi Kamada, Kristijan Jakic, Jesper Lindstrøm (80' Jens Hauge), Rafael Borré (90' Ragnar Ache), Ansgar Knauff (90+9' Timothy Chandler). Coach: Oliver Glasner.
Goals: 4' Filip Kostic 0-1 (p), 36' Rafael Borré 0-2, 67' Filip Kostic 0-3, 90+1' Sergio Busquets 1-3, 90+11' Memphis Depay 2-3 (p).
Referee: Artur Soares Dias (POR)   Attendance: 79,468
Sent-off: Evan N'Dicka (90+10').

14.04.22 Groupama Stadium, Décines-Charpieu: Lyon – West Ham United 0-3 (0-2)
Olympique Lyonnais: Julian Pollersbeck, Emerson, Jason Denayer (89' Jeff Reine-Adélaïde), Castello Lukeba, Malo Gusto, Thiago Mendes, Tanguy NDombèlé (46' Lucas Paquetá), Romain Faivre (46' Tetê), Houssem Aouar (71' Bradley Barcola), Karl Toko Ekambi, Moussa Dembélé. Coach: Peter Bosz.
West Ham United: Alphonse Aréola, Craig Dawson, Vladimír Coufal, Issa Diop, Ben Johnson, Manuel Lanzini (77' Mark Noble), Tomás Soucek, Declan Rice (90' Saïd Benrahma), Pablo Fornals, Michail Antonio (84' Andrey Yarmolenko), Jarrod Bowen. Coach: David Moyes.
Goals: 38' Craig Dawson 0-1, 44' Declan Rice 0-2, 48' Jarrod Bowen 0-3.
Referee: Sandro Schärer (SUI)   Attendance: 50,065

14.04.22 Ibrox Stadium, Glasgow:
Glasgow Rangers FC – Sporting Braga 3-1 (2-0,2-1) (AET)
Glasgow Rangers FC: Allan McGregor, James Tavernier, Connor Goldson, Borna Barisic (90+1' Leon Balogun), Calvin Bassey, Ryan Jack (80' Glen Kamara), Aaron Ramsey (80' Scott Wright), John Lundstram, Joe Ayodele-Aribo (106' Fashion Sakala), Kemar Roofe (106' Scott Arfield), Ryan Kent. Coach: Giovanni van Bronckhorst.
Sporting Braga: Matheus Magalhães, Paulo Oliveira, Vítor Tormena, Fabiano Silva, David Carmo (118' Miguel Falé), André Castro (106' Jean-Baptiste Gorby), Ali Musrati (100' Lucas Mineiro), André Horta (46' Francisco Moura), Ricardo Horta, Abel Ruiz (61' Vítor Oliveira "Vitinha"), Rodrigo Gomes (61' Iuri Medeiros). Coach: Carlos Carvalhal.
Goals: 2', 44' James Tavernier 1-0, 2-0 (p), 83' David Carmo 2-1, 101' Kemar Roofe 3-1.
Referee: François Letexier (FRA)   Attendance: 48,894
Sent-off: Vítor Tormena (42'), Iuri Medeiros (105').

Glasgow Rangers FC won after extra time.

SEMI-FINALS

28.04.22 Red Bull Arena, Leipzig: RB Leipzig – Glasgow Rangers FC 1-0 (0-0)
RB Leipzig: Péter Gulácsi, Marcel Halstenberg, Lukas Klostermann, Benjamin Henrichs (90' Nordi Mukiele), Angeliño, Josko Gvardiol, Konrad Laimer, Christopher Nkunku (89' Yussuf Poulsen), Dani Olmo (71' Emil Forsberg), Tyler Adams, Dominik Szoboszlai (71' André Silva). Coach: Domenico Tedesco.
Glasgow Rangers FC: Allan McGregor, James Tavernier, Connor Goldson, Borna Barisic, Calvin Bassey, Ryan Jack (83' James Sands), John Lundstram, Glen Kamara, Scott Wright (69' Fashion Sakala), Joe Ayodele-Aribo (83' Scott Arfield), Ryan Kent.
Coach: Giovanni van Bronckhorst.
Goal: 85' Angeliño 1-0.
Referee: Benoît Bastien (FRA)   Attendance: 40,303

28.04.22 London Stadium, London: West Ham United – Eintracht Frankfurt 1-2 (1-1)
West Ham United: Alphonse Aréola, Aaron Cresswell, Craig Dawson, Kurt Zouma, Ben Johnson, Manuel Lanzini (66' Saïd Benrahma), Tomás Soucek, Declan Rice, Pablo Fornals, Michail Antonio, Jarrod Bowen. Coach: David Moyes.
Eintracht Frankfurt: Kevin Trapp, Martin Hinteregger, Almany Touré, Tuta, Sebastian Rode, Filip Kostic, Djibril Sow, Daichi Kamada, Jesper Lindstrøm (62' Jens Hauge), Rafael Borré (90+3' Ragnar Ache), Ansgar Knauff. Coach: Oliver Glasner.
Goals: 1' Ansgar Knauff 0-1, 21' Michail Antonio 1-1, 54' Daichi Kamada 1-2.
Referee: Serdar Gözübüyük (HOL)   Attendance: 58,108

05.05.22   Ibrox Stadium, Glasgow: Glasgow Rangers FC – RB Leipzig 3-1 (2-0)
Glasgow Rangers FC: Allan McGregor, James Tavernier, Connor Goldson, Borna Barisic, Calvin Bassey, Ryan Jack (59' Leon Balogun), John Lundstram, Glen Kamara, Scott Wright (59' Scott Arfield), Joe Ayodele-Aribo (45+3' Fashion Sakala), Ryan Kent.
Coach: Giovanni van Bronckhorst.
RB Leipzig: Péter Gulácsi, Willi Orban, Lukas Klostermann, Benjamin Henrichs, Angeliño (81' Marcel Halstenberg), Josko Gvardiol, Kevin Kampl, Konrad Laimer, Christopher Nkunku, Dani Olmo (62' Dominik Szoboszlai), Yussuf Poulsen (82' André Silva).
Coach: Domenico Tedesco.
Goals: 19' James Tavernier 1-0, 24' Glen Kamara 2-0, 71' Christopher Nkunku 2-1, 81' John Lundstram 3-1.
Referee: Artur Soares Dias (POR)   Attendance: 49,397

05.05.22   Deutsche Bank Park, Frankfurt am Main:
    Eintracht Frankfurt – West Ham United 1-0 (1-0)
Eintracht Frankfurt: Kevin Trapp, Martin Hinteregger (8' Almany Touré), Evan N'Dicka, Tuta, Sebastian Rode (76' Kristijan Jakic), Filip Kostic, Djibril Sow, Daichi Kamada, Jens Hauge (82' Ajdin Hrustic), Rafael Borré (83' Gonçalo Paciência), Ansgar Knauff.
Coach: Oliver Glasner.
West Ham United: Alphonse Aréola, Aaron Cresswell, Craig Dawson, Vladimír Coufal (87' Andrey Yarmolenko), Kurt Zouma, Manuel Lanzini (22' Ben Johnson), Tomás Soucek, Declan Rice, Pablo Fornals (74' Saïd Benrahma), Michail Antonio, Jarrod Bowen.
Coach: David Moyes.
Goal: 26' Rafael Borré 1-0.
Referee: Jesús Gil Manzano (ESP)   Attendance: 48,000
Sent-off: 19' Aaron Cresswell.

FINAL

18.05.22   Estadio Ramón Sánchez Pizjuán, Sevilla:
    Eintracht Frankfurt – Glasgow Rangers FC 1-1 (0-0,1-1) (AET)
Eintracht Frankfurt: Kevin Trapp, Almany Touré, Evan N'Dicka (100' Christopher Lenz), Tuta (58' Makoto Hasebe), Sebastian Rode (90' Kristijan Jakic), Filip Kostic, Djibril Sow (106' Ajdin Hrustic), Daichi Kamada, Jesper Lindstrøm (71' Jens Hauge), Rafael Borré, Ansgar Knauff. Coach: Oliver Glasner.
Glasgow Rangers FC: Allan McGregor, James Tavernier, Connor Goldson, Borna Barisic (117' Kemar Roofe), Calvin Bassey, Ryan Jack (74' Steven Davis), John Lundstram, Glen Kamara (91' Scott Arfield), Scott Wright (74' Fashion Sakala, 118' Aaron Ramsey), Joe Ayodele-Aribo (101' James Sands), Ryan Kent. Coach: Giovanni van Bronckhorst.
Goals: 57' Joe Ayodele-Aribo 0-1, 69' Rafael Borré 1-1.
Referee: Slavko Vincic (SVN)   Attendance: 37,000

Eintracht Frankfurt won on penalties (5:4).

Penalties: Tavernier 1-0, Lenz 1-1, Davis 2-1, Hrustic 2-2, Arfield 3-2, Kamada 3-3, Ramsey (missed), Kostic 3-4, Roofe 4-4, Borré 4-5.

UEFA EUROPA LEAGUE 2022-2023

THIRD QUALIFYING ROUND

The winners of the ties advanced to the **Play-off Round**.

The losers transferred to the **UEFA Europa Conference League Play-off Round** of their respective path.

(Champions Path)

04.08.22   Eleda Stadion, Malmö: Malmö FF – F91 Dudelange 3-0 (0-0)
Malmö FF: Johan Dahlin, Martin Olsson (76' Eric Larsson), Niklas Moisander, Lasse Nielsen, Felix Beijmo, Jo Inge Berget (69' Veljko Birmancevic), Sergio Peña (76' Hugo Larsson), Erdal Rakip, Moustafa Zeidan, Joseph Ceesay (82' Mohamed Buya Turay), Isaac Kiese Thelin (76' Ola Toivonen). Coach: Andreas Georgson.
F91 Dudelange: Lucas Fox, Manuel da Costa, Jules Diouf (64' Ninte Junior), Mehdi Kirch, Sylvio Ouassiero (42' Eliot Gashi), Dejvid Sinani (63' Vova), Aldin Skenderovic, Charles Morren, Bruno Frere (63' Chris Stumpf), Samir Hadji (38' Filip Bojic), João Magno. Coach: Fangueiro.
Goals: 54' Isaac Kiese Thelin 1-0, 81' Ola Toivonen 2-0, 85' Veljko Birmancevic 3-0.
Referee: Enea Jorgji (ALB)   Attendance: 11,172.
Sent off: 31' Charles Morren.

Jo Inge Berget missed a penalty kick (50').

04.08.22   Ljudski vrt, Maribor: NK Maribor – HJK Helsinki 0-2 (0-0)
NK Maribor: Menno Bergsen, Nemanja Mitrovic, Gregor Sikosek, Max Watson, Andraz Zinic (76' Marin Lausic), Jan Repas, Vladan Vidakovic (76' Sven Karic), Aljaz Antolin (87' Luka Bozickovic), Roko Baturina, Zan Vipotnik (65' Rok Kronaveter), Ivan Brnic (65' Marko Bozic). Coach: Radovan Karanovic.
HJK Helsinki: Conor Hazard, Jukka Raitala, Miro Tenho, Murilo, Matti Peltola, Lucas Lingman (73' Johannes Yli-Kokko), Santeri Väänänen (46' Atomu Tanaka), David Browne (53' Pyry Soiri), Santeri Hostikka, Anthony Olusanya (46' Bojan Radulovic), Malik Abubakari (87' Fabian Serrarens). Coach: Toni Koskela.
Goals: 47' David Browne 0-1, 64' Bojan Radulovic 0-2.
Referee: Georgi Kabakov (BUL)   Attendance: 6,000.

04.08.22   Windsor Park, Belfast: Linfield FC – FC Zürich 0-2 (0-1)
Linfield FC: Chris Johns, Matthew Clarke (87' Ethan Devine), Ben Hall, Sam Roscoe-Byrne, Danny Finlayson, Jamie Mulgrew (68' Cammy Palmer), Chris Shields, Stephen Fallon, Kyle McClean (68' Jordan Stewart), Robbie McDaid (53' Joel Cooper), Eetu Vertainen (68' Chris McKee). Coach: David Healy.
FC Zürich: Yanick Brecher, Nikola Boranijasevic, Fidan Aliti, Mirlind Kryeziu, Lindrit Kamberi, Antonio Marchesano (72' Donis Avdijaj), Ole Selnæs (62' Marc Hornschuh), Cheick Oumar Condé, Jonathan Okita (62' Karol Mets), Aiyegun Tosin (72' Fabian Rohner), Wilfried Gnonto (85' Bledian Krasniqi). Coach: Franco Foda.
Goals: 8' Aiyegun Tosin 0-1, 64' Wilfried Gnonto 0-2.
Referee: Marco Di Bello (ITA)   Attendance: 3,044.

04.08.22   Tallaght Stadium, Dublin: Shamrock Rovers – KF Shkupi 3-1 (2-0)
Shamrock Rovers: Alan Mannus, Sean Gannon, Sean Hoare, Lee Grace, Andy Lyons, Ronan Finn (73' Neil Farrugia), Chris McCann (61' Richie Towell), Gary O'Neill, Dylan Watts (73' Sean Kavanagh), Rory Gaffney (73' Aidomo Emakhu), Graham Burke (54' Aaron Greene). Coach: Stephen Bradley.
KF Shkupi: Kristijan Naumovski, Gagi Margvelashvili, Faustin Senghor, Angelce Timovski, Freddy Álvarez (64' Ali Adem), Besir Demiri (46' Vladica Brdarovski), Queven (90' Dzhelil Abdula), Walid Hamidi, Sunday Adetunji (64' Pepi Georgiev), Albert Diène, Renaldo Cephas (64' Kristijan Trapanovski). Coach: Goce Sedloski.
Goals: 13' Graham Burke 1-0 (p), 29' Dylan Watts 2-0, 77' Queven 2-1, 90+7' Gary O'Neill 3-1.
Referee: Bartosz Frankowski (POL)   Attendance: 6,455.
Sent off: 84' Walid Hamidi.

04.08.22   Stadio Georgios Karaiskáki, Piraeus:
           Olympiakos Piraeus – Slovan Bratislava 1-1 (0-0)
Olympiakos Piraeus: Tomás Vaclík, Sokratis Papastathopoulos, Pape Cissé, Pipa Ávila, Oleg Reabciuk, Yann M'Vila, Pierre Kunde Malong, Georgios Masouras (78' Garry Rodrigues), Mady Camara (68' Mathieu Valbuena), Tiquinho Soares (68' Youssef El-Arabi), Philip Zinckernagel (55' Lazar Randjelovic). Coach: Carlos Corberán.
Slovan Bratislava: Adrián Chovan, Guram Kashia, Lukás Pauschek, Vernon De Marco, Myenty Abena, Juraj Kucka (90+1' Uche Agbo), Jaba Kankava, Jaromír Zmrhal (85' Jurij Medvedev), Giorgi Chakvetadze (90+1' Aleksandar Cavric), Tigran Barseghyan (82' Eric Ramírez), Andre Green. Coach: Vladimir Weiss.
Goals: 63' Andre Green 0-1, 86' Youssef El-Arabi 1-1.
Referee: Lawrence Visser (BEL)   Attendance: 15,585.

09.08.22   Tose Proeski Arena, Skopje: KF Shkupi – Shamrock Rovers 1-2 (0-0)
KF Shkupi: Kristijan Naumovski, Gagi Margvelashvili, Faustin Senghor, Blerton Sheji (46' Vladica Brdarovski), Angelce Timovski (79' Besir Demiri), Freddy Álvarez, Queven, Ali Adem (46' Kristijan Trapanovski), Pepi Georgiev (79' Antonio Kalanoski), Sunday Adetunji, Albert Diène (46' Dzhelil Abdula). Coach: Goce Sedloski.
Shamrock Rovers: Alan Mannus, Sean Hoare, Dan Cleary, Lee Grace, Andy Lyons (81' Neil Farrugia), Ronan Finn (68' Sean Gannon), Richie Towell (62' Graham Burke), Gary O'Neill, Dylan Watts, Rory Gaffney (69' Sean Kavanagh), Aaron Greene (81' Aidomo Emakhu). Coach: Stephen Bradley.
Goals: 65' Rory Gaffney 0-1, 85' Aidomo Emakhu 0-2, 90+4' Sunday Adetunji 1-2.
Referee: Aleksei Kulbakov (BLS)   Attendance: 4,870.

KF Shkupi played their home match at Tose Proeski Arena, Skopje, instead of their regular stadium Cair Stadium, Skopje, which did not meet UEFA requirements.

11.08.22   Bolt Arena, Helsinki: HJK Helsinki – NK Maribor 1-0 (0-0)
HJK Helsinki: Conor Hazard, Jukka Raitala, Miro Tenho, Murilo (84' Casper Terho), Arttu Hoskonen, Lucas Lingman (70' Përparim Hetemaj), Santeri Väänänen (57' Atomu Tanaka), David Browne, Santeri Hostikka (84' Anthony Olusanya), Bojan Radulovic, Malik Abubakari (57' Pyry Soiri). Coach: Toni Koskela.
NK Maribor: Menno Bergsen, Nemanja Mitrovic, Gregor Sikosek, Sven Karic, Andraz Zinic (72' Ignacio Guerrico), Rok Kronaveter (46' Zan Vipotnik), Jan Repas, Vladan Vidakovic (72' Aljaz Antolin), Marko Bozic (60' Rok Sirk), Roko Baturina, Ivan Brnic (46' Marin Lausic). Coach: Radovan Karanovic.
Goal: 54' Santeri Hostikka 1-0.
Referee: Tobias Stieler (GER)   Attendance: 6,487.

11.08.22   Stadion Letzigrund, Zürich: FC Zürich – Linfield FC 3-0 (2-0)
FC Zürich: Yanick Brecher, Nikola Boranijasevic (66' Fabian Rohner), Fidan Aliti, Mirlind Kryeziu, Adrián Guerrero, Lindrit Kamberi, Antonio Marchesano (74' Ivan Santini), Ole Selnæs (74' Blerim Dzemaili), Cheick Oumar Condé (46' Marc Hornschuh), Donis Avdijaj (46' Bledian Krasniqi), Aiyegun Tosin. Coach: Franco Foda.
Linfield FC: Chris Johns, Matthew Clarke, Conor Pepper (85' Kirk Millar), Michael Newberry, Sam Roscoe-Byrne, Danny Finlayson, Jamie Mulgrew (85' Joshua Archer), Joel Cooper (63' Ethan Devine), Kyle McClean, Cammy Palmer (78' Andrew Clarke), Chris McKee (63' Eetu Vertainen). Coach: David Healy.
Goals: 11', 25' Donis Avdijaj 1-0, 2-0, 84' Ivan Santini 3-0.
Referee: Harm Osmers (GER)   Attendance: 7,904.

11.08.22 Stade de Luxembourg, Luxembourg City: F91 Dudelange – Malmö FF 2-2 (0-0)
F91 Dudelange: Lucas Fox, Mehdi Kirch, Vincent Decker (77' Chris Stumpf), Dejvid Sinani, Vova, Eliot Gashi (67' Evann Mendes), Filip Bojic (77' Jules Diouf), Aldin Skenderovic, Samir Hadji, Edis Agovic (60' Bruno Frere), João Magno. Coach: Fangueiro.
Malmö FF: Johan Dahlin, Martin Olsson (78' Eric Larsson), Lasse Nielsen, Dennis Hadzikadunic, Felix Beijmo, Anders Christiansen (88' Moustafa Zeidan), Sergio Peña (67' Niklas Moisander), Joseph Ceesay, Hugo Larsson, Ola Toivonen (67' Isaac Kiese Thelin), Mohamed Buya Turay (68' Søren Rieks). Coach: Andreas Georgson.
Goals: 50' Mohamed Buya Turay 0-1, 52' Ola Toivonen 0-2, 56' Samir Hadji 1-2, 60' Dejvid Sinani 2-2.
Referee: Ricardo de Burgos Bengoetxea (ESP) Attendance: 898

F91 Dudelange played the match at Stade de Luxembourg, Luxembourg City, instead of their regular stadium, Stade Jos Nosbaum, Dudelange, which did not meet UEFA requirements.

11.08.22   Stadion Tehelné pole, Bratislava:
Slovan Bratislava – Olympiakos Piraeus 2-2 (0-0,1-1) (AET)
Slovan Bratislava: Adrián Chovan, Guram Kashia, Lukás Pauschek (90+1' Jurij Medvedev), Vernon De Marco (69' Uche Agbo), Myenty Abena, Juraj Kucka, Jaba Kankava (90+1' Aleksandar Cavric), Jaromír Zmrhal (85' Eric Ramírez), Giorgi Chakvetadze, Tigran Barseghyan (69' Iván Saponjic), Andre Green. Coach: Vladimir Weiss.
Olympiakos Piraeus: Tomás Vaclík, Pape Cissé, Pipa Ávila, Oleg Reabciuk, Ousseynou Ba (85' Andreas Bouchalakis), Yann M'Vila, Pierre Kunde Malong, Georgios Masouras, Lazar Randjelovic (80' Kostas Manolas), Youssef El-Arabi (68' Tiquinho Soares, 91' Mamadou Kané, 110' Mathieu Valbuena), Philip Zinckernagel (69' Aguibou Camara).
Coach: Carlos Corberán.
Goals: 54' Philip Zinckernagel 0-1, 90+4' Iván Saponjic 1-1, 101' Aguibou Camara 1-2, 108' Andre Green 2-2.
Referee: Glenn Nyberg (SWE)   Attendance: 18,133.
Sent off: 90+7' Myenty Abena.

Olympiakos Piraeus won after extra time on penalties (4:3).
Penalties: Ramírez 1-0, Kunde missed, Saponjic 2-0, Bouchalakis 2-1, Kucka missed, Masouras 2-2, Green 3-2, Pipa Ávila 3-3, Chakvetadze missed, Valbuena 3-4.

(Main Path)

04.08.22   AEK Arena – George Karapatakis, Larnaca:
AEK Larnaca – Partizan Beograd 2-1 (1-1)
AEK Larnaca: Kenan Piric, Roberto Rosales, Nenad Tomovic, Oier, Ángel García (81' Kypros Christoforou), Gus Ledes, Hrvoje Milicevic, Ádám Gyurcsó (61' Bruno Gama), Ivan Trickovski (62' Omri Altman), Imad Faraj (89' Rafail Mamas), Victor Olatunji (61' Rafael Lopes). Coach: José Luis Oltra.
Partizan Beograd: Nemanja Stevanovic, Aleksander Filipovic (63' Marko Zivkovic), Igor Vujacic, Slobodan Urosevic, Sinisa Sanicanin, Ljubomir Fejsa, Bibras Natcho (74' Samed Bazdar), Patrick Andrade (81' Kristijan Belic), Ricardo Gomes, Queensy Menig (81' Aleksandar Lutovac), Fousséni Diabaté (81' Nikola Terzic).
Coaches: Aleksandar Stanojevic & Ilija Stolica.
Goals: 18' Queensy Menig 0-1, 34' Ángel García 1-1, 70' Hrvoje Milicevic 2-1.
Referee: Andris Treimanis (LAT)   Attendance: 4,250.

04.08.22   Ülker Stadyumu Fenerbahçe Sükrü Saracoglu Spor Kompleksi, Istanbul:
Fenerbahçe – 1.FC Slovácko 3-0 (2-0)
Fenerbahçe: Ertugrul Çetin, Gustavo Henrique, Attila Szalai, Miha Zajc (60' Miguel Crespo), Willian Arão, Emre Mor (60' Bruma), Lincoln, Bright Osayi-Samuel, Ferdi Kadioglu (77' Filip Novák), Enner Valencia (77' Arda Güler), Diego Rossi (60' Serdar Dursun).
Coach: Jorge Jesus.
1.FC Slovácko: Filip Nguyen, Michal Kadlec, Petr Reinberk (69' Filip Vecheta), Stanislav Hofmann, Jan Kalabiska, Milan Petrzela (63' Michal Tomic), Vlastimil Danícek, Marek Havlík (46' Vladislav Levin), Michal Trávník (86' Michal Kohút), Daniel Holzer (63' Vlasiy Sinyavskiy), Merchas Doski. Coach: Martin Svedík.
Goals: 17' Emre Mor 1-0, 45+2', 81' Lincoln 2-0, 3-0.
Referee: João Pedro Pinheiro (POR)   Attendance: 35,536.
Sent off: 48' Stanislav Hofmann.

11.08.22   Mestský fotbalový stadion Miroslava Valenty, Uherské Hradiste:
1.FC Slovácko – Fenerbahçe 1-1 (0-0)
1.FC Slovácko: Filip Nguyen, Michal Kadlec, Patrik Simko (63' Petr Reinberk), Michal Tomic (84' Vlasiy Sinyavskiy), Milan Petrzela, Vlastimil Danícek, Michal Trávník, Daniel Holzer (64' Jan Kalabiska), Vladislav Levin (64' Michal Kohút), Merchas Doski, Ondrej Sasinka (72' Libor Kozák). Coach: Martin Svedík.
Fenerbahçe: Altay Bayindir, Luan Peres (65' Filip Novák), Mauricio Lemos (74' Gustavo Henrique), Attila Szalai, Bright Osayi-Samuel, Miguel Crespo (65' Miha Zajc), Ismail Yüksek, Arda Güler (80' Lincoln), Serdar Dursun, Bruma (65' Emre Mor), Diego Rossi.
Coach: Jorge Jesus.
Goals: 56' Serdar Dursun 0-1, 58' Ondrej Sasinka 1-1.
Referee: Nikola Dabanovic (MNE)   Attendance: 6,520.

11.08.22   Stadion Partizana, Beograd: Partizan Beograd – AEK Larnaca 2-2 (1-0)
Partizan Beograd: Aleksandar Popovic, Aleksander Filipovic, Igor Vujacic, Slobodan Urosevic, Svetozar Markovic, Ljubomir Fejsa, Bibras Natcho (64' Nemanja Jovic), Patrick Andrade, Ricardo Gomes (84' Samed Bazdar), Queensy Menig (80' Aleksandar Lutovac), Fousséni Diabaté. Coaches: Aleksandar Stanojevic & Ilija Stolica.
AEK Larnaca: Kenan Piric, Roberto Rosales, Nenad Tomovic, Oier, Gus Ledes, Hrvoje Milicevic, Ádám Gyurcsó (66' Bruno Gama), Omri Altman (79' Rafail Mamas), Nikos Englezou (66' Ismael Casas), Rafael Lopes (79' Victor Olatunji), Imad Faraj (89' Mikel González). Coach: José Luis Oltra.
Goals: 24' Ricardo Gomes 1-0, 51' Ádám Gyurcsó 1-1, 54' Ricardo Gomes 2-1, 56' Imad Faraj 2-2.
Referee: José María Sánchez Martínez (ESP)   Attendance: 10,802.

PLAY-OFF ROUND

The winners of the ties advanced to the Group Stage.
The losers were transferred to the UEFA Europa Conference League Group Stage.

18.08.22 Bolt Arena, Helsinki: HJK Helsinki – Silkeborg IF 1-0 (0-0)
HJK Helsinki: Conor Hazard, Jukka Raitala, Miro Tenho, Murilo, Arttu Hoskonen, Lucas Lingman, Santeri Väänänen (73' Nassim Boujellab), Atomu Tanaka (62' Përparim Hetemaj), David Browne, Santeri Hostikka (73' Bojan Radulovic), Malik Abubakari (88' Anthony Olusanya). Coach: Toni Koskela.
Silkeborg IF: Nicolai Larsen, André Calisir, Tobias Salquist, Lukas Engel, Oliver Sonne, Mark Brink (90+1' Pelle Mattsson), Stefán Teitur Thórdarson (71' Joel Felix, Nicolai Vallys, Sebastian Jørgensen (70' Søren Tengstedt), Anders Klynge (85' Mads Kaalund), Nicklas Helenius. Coach: Kent Nielsen.
Goal: 80' David Browne 1-0.
Referee: João Pedro Pinheiro (POR)   Attendance: 8,237.
Sent off: 68' André Calisir.

18.08.22 Groupama Aréna, Budapest: Ferencvárosi TC – Shamrock Rovers 4-0 (2-0)
Ferencvárosi TC: Dénes Dibusz, Endre Botka, Henry Wingo, Lóránd Pászka (84' Eldar Civic), Mats Knoester, Muhamed Besic (70' Bálint Vécsei), Aïssa Laïdouni, Carlos Auzqui (63' Marquinhos), Tokmac Nguen, Adama Traoré (I) (84' Xavier Mercier), Ryan Mmaee (64' Franck Boli). Coach: Stanislav Cherchesov.
Shamrock Rovers: Alan Mannus, Sean Kavanagh (60' Richie Towell), Sean Gannon (61' Neil Farrugia), Sean Hoare, Dan Cleary, Lee Grace, Andy Lyons, Gary O'Neill, Dylan Watts (70' Justin Ferizaj), Rory Gaffney (60' Jack Byrne), Aaron Greene (79' Gideon Tetteh).
Coach: Stephen Bradley.
Goals: 13' Carlos Auzqui 1-0, 34', 48' Adama Traoré 2-0, 3-0, 90+3' Eldar Civic 4-0.
Referee: Glenn Nyberg (SWE)   Attendance: 15,239.

18.08.22 Kybunpark, St. Gallen: FC Zürich – Heart of Midlothian 2-1 (2-1)
FC Zürich: Yanick Brecher, Karol Mets (83' Fidan Aliti), Nikola Boranijasevic, Mirlind Kryeziu, Becir Omeragic, Blerim Dzemaili (74' Cheick Oumar Condé), Antonio Marchesano, Ole Selnæs, Adrián Guerrero, Donis Avdijaj (71' Wilfried Gnonto), Bogdan Vyunnyk (71' Fabian Rohner). Coach: Franco Foda.
Heart of Midlothian: Craig Gordon, Stephen Kingsley, Criag Halkett (7' Toby Sibbick), Kye Rowles, Alex Cochrane, Nathaniel Atkinson (46' Michael Smith), Peter Haring (70' Liam Boyce), Jorge Grant (70' Alan Forrest), Cameron Devlin, Lawrence Shankland (90+3' Josh Ginnelly), Barrie McKay. Coach: Robbie Neilson.
Goals: 22' Lawrence Shankland 0-1 (p), 32' Adrián Guerrero 1-1, 34' Blerim Dzemaili 2-1.
Referee: Bartosz Frankowski (POL)   Attendance: 7,958.

FC Zürich played their home match at Kybunpark, St. Gallen, instead of their regular stadium Stadion Letzigrund, Zürich, which was hosting a concert.

18.08.22   Eleda Stadion, Malmö: Malmö FF – Sivasspor 3-1 (2-1)
Malmö FF: Johan Dahlin, Niklas Moisander, Lasse Nielsen, Dennis Hadzikadunic, Felix
Beijmo, Anders Christiansen (84' Hugo Larsson), Erdal Rakip (71' Sergio Peña), Moustafa
Zeidan (71' Emmanuel Lomotey), Veljko Birmancevic, Joseph Ceesay, Isaac Kiese Thelin (88'
Jo Inge Berget). Coach: Andreas Georgson.
Sivasspor: Muammer Yildirim, Caner Osmanpasa, Ugur Çiftçi, Dimitrios Goutas, Max Gradel,
Hakan Arslan (84' Kader Keita), Fredrik Ulvestad (74' Clinton N'Jie), Robin Yalçin (74'
Mustapha Yatabaré), Erdogan Yesilyurt, Kerem Kesgin (61' Charilaos Charisis), Leke James.
Coach: Riza Çalimbay.
Goals: 18' Moustafa Zeidan 1-0, 30' Leke James 1-1, 37' Anders Christiansen 2-1,
68' Niklas Moisander 3-1.
Referee: William Collum (SCO)   Attendance: 12,167.

18.08.22   Neo GSP Stadium, Nicosia: Apollon Limassol – Olympiacos Piraeus 1-1 (1-1)
Apollon Limassol: Aleksandar Jovanovic, Valentin Roberge, Mathieu Peybernes, Chambos
Kyriakou (60' El-Hadji Ba), Amine Khammas, Euclides Cabral, Nicolas Diguiny (74' Ezekiel
Henty), Israel Coll, Rangelo Janga (60' Ido Shahar), Ioannis Pittas, Vá (46' Hervin Ongenda).
Coach: David Català.
Olympiakos Piraeus: Tomás Vaclík, Pape Cissé, Pipa Ávila, Oleg Reabciuk, Ousseynou Ba,
Yann M'Vila, Pierre Kunde Malong (90+2' Andreas Bouchalakis), Hwang In-Beom (66'
Aguibou Camara), Lazar Randjelovic (79' Marios Vrousai), Youssef El-Arabi (66' Ahmed
Hassan "Koka"), Philip Zinckernagel (79' Konrad de la Fuente). Coach: Carlos Corberán.
Goals: 18' Rangelo Janga 1-0, 28' Hwang In-Beom 1-1.
Referee: José María Sánchez Martínez (ESP)   Attendance: 10,479.

*Apollon Limassol played their home match at Neo GSP Stadium, Nicosia, instead of their
regular stadium Tsirio Stadium, Limassol, which did not meet UEFA requirements,*

18.08.22   Vazgen Sargsyan anvan Hanrapetakan Marzadasht, Yerevan:
            Pyunik Erevan FC – Sheriff Tiraspol 0-0
Pyunik Erevan FC: David Yurchenko, Zoran Gajic (44' Mikhail Kovalenko), Alexander
González, Anton Bratkov, Sergiy Vakulenko, Juninho, Artak Dashyan, Eugeniu Cociuc,
Hovhannes Harutyunyan (61' Renzo Zambrano), Yusuf Otubanjo (61' Marjan Radeski), Luka
Juricic (73' Uros Nenadovic). Coach: Eghishe Melikyan.
Sheriff Tiraspol: Dumitru Celeadnic, Patrick Kpozo, Gaby Kiki, Renan Guedes, Heron, Abou
Ouattara (72' Iyayi Atiemwen), Cédric Badolo, Moussa Kyabou, Mouhamed Diop (83' Salifu
Mudasiru), Kay Tejan, Ibrahim Rasheed. Coach: Stjepan Tomas.
Referee: Alejandro Hernández Hernández (ESP)   Attendance: 9,000.

18.08.22   Huvepharma Arena, Razgrad: PFC Ludogorets Razgrad – FK Zalgiris 1-0 (1-0)
PFC Ludogorets Razgrad: Simon Sluga, Cicinho, Anton Nedyalkov, Olivier Verdon, Jakub
Piotrowski, Ivan Yordanov (90' Petar Georgiev), Danny Gruper, Spas Delev (66' Matías
Tissera), Kiril Despodov, Bernard Tekpetey (79' Jorghinho), Thiago (79' Show).
Coach: Ante Simundza.
FK Zalgiris: Edvinas Gertmonas, Saulius Mikoliūnas, Ivan Tatomirovic, Mario Pavelic, Kipras
Kazukolovas (72' Marko Milickovic), Nemanja Ljubisavljevic, Nicolás Gorobsov, Oliver Buff
(83' Gustas Jarusevicius), Fabien Ourega (90+3' Mantas Kuklys), Renan Oliveira (72' Josip
Tadic), Mathias Oyewusi (72' Donatas Kazlauskas). Coach: Vladimir Cheburin.
Goal: 2' IvanTatomirovic 1-0 (og).
Referee: Ivan Kruzliak (SVK)   Attendancce: 4,951.
Sent off: 90+4' Donatas Kazlauskas.

18.08.22   Kosická futbalová aréna, Kosice (SVK)): SK Dnipro-1 – AEK Larnaca 1-2 (0-2)
SK Dnipro-1: Max Walef, Volodymyr Tanchyk, Volodymyr Adamyuk, Oleksandr Svatok, Emiliano Purita (61' Oleksandr Nazarenko), Busanello, Domingo Blanco, Oleksandr Pikhalyonok, Igor Kogut (46' Artem Gromov), Eduard Sarapyi, Artem Dovbyk.
Coach: Oleksandr Kucher.
AEK Larnaca: Ioakim Toumpas, Mikel González, Roberto Rosales, Oier, Gus Ledes (86' Rafail Mamas), Hrvoje Milicevic, Ádám Gyurcsó (86' Ivan Trickovski), Omri Altman, Nikos Englezou (59' Ismael Casas), Rafael Lopes (59' José Romo), Imad Faraj (66' Bruno Gama).
Coach: José Luis Oltra.
Goals: 16' Omri Altman 0-1, 29' Oleksandr Svatok 0-2 (og), 90' Oleksandr Svatok 1-2.
Referee: Tobias Stieler (GER)   Attendance: 3,450.
Sent off: 90+5' Eduard Sarapyi.

Due to the Russian invasion of Ukraine, Ukrainian teams were required to play their home matches at neutral venues until further notice.

18.08.22   GHELAMCO-arena, Gent: KAA Gent – Omonia Nicosia 0-2 (0-1)
KAA Gent: Dany Roef, Michael Ngadeu-Ngadjui, Núrio Fortuna (46' Vadis Odjidja-Ofoe), Jordan Torunarigha (81' Bruno Godeau), Andreas Hanche-Olsen (80' Joseph Okumu), Sven Kums, Andrew Hjulsager, Alessio Castro-Montes (81' Matisse Samoise), Hong Hyun-seok, Hugo Cuypers, Jens Hauge (62' Laurent Depoitre). Coach: Hein Vanhaezebrouck.
Omonia Nicosia: Fabiano, Jan Lecjaks, Adam Matthews, Nemanja Miletic, Héctor Yuste, Mix Diskerud (70' Roman Bezus), Fouad Bachirou, Bruno Souza (74' Fotis Papoulis), Nikos Panagiotou, Charalampos Charalampous (74' Brandon Barker), Andronikos Kakoullis (86' Tim Matavz). Coach: Neil Lennon.
Goals: 19' Charalampos Charalampous 0-1, 76' Brandon Barker 0-2.
Referee: Irfan Peljto (BIH)   Attendance: 10,496.

18.08.22   Generali Arena, Vienna: Austria Wien – Fenerbahçe 0-2 (0-1)
Austria Wien: Christian Früchtl, Lucas Galvão, Marvin Martins, Lukas Mühl, Billy Koumetio, Reinhold Ranftl, Manfred Fischer, Matthias Braunöder, Florian Wustinger (22' Haris Tabakovic, 86' Johannes Handl), Dominik Fitz (75' Can Keles), Muharem Huskovic (46' Aleksandar Jukic). Coach: Manfred Schmid.
Fenerbahçe: Altay Bayindir, Ezgjan Alioski (79' Filip Novák), Luan Peres, Mauricio Lemos (75' Gustavo Henrique), Attila Szalai, Miguel Crespo (60' Miha Zajc), Ferdi Kadioglu, Ismail Yüksek (79' Willian Arão), Joshua King (59' Lincoln), Serdar Dursun, Diego Rossi.
Coach: Jorge Jesus.
Goals: 8' Joshua King 0-1, 89' Serdar Dursun 0-2.
Referee: Daniel Siebert (GER)   Attendance: 14,000.
Sent off: 83' Lucas Galvão.

25.08.22   AEK Arena – George Karapatakis, Larnaca: AEK Larnaca – SK Dnipro-1 3-0 (2-0)
AEK Larnaca: Kenan Piric, Mikel González, Roberto Rosales, Oier, Gus Ledes, Hrvoje Milicevic, Ádám Gyurcsó (83' Giorgos Naoum), Omri Altman (74' Ángel García), Nikos Englezou (87' Bruno Gama), Rafael Lopes (74' Victor Olatunji), Imad Faraj (74' Rafail Mamas). Coach: José Luis Oltra.
SK Dnipro-1: Max Walef, Volodymyr Tanchyk, Sergiy Loginov (73' Valentyn Rubchynskyi), Oleksandr Svatok, Busanello, Ruslan Babenko, Domingo Blanco, Oleksandr Pikhalyonok, Oleksiy Hutsulyak (58' Oleksandr Nazarenko), Artem Gromov (69' Igor Kogut), Artem Dovbyk. Coach: Oleksandr Kucher.
Goals: 21' Ádám Gyurcsó 1-0, 45' Rafael Lopes 2-0, 78' Nikos Englezou 3-0.
Referee: Davide Massa (ITA)   Attendance: 4,893.

25.08.22   Vilniaus LFF stadionas, Vilnius:
    FK Zalgiris – PFC Ludogorets Razgrad 3-3 (2-1,3-2) (AET)
FK Zalgiris: Edvinas Gertmonas, Mario Pavelic, Joël Bopesu, Kipras Kazukolovas, Nemanja Ljubisavljevic, Nicolás Gorobsov, Oliver Buff (100' Mantas Kuklys), Fabien Ourega (101' Petar Mamic), Marko Milickovic (109' Motiejus Burba), Renan Oliveira (71' Francis Kyeremeh), Mathias Oyewusi (71' Josip Tadic). Coach: Vladimir Cheburin.
PFC Ludogorets Razgrad: Simon Sluga, Cicinho, Anton Nedyalkov, Olivier Verdon, Jakub Piotrowski, Ivan Yordanov (80' Show), Danny Gruper (71' Zan Karnicnik), Bernard Tekpetey (64' Spas Delev), Matías Tissera (64' Cauly), Rick (100' Jorghinho), Thiago.
Coach: Ante Simundza.
Goals: 1' Fabien Ourega 1-0, 8' Matías Tissera 1-1, 15' Oliver Buff 2-1, 57' Matías Tissera 2-2, 63' Renan Oliveira 3-2, 120' Olivier Verdon 3-3 (p).
Referee: Harm Osmers (GER)   Attendance: 4,601.

PFC Ludogorets Razgrad won after extra time.

25.08.22   JYSK park, Silkeborg: Silkeborg IF – HJK Helsinki 1-1 (0-1)
Silkeborg IF: Nicolai Larsen, Tobias Salquist, Joel Felix, Lukas Engel, Oliver Sonne, Mark Brink, Stefán Teitur Thórdarson (46' Mads Kaalund), Nicolai Vallys, Sebastian Jørgensen (60' Tonni Adamsen), Anders Klynge (85' Søren Tengstedt), Nicklas Helenius.
Coach: Kent Nielsen.
HJK Helsinki: Conor Hazard, Jukka Raitala, Aapo Halme (66' Matti Peltola), Murilo, Arttu Hoskonen, Lucas Lingman, Santeri Väänänen, Atomu Tanaka (46' Përparim Hetemaj), David Browne (78' Pyry Soiri), Santeri Hostikka (78' Nassim Boujellab), Malik Abubakari (86' Anthony Olusanya). Coach: Toni Koskela.
Goals: 40' Malik Abubakari 0-1, 74' Joel Felix 1-1.
Referee: Maurizio Mariani (ITA)   Attendance: 6,334.

25.08.22   Neo GSP Stadium, Nicosia: Omonia Nicosia – KAA Gent 2-0 (2-0)
Omonia Nicosia: Fabiano, Jan Lecjaks, Adam Matthews, Nemanja Miletic, Héctor Yuste, Mix Diskerud (79' Fotis Papoulis), Fouad Bachirou, Bruno Souza (67' Brandon Barker), Nikos Panagiotou, Charalampos Charalampous (67' Roman Bezus), Andronikos Kakoullis (79' Pangiotis Zachariou). Coach: Neil Lennon.
KAA Gent: Dany Roef, Michael Ngadeu-Ngadjui, Jordan Torunarigha, Joseph Okumu (84' Andreas Hanche-Olsen), Vadis Odjidja-Ofoe (63' Andrew Hjulsager), Sven Kums (72' Jens Hauge), Alessio Castro-Montes, Hong Hyun-seok (72' Sulayman Marreh), Matisse Samoise, Laurent Depoitre (63' Darko Lemajic), Hugo Cuypers. Coach: Hein Vanhaezebrouck.
Goals: 18' Andronikos Kakoullis 1-0, 36' Charalampos Charalampous 2-0.
Referee: Georgi Kabakov (BUL)   Attendance: 17,002.

25.08.22   Ülker Stadyumu Fenerbahçe Sükrü Saracoglu spor Kompleksi, Istanbul:
Fenerbahçe – Austria Wien 4-1 (2-1)
Fenerbahçe: Altay Bayindir, Ezgjan Alioski, Gustavo Henrique, Luan Peres (80' Attila Szalai), Mauricio Lemos, İrfan Kahveci (77' Arda Güler), Bright Osayi-Samuel, Miguel Crespo (77' Mert Hakan Yandas), İsmail Yüksek, Serdar Dursun (80' Enner Valencia), Diego Rossi (85' Emre Mor). Coach: Jorge Jesus.
Austria Wien: Christian Früchtl, Marvin Martins (46' Can Keles), Johannes Handl (81' Dario Kreiker), Lukas Mühl, Billy Koumetio, Reinhold Ranftl, Manfred Fischer, Matthias Braunöder (46' James Holland), Andreas Gruber (66' Marco Djuricin), Haris Tabakovic, Dominik Fitz (65' Romeo Vucic). Coach: Manfred Schmid.
Goals: 12' İsmail Yüksek 1-0, 44' İrfan Kahveci 2-0, 45+1' Marvin Martins 2-1, 70' İrfan Kahveci 3-1, 79' Mert Hakan Yandas 4-1.
Referee: Jesús Gil Manzano (ESP)   Attendance: 35,350.

25.08.22   Yeni Sivas 4 Eylül Stadyumu, Sivas: Sivasspor – Malmö FF 0-2 (0-0)
Sivasspor: Ali Vural, Ugur Çiftçi, Dimitrios Goutas, Aaron Appindangoyé, Max Gradel, Fredrik Ulvestad, Erdogan Yesilyurt, Charilaos Charisis (69' Hakan Arslan), Kader Keita, Mustapha Yatabaré (80' Clinton N'Jie), Leke James (80' Karol Angielski).
Coach: Riza Çalimbay.
Malmö FF: Ismael Diawara, Niklas Moisander, Lasse Nielsen, Dennis Hadzikadunic, Felix Beijmo, Anders Christiansen, Jo Inge Berget, Erdal Rakip, Moustafa Zeidan (82' Hugo Larsson), Veljko Birmancevic (89' Joseph Ceesay), Isaac Kiese Thelin.
Coach: Andreas Georgson.
Goals: 76' Veljko Birmancevic 0-1, 89' Isaac Kiese Thelin 0-2.
Referee: Srdjan Jovanovic (SRB)   Attendance: 16,873.

25.08.22   Stadionul Zimbru, Chisinau: Sheriff Tiraspol – Pyunik Erevan FC 0-0 (AET)
Sheriff Tiraspol: Dumitru Celeadnic, Patrick Kpozo, Stjepan Radeljic, Gaby Kiki, Renan Guedes, Iyayi Atiemwen (72' Kay Tejan), Abou Ouattara (81' Steve Ambri), Cédric Badolo (102' Salifu Mudasiru), Moussa Kyabou, Mouhamed Diop, Ibrahim Rasheed (90+4' Giannis Botos). Coach: Stjepan Tomas.
Pyunik Erevan FC: David Yurchenko, Alexander González (80' Renzo Zambrano), Anton Bratkov, Sergiy Vakulenko, Mikhail Kovalenko, Juninho (90' Yuri Gareginyan), Artak Dashyan, Eugeniu Cociuc (80' Aleksandar Miljkovic), Hovhannes Harutyunyan, Yusuf Otubanjo (70' Uros Nenadovic, 105' Boris Varga), Marjan Radeski (46' Luka Juricic).
Coach: Eghishe Melikyan.
Referee: Andreas Ekberg (SWE)   Attendance: 6,154.

Sheriff Tiraspol won on penalties after extra time (3:2).

Penalties: Harutyunyan missed, Tejan 0-1, Dashyan missed, Steve Ambri missed,
Zambrano missed, Diop missed, Gareginyan 1-1, Kpozo 1-2, Vakulenko 2-2,
Kiki missed, Kovalenko missed, Radeljic 2-3.

Sheriff Tiraspol played their home match at Stadionul Zimbru, Chisinau, instead of their regular stadium Sheriff Stadium, Tiraspol, due to Transnistria's involvement in the Russian invasion of Ukraine.

25.08.22 Tynecastle Park, Edinburgh: Heart of Midlothian – FC Zürich 0-1 (0-0)
Heart of Midlothian: Craig Gordon, Michael Smith, Stephen Kingsley (78' Toby Sibbick), Kye Rowles, Alex Cochrane, Jorge Grant, Cameron Devlin (84' Connor Smith), Liam Boyce (64' Peter Haring), Lawrence Shankland, Barrie McKay, Alan Forrest (64' Josh Ginnelly).
Coach: Robbie Neilson.
FC Zürich: Yanick Brecher, Karol Mets, Nikola Boranijasevic, Mirlind Kryeziu, Becir Omeragic, Antonio Marchesano (79' Fabian Rohner), Ole Selnæs, Adrián Guerrero (90+1' Fidan Aliti), Cheick Oumar Condé (46' Marc Hornschuh), Donis Avdijaj (46' Wilfried Gnonto), Bogdan Vyunnyk (63' Aiyegun Tosin). Coach: Franco Foda.
Goal: 80' Fabian Rohner 0-1.
Referee: Lawrence Visser (BEL)   Attendance: 17,225.
Sent off: 54' Jorge Grant.

25.08.22 Tallaght Stadium, Dublin: Shamrock Rovers – Ferencvárosi TC 1-0 (0-0)
Shamrock Rovers: Alan Mannus, Sean Kavanagh (73' Dylan Watts), Sean Gannon, Sean Hoare, Lee Grace, Ronan Finn (64' Andy Lyons), Richie Towell (73' Jack Byrne), Gary O'Neill, Neil Farrugia, Justin Ferizaj (72' Gideon Tetteh), Aidomo Emakhu (64' Aaron Greene). Coach: Stephen Bradley.
Ferencvárosi TC: Ádám Bogdán, Adnan Kovacevic, Eldar Civic, Henry Wingo, Mats Knoester, Anderson Esiti (57' Bálint Vécsei), Aïssa Laïdouni, Carlos Auzqui (57' Marquinhos), Tokmac Nguen (71' Xavier Mercier), Adama Traoré (I) (79' Krisztián Lisztes), Ryan Mmaee (71' Franck Boli). Coach: Stanislav Cherchesov.
Goal: 89' Andy Lyons 1-0.
Referee: François Letexier (FRA)   Attendance: 7,163.

25.08.22 Stadio Georgios Karaiskáki, Piraeus:
         Olympiakos Piraeus – Apollon Limassol 1-1 (1-0,1-1) (AET)
Olympiakos Piraeus: Tomás Vaclík, Pape Cissé, Pipa Ávila, Oleg Reabciuk, Ousseynou Ba, Yann M'Vila, Pierre Kunde Malong (84' Aguibou Camara), Georgios Masouras (84' Konrad de la Fuente), Hwang In-Beom (79' Mathieu Valbuena), Youssef El-Arabi (103' Kostas Manolas), Philip Zinckernagel (55' Lazar Randjelovic). Coach: Carlos Corberán.
Apollon Limassol: Aleksandar Jovanovic, Valentin Roberge, Mathieu Peybernes, Amine Khammas, Nicolas Diguiny (81' Rangelo Janga), Charis Mavrias, Israel Coll (81' Chambos Kyriakou), Ido Shahar (67' El-Hadji Ba), Ezekiel Henty (57' Bassel Jradi, 97' Euclides Cabral), Ioannis Pittas, Vá (67' Hervin Ongenda). Coach: David Catalá.
Goals: 2' Giannis Masouras 1-0, 90' Ioannis Pittas 1-1.
Referee: Sandro Schärer (SUI)   Attendance: 20,054.
Sent off: 100' Ousseynou Ba.

Olympiakos Piraeus won on penalties after extra time (3:1).

Penalties: M'Vila 1-0, Kyriakou missed, De la Fuente 2-0, Pittas 2-1, Pipa Ávila 3-1, Ongenda missed, Randjelovic missed, Ba missed.

GROUP STAGE

The group winners advance to Round of 16
The second-placed team in the group advance to Knockout Round Play-offs
The third-placed team in the group transfer to UEFA Europa Conference League

GROUP A

Arsenal	6	5	0	1	8	-	3	15
PSV Eindhoven	6	4	1	1	15	-	4	13
FK Bodø/Glimt	6	1	1	4	5	-	10	4
FC Zürich	6	1	0	5	5	-	16	3

GROUP B

Fenerbahçe	6	4	2	0	13	-	7	14
Stade Rennes	6	3	3	0	11	-	8	12
AEK Larnaca	6	1	2	3	7	-	10	5
Dynamo Kyiv	6	0	1	5	5	-	11	1

GROUP C

Real Betis	6	5	1	0	12	-	4	16
AS Roma	6	3	1	2	11	-	7	10
PFC Ludogorets Razgrad	6	2	1	3	8	-	9	7
HJK Helsinki	6	0	1	5	2	-	13	1

GROUP D

Union Saint-Gilloise	6	4	1	1	11	-	7	13
Union Berlin	6	4	0	2	4	-	2	12
Sporting Braga	6	3	1	2	9	-	7	10
Malmö FF	6	0	0	6	3	-	11	0

GROUP E

Real Sociedad	6	5	0	1	10	-	2	15
Manchester United	6	5	0	1	10	-	3	15
Sheriff Tiraspol	6	2	0	4	4	-	10	6
Omonia Nicosia	6	0	0	6	3	-	12	0

GROUP F

Feyenoord Rotterdam	6	2	2	2	13	-	9	8
FC Midtjylland	6	2	2	2	12	-	8	8
Lazio Roma	6	2	2	2	9	-	11	8
Sturm Graz	6	2	2	2	4	-	10	8

GROUP G

SC Freiburg	6	4	2	0	13	-	3	14
FC Nantes	6	3	0	3	6	-	11	9
Qarabag FK	6	2	2	2	9	-	5	8
Olympiakos Piraeus	6	0	2	4	2	-	11	2

GROUP H

Ferencvárosi TC	6	3	1	2	8	-	9	10
AS Monaco	6	3	1	2	9	-	8	10
Trabzonspor	6	3	0	3	11	-	9	9
Crvena Zvezda Beograd	6	2	0	4	9	-	11	6

GROUP A

08.09.22   Kybunpark, St. Gallen: FC Zürich – Arsenal 1-2 (1-1)
FC Zürich: Yanick Brecher, Nikola Boranijasevic, Fidan Aliti, Mirlind Kryeziu, Lindrit Kamberi, Blerim Dzemaili (67' Cheick Condé), Ole Selnæs, Adrián Guerrero (67' Fabian Rohner), Bledian Krasniqi (67' Antonio Marchesano), Jonathan Okita (80' Donis Avdijaj), Aiyegun Tosin (80' Ivan Santini). Coach: Franco Foda.
Arsenal: Matt Turner, Kieran Tierney (69' Oleksandr Zinchenko), Rob Holding, Takehiro Tomiyasu, Gabriel Magalhães, Granit Xhaka, Albert Lokonga, Fábio Vieira (69' Martin Ødegaard), Eddie Nketiah (78' Gabriel Jesus), Gabriel Martinelli, Marquinhos (69' Bukayo Saka). Coach: Mikel Arteta.
Goals: 17' Marquinhos 0-1, 44' Mirlind Kryeziu 1-1 (p), 62' Eddie Nketiah 1-2.
Referee: Mohammed Al-Hakim (SWE)   Attendance: 17,070.

FC Zürich played their home match at Kybunpark, St. Gallen, instead of their regular stadium, Stadion Letzigrund, Zürich, due to a music concert and athletic event.

08.09.22   Philips Stadion, Eindhoven: PSV Eindhoven – FK Bodø/Glimt 1-1 (0-1)
PSV Eindhoven: Walter Benítez, Phillipp Mwene, Philipp Max, Armando Obispo, Jordan Teze, Ibrahim Sangaré, Joey Veerman, Xavi Simons, Cody Gakpo, Yorbe Vertessen (62' Anwar El Ghazi), Ismael Saibari (62' Sávio). Coach: Ruud van Nistelrooij.
FK Bodø/Glimt: Nikita Haikin, Marius Høibråten, Marius Lode (70' Isak Amundsen), Brice Wembangomo, Alfons Sampsted, Ulrik Saltnes, Patrick Berg, Hugo Vetlesen, Albert Grønbæk Erlykke, Runar Espejord (58' Lars-Jørgen Salvesen), Joel Mvuka. Coach: Kjetil Knutsen.
Goals: 44' Albert Grønbæk Erlykke 0-1, 62' Cody Gakpo 1-1.
Referee: Georgi Kabakov (BUL)   Attendance: 28,627.

15.09.22   Aspmyra Stadion, Bodø: FK Bodø/Glimt – FC Zürich 2-1 (0-0)
FK Bodø/Glimt: Nikita Haikin, Marius Høibråten, Marius Lode (77' Isak Amundsen), Brice Wembangomo, Alfons Sampsted, Ulrik Saltnes, Patrick Berg, Hugo Vetlesen, Lars-Jørgen Salvesen (46' Runar Espejord), Ola Solbakken (77' Albert Grønbæk Erlykke), Joel Mvuka (67' Amahl Pellegrino). Coach: Kjetil Knutsen.
FC Zürich: Yanick Brecher, Nikola Boranijasevic, Mirlind Kryeziu, Lindrit Kamberi, Blerim Dzemaili (71' Cheick Condé), Ole Selnæs, Adrián Guerrero, Fabian Rohner (61' Donis Avdijaj), Bledian Krasniqi (61' Antonio Marchesano), Jonathan Okita (71' Bogdan Viunnyk), Aiyegun Tosin (82' Ivan Santini). Coach: Franco Foda.
Goals: 54' Ole Selnæs 1-0 (og), 58' Hugo Vetlesen 2-0, 81' Donis Avdijaj 2-1.
Referee: Stéphanie Frappart (FRA)   Attendance: 8,000.

06.10.22   Stadion Letzigrund, Zürich: FC Zürich – PSV Eindhoven 1-5 (0-4)
FC Zürich: Yanick Brecher, Nikola Boranijasevic (56' Jonathan Okita), Fidan Aliti (56' Karol Mets), Mirlind Kryeziu (71' Nikola Katic), Lindrit Kamberi, Blerim Dzemaili (56' Marc Hornschuh), Antonio Marchesano (71' Donis Avdijaj), Ole Selnæs, Adrián Guerrero, Fabian Rohner, Aiyegun Tosin. Coach: Genesio Colatrella.
PSV Eindhoven: Walter Benítez, Phillipp Mwene, André Ramalho, Philipp Max (66' Ki-Jana Hoever), Armando Obispo (46' Jordan Teze), Ibrahim Sangaré, Joey Veerman, Xavi Simons (61' Guus Til), Cody Gakpo (62' Johan Bakayoko), Yorbe Vertessen (61' Anwar El Ghazi), Ismael Saibari. Coach: Ruud van Nistelrooij.
Goals: 10', 16' Yorbe Vertessen 0-1, 0-2, 21' Cody Gakpo 0-3, 35' Xavi Simons 0-4, 55' Cody Gakpo 0-5, 87' Jonathan Okita 1-5.
Referee: William Collum (SCO)   Attendance: 10,626.

06.10.22   Emirates Stadium, London: Arsenal – FK Bodø/Glimt 3-0 (2-0)
Arsenal: Matt Turner, Kieran Tierney (70' Ben White), Rob Holding, Takehiro Tomiyasu, Gabriel Magalhães, Granit Xhaka (58' Martin Ødegaard), Albert Lokonga, Fábio Vieira, Eddie Nketiah (82' Reiss Nelson), Gabriel Martinelli (59' Gabriel Jesus), Marquinhos (59' Bukayo Saka). Coach: Mikel Arteta.
FK Bodø/Glimt: Nikita Haikin, Brede Moe, Marius Lode (88' Marius Høibråten), Brice Wembangomo, Alfons Sampsted (88' Morten Konradsen), Ulrik Saltnes, Patrick Berg, Hugo Vetlesen (73' Albert Grønbæk Erlykke), Amahl Pellegrino, Runar Espejord (88' Lars-Jørgen Salvesen), Joel Mvuka (73' Ola Solbakken). Coach: Kjetil Knutsen.
Goals: 23' Eddie Nketiah 1-0, 27' Rob Holding 2-0, 84' Fábio Vieira 3-0.
Referee: Harm Osmers (GER)   Attendance: 59,724.

13.10.22   Aspmyra Stadion, Bodø: FK Bodø/Glimt – Arsenal 0-1 (0-1)
FK Bodø/Glimt: Nikita Haikin, Marius Høibråten (89' Brede Moe), Marius Lode, Brice Wembangomo, Alfons Sampsted, Ulrik Saltnes (12' Albert Grønbæk Erlykke), Patrick Berg, Hugo Vetlesen, Amahl Pellegrino (89' Joel Mvuka), Runar Espejord (76' Lars-Jørgen Salvesen), Ola Solbakken. Coach: Kjetil Knutsen.
Arsenal: Matt Turner, Kieran Tierney, Rob Holding, Ben White (70' Takehiro Tomiyasu), William Saliba, Martin Ødegaard (70' Marquinhos), Albert Lokonga (84' Thomas Partey), Bukayo Saka (59' Granit Xhaka), Fábio Vieira, Eddie Nketiah, Reiss Nelson (59' Gabriel Martinelli). Coach: Mikel Arteta.
Goal: 24' Bukayo Saka 0-1.
Referee: Irfan Peljto (BIH)   Attendance: 7,922.

13.10.22   Philips Stadion, Eindhoven: PSV Eindhoven – FC Zürich 5-0 (3-0)
PSV Eindhoven: Walter Benítez, Phillipp Mwene, André Ramalho, Philipp Max, Armando Obispo (74' Jordan Teze), Érick Gutiérrez, Ibrahim Sangaré (63' Sávio), Guus Til, Joey Veerman (56' Johan Bakayoko), Xavi Simons (46' Richy Ledezma), Cody Gakpo (46' Anwar El Ghazi). Coach: Ruud van Nistelrooij.
FC Zürich: Yanick Brecher, Marc Hornschuh (82' Fabian Rohner), Karol Mets, Nikola Boranijasevic, Nikola Katic, Lindrit Kamberi, Antonio Marchesano (70' Bledian Krasniqi), Adrián Guerrero, Cheick Condé (59' Ole Selnæs), Aiyegun Tosin (70' Donis Avdijaj), Bogdan Viunnyk (59' Jonathan Okita). Coach: Bo Henriksen.
Goals: 9' Érick Gutiérrez 1-0, 15' Joey Veerman 2-0, 34' Ibrahim Sangaré 3-0, 55' Joey Veerman 4-0, 84' Anwar El Ghazi 5-0.
Referee: Ali Palabiyik (TUR)   Attendance: 30,000.

20.10.22   Emirates Stadium, London: Arsenal – PSV Eindhoven 1-0 (0-0)
Arsenal: Matt Turner, Kieran Tierney, Rob Holding, Takehiro Tomiyasu (76' Ben White), Gabriel Magalhães, Granit Xhaka, Albert Lokonga (67' Thomas Partey), Bukayo Saka (85' Reiss Nelson), Fábio Vieira (67' Martin Ødegaard), Gabriel Jesus (76' Gabriel Martinelli), Eddie Nketiah. Coach: Mikel Arteta.
PSV Eindhoven: Walter Benítez, Phillipp Mwene, André Ramalho, Philipp Max (66' Jordan Teze), Armando Obispo, Érick Gutiérrez, Ibrahim Sangaré, Guus Til (65' Noni Madueke), Joey Veerman (77' Luuk de Jong), Xavi Simons (90+1' Richy Ledezma), Cody Gakpo. Coach: Ruud van Nistelrooij.
Goal: 71' Granit Xhaka 1-0.
Referee: Alejandro Hernández Hernández (ESP)   Attendance: 52,200.

The match was originally due to be played on 15th September 2022, but was rescheduled to 20th October 2022, following the death of Queen Elizabeth II.

27.10.22   Stadion Letzigrund, Zürich: FC Zürich – FK Bodø/Glimt 2-1 (0-1)
FC Zürich: Yanick Brecher, Nikola Boranijasevic, Fidan Aliti (84' Karol Mets), Nikola Katic, Lindrit Kamberi, Blerim Dzemaili (71' Antonio Marchesano), Ole Selnæs, Adrián Guerrero (60' Fabian Rohner), Cheick Condé, Jonathan Okita (84' Bogdan Viunnyk), Aiyegun Tosin (84' Selmin Hodza). Coach: Bo Henriksen.
FK Bodø/Glimt: Nikita Haikin, Marius Høibråten, Brede Moe (82' Marius Lode), Brice Wembangomo, Alfons Sampsted, Ulrik Saltnes, Hugo Vetlesen, Albert Grønbæk Erlykke (87' Elias Hagen), Amahl Pellegrino (78' Joel Mvuka), Runar Espejord (78' Lars-Jørgen Salvesen), Ola Solbakken. Coach: Kjetil Knutsen.
Goals: 45+1' Amahl Pellegrino 0-1, 67' Nikola Boranijasevic 1-1, 90+4' Antonio Marchesano 2-1.
Referee: Yevhen Aranovskyi (UKR)   Attendance: 10,168.

27.10.22   Philips Stadion, Eindhoven: PSV Eindhoven – Arsenal 2-0 (0-0)
PSV Eindhoven: Walter Benítez, Phillipp Mwene, André Ramalho, Philipp Max, Jarrad Branthwaite (81' Jordan Teze), Érick Gutiérrez, Ibrahim Sangaré, Joey Veerman (81' Guus Til), Xavi Simons (80' Noni Madueke), Anwar El Ghazi (46' Luuk de Jong), Cody Gakpo (84' Mauro Júnior). Coach: Ruud van Nistelrooij.
Arsenal: Aaron Ramsdale, Kieran Tierney (74' Gabriel Magalhães), Rob Holding (64' Gabriel Jesus), Takehiro Tomiyasu (74' Ben White), William Saliba, Granit Xhaka, Martin Ødegaard (57' Bukayo Saka), Albert Lokonga (56' Thomas Partey), Fábio Vieira, Eddie Nketiah, Gabriel Martinelli. Coach: Mikel Arteta.
Goals: 55' Joey Veerman 1-0, 63' Luuk de Jong 2-0.
Referee: Marco Di Bello (ITA)   Attendance: 35,000.

03.11.22   Emirates Stadium, London: Arsenal – FC Zürich 1-0 (1-0)
Arsenal: Aaron Ramsdale, Kieran Tierney, Rob Holding, Gabriel Magalhães, Ben White (73' Takehiro Tomiyasu, 88' Cédric Soares), Mohamed Elneny (63' Thomas Partey), Albert Lokonga, Fábio Vieira (73' Martin Ødegaard), Gabriel Jesus (63' Bukayo Saka), Eddie Nketiah, Reiss Nelson. Coach: Mikel Arteta.
FC Zürich: Yanick Brecher, Nikola Boranijasevic, Fidan Aliti (89' Ivan Santini), Nikola Katic, Lindrit Kamberi, Ole Selnæs (77' Marc Hornschuh), Adrián Guerrero, Fabian Rohner (46' Antonio Marchesano), Cheick Condé (82' Bledian Krasniqi), Jonathan Okita, Aiyegun Tosin (78' Bogdan Viunnyk). Coach: Bo Henriksen.
Goal: 17' Kieran Tierney 1-0.
Referee: Erik Lambrechts (BEL)   Attendance: 48,500.

03.11.22   Aspmyra Stadion, Bodø: FK Bodø/Glimt – PSV Eindhoven 1-2 (0-1)
FK Bodø/Glimt: Nikita Haikin, Marius Høibråten, Marius Lode, Alfons Sampsted, Japhet Sery Larsen (75' Morten Konradsen), Patrick Berg, Hugo Vetlesen (75' Ulrik Saltnes), Albert Grønbæk Erlykke, Runar Espejord (83' Lars-Jørgen Salvesen), Ola Solbakken (75' Nino Zugelj), Joel Mvuka (75' Amahl Pellegrino). Coach: Kjetil Knutsen.
PSV Eindhoven: Joël Drommel, Armando Obispo (46' André Ramalho), Jordan Teze, Ki-Jana Hoever (90+1' Emmanuel van de Blaak), Fredrik Oppegård, Guus Til, Joey Veerman (46' Érick Gutiérrez), Richy Ledezma, Luuk de Jong (46' Anwar El Ghazi), Noni Madueke (70' Yorbe Vertessen), Johan Bakayoko. Coach: Ruud van Nistelrooij.
Goals: 36' Alfons Sampsted 0-1 (og), 52' Johan Bakayoko 0-2, 90+3' Nino Zugelj 1-2.
Referee: Donatas Rumsas (LTU)   Attendance: 7,985.

GROUP B

08.09.22   AEK Arena – Georgios Karapatakis, Larnaca:
AEK Larnaca – Stade Rennes 1-2 (1-1)
AEK Larnaca: Kenan Piric, Roberto Rosales (46' Kypros Christoforou), Nenad Tomovic, Oier, Ángel García, Gus Ledes, Hrvoje Milicevic, Omri Altman (63' Ádám Gyurcsó), Ivan Trickovski (79' Pere Pons), Imad Faraj (90+3' Giorgos Naoum), Victor Olatunji (80' Rafael Lopes). Coach: José Luis Oltra.
Stade Rennes: Steve Mandanda, Hamari Traoré, Birger Meling (57' Martin Terrier), Joe Rodon, Arthur Theate, Adrien Truffert, Flavien Tait, Baptiste Santamaría, Lovro Majer (83' Lorenz Assignon), Kamaldeen Sulemana, Matthis Abline (58' Benjamin Bourigeaud).
Coach: Bruno Génésio.
Goals: 29' Arthur Theate 0-1, 33' Oier 1-1, 90+4' Lorenz Assignon 1-2.
Referee: Giorgi Kruashvili (GEO)   Attendance: 4,103.

08.09.22   Sükrü Saracoglu Stadium, Istanbul: Fenerbahçe – Dynamo Kyiv 2-1 (1-0)
Fenerbahçe: Altay Bayindir, Ezgjan Alioski (83' Lincoln), Gustavo Henrique, Luan Peres, Attila Szalai, Willian Arão, Miguel Crespo (83' Mert Hakan Yandas), Ferdi Kadioglu, Joshua King (69' Enner Valencia), João Pedro (69' Michy Batshuayi), Diego Rossi (69' Irfan Kahveci). Coach: Jorge Jesus.
Dynamo Kyiv: Georgiy Bushchan, Tomasz Kedziora, Mykyta Burda, Vladyslav Dubinchak (59' Kostiantyn Vivcharenko), Oleksandr Syrota, Sergiy Sydorchuk, Denys Garmash (88' Mykyta Kravchenko), Vitaliy Buyalskyi, Viktor Tsygankov, Mykola Shaparenko (68' Volodymyr Shepelyev), Vladyslav Kabaev. Coach: Mircea Lucescu.
Goals: 35' Gustavo Henrique 1-0, 63' Viktor Tsygankov 1-1, 90+3' Michy Batshuayi 2-1.
Referee: Tamás Bognár (HUN)   Attendance: 41,895.

15.09.22   Stadion Cracovii im. Józefa Pilsudskiego, Kraków (POL):
Dynamo Kyiv – AEK Larnaca 0-1 (0-1)
Dynamo Kyiv: Denis Boyko, Tomasz Kedziora (67' Oleksandr Karavaev), Vladyslav Dubinchak, Oleksandr Syrota, Ilya Zabarnyi, Sergiy Sydorchuk, Denys Garmash (46' Artem Besedin), Vitaliy Buyalskyi, Oleksandr Andriyevskyi (67' Volodymyr Shepelyev), Viktor Tsygankov, Vladyslav Kabaev (84' Vladyslav Vanat). Coach: Mircea Lucescu.
AEK Larnaca: Kenan Piric, Nenad Tomovic, Ángel García, Kypros Christoforou, Hrvoje Milicevic, Ádám Gyurcsó (77' Nikos Englezou), Omri Altman, Pere Pons (74' Giorgos Naoum), Rafail Mamas (64' Oier), Ivan Trickovski (64' Gus Ledes), Victor Olatunji (73' Rafael Lopes). Coach: José Luis Oltra.
Goal: 8' Ádám Gyurcsó 0-1.
Referee: Jakob Kehlet (DEN)   Attendance: 3,362.

Due to the Russian invasion of Ukraine, Ukrainian teams were required to play their home matches at neutral venues until further notice. Therefore, Dynamo Kyiv played at Stadion Cracovii im. Józefa Pilsudskiego, Kraków, Poland, instead of their regular stadium NSC Olimpiyskiy, Kyiv.

15.09.22   Roazhon Park, Rennes: Stade Rennes – Fenerbahçe 2-2 (0-0)
Stade Rennes: Steve Mandanda, Hamari Traoré, Birger Meling, Joe Rodon, Arthur Theate, Benjamin Bourigeaud, Lovro Majer (78' Flavien Tait), Lesley Chimuanya Ugochukwu (78' Jérémy Doku), Kamaldeen Sulemana (65' Désiré Doué), Martin Terrier (74' Matthis Abline), Amine Gouiri (64' Adrien Truffert). Coach: Bruno Génésio.
Fenerbahçe: Altay Bayindir, Gustavo Henrique, Luan Peres (57' Ezgjan Alioski), Attila Szalai, Irfan Kahveci, Mert Hakan Yandas (86' Diego Rossi), Lincoln (67' Emre Mor), Bright Osayi-Samuel, Ismail Yüksek, Joshua King (67' João Pedro), Michy Batshuayi (66' Enner Valencia). Coach: Jorge Jesus.
Goals: 52' Martin Terrier 1-0, 54' Lovro Majer 2-0, 60' Irfan Kahveci 2-1, 90+3' Enner Valencia 2-2 (p).
Referee: Aleksei Kulbakov (BLS)   Attendance: 20,993.
Sent off: 83' Hamari Traoré.

06.10.22   Roazhon Park, Rennes: Stade Rennes – Dynamo Kyiv 2-1 (1-1)
Stade Rennes: Steve Mandanda, Birger Meling, Joe Rodon, Arthur Theate, Lorenz Assignon, Flavien Tait, Benjamin Bourigeaud (85' Adrien Truffert), Lovro Majer (65' Arnaud Kalimuendo), Lesley Chimuanya Ugochukwu, Martin Terrier (79' Matthis Abline), Amine Gouiri (64' Désiré Doué). Coach: Bruno Génésio.
Dynamo Kyiv: Denis Boyko, Tomasz Kedziora, Vladyslav Dubinchak, Denys Popov (90+2' Kostiantyn Vivcharenko), Ilya Zabarnyi, Sergiy Sydorchuk, Vitaliy Buyalskyi, Viktor Tsygankov (86' Oleksandr Karavaev), Volodymyr Shepelyev, Vladyslav Kabaev (79' Vladyslav Vanat), Artem Besedin. Coach: Mircea Lucescu.
Goals: 23' Martin Terrier 1-0, 33' Viktor Tsygankov 1-1, 89' Désiré Doué 2-1.
Referee: José María Sánchez Martínez (ESP)   Attendance: 24,671.

06.10.22   Sükrü Saracoglu Stadium, Istanbul: Fenerbahçe – AEK Larnaca 2-0 (1-0)
Fenerbahçe: Altay Bayindir, Ezgjan Alioski, Gustavo Henrique, Attila Szalai, Emre Mor (72' Irfan Kahveci), Lincoln (72' Enner Valencia), Bright Osayi-Samuel (72' Ferdi Kadioglu), Miguel Crespo, Ismail Yüksek, Michy Batshuayi (88' Arda Güler), Diego Rossi (87' Serdar Aziz). Coach: Jorge Jesus.
AEK Larnaca: Kenan Piric, Roberto Rosales, Nenad Tomovic, Oier (70' Giorgos Naoum), Ángel García, Gus Ledes (80' Pere Pons), Hrvoje Milicevic, Omri Altman (69' Victor Olatunji), Rafail Mamas, Rafael Lopes (81' Ivan Trickovski), Imad Faraj. Coach: José Luis Oltra.
Goals: 26' Michy Batshuayi 1-0, 79' Rafail Mamas 2-0 (og).
Referee: Chris Kavanagh (ENG)   Attendance: 38,860.

13.10.22   Stadion Cracovii im. Józefa Pilsudskiego, Kraków (POL):
Dynamo Kyiv – Stade Rennes 0-1 (0-0)
Dynamo Kyiv: Ruslan Neshcheret, Oleksandr Tymchyk (77' Oleksandr Karavaev), Vladyslav Dubinchak (67' Kostiantyn Vivcharenko), Oleksandr Syrota, Ilya Zabarnyi, Sergiy Sydorchuk, Denys Garmash (66' Vladyslav Kabaev), Vitaliy Buyalskyi, Viktor Tsygankov, Volodymyr Shepelyev (70' Oleksandr Andriyevskyi), Artem Besedin (66' Vladyslav Vanat). Coach: Mircea Lucescu.
Stade Rennes: Steve Mandanda, Birger Meling, Christopher Wooh, Arthur Theate, Lorenz Assignon, Benjamin Bourigeaud (84' Adrien Truffert), Lovro Majer, Lesley Chimuanya Ugochukwu, Désiré Doué (73' Flavien Tait), Martin Terrier (66' Kamaldeen Sulemana), Arnaud Kalimuendo (73' Amine Gouiri). Coach: Bruno Génésio.
Goal: 48' Christopher Wooh 0-1.
Referee: Serdar Gözübüyük (HOL)   Attendance: 5,398.

13.10.22   AEK Arena – Georgios Karapatakis, Larnaca: AEK Larnaca – Fenerbahçe 1-2 (0-1)
AEK Larnaca: Kenan Piric, Roberto Rosales, Nenad Tomovic, Oier (82' Mikel González), Ángel García, Gus Ledes (75' Pere Pons), Hrvoje Milicevic, Omri Altman (75' Victor Olatunji), Rafail Mamas (64' Giorgos Naoum), Ivan Trickovski (75' Rafael Lopes), Imad Faraj. Coach: José Luis Oltra.
Fenerbahçe: Altay Bayindir, Serdar Aziz, Ezgjan Alioski (68' Bright Osayi-Samuel), Gustavo Henrique, Attila Szalai, Lincoln (76' Miguel Crespo), Ferdi Kadioglu, Ismail Yüksek, Arda Güler (69' Michy Batshuayi), João Pedro (69' Enner Valencia), Diego Rossi (90+2' Irfan Kahveci). Coach: Jorge Jesus.
Goals: 16' João Pedro 0-1, 52' Ivan Trickovski 1-1 (p), 80' Michy Batshuayi 1-2 (p).
Referee: Pawel Raczkowski (POL)   Attendance: 6,947.
Sent off: 84' Ángel García.

Enner Valencia missed a penalty kick (86').

27.10.22 Sükrü Saracoglu Stadium, Istanbul: Fenerbahçe – Stade Rennes 3-3 (1-3)
Fenerbahçe: Altay Bayindir, Serdar Aziz, Gustavo Henrique (60' Ezgjan Alioski), Attila Szalai, Willian Arão (61' Miha Zajc), Irfan Kahveci (60' Emre Mor), Lincoln (78' Arda Güler), Bright Osayi-Samuel, Miguel Crespo, Enner Valencia, João Pedro (61' Michy Batshuayi). Coach: Jorge Jesus.
Stade Rennes: Steve Mandanda (52' Dogan Alemdar), Hamari Traoré, Joe Rodon, Arthur Theate, Adrien Truffert, Flavien Tait, Benjamin Bourigeaud (70' Lorenz Assignon), Lovro Majer (70' Désiré Doué), Lesley Chimuanya Ugochukwu, Martin Terrier (83' Kamaldeen Sulemana), Amine Gouiri (84' Arnaud Kalimuendo). Coach: Bruno Génésio.
Goals: 5' Amine Gouiri 0-1,16' Martin Terrier 0-2, 30' Amine Gouiri 0-3, 42' Enner Valencia 1-3, 82' Miha Zajc 2-3, 88' Emre Mor 3-3.
Referee: Novak Simovic (SRB)   Attendance: 34,840.

27.10.22 AEK Arena – Georgios Karapatakis, Larnaca:
AEK Larnaca – Dynamo Kyiv 3-3 (1-1)
AEK Larnaca: Kenan Piric, Roberto Rosales (88' Mikel González), Nenad Tomovic, Gus Ledes, Hrvoje Milicevic, Ádám Gyurcsó (89' Giorgos Naoum), Omri Altman (83' Victor Olatunji), Pere Pons, Nikos Englezou, Rafael Lopes (66' Rafail Mamas), Imad Faraj (84' Kypros Christoforou). Coach: José Luis Oltra.
Dynamo Kyiv: Ruslan Neshcheret, Oleksandr Tymchyk, Oleksandr Syrota, Kostiantyn Vivcharenko, Ilya Zabarnyi, Sergiy Sydorchuk, Vitaliy Buyalskyi (75' Kaheem Parris), Viktor Tsygankov, Volodymyr Shepelyev (83' Samba Diallo), Vladyslav Kabaev (65' Denys Garmash), Vladyslav Vanat (83' Artem Besedin). Coach: Mircea Lucescu.
Goals: 26' Omri Altman 1-0, 45' Vladyslav Vanat 1-1, 53' Rafael Lopes 2-1, 72' Omri Altman 3-1, 82', 90+2' Denys Garmash 3-2, 3-3.
Referee: John Beaton (SCO)   Attendance: 4,321.

03.11.22 Stadion Cracovii im. Józefa Pilsudskiego, Kraków (POL):
Dynamo Kyiv – Fenerbahçe 0-2 (0-2)
Dynamo Kyiv: Georgiy Bushchan, Oleksandr Tymchyk, Denys Popov, Kostiantyn Vivcharenko (70' Oleksandr Syrota), Ilya Zabarnyi, Sergiy Sydorchuk, Vitaliy Buyalskyi (70' Oleksandr Karavaev), Viktor Tsygankov (86' Samba Diallo), Volodymyr Shepelyev (46' Denys Garmash), Artem Besedin (46' Vladyslav Kabaev), Vladyslav Vanat.
Coach: Mircea Lucescu.
Fenerbahçe: Altay Bayindir, Serdar Aziz, Attila Szalai, Willian Arão (73' Miha Zajc), Lincoln (79' Ezgjan Alioski), Bright Osayi-Samuel, Miguel Crespo, Ferdi Kadioglu, Arda Güler (64' Emre Mor), Enner Valencia (64' Irfan Kahveci), Michy Batshuayi (64' João Pedro).
Coach: Jorge Jesus.
Goals: 23' Arda Güler 0-1, 45+2' Willian Arão 0-2.
Referee: Duje Strukan (CRO)   Attendance: 6,304.
Sent off: 68' Ilya Zabarnyi.

03.11.22   Roazhon Park, Rennes: Stade Rennes – AEK Larnaca 1-1 (1-0)
Stade Rennes: Dogan Alemdar, Birger Meling, Joe Rodon, Lorenz Assignon, Jeanuël Belocian, Flavien Tait, Benjamin Bourigeaud (63' Désiré Doué), Lovro Majer (63' Lesley Chimuanya Ugochukwu), Martin Terrier (56' Jérémy Doku), Arnaud Kalimuendo (71' Adrien Truffert), Matthis Abline (56' Amine Gouiri). Coach: Bruno Génésio.
AEK Larnaca: Kenan Piric, Roberto Rosales, Nenad Tomovic, Ángel García, Kypros Christoforou, Gus Ledes (88' Mikel González), Hrvoje Milicevic, Ádám Gyurcsó (88' Nikos Englezou), Pere Pons, Rafail Mamas (74' Rafael Lopes), Victor Olatunji (90+2' Henry Andreou). Coach: José Luis Oltra.
Goals: 17' MatthisAbline 1-0, 76' Rafael Lopes 1-1.
Referee: Mohammed Al-Hakim (SWE)   Attendance: 27,210.

GROUP C

08.09.22   Huvepharma Arena, Razgrad: PFC Ludogorets Razgrad – AS Roma 2-1 (0-0)
PFC Ludogorets Razgrad: Sergio Padt, Cicinho, Anton Nedyalkov, Aslak Witry (87' Georgi Terziev), Olivier Verdon, Cauly (86' Spas Delev), Jakub Piotrowski, Show (77' Nonato), Kiril Despodov (71' Rick), Bernard Tekpetey, Thiago. Coach: Ante Simundza.
AS Roma: Mile Svilar, Chris Smalling, Zeki Çelik (67' Leonardo Spinazzola), Gianluca Mancini (75' Cristian Volpato), Ibañez, Nemanja Matic (76' Mady Camara), Bryan Cristante (76' Edoardo Bove), Lorenzo Pellegrini, Paulo Dybala, Andrea Belotti (67' Eldor Shomurodov), Nicola Zalewski. Coach: José Mourinho.
Goals: 72' Cauly 1-0, 86' Eldor Shomurodov 1-1, 88' Nonato 2-1.
Referee: Craig Pawson (ENG)   Attendance: 10,011.

08.09.22   Bolt Arena, Helsinki: HJK Helsinki – Real Betis 0-2 (0-1)
HJK Helsinki: Conor Hazard, Jukka Raitala, Miro Tenho, Arttu Hoskonen (87' Matti Peltola), Pyry Soiri (74' Casper Terho), Lucas Lingman (88' Përparim Hetemaj), Nassim Boujellab (74' Murilo), Santeri Väänänen, David Browne, Santeri Hostikka, Malik Abubakari (74' Anthony Olusanya). Coach: Toni Koskela.
Real Betis: Claudio Bravo, Víctor Ruíz (46' Luiz Felipe), Germán Pezzella, Juan Miranda, Joaquín (60' Sergio Canales), William Carvalho (75' Guido Rodríguez), Paul Akouokou, Willian José, Juanmi (6' Rodri), Aitor Ruibal, Luiz Henrique (74' Andrés Guardado). Coach: Manuel Pellegrini.
Goals: 45+3', 64' Willian José 0-1 (p), 0-2.
Referee: Roi Reinshreiber (ISR)   Attendance: 10,164.

15.09.22   Estadio Benito Villamarín, Sevilla: Real Betis – PFC Ludogorets Razgrad 3-2 (2-1)
Real Betis: Claudio Bravo, Édgar González, Luiz Felipe (73' Germán Pezzella), Juan Miranda, Joaquín (72' Rodri), Andrés Guardado, Sergio Canales (85' Álex Moreno), Paul Akouokou (56' Guido Rodríguez), Willian José, Aitor Ruibal, Luiz Henrique (84' William Carvalho). Coach: Manuel Pellegrini.
PFC Ludogorets Razgrad: Sergio Padt, Cicinho, Anton Nedyalkov, Aslak Witry (62' Danny Gruper), Olivier Verdon, Cauly, Jakub Piotrowski, Show (62' Nonato), Kiril Despodov (69' Spas Delev), Bernard Tekpetey (70' Rick), Thiago (80' Matías Tissera).
Coach: Ante Simundza.
Goals: 25' Luiz Henrique 1-0, 39' Joaquín 2-0, 45+2' Kiril Despodov 2-1, 59' Sergio Canales 3-1, 74' Rick 3-2.
Referee: Andris Treimanis (LAT)   Attendance: 43,113.

15.09.22   Stadio Olimpico, Roma: AS Roma – HJK Helsinki 3-0 (0-0)
AS Roma: Rui Patrício, Leonardo Spinazzola, Rick Karsdorp, Gianluca Mancini, Matías Viña (46' Paulo Dybala), Ibañez (46' Chris Smalling), Nemanja Matic, Bryan Cristante (64' Mady Camara), Lorenzo Pellegrini (69' Edoardo Bove), Nicolò Zaniolo (76' Tammy Abraham), Andrea Belotti. Coach: José Mourinho.
HJK Helsinki: Conor Hazard, Jukka Raitala, Miro Tenho, Arttu Hoskonen (46' Paulus Arajuuri), Përparim Hetemaj (46' Aapo Halme), Pyry Soiri (66' Anthony Olusanya), Lucas Lingman (69' Nassim Boujellab), Santeri Väänänen, David Browne, Santeri Hostikka (23' Matti Peltola), Malik Abubakari. Coach: Toni Koskela.
Goals: 47' Paulo Dybala 1-0, 49' Lorenzo Pellegrini 2-0, 68' Andrea Belotti 3-0.
Referee: Radu Petrescu (ROM)   Attendance: 60,193.
Sent off: 14' Miro Tenho.

06.10.22   Bolt Arena, Helsinki: HJK Helsinki – PFC Ludogorets Razgrad 1-1 (0-1)
HJK Helsinki: Conor Hazard, Jukka Raitala, Arttu Hoskonen, Matti Peltola, Përparim Hetemaj (74' Bojan Radulovic), Pyry Soiri, Lucas Lingman, Santeri Väänänen, David Browne, Santeri Hostikka (74' Nassim Boujellab), Malik Abubakari (64' Anthony Olusanya).
Coach: Toni Koskela.
PFC Ludogorets Razgrad: Sergio Padt, Igor Plastun, Anton Nedyalkov, Aslak Witry, Olivier Verdon, Cauly, Jakub Piotrowski, Show (69' Nonato), Kiril Despodov (87' Pedro Naressi), Bernard Tekpetey (61' Rick), Matías Tissera (70' Thiago). Coach: Ante Simundza.
Goals: 10' Matías Tissera 0-1, 55' Përparim Hetemaj 1-1.
Referee: Yevhen Aranovskyi (UKR)   Attendance: 9,751.

06.10.22   Stadio Olimpico, Roma: AS Roma – Real Betis 1-2 (1-1)
AS Roma: Rui Patrício, Chris Smalling, Zeki Çelik (5' Leonardo Spinazzola), Gianluca Mancini, Ibañez, Nemanja Matic, Bryan Cristante (80' Mady Camara), Nicolò Zaniolo, Paulo Dybala (80' Stephan El Shaarawy), Tammy Abraham (72' Andrea Belotti), Nicola Zalewski. Coach: José Mourinho.
Real Betis: Claudio Bravo, Germán Pezzella, Luiz Felipe, Juan Miranda (76' Álex Moreno), Joaquín (61' Rodri), Andrés Guardado (75' William Carvalho), Sergio Canales, Guido Rodríguez, Willian José (76' Borja Iglesias), Nabil Fekir (22' Luiz Henrique), Aitor Ruibal.
Coach: Manuel Pellegrini.
Goals: 34' Paulo Dybala 1-0 (p), 40' Guido Rodríguez 1-1, 88' Luiz Henrique 1-2.
Referee: Matej Jug (SVN)   Attendance: 62,294.
Sent off: 90+3' Nicolò Zaniolo.

13.10.22   Estadio Benito Villamarín, Sevilla: Real Betis – AS Roma 1-1 (1-0)
Real Betis: Claudio Bravo, Germán Pezzella, Luiz Felipe, Juan Miranda (86' Álex Moreno), Joaquín (69' Luiz Henrique), Andrés Guardado (80' William Carvalho), Sergio Canales (81' Guido Rodríguez), Paul Akouokou, Rodri, Willian José (69' Borja Iglesias), Aitor Ruibal.
Coach: Manuel Pellegrini.
AS Roma: Rui Patrício, Chris Smalling, Leonardo Spinazzola (71' Matías Viña), Gianluca Mancini, Ibañez, Nemanja Matic (46' Mady Camara), Bryan Cristante, Lorenzo Pellegrini (88' Stephan El Shaarawy), Andrea Belotti (76' Edoardo Bove), Tammy Abraham, Nicola Zalewski. Coach: José Mourinho.
Goals: 34' Sergio Canales 1-0, 53' Andrea Belotti 1-1.
Referee: Anastasios Sidiropoulos (GRE)   Attendance: 52,472.

13.10.22 Huvepharma Arena, Razgrad: PFC Ludogorets Razgrad – HJK Helsinki 2-0 (1-0)
PFC Ludogorets Razgrad: Sergio Padt, Cicinho, Anton Nedyalkov, Olivier Verdon, Cauly, Jakub Piotrowski (86' Nonato), Show (77' Pedro Naressi), Danny Gruper, Bernard Tekpetey (86' Spas Delev), Matías Tissera (67' Thiago), Rick. Coach: Ante Simundza.
HJK Helsinki: Conor Hazard, Jukka Raitala, Miro Tenho, Arttu Hoskonen, Përparim Hetemaj, Pyry Soiri (58' Casper Terho), Lucas Lingman (70' Atomu Tanaka), Santeri Väänänen (59' Nassim Boujellab), David Browne (46' Matti Peltola), Santeri Hostikka (70' Anthony Olusanya), Malik Abubakari. Coach: Toni Koskela.
Goals: 39' Danny Gruper 1-0, 64' Rick 2-0.
Referee: Kristo Tohver (EST) Attendance: 4,623.
Sent off: 90+3' Jukka Raitala.

27.10.22 Huvepharma Arena, Razgrad: PFC Ludogorets Razgrad – Real Betis 0-1 (0-0)
PFC Ludogorets Razgrad: Sergio Padt, Cicinho, Anton Nedyalkov, Aslak Witry (83' Danny Gruper), Olivier Verdon, Cauly, Jakub Piotrowski (74' Nonato), Pedro Naressi (84' Claude Gonçalves), Bernard Tekpetey, Rick (74' Spas Delev), Thiago (65' Matías Tissera). Coach: Ante Simundza.
Real Betis: Claudio Bravo, Víctor Ruíz, Édgar González, Juan Miranda (46' Álex Moreno), Joaquín (28' Luiz Henrique), Sergio Canales, Guido Rodríguez (73' Enrique "Quique" Fernández), Paul Akouokou (46' Nabil Fekir), Rodri, Willian José (83' Borja Iglesias), Aitor Ruibal. Coach: Manuel Pellegrini.
Goal: 56' Nabil Fekir 0-1.
Referee: Harald Lechner (AUT) Attendance: 9,487.

27.10.22 Bolt Arena, Helsinki: HJK Helsinki – AS Roma 1-2 (0-1)
HJK Helsinki: Conor Hazard, Aapo Halme, Arttu Hoskonen, Matti Peltola, Përparim Hetemaj (69' Nassim Boujellab), Pyry Soiri, Lucas Lingman, Santeri Väänänen, David Browne, Santeri Hostikka, Anthony Olusanya (46' Malik Abubakari). Coach: Toni Koskela.
AS Roma: Rui Patrício, Chris Smalling, Gianluca Mancini, Matías Viña, Bryan Cristante (84' Marash Kumbulla), Lorenzo Pellegrini (78' Eldor Shomurodov), Mady Camara (78' Edoardo Bove), Cristian Volpato (77' Giacomo Faticanti), Stephan El Shaarawy (89' Leonardo Spinazzola), Tammy Abraham, Nicola Zalewski. Coach: José Mourinho.
Goals: 41' Tammy Abraham 0-1, 54' Përparim Hetemaj 1-1, 62' Arttu Hoskonen 1-2 (og).
Referee: Tiago Martins (POR) Attendance: 9,751.

03.11.22 Stadio Olimpico, Roma: AS Roma – PFC Ludogorets Razgrad 3-1 (0-1)
AS Roma: Rui Patrício, Chris Smalling, Rick Karsdorp (46' Bryan Cristante), Matías Viña, Ibañez, Nemanja Matic (61' Nicola Zalewski), Lorenzo Pellegrini, Mady Camara (46' Cristian Volpato, 80' Edoardo Bove), Stephan El Shaarawy, Andrea Belotti (46' Nicolò Zaniolo), Tammy Abraham. Coach: José Mourinho.
PFC Ludogorets Razgrad: Sergio Padt, Cicinho (87' Danny Gruper), Anton Nedyalkov, Aslak Witry (87' Spas Delev), Olivier Verdon, Cauly, Jakub Piotrowski (71' Nonato), Pedro Naressi, Bernard Tekpetey (71' Kiril Despodov), Rick, Thiago (71' Matías Tissera). Coach: Ante Simundza.
Goals: 41' Rick 0-1, 56', 65' Lorenzo Pellegrini 1-1 (p), 2-1 (p), 85' Nicolò Zaniolo 3-1.
Referee: Nikola Dabanovic (MNE) Attendance: 60,807.
Sent off: 90' Olivier Verdon.

03.11.22   Estadio Benito Villamarín, Sevilla: Real Betis – HJK Helsinki 3-0 (2-0)
Real Betis: Rui Silva, Víctor Ruíz, Youssouf Sabaly (46' Sergio Canales), Édgar González, Juan Miranda, William Carvalho (46' Borja Iglesias), Paul Akouokou (77' Andrés Guardado), Rodri, Willian José (67' Dani Pérez), Aitor Ruibal, Luiz Henrique (67' Nabil Fekir).
Coach: Manuel Pellegrini.
HJK Helsinki: Conor Hazard, Jukka Raitala, Arttu Hoskonen, Matti Peltola (54' Joona Toivio), Pyry Soiri, Lucas Lingman, Nassim Boujellab (80' Johannes Yli-Kokko), Santeri Väänänen (80' Atomu Tanaka), David Browne, Santeri Hostikka (68' Anthony Olusanya), Malik Abubakari (80' Bojan Radulovic). Coach: Toni Koskela.
Goals: 20', 40' Aitor Ruibal 1-0, 2-0, 90+3' Nabil Fekir 3-0.
Referee: William Collum (SCO)   Attendance: 35,384.

GROUP D

08.09.22   Eleda Stadion, Malmö: Malmö FF – Sporting Braga 0-2 (0-1)
Malmö FF: Ismael Diawara, Martin Olsson (88' Jonas Knudsen), Niklas Moisander, Lasse Nielsen, Dennis Hadzikadunic, Felix Beijmo (56' Joseph Ceesay), Anders Christiansen, Jo Inge Berget, Oscar Lewicki (46' Sergio Peña), Erdal Rakip (25' Mohamed Buya Turay), Isaac Kiese Thelin (46' Ola Toivonen). Coach: Åge Hareide.
Sporting Braga: Matheus Magalhães, Paulo Oliveira, Nuno Sequeira (85' Cristian Borja), Fabiano Silva, Bruno Rodrigues, Ali Al Musrati, André Horta (73' Uros Racic), Diego Lainez (74' Rodrigo Gomes), Ricardo Horta (85' Andre Castro), Abel Ruiz, Vítinha (61' Álvaro Djaló). Coach: Artur Jorge.
Goals: 30' Bruno Rodrigues 0-1, 70' Ricardo Horta 0-2 (p).
Referee: Duje Strukan (CRO)   Attendance: 13,721.

08.09.22   Stadion An der Alten Försterei, Berlin:
              Union Berlin – Union Saint-Gilloise 0-1 (0-1)
Union Berlin: Frederik Rønnow, Christopher Trimmel (70' Julian Ryerson), Niko Gießelmann, Robin Knoche, Paul Jaeckel, Danilho Doekhi (82' Jamie Leweling), Genki Haraguchi (60' András Schäfer), Rani Khedira, Janik Haberer (69' Tim Skarke), Kevin Behrens (60' Sven Michel), Sheraldo Becker. Coach: Urs Fischer.
Union Saint-Gilloise: Anthony Moris, Bart Nieuwkoop, Christian Burgess, Siebe Van Der Heyden, Ismaël Kandouss, José Rodríguez (69' Cameron Puertas), Teddy Teuma, Senne Lynen, Dante Vanzeir (75' Simon Adingra), Loïc Lapoussin, Victor Boniface (83' Dennis Eckert-Ayensa). Coach: Karel Geraerts.
Goal: 39' Senne Lynen 0-1.
Referee: Serhiy Boyko (UKR)   Attendance: 21,512.
Sent off: 90+6' Sven Michel.

15.09.22   King Power at Den Dreef Stadion, Heverlee:
Union Saint-Gilloise – Malmö FF 3-2 (1-1)
Union Saint-Gilloise: Anthony Moris, Guillaume François (66' Gustaf Nilsson), Christian Burgess, Siebe Van Der Heyden, Ismaël Kandouss, Teddy Teuma, Senne Lynen, Jean Lazare Amani, Dennis Eckert-Ayensa (53' Simon Adingra), Loïc Lapoussin, Victor Boniface (80' José Rodríguez). Coach: Karel Geraerts.
Malmö FF: Johan Dahlin, Martin Olsson, Lasse Nielsen, Jonas Knudsen (46' Søren Rieks), Dennis Hadzikadunic, Felix Beijmo, Jo Inge Berget, Oscar Lewicki, Moustafa Zeidan (61' Hugo Larsson), Joseph Ceesay (74' Ola Toivonen), Isaac Kiese Thelin. Coach: Åge Hareide.
Goals: 6' Joseph Ceesay 0-1, 17' Christian Burgess 1-1, 57' Isaac Kiese Thelin 1-2, 69' Teddy Teuma 2-2, 71' Victor Boniface 3-2.
Referee: Bartosz Frankowski (POL)   Attendance: 4,373.

Union Saint-Gilloise played their home matches at King Power at Den Dreef Stadion, Heverlee, instead of their regular stadium, Joseph Marien Stadium, Brussels, which did not meey UEFA requirements.

15.09.22   Estádio Municipal de Braga, Braga: Sporting Braga – Union Berlin 1-0 (0-0)
Sporting Braga: Matheus Magalhães, Paulo Oliveira, Nuno Sequeira, Vítor Tormena, Fabiano Silva, Ali Al Musrati, Uros Racic (61' André Horta), Ricardo Horta, Simon Banza (70' Abel Ruiz), Álvaro Djaló (61' Iuri Medeiros), Vítinha (86' Andre Castro). Coach: Artur Jorge.
Union Berlin: Frederik Rønnow, Robin Knoche (82' Jamie Leweling), Julian Ryerson, Paul Jaeckel, Diogo Leite, Tymoteusz Puchacz (64' Christopher Trimmel), Rani Khedira, Janik Haberer (82' Tim Skarke), András Schäfer (68' Genki Haraguchi), Sheraldo Becker (82' Kevin Behrens), Jordan Siebatcheu. Coach: Urs Fischer.
Goal: 77' Vítinha 1-0.
Referee: Filip Glova (SVK)   Attendance: 17,782.

06.10.22   Eleda Stadion, Malmö: Malmö FF – Union Berlin 0-1 (0-0)
Malmö FF: Ismael Diawara, Martin Olsson, Dennis Hadzikadunic, Felix Beijmo, Anders Christiansen, Jo Inge Berget (64' Ola Toivonen), Oscar Lewicki, Erdal Rakip, Joseph Ceesay (80' Patriot Sejdiu), Hugo Larsson (80' Moustafa Zeidan), Isaac Kiese Thelin. Coach: Åge Hareide.
Union Berlin: Frederik Rønnow, Christopher Trimmel, Robin Knoche, Julian Ryerson (74' Niko Gießelmann), Diogo Leite, Danilho Doekhi, Rani Khedira, Janik Haberer (84' Genki Haraguchi), András Schäfer, Sheraldo Becker (90+1' Morten Thorsby), Jordan Siebatcheu (74' Kevin Behrens). Coach: Urs Fischer.
Goal: 68' Sheraldo Becker 0-1.
Referee: Halil Umut Meler (TUR)   Attendance: 16,057.
Sent off: 45' András Schäfer.

06.10.22   Estádio Municipal de Braga, Braga: Sporting Braga – Union Saint-Gilloise 1-2 (0-0)
Sporting Braga: Matheus Magalhães, Paulo Oliveira, Nuno Sequeira, Vítor Tormena, Fabiano Silva, Andre Castro (90+1' Jean-Baptiste Gorby), André Horta (65' Rodrigo Gomes), Uros Racic, Ricardo Horta (79' Diego Lainez), Abel Ruiz (89' Álvaro Djaló), Vítinha (79' Simon Banza). Coach: Artur Jorge.
Union Saint-Gilloise: Anthony Moris, Bart Nieuwkoop (83' Guillaume François), Christian Burgess, Siebe Van Der Heyden, Ismaël Kandouss (83' Gustaf Nilsson), Teddy Teuma, Senne Lynen, Jean Lazare Amani (89' Cameron Puertas), Dante Vanzeir (90+1' Ross Sykes), Loïc Lapoussin (67' Simon Adingra), Victor Boniface. Coach: Karel Geraerts.
Goals: 49' Abel Ruiz 1-0, 86', 90+4' Gustaf Nilsson 1-1, 1-2.
Referee: Stéphanie Frappart (FRA)   Attendance: 14,044.

13.10.22   King Power at Den Dreef Stadion, Heverlee:
Union Saint-Gilloise – Sporting Braga 3-3 (1-3)
Union Saint-Gilloise: Anthony Moris, Bart Nieuwkoop (90+4' Ross Sykes), Christian Burgess (46' Loïc Lapoussin), Siebe Van Der Heyden, Ismaël Kandouss, Teddy Teuma, Senne Lynen, Jean Lazare Amani (63' Cameron Puertas), Dante Vanzeir (82' Gustaf Nilsson), Victor Boniface (90+5' Oussama El Azzouzi), Simon Adingra. Coach: Karel Geraerts.
Sporting Braga: Matheus Magalhães, Nuno Sequeira, Vítor Tormena, Sikou Niakaté (76' Paulo Oliveira), Fabiano Silva (46' Víctor Gómez), Ali Al Musrati, André Horta (69' Uros Racic), Ricardo Horta, Abel Ruiz (90+1' Simon Banza), Rodrigo Gomes (69' Iuri Medeiros), Vítinha. Coach: Artur Jorge.
Goals: 15' Vítinha 0-1, 20' Victor Boniface 1-1, 36', 41' Vítinha 1-2, 1-3, 49' Dante Vanzeir 2-3, 62' Victor Boniface 3-3.
Referee: Aliyar Aghayev (AZE)   Attendance: 7,851.

13.10.22   Stadion An der Alten Försterei, Berlin: Union Berlin – Malmö FF 1-0 (0-0)
Union Berlin: Frederik Rønnow, Christopher Trimmel, Robin Knoche, Julian Ryerson, Paul Jaeckel, Diogo Leite, Genki Haraguchi (67' Morten Thorsby), Rani Khedira, Janik Haberer (85' Kevin Behrens), Sheraldo Becker (90+6' Niko Gießelmann), Jordan Siebatcheu (67' Sven Michel). Coach: Urs Fischer.
Malmö FF: Ismael Diawara, Martin Olsson (84' Jonas Knudsen), Dennis Hadzikadunic, Felix Beijmo, Anders Christiansen, Jo Inge Berget (37' Erdal Rakip), Oscar Lewicki (81' Emmanuel Lomotey), Sergio Peña, Joseph Ceesay, Hugo Larsson, Isaac Kiese Thelin.
Coach: Åge Hareide.
Goal: 89' Robin Knoche 1-0 (p).
Referee: Aleksandar Stavrev (MKD)   Attendance: 21,800.
Sent off: 90+2' Emmanuel Lomotey.

27.10.22   Eleda Stadion, Malmö: Malmö FF – Union Saint-Gilloise 0-2 (0-2)
Malmö FF: Ismael Diawara, Dennis Hadzikadunic, Matej Chalus, Felix Beijmo, Søren Rieks (72' Jonas Knudsen), Anders Christiansen, Oscar Lewicki (46' Erdal Rakip), Patriot Sejdiu, Hugo Larsson (72' Sergio Peña), Isaac Kiese Thelin, Mohamed Buya Turay.
Coach: Åge Hareide.
Union Saint-Gilloise: Anthony Moris, Bart Nieuwkoop, Christian Burgess, Siebe Van Der Heyden, Ismaël Kandouss, Teddy Teuma (82' Oussama El Azzouzi), Senne Lynen, Jean Lazare Amani (46' Cameron Puertas), Dante Vanzeir (88' Guillaume François), Loïc Lapoussin (70' Simon Adingra), Victor Boniface (46' Gustaf Nilsson). Coach: Karel Geraerts.
Goals: 10' Teddy Teuma 0-1, 41' Jean Lazare Amani 0-2.
Referee: Roi Reinshreiber (ISR)   Attendance: 10,912.

27.10.22   Stadion An der Alten Försterei, Berlin: Union Berlin – Sporting Braga 1-0 (0-0)
Union Berlin: Frederik Rønnow, Christopher Trimmel, Robin Knoche, Julian Ryerson, Diogo Leite, Danilho Doekhi, Rani Khedira, Janik Haberer (90+4' Genki Haraguchi), Morten Thorsby (46' András Schäfer), Sheraldo Becker (90+1' Jamie Leweling), Jordan Siebatcheu (63' Kevin Behrens). Coach: Urs Fischer.
Sporting Braga: Matheus Magalhães, Paulo Oliveira, Nuno Sequeira (90+1' Álvaro Djaló), Vítor Tormena, Fabiano Silva (80' Simon Banza), Andre Castro (75' André Horta), Ali Al Musrati, Iuri Medeiros (75' Rodrigo Gomes), Ricardo Horta, Abel Ruiz, Vítinha.
Coach: Artur Jorge.
Goal: 68' Robin Knoche 1-0 (p).
Referee: Craig Pawson (ENG)   Attendance: 21,082.

03.11.22 King Power at Den Dreef Stadion, Heverlee:
Union Saint-Gilloise – Union Berlin 0-1 (0-1)
Union Saint-Gilloise: Anthony Moris, Bart Nieuwkoop, Christian Burgess, Ross Sykes, Ismaël Kandouss (72' Loïc Lapoussin), Teddy Teuma (72' José Rodríguez), Senne Lynen, Jean Lazare Amani (64' Oussama El Azzouzi), Gustaf Nilsson (46' Victor Boniface), Dante Vanzeir (64' Dennis Eckert-Ayensa), Simon Adingra. Coach: Karel Geraerts.
Union Berlin: Frederik Rønnow (46' Lennart Grill), Christopher Trimmel, Robin Knoche, Julian Ryerson, Diogo Leite, Danilho Doekhi, Genki Haraguchi (62' András Schäfer), Rani Khedira, Janik Haberer (62' Morten Thorsby), Sheraldo Becker (89' Jamie Leweling), Sven Michel (62' Kevin Behrens). Coach: Urs Fischer.
Goal: 6' Sven Michel 0-1.
Referee: Andris Treimanis (LAT)   Attendance: 5,597.

03.11.22 Estádio Municipal de Braga, Braga: Sporting Braga – Malmö FF 2-1 (1-0)
Sporting Braga: Matheus Magalhães, Paulo Oliveira, Nuno Sequeira (79' Cristian Borja), Vítor Tormena, Víctor Gómez, Andre Castro, Ali Al Musrati (60' Uros Racic), Ricardo Horta (74' Diego Lainez), Simon Banza, Abel Ruiz (46' Álvaro Djaló), Rodrigo Gomes (59' Hernâni Infande). Coach: Artur Jorge.
Malmö FF: Johan Dahlin, Dennis Hadzikadunic, Matej Chalus, Felix Beijmo, Søren Rieks, Anders Christiansen, Erdal Rakip (74' Sergio Peña), Romain Gall, Hugo Larsson, Ola Toivonen (61' Isaac Kiese Thelin), Mohamed Buya Turay (62' Patriot Sejdiu). Coach: Åge Hareide.
Goals: 36' Ricardo Horta 1-0, 55' Álvaro Djaló 2-0, 77' Patriot Sejdiu 2-1.
Referee: Ruddy Buquet (FRA)   Attendance: 11,805.

GROUP E

08.09.22 Old Trafford, Manchester: Manchester United – Real Sociedad 0-1 (0-0)
Manchester United: David de Gea, Victor Lindelöf, Harry Maguire, Diogo Dalot (46' Lisandro Martínez), Tyrell Malacia (83' Charlie McNeill), Christian Eriksen (46' Bruno Fernandes), Casemiro, Fred, Cristiano Ronaldo, Antony (71' Jadon Sancho), Anthony Elanga (71' Alejandro Garnacho). Coach: Erik ten Hag.
Real Sociedad: Álex Remiro, Aritz Elustondo, Andoni Gorosabel (84' Álex Sola), Aihen Muñoz, Jon Pacheco, David Silva (65' Mohamed Cho), Brais Méndez (84' Beñat Turrientes), Mikel Merino, Martín Zubimendi, Takefusa Kubo (78' Ander Barrenetxea), Umar Sadiq (46' Alexander Sørloth). Coach: Imanol Alguacil.
Goal: 59' Brais Méndez 0-1 (p).
Referee: Marco Di Bello (ITA)   Attendance: 74,310.

08.09.22 Neo GSP Stadium, Nicosia: Omonia Nicosia – Sheriff Tiraspol 0-3 (0-1)
Omonia Nicosia: Fabiano (46' Francis Uzoho), Jan Lecjaks, Adam Matthews, Ádám Lang, Nemanja Miletic, Mix Diskerud, Moreto Cassamá (73' Fotis Papoulis), Bruno Felipe (81' Roman Bezus), Nikos Panagiotou, Charalampos Charalampous (82' Ioannis Kousoulos), Brandon Barker (73' Karim Ansarifard). Coach: Neil Lennon.
Sheriff Tiraspol: Maksim Koval, Patrick Kpozo (90+10' Heron), Stjepan Radeljic, Gaby Kiki, Armel Zohouri (90+10' Renan Guedes), Iyayi Atiemwen (74' Mudasiru Salifu), Abou Ouattara (90+4' Pernambuco), Cédric Badolo, Moussa Kyabou, Mouhamed Diop, Ibrahim Rasheed (90+5' Felipe Vizeu). Coach: Stjepan Tomas.
Goals: 2' Ibrahim Rasheed 0-1, 55' Iyayi Atiemwen 0-2 (p), 76' Mouhamed Diop 0-3.
Referee: Rade Obrenovic (SVN)   Attendance: 11,271.

15.09.22   Stadionul Zimbru, Chisinau: Sheriff Tiraspol – Manchester United 0-2 (0-2)
Sheriff Tiraspol: Maksim Koval, Patrick Kpozo, Stjepan Radeljic, Gaby Kiki, Armel Zohouri, Iyayi Atiemwen (81' Mudasiru Salifu), Abou Ouattara (73' Pernambuco), Cédric Badolo, Moussa Kyabou, Mouhamed Diop, Ibrahim Rasheed (73' Felipe Vizeu).
Coach: Stjepan Tomas.
Manchester United: David de Gea, Raphaël Varane, Diogo Dalot (70' Luke Shaw), Tyrell Malacia, Lisandro Martínez (90' Harry Maguire), Christian Eriksen, Bruno Fernandes, Scott McTominay (46' Casemiro), Cristiano Ronaldo (81' Anthony Elanga), Jadon Sancho, Antony (90' Alejandro Garnacho). Coach: Erik ten Hag.
Goals: 17' Jadon Sancho 0-1, 39' Cristiano Ronaldo 0-2 (p).
Referee: Pawel Raczkowski (POL)   Attendance: 8,734.

Sheriff Tiraspol played their home matches at Stadionul Zimbru, Chisinau, instead of their regular stadium, Sheriff Stadium, Tiraspol, due to Transnistria's involvement in the Russian invasion of Ukraine.

15.09.22   Reale Arena, San Sebastián: Real Sociedad – Omonia Nicosia 2-1 (1-0)
Real Sociedad: Álex Remiro, Diego Rico, Aritz Elustondo, Álex Sola (75' Andoni Gorosabel), Illarramendi (75' Beñat Turrientes), Brais Méndez, Mikel Merino (61' Robert Navarro), Zubeldía, Guevara, Jon Karrikaburu (61' Alexander Sørloth), Mohamed Cho (61' Takefusa Kubo). Coach: Imanol Alguacil.
Omonia Nicosia: Fabiano, Nemanja Miletic, Paris Psaltis (65' Adam Matthews), Héctor Yuste (51' Ádám Lang), Mix Diskerud (65' Fotis Papoulis), Fouad Bachirou, Moreto Cassamá (13' Charalampos Charalampous), Nikos Panagiotou, Fotios Kitsos, Karim Ansarifard (66' Bruno Felipe), Loizos Loizou. Coach: Neil Lennon.
Goals: 30' Guevara 1-0, 72' Bruno Felipe 1-1, 80' Alexander Sørloth 2-1.
Referee: Kristo Tohver (EST)   Attendance: 28,587.

06.10.22   Stadionul Zimbru, Chisinau: Sheriff Tiraspol – Real Sociadad 0-2 (0-0)
Sheriff Tiraspol: Maksim Koval, Stjepan Radeljic, Gaby Kiki, Armel Zohouri, Iyayi Atiemwen (66' Mudasiru Salifu), Cédric Badolo, Moussa Kyabou, Mouhamed Diop, Felipe Vizeu (77' Patrick Kpozo), Pernambuco (67' Abou Ouattara), Ibrahim Rasheed. Coach: Stjepan Tomas.
Real Sociedad: Álex Remiro, Diego Rico, Aritz Elustondo, Álex Sola (69' Aritz Arambarri), Jon Pacheco, David Silva (69' Carlos Fernández), Brais Méndez (77' Beñat Turrientes), Mikel Merino (77' Illarramendi), Guevara, Takefusa Kubo, Alexander Sørloth (81' Jon Karrikaburu). Coach: Imanol Alguacil.
Goals: 53' David Silva 0-1, 62' Aritz Elustondo 0-2.
Referee: Harald Lechner (AUT)   Attendance: 5,427.
Sent off: 61' Moussa Kyabou.

06.10.22   Neo GSP Stadium, Nicosia: Omonia Nicosia – Manchester United 2-3 (1-0)
Omonia Nicosia: Fabiano, Jan Lecjaks, Adam Matthews, Ádám Lang, Nemanja Miletic (82' Roman Bezus), Héctor Yuste, Mix Diskerud (72' Nikos Panagiotou), Bruno Felipe (71' Loizos Loizou), Charalampos Charalampous, Karim Ansarifard (61' Andronikos Kakoullis), Brandon Barker (61' Fotis Papoulis). Coach: Neil Lennon.
Manchester United: David de Gea, Victor Lindelöf, Diogo Dalot, Tyrell Malacia (46' Luke Shaw), Lisandro Martínez, Christian Eriksen, Casemiro (82' Scott McTominay), Bruno Fernandes (61' Anthony Martial), Cristiano Ronaldo, Jadon Sancho (46' Marcus Rashford), Antony (74' Fred). Coach: Erik ten Hag.
Goals: 34' Karim Ansarifard 1-0, 53' Marcus Rashford 1-1, 63' Anthony Martial 1-2, 84' Marcus Rashford 1-3, 85' Nikos Panagiotou 2-3.
Referee: João Pedro Pinheiro (POR)   Attendance: 20,011.

13.10.22   Old Trafford, Manchester: Manchester United – Omonia Nicosia 1-0 (0-0)
Manchester United: David de Gea, Victor Lindelöf, Diogo Dalot, Tyrell Malacia (60' Luke Shaw), Lisandro Martínez, Casemiro (81' Scott McTominay), Fred (70' Christian Eriksen), Bruno Fernandes, Cristiano Ronaldo, Marcus Rashford, Antony (60' Jadon Sancho).
Coach: Erik ten Hag.
Omonia Nicosia: Francis Uzoho, Adam Matthews (65' Paris Psaltis), Ádám Lang, Nemanja Miletic, Héctor Yuste, Moreto Cassamá (86' Mix Diskerud), Bruno Felipe (74' Loizos Loizou), Nikos Panagiotou, Charalampos Charalampous (74' Fotis Papoulis), Fotios Kitsos, Andronikos Kakoullis (64' Karim Ansarifard). Coach: Neil Lennon.
Goal: 90+3' Scott McTominay 1-0.
Referee: Jérôme Brisard (FRA)   Attendance: 74,310.

13.10.22   Reale Arena, San Sebastián: Real Sociedad – Sheriff Tiraspol 3-0 (1-0)
Real Sociedad: Álex Remiro, Diego Rico, Aritz Elustondo (74' Aritz Arambarri), Robin Le Normand, Jon Pacheco, David Silva (46' Robert Navarro), Brais Méndez (62' Urko González), Guevara, Beñat Turrientes, Alexander Sørloth (62' Takefusa Kubo), Carlos Fernández (46' Jon Karrikaburu). Coach: Imanol Alguacil.
Sheriff Tiraspol: Dumitru Celeadnic, Patrick Kpozo, Stjepan Radeljic, Gaby Kiki (85' Danila Ignatov), Renan Guedes, Armel Zohouri, Cédric Badolo, Mudasiru Salifu, Mouhamed Diop, Pernambuco (75' Heron), Ibrahim Rasheed (80' Felipe Vizeu). Coach: Stjepan Tomas.
Goals: 45+1' Alexander Sørloth 1-0, 66' Diego Rico 2-0, 81' Robert Navarro 3-0.
Referee: Enea Jorgji (ALB)   Attendance: 25,806.
Sent off: 33' Armel Zohouri.

27.10.22   Old Trafford, Manchester: Manchester United – Sheriff Tiraspol 3-0 (1-0)
Manchester United: David de Gea, Victor Lindelöf, Diogo Dalot (63' Luke Shaw), Tyrell Malacia, Lisandro Martínez (46' Harry Maguire), Christian Eriksen, Casemiro (63' Scott McTominay), Bruno Fernandes, Cristiano Ronaldo, Antony (46' Marcus Rashford), Alejandro Garnacho (79' Donny van de Beek). Coach: Erik ten Hag.
Sheriff Tiraspol: Maksim Koval, Patrick Kpozo, Stjepan Radeljic, Gaby Kiki, Renan Guedes, Iyayi Atiemwen (89' Nichita Covali), Cédric Badolo (90+4' Eugeniu Gliga), Mudasiru Salifu, Moussa Kyabou, Mouhamed Diop (79' Adrian Hatman), Ibrahim Rasheed (79' Pernambuco). Coach: Victor Mihailov.
Goals: 44' Diogo Dalot 1-0, 65' Marcus Rashford 2-0, 81' Cristiano Ronaldo 3-0.
Referee: Anastasios Sidiropoulos (GRE)   Attendance: 73,764.

27.10.22   Neo GSP Stadium, Nicosia: Omonia Nicosia – Real Sociedad 0-2 (0-1)
Omonia Nicosia: Francis Uzoho, Jan Lecjaks, Adam Matthews (80' Nikos Panagiotou), Ádám Lang, Nemanja Miletic (64' Héctor Yuste), Roman Bezus, Moreto Cassamá, Bruno Felipe (64' Karim Ansarifard), Charalampos Charalampous (72' Ioannis Kousoulos), Brandon Barker (46' Fotis Papoulis), Andronikos Kakoullis. Coach: Yannick Ferrera.
Real Sociedad: Álex Remiro, Diego Rico (69' Aritz Arambarri), Aritz Elustondo, Jon Pacheco, Illarramendi (80' Beñat Turrientes), Mikel Merino (46' Brais Méndez), Zubeldía, Guevara, Takefusa Kubo (46' Pablo Marín), Robert Navarro, Jon Karrikaburu (70' Jon Magunazelaia). Coach: Imanol Alguacil.
Goals: 45+2' Robert Navarro 0-1, 60' Brais Méndez 0-2.
Referee: Tamás Bognár (HUN)   Attendance: 11,780.

03.11.22   Reale Arena, San Sebastián: Real Sociedad – Manchester United 0-1 (0-1)
Real Sociedad: Álex Remiro, Diego Rico, Andoni Gorosabel (58' Aritz Elustondo), Robin Le Normand, Jon Pacheco, Brais Méndez (83' Zubeldía), Mikel Merino, Martín Zubimendi, Pablo Marín (58' Robert Navarro), Alexander Sørloth (83' Jon Magunazelaia), Carlos Fernández (73' Guevara). Coach: Imanol Alguacil.
Manchester United: David de Gea, Victor Lindelöf (58' Scott McTominay), Luke Shaw, Diogo Dalot, Lisandro Martínez, Christian Eriksen (82' Fred), Casemiro, Bruno Fernandes, Donny van de Beek (58' Marcus Rashford), Cristiano Ronaldo, Alejandro Garnacho (82' Harry Maguire). Coach: Erik ten Hag.
Goal: 17' Alejandro Garnacho 0-1.
Referee: Georgi Kabakov (BUL)   Attendance: 36,744.

03.11.22   Stadionul Zimbru, Chisinau: Sheriff Tiraspol – Omonia Nicosia 1-0 (0-0)
Sheriff Tiraspol: Maksim Koval, Patrick Kpozo, Stjepan Radeljic, Gaby Kiki, Armel Zohouri, Cédric Badolo, Mudasiru Salifu (69' Iyayi Atiemwen), Moussa Kyabou (90+2' Heron), Mouhamed Diop, Pernambuco (86' Renan Guedes), Ibrahim Rasheed. Coach: Victor Mihailov.
Omonia Nicosia: Francis Uzoho, Jan Lecjaks (63' Paris Psaltis), Nemanja Miletic, Héctor Yuste, Roman Bezus, Moreto Cassamá (76' Mix Diskerud), Bruno Felipe (81' Brandon Barker), Charalampos Charalampous (63' Fotis Papoulis), Fotios Kitsos, Andronikos Kakoullis, Loizos Loizou (63' Pangiotis Zachariou). Coach: Yannick Ferrera.
Goal: 87' Ibrahim Rasheed 1-0.
Referee: Fran Jovic (CRO)   Attendance: 2,295.

GROUP F

08.09.22   Stadio Olimpico, Roma: Lazio Roma – Feyenoord Rotterdam 4-2 (3-0)
Lazio Roma: Ivan Provedel, Elseid Hysaj, Alessio Romagnoli (73' Patric), Adam Marusic (76' Stefan Radu), Mario Gila, Matías Vecino (70' Sergej Milinkovic-Savic), Luis Alberto (69' Toma Basic), Felipe Anderson, Mattia Zaccagni, Danilo Cataldi, Ciro Immobile (70' Matteo Cancellieri). Coach: Maurizio Sarri.
Feyenoord Rotterdam: Justin Bijlow, Gernot Trauner, Dávid Hancko, Marcus Pedersen, Quilindschy Hartman, Sebastian Szymanski (46' Alireza Jahanbakhsh), Quinten Timber (86' Igor Paixão), Orkun Kökçü, Javairô Dilrosun (64' Mats Wieffer), Danilo (64' Santiago Giménez), Patrik Wålemark (69' Oussama Idrissi). Coach: Arne Slot.
Goals: 4' Luis Alberto 1-0, 15' Felipe Anderson 2-0, 28', 63' Matías Vecino 3-0, 4-0, 69', 88' Santiago Giménez 4-1 (p), 4-2.
Referee: Ricardo de Burgos Bengoetxea (ESP)   Attendance: 22,763.

08.09.22   Merkur Arena, Graz: Sturm Graz – FC Midtjylland 1-0 (1-0)
Sturm Graz: Jörg Siebenhandl, Jon Gorenc Stankovic (79' Dominik Oroz), Gregory Wüthrich, Jusuf Gazibegovic, David Affengruber, Amadou Danté, Stefan Hierländer, Tomi Horvat (78' Ivan Ljubic), Alexander Prass, William Bøving (62' Mohammed Fuseini), Emanuel Emegha (69' Albian Ajeti). Coach: Christian Ilzer.
FC Midtjylland: Jonas Lössl, Erik Sviatchenko, Henrik Dalsgaard (81' Edward Chilufya), Paulinho (81' Mads Thychosen), Juninho, Evander, Oliver Sørensen (57' Kristoffer Olsson), Pione Sisto (70' Emiliano Martínez), Anders Dreyer, Gustav Isaksen, Sory Kaba.
Coach: Albert Capellas.
Goal: 8' Emanuel Emegha 1-0.
Referee: Aliyar Aghayev (AZE)   Attendance: 10,521.
Sent off: 73' Stefan Hierländer.

Tomi Horvat missed a penalty kick (42').

15.09.22   MCH Arena, Herning: FC Midtjylland – Lazio Roma 5-1 (2-0)
FC Midtjylland: Jonas Lössl, Erik Sviatchenko, Henrik Dalsgaard, Mads Thychosen, Paulinho, Kristoffer Olsson, Evander, Emiliano Martínez (62' Charles), Anders Dreyer (62' Pione Sisto), Gustav Isaksen (77' Edward Chilufya), Sory Kaba (87' Valdemar Andreasen).
Coach: Albert Capellas.
Lazio Roma: Ivan Provedel, Stefan Radu (53' Adam Marusic), Elseid Hysaj, Alessio Romagnoli, Mario Gila, Matías Vecino (52' Sergej Milinkovic-Savic), Luis Alberto, Felipe Anderson, Danilo Cataldi (69' Marcos Antônio), Pedro (53' Matteo Cancellieri), Ciro Immobile (76' Luka Romero). Coach: Maurizio Sarri.
Goals: 26' Paulinho 1-0, 30' Sory Kaba 2-0, 52' Evander 3-0 (p), 57' Sergej Milinkovic-Savic 3-1, 67' Gustav Isaksen 4-1, 72' Erik Sviatchenko 5-1.
Referee: Nikola Dabanovic (MNE)   Attendance: 9,052.

Evander missed a penalty kick (67').

15.09.22   De Kuip, Rotterdam: Feyenoord Rotterdam – Sturm Graz 6-0 (4-0)
Feyenoord Rotterdam: Justin Bijlow, Gernot Trauner, Dávid Hancko, Marcos López (55' Quilindschy Hartman), Marcus Pedersen, Alireza Jahanbakhsh (64' Patrik Wålemark), Quinten Timber (75' Mats Wieffer), Orkun Kökçü (75' Ezequiel Bullaude), Oussama Idrissi, Javairô Dilrosun, Danilo (64' Santiago Giménez). Coach: Arne Slot.
Sturm Graz: Jörg Siebenhandl, Jon Gorenc Stankovic (46' Dominik Oroz), Gregory Wüthrich (46' David Affengruber), Aleksandar Borkovic, Jusuf Gazibegovic, Amadou Danté, Tomi Horvat (72' Otar Kiteishvili), Alexander Prass, William Bøving (63' Christoph Lang), Manprit Sarkaria, Emanuel Emegha (19' Ivan Ljubic). Coach: Christian Ilzer.
Goals: 9' Alireza Jahanbakhsh 1-0, 31' Dávid Hancko 2-0, 34' Danilo 3-0, 41' Alireza Jahanbakhsh 4-0, 66' Santiago Giménez 5-0, 78' Oussama Idrissi 6-0.
Referee: Jérôme Brisard (FRA)   Attendance: 34,332.

06.10.22   Merkur Arena, Graz: Sturm Graz – Lazio Roma 0-0
Sturm Graz: Jörg Siebenhandl, Jon Gorenc Stankovic, Gregory Wüthrich, Jusuf Gazibegovic, David Affengruber, Amadou Danté, Stefan Hierländer (75' Ivan Ljubic), Tomi Horvat (69' Otar Kiteishvili), Alexander Prass (84' Sandro Ingolitsch), William Bøving (70' Mohammed Fuseini), Albian Ajeti (76' Manprit Sarkaria). Coach: Christian Ilzer.
Lazio Roma: Ivan Provedel, Elseid Hysaj, Alessio Romagnoli, Adam Marusic (46' Manuel Lazzari), Mario Gila (74' Patric), Luis Alberto, Felipe Anderson (46' Mattia Zaccagni), Danilo Cataldi, Sergej Milinkovic-Savic (63' Matías Vecino), Pedro (72' Matteo Cancellieri), Ciro Immobile. Coach: Maurizio Sarri.
Referee: Benoît Bastien (FRA)   Attendance: 14,171.
Sent off: 82' Jusuf Gazibegovic.

06.10.22   MCH Arena, Herning: FC Midtjylland – Feyenoord Rotterdam 2-2 (0-2)
FC Midtjylland: Jonas Lössl, Erik Sviatchenko (46' Juninho), Henrik Dalsgaard, Joel Andersson (73' Mads Thychosen), Paulinho (84' Nikolas Dyhr), Kristoffer Olsson, Evander, Emiliano Martínez, Pione Sisto (73' Edward Chilufya), Gustav Isaksen, Sory Kaba (46' Anders Dreyer). Coach: Albert Capellas.
Feyenoord Rotterdam: Justin Bijlow, Gernot Trauner, Dávid Hancko, Marcos López, Lutsharel Geertruida, Sebastian Szymanski (79' Santiago Giménez), Quinten Timber, Orkun Kökçü (66' Marcus Pedersen), Oussama Idrissi (32' Alireza Jahanbakhsh), Javairô Dilrosun (66' Patrik Wålemark), Danilo (80' Mats Wieffer). Coach: Arne Slot.
Goals: 21' Sebastian Szymanski 0-1, 45' Orkun Kökçü 0-2 (p), 54' Gustav Isaksen 1-2, 85' Juninho 2-2.
Referee: Mohammed Al-Hakim (SWE)   Attendance: 9,044.

13.10.22 De Kuip, Rotterdam: Feyenoord Rotterdam – FC Midtjylland 2-2 (1-1)
Feyenoord Rotterdam: Justin Bijlow, Gernot Trauner, Dávid Hancko, Marcos López, Lutsharel Geertruida, Marcus Pedersen, Alireza Jahanbakhsh (71' Patrik Wålemark), Sebastian Szymanski, Quinten Timber (71' Javairô Dilrosun), Orkun Kökçü, Santiago Giménez (77' Danilo). Coach: Arne Slot.
FC Midtjylland: Jonas Lössl, Erik Sviatchenko, Henrik Dalsgaard (42' Juninho), Mads Thychosen, Paulinho, Kristoffer Olsson, Evander (88' Oliver Sørensen), Emiliano Martínez (88' Charles), Pione Sisto (66' Sory Kaba), Anders Dreyer (88' Edward Chilufya), Gustav Isaksen. Coach: Albert Capellas.
Goals: 16' Emiliano Martínez 0-1, 32' Quinten Timber 1-1, 48' Dávid Hancko 2-1, 58' Erik Sviatchenko 2-2.
Referee: Rade Obrenovic (SVN)   Attendance: 43,086.

13.10.22 Stadio Olimpico, Roma: Lazio Roma – Sturm Graz 2-2 (1-0)
Lazio Roma: Ivan Provedel, Elseid Hysaj, Patric, Mario Gila, Luis Alberto (58' Felipe Anderson), Manuel Lazzari, Mattia Zaccagni (46' Adam Marusic), Danilo Cataldi (57' Matías Vecino), Toma Basis (57' Sergej Milinkovic-Savic), Pedro, Ciro Immobile (79' Matteo Cancellieri). Coach: Maurizio Sarri.
Sturm Graz: Jörg Siebenhandl, Jon Gorenc Stankovic (79' Ivan Ljubic), Gregory Wüthrich, Sandro Ingolitsch, David Affenbruber, Amadou Danté, Stefan Hierländer (79' Manprit Sarkaria), Otar Kiteishvili (57' Tomi Horvat), Alexander Prass, Albian Ajeti (79' Jakob Jantscher), Emanuel Emegha (46' William Bøving). Coach: Christian Ilzer.
Goals: 45' Ciro Immobile 1-0 (p), 56' William Bøving 1-1, 71' Pedro 2-1, 83' William Bøving 2-2.
Referee: Sascha Stegemann (GER)   Attendance: 21,059.
Sent off: 45+2' Manuel Lazzari.

27.10.22 Stadio Olimpico, Roma: Lazio Roma – FC Midtjylland 2-1 (1-1)
Lazio Roma: Ivan Provedel, Elseid Hysaj, Alessio Romagnoli, Adam Marusic, Mario Gila (82' Nicolò Casale), Felipe Anderson, Mattia Zaccagni (73' Luka Romero), Sergej Milinkovic-Savic, Toma Basis (55' Matías Vecino), Marcos Antônio (55' Danilo Cataldi), Matteo Cancellieri (55' Pedro). Coach: Maurizio Sarri.
FC Midtjylland: Jonas Lössl, Erik Sviatchenko, Henrik Dalsgaard, Joel Andersson (53' Mads Thychosen), Paulinho (82' Nikolas Dyhr), Evander, Charles (61' Sory Kaba), Emiliano Martínez (82' Juninho), Anders Dreyer, Gustav Isaksen, Edward Chilufya (53' Pione Sisto). Coach: Albert Capellas.
Goals: 8' Gustav Isaksen 0-1, 36' Sergej Milinkovic-Savic 1-1, 58' Pedro 2-1.
Referee: Daniel Stefanski (POL)   Attendance: 17,756.

27.10.22 Merkur Arena, Graz: Sturm Graz – Feyenoord Rotterdam 1-0 (0-0)
Sturm Graz: Jörg Siebenhandl, Gregory Wüthrich, Jusuf Gazibegovic, David Affenbruber, Amadou Danté (90+1' David Schnegg), Stefan Hierländer (56' Otar Kiteishvili, Ivan Ljubic), Tomi Horvat, Alexander Prass, William Bøving (83' Jakob Jantscher), Albian Ajeti (56' Emanuel Emegha). Coach: Christian Ilzer.
Feyenoord Rotterdam: Justin Bijlow, Gernot Trauner, Dávid Hancko, Marcos López, Lutsharel Geertruida, Alireza Jahanbakhsh (60' Patrik Wålemark), Sebastian Szymanski (68' Marcus Pedersen), Quinten Timber, Orkun Kökçü, Javairô Dilrosun, Danilo (85' Santiago Giménez). Coach: Arne Slot.
Goal: 90+3' Otar Kiteishvili 1-0.
Referee: Espen Eskås (NOR)   Attendance: 13,987.

03.11.22 MCH Arena, Herning: FC Midtjylland – Sturm Graz 2-0 (1-0)
FC Midtjylland: Jonas Lössl, Erik Sviatchenko (89' Juninho), Joel Andersson, Stefan Gartenmann, Paulinho (67' Nikolas Dyhr), Kristoffer Olsson, Evander (66' Oliver Sørensen), Emiliano Martínez, Anders Dreyer (90+1' Gustav Christensen), Gustav Isaksen, Edward Chilufya (66' Valdemar Andreasen). Coach: Albert Capellas.
Sturm Graz: Jörg Siebenhandl, Jon Gorenc Stankovic, Gregory Wüthrich, Jusuf Gazibegovic, David Affengruber (80' Aleksandar Borkovic), Amadou Danté (46' David Schnegg), Otar Kiteishvili (80' Manprit Sarkaria), Tomi Horvat, Alexander Prass, William Bøving (46' Emanuel Emegha), Albian Ajeti (74' Jakob Jantscher). Coach: Christian Ilzer.
Goals: 15', 72' Anders Dreyer 1-0, 2-0.
Referee: Matej Jug (SVN)   Attendance: 9,134.

03.11.22 De Kuip, Rotterdam: Feyenoord Rotterdam – Lazio Roma 1-0 (0-0)
Feyenoord Rotterdam: Justin Bijlow, Gernot Trauner, Dávid Hancko, Marcos López (46' Quilindschy Hartman), Lutsharel Geertruida, Sebastian Szymanski, Quinten Timber (90+2' Mats Wieffer), Orkun Kökçü, Javairô Dilrosun, Danilo (63' Santiago Giménez), Igor Paixão (73' Patrik Wålemark). Coach: Arne Slot.
Lazio Roma: Ivan Provedel, Elseid Hysaj, Patric, Nicolò Casale, Felipe Anderson, Manuel Lazzari (46' Adam Marusic), Mattia Zaccagni (63' Pedro), Sergej Milinkovic-Savic, Toma Basis (67' Matías Vecino), Marcos Antônio (67' Danilo Cataldi), Matteo Cancellieri (81' Luka Romero). Coach: Maurizio Sarri.
Goal: 64' Santiago Giménez 1-0.
Referee: Irfan Peljto (BIH)   Attendance: 43,268.
Sent off: 90+6' Luka Romero.

GROUP G

08.09.22 Stade de la Beaujoire – Louis Fonteneau, Nantes:
FC Nantes – Olympiakos Piraeus 2-1 (1-0)
FC Nantes: Alban Lafont, Nicolas Pallois, Dennis Appiah, Andrei Girotto, Pedro Chirivella, Samuel Moutoussamy (69' Moussa Sissoko), Ludovic Blas, Quentin Merlin, Mostafa Mohamed, Ignatius Ganago (69' Moses Simon), Evann Guessand.
Coach: Antoine Kombouaré.
Olympiakos Piraeus: Tomáš Vaclík, Kostas Manolas, Panagiotis Retsos, Pape Cissé, Pipa, Oleg Reabciuk, Andreas Bouchalakis, Pep Biel (86' Youssef El-Arabi), Pierre Kunde, Georgios Masouras (59' Josh Bowler), Ui-Jo Hwang (77' Aboubakar Kamara).
Coach: Carlos Corberán.
Goals: 32' Mostafa Mohamed 1-0, 50' Samuel Moutoussamy 1-1 (og), 90+3' Evann Guessand 2-1.
Referee: Harald Lechner (AUT)   Attendance: 31,276.

08.09.22 Europa-Park Stadion, Freiburg im Breisgau: SC Freiburg – Qarabag FK 2-1 (2-1)
SC Freiburg: Mark Flekken, Matthias Ginter, Christian Günter, Philipp Lienhart, Kiliann Sildillia, Nicolas Höfler, Vincenzo Grifo (71' Daniel Kyereh), Maximilian Eggestein, Wooyeong Jeong (88' Noah Weißhaupt), Nils Petersen (71' Michael Gregoritsch), Ritsu Dōan (90+3' Yannik Keitel). Coach: Christian Streich.
Qarabag FK: Sahrudin Mahammadaliyev, Marko Vesovic, Qara Qarayev (77' Richard Almeyda), Badavi Hüseynov, Bahlul Mustafazada, Abdellah Zoubir, Kady, Toral Bayramov (90+2' Elvin Cafarquliyev), Marko Jankovic (84' Leandro Andrade), Ramil Sheydayev (76' Júlio Romão), Owusu Kwabena. Coach: Qurban Qurbanov.
Goals: 7' Vincenzo Grifo 1-0 (p), 15' Ritsu Dōan 2-0, 39' Marko Vesovic 2-1.
Referee: Erik Lambrechts (BEL)   Attendance: 31,500.

15.09.22 Stadio Georgios Karaiskáki, Piraeus: Olympiakos Piraeus – SC Freiburg 0-3 (0-2)
Olympiakos Piraeus: Tomás Vaclík, Sime Vrsaljko (71' Pipa), Panagiotis Retsos (46' Pierre Kunde), Pape Cissé, Ousseynou Ba, Yann M'Vila, Andreas Bouchalakis (46' Oleg Reabciuk), Pep Biel, Georgios Masouras (63' Garry Rodrigues), Josh Bowler (63' Youssef El-Arabi), Ui-Jo Hwang. Coach: Carlos Corberán.
SC Freiburg: Mark Flekken, Matthias Ginter, Christian Günter, Philipp Lienhart, Kiliann Sildillia (78' Lukas Kübler), Nicolas Höfler, Vincenzo Grifo (78' Yannik Keitel), Maximilian Eggestein, Daniel Kyereh (62' Woo-yeong Jeong), Michael Gregoritsch (62' Kevin Schade), Ritsu Dōan (69' Nils Petersen). Coach: Christian Streich.
Goals: 5' Nicolas Höfler 0-1, 25', 52' Michael Gregoritsch 0-2, 0-3.
Referee: Matej Jug (SVN)   Attendance: 23,104.

15.09.22 Tofiq Bahramov adina Respublika stadionu, Baku:
          Qarabag FK – FC Nantes 3-0 (0-0)
Qarabag FK: Sahrudin Mahammadaliyev, Marko Vesovic, Qara Qarayev (89' Júlio Romão), Badavi Hüseynov, Bahlul Mustafazada, Filip Ozobic (62' Ramil Sheydayev), Abdellah Zoubir (90+1' Musa Qurbanli), Kady, Elvin Cafarquliyev, Marko Jankovic (88' Richard Almeyda), Owusu Kwabena (88' Leandro Andrade). Coach: Qurban Qurbanov.
FC Nantes: Alban Lafont, Fábio, Sébastien Corchia, Nicolas Pallois, Jean-Charles Castelletto, Moussa Sissoko (65' Pedro Chirivella), Samuel Moutoussamy (76' Andrei Girotto), Ludovic Blas, Moses Simon (76' Marcus Coco), Mostafa Mohamed (84' Dennis Appiah), Ignatius Ganago (64' Evann Guessand). Coach: Antoine Kombouaré.
Goals: 60' Owusu Kwabena 1-0, 65' Abdellah Zoubir 2-0, 72' Marko Jankovic 3-0.
Referee: Enea Jorgji (ALB)   Attendance: 26,495.

06.10.22 Stadio Georgios Karaiskáki, Piraeus: Olympiakos Piraeus – Qarabag FK 0-3 (0-0)
Olympiakos Piraeus: Konstantinos Tzolakis, Sime Vrsaljko, Pape Cissé (83' Mathieu Valbuena), Pipa, Oleg Reabciuk, Yann M'Vila, Andreas Bouchalakis (60' Marcelo), Pep Biel, Pierre Kunde (74' In-Beom Hwang), Garry Rodrigues (60' Georgios Masouras), Ui-Jo Hwang (74' Aboubakar Kamara). Coach: Míchel.
Qarabag FK: Sahrudin Mahammadaliyev, Marko Vesovic (90+1' Abbas Hüseynov), Qara Qarayev, Badavi Hüseynov, Bahlul Mustafazada, Richard Almeyda (65' Júlio Romão), Abdellah Zoubir, Kady, Elvin Cafarquliyev (46' Toral Bayramov), Leandro Andrade (65' Ramil Sheydayev), Owusu Kwabena (90+1' Filip Ozobic). Coach: Qurban Qurbanov.
Goals: 68' Owusu Kwabena 0-1, 82' Marko Vesovic 0-2, 86' Ramil Sheydayev 0-3.
Referee: Irfan Peljto (BIH)   Attendance: 21,677.

06.10.22 Europa-Park Stadion, Freiburg im Breisgau: SC Freiburg – FC Nantes 2-0 (0-0)
SC Freiburg: Mark Flekken, Matthias Ginter, Christian Günter, Philipp Lienhart, Kiliann Sildillia, Nicolas Höfler, Vincenzo Grifo (82' Noah Weißhaupt), Maximilian Eggestein (71' Yannik Keitel), Daniel Kyereh (82' Kevin Schade), Michael Gregoritsch (20' Nils Petersen), Ritsu Dōan (83' Lukas Kübler). Coach: Christian Streich.
FC Nantes: Alban Lafont, Nicolas Pallois, Dennis Appiah (78' Sébastien Corchia), Andrei Girotto (78' Evann Guessand), Jean-Charles Castelletto, Pedro Chirivella (69' Moussa Sissoko), Samuel Moutoussamy, Ludovic Blas, Quentin Merlin, Moses Simon (69' Ignatius Ganago), Mostafa Mohamed (84' Abdoul Kader Bamba). Coach: Antoine Kombouaré.
Goals: 48' Daniel Kyereh 1-0, 72' Vincenzo Grifo 2-0.
Referee: Glenn Nyberg (SWE)   Attendance: 33,200.

13.10.22   Stade de la Beaujoire – Louis Fonteneau, Nantes:
           FC Nantes – SC Freiburg 0-4 (0-1)
FC Nantes: Alban Lafont, Sébastien Corchia, Nicolas Pallois (80' Jean-Charles Castelletto), Andrei Girotto (88' Dennis Appiah), Moussa Sissoko (73' Marcus Coco), Pedro Chirivella (80' Samuel Moutoussamy), Ludovic Blas, Quentin Merlin, Moses Simon (73' Abdoul Kader Bamba), Mostafa Mohamed, Evann Guessand. Coach: Antoine Kombouaré.
SC Freiburg: Mark Flekken, Lukas Kübler, Matthias Ginter, Christian Günter, Philipp Lienhart, Nicolas Höfler (87' Keven Schlotterbeck), Vincenzo Grifo (65' Kevin Schade), Yannik Keitel (75' Maximilian Eggestein), Woo-yeong Jeong, Nils Petersen (65' Michael Gregoritsch), Ritsu Dōan (75' Noah Weißhaupt). Coach: Christian Streich.
Goals: 26' Lukas Kübler 0-1, 71' Michael Gregoritsch 0-2, 82' Kevin Schade 0-3, 87' Woo-yeong Jeong 0-4.
Referee: Horatiu Fesnic (ROM)   Attendance: 31,845.

13.10.22   Tofiq Bahramov adina Respublika stadionu, Baku:
           Qarabag FK – Olympiakos Piraeus 0-0
Qarabag FK: Sahrudin Mahammadaliyev, Marko Vesovic, Qara Qarayev (68' Júlio Romão), Badavi Hüseynov, Bahlul Mustafazada, Richard Almeyda (68' Marko Jankovic), Abdellah Zoubir, Kady (62' Filip Ozobic), Elvin Cafarquliyev (85' Toral Bayramov), Ramil Sheydayev, Owusu Kwabena (85' Abbas Hüseynov). Coach: Qurban Qurbanov.
Olympiakos Piraeus: Alexandros Paschalakis, Sokratis Papastathopoulos, Sime Vrsaljko, Oleg Reabciuk, Andreas Bouchalakis (86' In-Beom Hwang), Pep Biel (60' Mathieu Valbuena), Pierre Kunde (69' Yann M'Vila), Andreas Ntoj, Ui-Jo Hwang (60' Marcelo), Aboubakar Kamara, Marios Vrousai (86' Garry Rodrigues). Coach: Míchel.
Referee: Craig Pawson (ENG)   Attendance: 31,200.

27.10.22   Europa-Park Stadion, Freiburg im Breisgau:
           SC Freiburg – Olympiakos Piraeus 1-1 (0-1)
SC Freiburg: Mark Flekken, Lukas Kübler, Matthias Ginter, Christian Günter, Philipp Lienhart (78' Kiliann Sildillia), Nicolas Höfler, Vincenzo Grifo, Daniel Kyereh (64' Woo-yeong Jeong), Yannik Keitel (63' Maximilian Eggestein), Michael Gregoritsch (72' Nils Petersen), Ritsu Dōan (64' Noah Weißhaupt). Coach: Christian Streich.
Olympiakos Piraeus: Alexandros Paschalakis, Pipa, Ousseynou Ba, Yann M'Vila, Pep Biel (69' Pierre Kunde), Georgios Masouras (82' Mathieu Valbuena), In-Beom Hwang, Andreas Ntoj, Youssef El-Arabi (83' Ui-Jo Hwang), Garry Rodrigues (39' Oleg Reabciuk), Marios Vrousai (82' Panagiotis Retsos). Coach: Míchel.
Goals: 17' Youssef El-Arabi 0-1, 90+3' Lukas Kübler 1-1.
Referee: Kristo Tohver (EST)   Attendance: 33,000.
Sent off: 90+6' Ousseynou Ba.

27.10.22   Stade de la Beaujoire – Louis Fonteneau, Nantes:
           FC Nantes – Qarabag FK 2-1 (1-0)
FC Nantes: Alban Lafont, Sébastien Corchia (68' Moussa Sissoko), Andrei Girotto, Jean-Charles Castelletto, Pedro Chirivella (88' Marcus Coco), Samuel Moutoussamy (78' Ignatius Ganago), Ludovic Blas, Quentin Merlin, Abdoul Kader Bamba (68' Dennis Appiah), Mostafa Mohamed, Evann Guessand (67' Moses Simon). Coach: Antoine Kombouaré.
Qarabag FK: Sahrudin Mahammadaliyev, Marko Vesovic (88' Abbas Hüseynov), Qara Qarayev (79' Júlio Romão), Bahlul Mustafazada, Kevin Medina, Richard Almeyda (69' Marko Jankovic), Filip Ozobic (69' Ramil Sheydayev), Abdellah Zoubir, Kady, Toral Bayramov (88' Elvin Cafarquliyev), Owusu Kwabena. Coach: Qurban Qurbanov.
Goals: 16' Ludovic Blas 1-0, 56' Filip Ozobic 1-1 (p), 90+5' Ignatius Ganago 2-1.
Referee: Jakob Kehlet (DEN)   Attendance: 30,927.

03.11.22   Tofiq Bahramov adina Respublika stadionu, Baku:
Qarabag FK – SC Freiburg 1-1 (0-1)
Qarabag FK: Sahrudin Mahammadaliyev, Marko Vesovic (88' Abbas Hüseynov), Bahlul Mustafazada, Kevin Medina, Richard Almeyda (87' Musa Qurbanli), Abdellah Zoubir, Kady, Elvin Cafarquliyev (88' Toral Bayramov), Marko Jankovic (88' Júlio Romão), Ramil Sheydayev (63' Maksim Medvedev), Owusu Kwabena. Coach: Qurban Qurbanov.
SC Freiburg: Noah Atubolu, Christian Günter (46' Lukas Kübler), Keven Schlotterbeck, Hugo Siquet (73' Matthias Ginter), Kiliann Sildillia, Yannik Keitel, Robert Wagner, Nils Petersen, Lucas Höler (84' Vincenzo Grifo), Noah Weißhaupt (72' Woo-yeong Jeong), Kevin Schade (62' Roland Sallai). Coach: Christian Streich.
Goals: 25' Nils Petersen 0-1 (p), 90+2' Owusu Kwabena 1-1.
Referee: Aleksei Kulbakov (BLS)   Attendance: 30,430.
Sent off: 62' Kevin Medina.

03.11.22   Stadio Georgios Karaiskáki, Piraeus: Olympiakos Piraeus – FC Nantes 0-2 (0-0)
Olympiakos Piraeus: Konstantinos Tzolakis, Panagiotis Retsos, Alexios Kalogeropoulos (60' Pape Cissé), Andreas Bouchalakis, Pierre Kunde, Athanasios Androutsos, Josh Bowler (85' Pipa), Youssef El-Arabi (46' Anastasios Sapountzis), Ui-Jo Hwang, Aboubakar Kamara (69' Marcelo), Marios Vrousai (46' Sime Vrsaljko). Coach: Míchel.
FC Nantes: Alban Lafont, Fábio (5' Dennis Appiah), Sébastien Corchia, Nicolas Pallois, Jean-Charles Castelletto, Moussa Sissoko, Samuel Moutoussamy (73' Pedro Chirivella), Moses Simon (46' Ludovic Blas), Mostafa Mohamed, Ignatius Ganago (73' Abdoul Kader Bamba), Evann Guessand (80' Marcus Coco). Coach: Antoine Kombouaré.
Goals: 79' Mostafa Mohamed 0-1, 90' Ludovic Blas 0-2.
Referee: Serhiy Boyko (UKR)   Attendance: 16,254.

GROUP H

08.09.22   Stadion Rajko Mitic, Beograd: Crvena Zvezda Beograd – AS Monaco 0-1 (0-0)
Crvena Zvezda Beograd: Milan Borjan, Aleksandar Dragovic, Nemanja Milunovic, Milan Rodic, Strahinja Erakovic, Aleksandar Katai (87' Kalifa Coulibaly), Slavoljub Srnic (76' Veljko Nikolic), Sékou Sanogo (88' Stefan Mitrovic), Guélor Kanga, Aleksandar Pesic (54' El Fardou Ben Mohamed), Osman Bukari. Coach: Milos Milojevic.
AS Monaco: Alexander Nübel, Guillermo Maripán, Axel Disasi, Caio Henrique, Benoît Badiashile, Vanderson, Takumi Minamino (57' Krépin Diatta), Aleksandr Golovin (83' Ismail Jakobs), Youssouf Fofana (57' Jean Lucas), Mohamed Camara, Wissam Ben Yedder (66' Breel Embolo). Coach: Philippe Clement.
Goal: 74' Breel Embolo 0-1 (p).
Referee: Harm Osmers (GER)   Attendance: 40,226.

08.09.22 Groupama Aréna, Budapest: Ferencvárosi TC – Trabzonspor 3-2 (3-1)
Ferencvárosi TC: Dénes Dibusz, Eldar Civic, Henry Wingo, Samy Mmaee, Mats Knoester, Muhamed Besic (90' Adnan Kovacevic), Bálint Vécsei (76' Aïssa Laïdouni), Kristoffer Zachariassen, Tokmac Nguen (76' Amer Gojak), Franck Boli (20' Endre Botka), Adama Traoré (I). Coach: Stanislav Cherchesov.
Trabzonspor: Muhammet Taha Tepe, Jens Stryger Larsen, Vitor Hugo (46' Eren Elmali), Marc Bartra, Stefano Denswil (72' Djaniny), Anastasios Bakasetas, Trézéguet, Jean-Philippe Gbamin (46' Marek Hamsík), Enis Bardhi (46' Yusuf Yazici), Abdülkadir Ömür (60' Umut Bozok), Maximiliano Gómez. Coach: Abdullah Avci.
Goals: 5' Tokmac Nguen 1-0, 29' Adama Traoré 2-0, 39' Maximiliano Gómez 2-1, 44' Tokmac Nguen 3-1 (p), 71' Umut Bozok 3-2.
Referee: Fabio Maresca (ITA)   Attendancce: 17,987.
Sent off: 16' Eldar Civic.

15.09.22 Senol Günes Spor Kompleksi, Trabzon:
Trabzonspor – Crvena Zveda Beograd 2-1 (1-0)
Trabzonspor: Ugurcan Çakir, Jens Stryger Larsen (69' Vitor Hugo), Marc Bartra, Stefano Denswil, Eren Elmali, Marek Hamsík (61' Enis Bardhi), Anastasios Bakasetas, Emmanouil "Manolis" Siopis, Trézéguet, Djaniny (79' Umut Bozok), Maximiliano Gómez (61' Abdülkadir Ömür, 79' Montassir Lahtimi). Coach: Abdullah Avci.
Crvena Zvezda Beograd: Milan Borjan, Aleksandar Dragovic, Nemanja Milunovic, Milan Rodic, Strahinja Erakovic, Slavoljub Srnic (46' Aleksandar Katai), Sékou Sanogo (59' Ibrahim Mustapha), Guélor Kanga (84' Radovan Pankov), Kings Kangwa, Aleksandar Pesic (59' Kalifa Coulibaly), Osman Bukari (70' Veljko Nikolic). Coach: Milos Milojevic.
Goals: 16' Marek Hamsík 1-0, 68' Trézéguet 2-0, 89' Veljko Nikolic 2-1.
Referee: Sascha Stegemann (GER)   Attendance: 24,884.
Sent off: 63' Kings Kangwa.

15.09.22 Stade Louis II, Monaco: AS Monaco – Ferencvárosi TC 0-1 (0-0)
AS Monaco: Alexander Nübel, Axel Disasi, Malang Sarr (81' Myron Boadu), Caio Henrique, Benoît Badiashile, Vanderson (46' Ruben Aguilar), Aleksandr Golovin (73' Ismail Jakobs), Youssouf Fofana, Mohamed Camara, Wissam Ben Yedder (66' Breel Embolo), Krépin Diatta (46' Maghnes Akliouche). Coach: Philippe Clement.
Ferencvárosi TC: Dénes Dibusz, Endre Botka, Henry Wingo, Samy Mmaee, Mats Knoester, Muhamed Besic (70' Bálint Vécsei), Kristoffer Zachariassen (90' Anderson Esiti), Aïssa Laïdouni, Tokmac Nguen (63' Amer Gojak), Adama Traoré (I), Ryan Mmaee (64' Franck Boli). Coach: Stanislav Cherchesov.
Goal: 79' Bálint Vécsei 0-1.
Referee: Espen Eskås (NOR)   Attendance: 3,931.

06.10.22 Stadion Rajko Mitic, Beograd: Crvena Zvezda Beograd – Ferencvárosi TC 4-1 (2-0)
Crvena Zvezda Beograd: Milan Borjan, Aleksandar Dragovic (72' Veljko Nikolic), Milan Rodic, Marko Gobeljic, Strahinja Erakovic, Aleksandar Katai (72' Nemanja Motika), Sékou Sanogo (62' Slavoljub Srnic), Guélor Kanga (80' Ibrahim Mustapha), Mirko Ivanic, Aleksandar Pesic, Stefan Mitrovic (62' Radovan Pankov). Coach: Milos Milojevic.
Ferencvárosi TC: Dénes Dibusz, Endre Botka (77' Lóránd Pászka), Henry Wingo, Samy Mmaee, Mats Knoester, Muhamed Besic (57' Bálint Vécsei), Kristoffer Zachariassen, Aïssa Laïdouni (67' Amer Gojak), Tokmac Nguen (66' Marquinhos), Franck Boli (57' Ryan Mmaee), Adama Traoré (I). Coach: Stanislav Cherchesov.
Goals: 27' Guélor Kanga 1-0 (p), 35' Stefan Mitrovic 2-0, 50' Aleksandar Katai 3-0, 60' Guélor Kanga 4-0, 71' Kristoffer Zachariassen 4-1.
Referee: Lawrence Visser (BEL)   Attendance: 26,244.

06.10.22 Stade Louis II, Monaco: AS Monaco – Trabzonspor 3-1 (2-0)
AS Monaco: Alexander Nübel, Axel Disasi, Caio Henrique, Benoît Badiashile, Vanderson (65'
Guillermo Maripán), Aleksandr Golovin (73' Takumi Minamino), Youssouf Fofana, Mohamed
Camara (65' Jean Lucas), Wissam Ben Yedder (57' Myron Boadu), Breel Embolo (57' Kevin
Volland), Krépin Diatta. Coach: Philippe Clement.
Trabzonspor: Ugurcan Çakir, Jens Stryger Larsen, Marc Bartra, Stefano Denswil, Eren Elmali,
Marek Hamsík (56' Anastasios Bakasetas), Emmanouil "Manolis" Siopis (72' Abdülkadir
Ömür), Trézéguet (72' Djaniny), Enis Bardhi (82' Naci Ünüvar), Yusuf Yazici (56' Umut
Bozok), Maximiliano Gómez. Coach: Abdullah Avci.
Goals: 14', 45+2' Wissam Ben Yedder 1-0, 2-0 (p), 55' Axel Disasi 3-0,
72' Anastasios Bakasetas 3-1.
Referee: Giorgi Kruashvili (GEO)   Attendance: 5,050.
Sent off: 11' Maximiliano Gómez.

13.10.22 Senol Günes Spor Kompleksi, Trabzon: Trabzonspor – AS Monaco 4-0 (1-0)
Trabzonspor: Ugurcan Çakir, Marc Bartra, Stefano Denswil, Hüseyin Türkmen (46' Vitor
Hugo), Eren Elmali (77' Yusuf Erdogan), Marek Hamsík (58' Emmanouil "Manolis" Siopis),
Anastasios Bakasetas, Jean-Philippe Gbamin, Enis Bardhi (64' Trézéguet), Djaniny (58'
Abdülkadir Ömür), Umut Bozok. Coach: Abdullah Avci.
AS Monaco: Alexander Nübel, Axel Disasi, Malang Sarr, Caio Henrique (83' Ismail Jakobs),
Vanderson, Aleksandr Golovin (60' Takumi Minamino), Youssouf Fofana, Mohamed Camara,
Wissam Ben Yedder (68' Kevin Volland), Breel Embolo (60' Myron Boadu), Krépin Diatta
(60' Gelson Martins). Coach: Philippe Clement.
Goals: 44' Malang Sarr 1-0 (og), 48' Vitor Hugo 2-0, 57' Enis Bardhi 3-0, 69' Trézéguet 4-0.
Referee: Jakob Kehlet (DEN)   Attendance: 24,343.

13.10.22 Groupama Aréna, Budapest: Ferencvárosi TC – Crvena Zvezda Beograd 2-1 (1-0)
Ferencvárosi TC: Dénes Dibusz, Endre Botka, Lóránd Pászka, Samy Mmaee, Mats Knoester,
Muhamed Besic (81' Anderson Esiti), Bálint Vécsei, Amer Gojak (66' Tokmac Nguen),
Kristoffer Zachariassen, Adama Traoré (I), Ryan Mmaee (90+4' Franck Boli).
Coach: Stanislav Cherchesov.
Crvena Zvezda Beograd: Milan Borjan, Aleksandar Dragovic (81' Nemanja Milunovic), Milan
Rodic, Marko Gobeljic, Strahinja Erakovic, Aleksandar Katai (61' Osman Bukari), Sékou
Sanogo (27' Kings Kangwa), Guélor Kanga (82' Jovan Mijatovic), Mirko Ivanic, Aleksandar
Pesic, Stefan Mitrovic. Coach: Milos Milojevic.
Goals: 23' Kristoffer Zachariassen 1-0, 55' Stefan Mitrovic 1-1, 61' Samy Mmaee 2-1.
Referee: Daniel Stefanski (POL)   Attendance: 20,675.

27.10.22 Stadion Rakjo Mitic, Beograd: Crvena Zvezda Beograd – Trabzonspor 2-1 (1-1)
Crvena Zvezda Beograd: Milan Borjan, Aleksandar Dragovic, Nemanja Milunovic, Milan
Rodic, Strahinja Erakovic, Aleksandar Katai (75' Kings Kangwa), Slavoljub Srnic (60' Mirko
Ivanic), Guélor Kanga, Aleksandar Pesic (83' Jovan Mijatovic), Osman Bukari, Stefan
Mitrovic (83' Ibrahim Mustapha). Coach: Milos Milojevic.
Trabzonspor: Ugurcan Çakir, Jens Stryger Larsen, Vitor Hugo, Marc Bartra, Eren Elmali,
Marek Hamsík (82' Yusuf Yazici), Anastasios Bakasetas, Trézéguet, Jean-Philippe Gbamin
(68' Abdülkadir Ömür), Enis Bardhi (83' Montassir Lahtimi), Umut Bozok (69' Djaniny).
Coach: Abdullah Avci.
Goals: 37' Aleksandar Katai 1-0, 39' Anastasios Bakasetas 1-1, 64' Aleksandar Pesic 2-1.
Referee: João Pedro Pinheiro (POR)   Attendance: 30,431.

27.10.22   Groupama Aréna, Budapest: Ferencvárosi TC – AS Monaco 1-1 (0-1)
Ferencvárosi TC: Dénes Dibusz, Endre Botka, Henry Wingo, Lóránd Pászka (65' Tokmac Nguen), Samy Mmaee, Bálint Vécsei (56' Muhamed Besic), Amer Gojak (46' Marquinhos, 90+1' Anderson Esiti), Kristoffer Zachariassen, Aïssa Laïdouni, Adama Traoré (I), Ryan Mmaee. Coach: Stanislav Cherchesov.
AS Monaco: Alexander Nübel, Guillermo Maripán, Axel Disasi, Caio Henrique, Benoît Badiashile, Vanderson (41' Krépin Diatta), Aleksandr Golovin, Youssouf Fofana (83' Jean Lucas), Mohamed Camara, Kevin Volland (83' Breel Embolo), Wissam Ben Yedder. Coach: Philippe Clement.
Goals: 31' Wissam Ben Yedder 0-1, 81' Kristoffer Zachariassen 1-1.
Referee: Enea Jorgji (ALB)   Attendance: 20,517.

03.11.22   Senol Günes Spor Kompleksi, Trabzon: Trabzonspor – Ferencvárosi TC 1-0 (1-0)
Trabzonspor: Ugurcan Çakir, Jens Stryger Larsen, Vitor Hugo, Marc Bartra, Eren Elmali, Marek Hamsík (62' Jean-Philippe Gbamin), Anastasios Bakasetas (70' Naci Ünüvar), Emmanouil "Manolis" Siopis, Trézéguet (85' Dogucan Haspolat), Abdülkadir Ömür (69' Enis Bardhi), Yusuf Yazici (62' Djaniny). Coach: Abdullah Avci.
Ferencvárosi TC: Dénes Dibusz, Henry Wingo, Lóránd Pászka (90+1' Damir Redzic), Samy Mmaee, Mats Knoester, Bálint Vécsei, Anderson Esiti (61' Xavier Mercier), Kristoffer Zachariassen, Aïssa Laïdouni, Tokmac Nguen (82' Adnan Kovacevic), Ryan Mmaee. Coach: Stanislav Cherchesov.
Goal: 7' Anastasios Bakasetas 1-0.
Referee: Harm Osmers (GER)   Attendance: 22,840.

03.11.22   Stade Louis II, Monaco: AS Monaco – Crvena Zvezda Beograd 4-1 (2-0)
AS Monaco: Alexander Nübel, Guillermo Maripán, Axel Disasi, Caio Henrique, Benoît Badiashile, Aleksandr Golovin (85' Ismail Jakobs), Youssouf Fofana, Mohamed Camara (85' Eliot Matazo), Kevin Volland (90' Eliesse Ben Seghir), Wissam Ben Yedder (76' Breel Embolo), Krépin Diatta (75' Vanderson). Coach: Philippe Clement.
Crvena Zvezda Beograd: Milan Borjan, Nemanja Milunovic, Milan Rodic (84' Irakli Azarov), Marko Gobeljic, Strahinja Erakovic, Aleksandar Katai (60' Kings Kangwa), Guélor Kanga (71' Ibrahim Mustapha), Mirko Ivanic, Aleksandar Pesic, Osman Bukari (71' El Fardou Ben Mohamed), Stefan Mitrovic (46' Slavoljub Srnic). Coach: Milos Milojevic.
Goals: 5', 27' Kevin Volland 1-0, 2-0, 50' Milan Rodic 3-0 (og), 54' Guélor Kanga 3-1 (p), 87' Kevin Volland 4-1.
Referee: Serdar Gözübüyük (HOL)   Attendance: 6,341.

KNOCKOUT ROUND PLAY-OFFS

16.02.23   Camp Nou, Barcelona: FC Barcelona – Manchester United 2-2 (0-0)
FC Barcelona: Marc-André ter Stegen, Jordi Alba (67' Alejandro (Álex) Baldé), Marcos Alonso (67' Andreas Christensen), Jules Koundé, Ronald Araújo, Franck Kessié (67' Ansu Fati), Frenkie de Jong, Pedri (41' Sergi Roberto), Gavi, Robert Lewandowski, Raphinha (83' Ferrán Torres). Coach: Xavi.
Manchester United: David de Gea, Raphaël Varane, Luke Shaw, Tyrell Malacia, Aaron Wan-Bissaka, Casemiro, Fred, Bruno Fernandes, Wout Weghorst, Marcus Rashford, Jadon Sancho (81' Alejandro Garnacho). Coach: Erik ten Hag.
Goals: 50' Marcos Alonso 1-0, 53' Marcus Rashford 1-1, 59' Jules Koundé 1-2 (og), 76' Raphinha 2-2.
Referee: Maurizio Mariani (ITA)   Attendance: 90,225.

16.02.23   Stadion Wojska Polskiego, Warszawa (POL):
Shakhtar Donetsk – Stade Rennes 2-1 (2-0)
Shakhtar Donetsk: Anatoliy Trubin, Mykola Matviyenko, Bogdan Mykhailichenko, Valeriy Bondar, Yukhym Konoplya, Taras Stepanenko, Dmytro Kryskiv (76' Ivan Petryak), Artem Bondarenko, Georgiy Sudakov, Oleksandr Zubkov, Lassina Traoré (77' Danylo Sikan).
Coach: Igor Jovicevic.
Stade Rennes: Steve Mandanda, Djed Spence, Warmed Omari, Adrien Truffert, Jeanuël Belocian, Benjamin Bourigeaud, Lesley Chimuanya Ugochukwu (77' Baptiste Santamaría), Karl Toko Ekambi (77' Lovro Majer), Amine Gouiri (71' Désiré Doué), Jérémy Doku (71' Ibrahim Salah), Arnaud Kalimuendo (86' Birger Meling). Coach: Bruno Génésio.
Goals: 11' Dmytro Kryskiv 1-0, 45' Artem Bondarenko 2-0 (p), 59' Karl Toko Ekambi 2-1.
Referee: Irfan Peljto (BIH)   Attendance: 13,415.

16.02.23   Johan Cruyff Arena, Amsterdam: AFC Ajax – Union Berlin   0-0
AFC Ajax: Gerónimo Rulli, Owen Wijndal (46' Brian Brobbey), Calvin Bassey, Jurriën Timber, Devyne Rensch, Edson Álvarez, Kenneth Taylor, Mohammed Kudus, Dusan Tadic, Steven Berghuis, Steven Bergwijn (75' Davy Klaassen). Coach: John Heitinga.
Union Berlin: Frederik Rønnow, Robin Knoche, Jérôme Roussillon (90' Niko Gießelmann), Josip Juranovic, Diogo Leite, Danilho Doekhi, Rani Khedira, Morten Thorsby, Aïssa Laïdouni, Kevin Behrens (70' Jordan Siebatcheu), Sheraldo Becker (82' Sven Michel).
Coach: Urs Fischer.
Referee: Halil Umut Meler (TUR)   Attendance: 54,322.

16.02.23   Red Bull Arena, Wals-Siezenheim: Red Bull Salzburg – AS Roma 1-0 (0-0)
Red Bull Salzburg: Philipp Köhn, Andreas Ulmer, Oumar Solet, Strahinja Pavlovic, Amar Dedic, Nicolas Seiwald, Luka Sucic (82' Oscar Gloukh), Nicolás Capaldo, Lucas Gourna-Douath, Noah Okafor (82' Sékou Koïta), Fernando (60' Junior Chikwubuike Adamu).
Coach: Matthias Jaissle.
AS Roma: Rui Patrício, Chris Smalling, Gianluca Mancini, Ibañez, Nemanja Matic, Bryan Cristante, Lorenzo Pellegrini (74' Georginio Wijnaldum), Stephan El Shaarawy, Paulo Dybala (46' Zeki Çelik), Tammy Abraham (74' Andrea Belotti), Nicola Zalewski. Coach: José Mourinho.
Goal: 88' Nicolás Capaldo 1-0.
Referee: Dennis Higler (HOL)   Attendance: 29,520.

16.02.23   Allianz Stadium, Torino: FC Juventus – FC Nantes 1-1 (1-0)
FC Juventus: Wojciech Szczesny, Danilo, Alex Sandro, Mattia De Sciglio (73' Juan Cuadrado), Bremer, Ángel Di María (73' Matías Soulé), Leandro Paredes (63' Manuel Locatelli), Adrien Rabiot, Nicolò Fagioli (63' Filip Kostic), Dusan Vlahovic (86' Moise Kean), Federico Chiesa. Coach: Massimiliano Allegri.
FC Nantes: Alban Lafont, Nicolas Pallois (83' Sébastien Corchia), Andrei Girotto, Jean-Charles Castelletto (88' Evann Guessand), Fabien Centonze, Moussa Sissoko, Pedro Chirivella (77' Florent Mollet), Samuel Moutoussamy, Ludovic Blas, Marcus Coco (77' Charles Traoré), Mostafa Mohamed (77' Moses Simon). Coach: Antoine Kombouaré.
Goals: 13' Dusan Vlahovic 1-0, 60' Ludovic Blas 1-1.
Referee: João Pedro Pinheiro (POR)   Attendance: 41,019.

16.02.23   Estádio José Alvalade, Lisboa: Sporting CP – FC Midtjylland 1-1 (0-0)
Sporting CP: Antonio Adán, Sebastián Coates, Ricardo Esgaio (65' Héctor Bellerín), Matheus Reis (78' Gonçalo Inácio), Jerry St.Juste, Nuno Santos, Arthur Gomes (65' Trincão), Manuel Ugarte (86' Mateo Tanlongo), Pedro Gonçalves "Pote", Paulinho (77' Youssef Chermiti), Marcus Edwards. Coach: Rúben Amorim.
FC Midtjylland: Jonas Lössl, Henrik Dalsgaard, Joel Andersson, Stefan Gartenmann, Paulinho (67' Victor Bak), Kristoffer Olsson, Emiliano Martínez (67' Emam Ashour), Armin Gigovic, Valdemar Andreasen (46' Edward Chilufya), Gustav Isaksen (86' Aral Simsir), Frederik Heiselberg (59' Oliver Sørensen). Coach: Albert Capellas.
Goals: 77' Emam Ashour 0-1, 90+4' Sebastián Coates 1-1.
Referee: François Letexier (FRA)   Attendance: 23,279.

16.02.23   BayArena, Leverkusen: Bayer Leverkusen – AS Monaco 2-3 (0-1)
Bayer Leverkusen: Lukás Hrádecký, Jonathan Tah, Jeremie Frimpong (88' Callum Hudson-Odoi), Edmond Tapsoba, Piero Hincapié, Robert Andrich, Nadiem Amiri (68' Odilon Kossounou), Exequiel Palacios, Florian Wirtz, Moussa Diaby (56' Amine Adli), Adam Hlozek (88' Patrik Schick). Coach: Xabi Alonso.
AS Monaco: Alexander Nübel, Ruben Aguilar (80' Chrislain Matsima), Guillermo Maripán, Axel Disasi, Caio Henrique, Takumi Minamino (46' Eliesse Ben Seghir), Aleksandr Golovin (71' Ismail Jakobs), Youssouf Fofana, Mohamed Camara (71' Eliot Matazo), Breel Embolo (62' Wissam Ben Yedder), Krépin Diatta. Coach: Philippe Clement.
Goals: 9' Lukás Hrádecký 0-1 (og), 48' Moussa Diaby 1-1, 59' Florian Wirtz 2-1, 74' Krépin Diatta 2-2, 90+2' Axel Disasi 2-3.
Referee: Orel Grinfeld (ISR)   Attendance: 27,864.

16.02.23   Estadio Ramón Sánchez Pizjuán, Sevilla: Sevilla FC – PSV Eindhoven 3-0 (1-0)
Sevilla FC: Yassine Bounou "Bono", Jesús Navas, Marcos Acuña (70' Gonzalo Montiel), Loïc Badé (16' Fernando), Tanguy Nianzou, Ivan Rakitic, Nemanja Gudelj, Óliver Torres (70' Érik Lamela), Joan Jordán, Youssef En-Nesyri (63' Suso), Bryan Gil (46' Lucas Ocampos). Coach: Jorge Sampaoli.
PSV Eindhoven: Walter Benítez, Patrick van Aanholt (75' Mauro Júnior), André Ramalho (90+1' Armando Obispo), Jordan Teze, Jarrad Branthwaite, Ibrahim Sangaré, Guus Til (62' Thorgan Hazard), Joey Veerman, Xavi Simons, Luuk de Jong (62' Fábio Silva), Ismael Saibari (90+1' Philipp Mwene). Coach: Ruud van Nistelrooij.
Goals: 45+2' Youssef En-Nesyri 1-0, 50' Lucas Ocampos 2-0, 55' Nemanja Gudelj 3-0).
Referee: Radu Petrescu (ROM)   Attendance: 29,593.

23.02.23   Stade de la Beaujoire, Nantes: FC Nantes – FC Juventus 0-3 (0-2)
FC Nantes: Alban Lafont, Nicolas Pallois, Andrei Girotto, Jean-Charles Castelletto, Fabien Centonze, Moussa Sissoko (46' Samuel Moutoussamy), Florent Mollet (73' Evann Guessand), Pedro Chirivella (24' Charles Traoré), Ludovic Blas, Andy Delort (46' Ignatius Ganago), Moses Simon (73' Mostafa Mohamed). Coach: Antoine Kombouaré.
FC Juventus: Wojciech Szczesny, Danilo (82' Leonardo Bonucci), Alex Sandro, Mattia De Sciglio (65' Juan Cuadrado), Bremer, Ángel Di María (82' Leandro Paredes), Filip Kostic (82' Samuel Iling-Junior), Adrien Rabiot, Manuel Locatelli, Nicolò Fagioli, Moise Kean (64' Dusan Vlahovic). Coach: Massimiliano Allegri.
Goals: 5', 20', 78' Ángel Di María 0-1, 0-2 (p), 0-3.
Referee: José María Sánchez Martínez (ESP)   Attendance: 34,420.
Send off: 17' Nicolas Pallois.

23.02.23   MCH Arena, Herning: FC Midtjylland – Sporting CP 0-4 (0-1)
FC Midtjylland: Jonas Lössl, Henrik Dalsgaard, Joel Andersson (72' Mads Thychosen), Stefan Gartenmann, Paulinho, Kristoffer Olsson, Oliver Sørensen (46' Victor Bak), Armin Gigovic, Valdemar Andreasen (46' Emam Ashour), Astrit Selmani (46' Edward Chilufya), Gustav Isaksen (79' Frederik Heiselberg). Coach: Albert Capellas.
Sporting CP: Antonio Adán, Sebastián Coates, Ricardo Esgaio (46' Héctor Bellerín), Jerry St.Juste, Gonçalo Inácio, Arthur Gomes (65' Nuno Santos), Manuel Ugarte (78' Mateo Tanlongo), Pedro Gonçalves "Pote", Hidemasa Morita (53' Mateus Fernandes), Paulinho, Marcus Edwards (65' Trincão). Coach: Rúben Amorim.
Goals: 21' Sebastián Coates 0-1, 50', 77' Pedro Gonçalves "Pote" 0-2, 0-3, 85' Stefan Gartenmann 0-4 (og).
Referee: Ivan Kruzliak (SVK)   Attendance: 9,576.
Send off: 38' Paulinho.

23.02.23   Stade Louis II, Monaco: AS Monaco – Bayer Leverkusen 2-3 (1-2,2-3) (AET)
AS Monaco: Alexander Nübel, Axel Disasi, Malang Sarr, Caio Henrique, Chrislain Matsima (61' Edan Diop), Aleksandr Golovin (78' Myron Boadu), Youssouf Fofana, Mohamed Camara (70' Eliot Matazo), Eliesse Ben Seghir (78' Ismail Jakobs), Wissam Ben Yedder (78' Breel Embolo), Krépin Diatta (110' Kevin Volland). Coach: Philippe Clement.
Bayer Leverkusen: Lukás Hrádecký, Jonathan Tah, Jeremie Frimpong (103' Moussa Diaby), Mitchel Bakker, Edmond Tapsoba, Piero Hincapié, Robert Andrich, Exequiel Palacios, Florian Wirtz (115' Sardar Azmoun), Adam Hlozek (70' Patrik Schick), Amine Adli (74' Nadiem Amiri). Coach: Xabi Alonso.
Goals: 13' Florian Wirtz 0-1, 19' Wissam Ben Yedder 1-1 (p), 21' Exequiel Palacios 1-2, 58' Amine Adli 1-3, 84' Breel Embolo 2-3.
Referee: Alejandro Hernández Hernández (ESP)   Attendance: 8,504.

Bayer Leverkusen won on penalties after extra time (5:3).
Penalties: Azmoun 1-0, Disasi 1-1, Amiri 2-1, Matazo missed, Tapsoba 3-1, Embolo 3-2, Schick 4-2, Volland 4-3, Diaby 5-3.

23.02.23   Philips Stadion, Eindhoven: PSV Eindhoven – Sevilla 2-0 (0-0)
PSV Eindhoven: Walter Benítez, Patrick van Aanholt (62' Mauro Júnior), Philipp Mwene, André Ramalho, Jarrad Branthwaite, Érick Gutiérrez (62' Fábio Silva), Guus Til, Joey Veerman, Xavi Simons, Luuk de Jong, Johan Bakayoko. Coach: Ruud van Nistelrooij.
Sevilla FC: Marko Dmitrovic, Jesús Navas (80' Gonzalo Montiel), Alex Telles, Marcos Acuña, Tanguy Nianzou, Ivan Rakitic, Fernando, Óliver Torres (68' Suso), Joan Jordán, Youssef En-Nesyri (69' Lucas Ocampos), Bryan Gil (86' Rafa Mir). Coach: Jorge Sampaoli.
Goals: 77' Luuk de Jong 1-0, 90+5' Fábio Silva 2-0.
Referee: Daniele Orsato (ITA)   Attendance: 34,000.
Send off: 90+7' Mauro Júnior.

23.02.23   Old Trafford, Manchester: Manchester United – FC Barcelona 2-1 (0-1)
Manchester United: David de Gea, Raphaël Varane, Luke Shaw, Aaron Wan-Bissaka (67'
Diogo Dalot), Lisandro Martínez, Casemiro, Fred, Bruno Fernandes, Wout Weghorst (46'
Antony), Marcus Rashford (88' Scott McTominay), Jadon Sancho (67' Alejandro Garnacho).
Coach: Erik ten Hag.
FC Barcelona: Marc-André ter Stegen, Sergi Roberto (70' Ferrán Torres), Andreas
Christensen, Jules Koundé, Ronald Araújo (82' Marcos Alonso), Alejandro (Álex) Baldé,
Sergio Busquets, Franck Kessié, Frenkie de Jong, Robert Lewandowski, Raphinha (75' Ansu
Fati). Coach: Xavi.
Goals: 18' Robert Lewandowski 0-1 (p), 47' Fred 1-1, 73' Antony 2-1.
Referee: Clément Turpin (FRA)   Attendance: 73,021.

23.02.23   Roazhon Park, Rennes: Stade Rennes – Shakhtar Donetsk 2-1 (0-0,1-0) (AET)
Stade Rennes: Steve Mandanda, Djed Spence, Warmed Omari, Adrien Truffert (97' Birger
Meling), Jeanuël Belocian, Baptiste Santamaría (96' Désiré Doué), Lovro Majer (71' Lesley
Chimuanya Ugochukwu), Karl Toko Ekambi (96' Ibrahim Salah), Amine Gouiri, Jérémy
Doku, Arnaud Kalimuendo (84' Flavien Tait). Coach: Bruno Génésio.
Shakhtar Donetsk: Anatoliy Trubin, Mykola Matviyenko, Bogdan Mykhailichenko, Valeriy
Bondar, Yukhym Konoplya, Taras Stepanenko (100' Yegor Nazaryna), Artem Bondarenko,
Georgiy Sudakov, Oleksandr Zubkov (112' Kevin Kelsy), Dmytro Topalov (80' Neven
Djurasek), Lassina Traoré (79' Danylo Sikan). Coach: Igor Jovicevic.
Goals: 52' Karl Toko Ekambi 1-0, 106' Ibrahim Salah 2-0, 119' Jeanuël Belocian 2-1 (og).
Referee: Tobias Stieler (GER)   Attendance: 27,781.

Shakhtar Donetsk won on penalties after extra time (5:4).

*Penalties: Doué 1-0, Nazaryna 1-1, Doku missed, Sudakov 1-2, Meling missed,
Bondarenko 1-3, Gouiri 2-3, Bondar missed, Tait 3-3, Sikan missed, Omari 4-3,
Konoplya 4-4, Ugochukwu missed, Kelsy 4-5.*

23.02.23   Stadion An der Alten Försterei, Berlin: Union Berlin – AFC Ajax 3-1 (2-0)
Union Berlin: Frederik Rønnow, Robin Knoche, Jérôme Roussillon (90+4' Niko Gießelmann),
Josip Juranovic (90+4' Christopher Trimmel), Diogo Leite, Danilho Doekhi, Rani Khedira,
Janik Haberer, Aïssa Laïdouni (65' Morten Thorsby), Kevin Behrens (65' Jordan Siebatcheu),
Sheraldo Becker (85' Jamie Leweling). Coach: Urs Fischer.
AFC Ajax: Gerónimo Rulli, Calvin Bassey, Jurriën Timber, Devyne Rensch (84' Francisco
Conceição), Davy Klaassen (64' Brian Brobbey), Edson Álvarez, Kenneth Taylor, Mohammed
Kudus, Dusan Tadic, Steven Berghuis, Steven Bergwijn (80' Lorenzo Lucca).
Coach: John Heitinga.
Goals: 20' Robin Knoche 1-0 (p), 44' Josip Juranovic 2-0, 47' Mohammed Kudus 2-1,
50' Danilho Doekhi 3-1.
Referee: Ricardo de Burgos Bengoetxea (ESP)   Attendance: 21,800.
Send off: 90+7' Edson Álvarez.

23.02.23   Stadio Olimpico, Roma: AS Roma – Red Bull Salzburg 2-0 (2-0)
AS Roma: Rui Patrício, Chris Smalling, Leonardo Spinazzola, Gianluca Mancini, Ibañez, Nemanja Matic, Bryan Cristante, Lorenzo Pellegrini (81' Georginio Wijnaldum), Paulo Dybala (90+3' Stephan El Shaarawy), Andrea Belotti (87' Tammy Abraham), Nicola Zalewski (81' Rick Karsdorp). Coach: José Mourinho.
Red Bull Salzburg: Philipp Köhn, Andreas Ulmer, Bernardo, Oumar Solet, Amar Dedic (74' Ignace Van Der Brempt), Nicolas Seiwald (75' Oscar Gloukh), Nicolás Capaldo (84' Sékou Koïta), Maurits Kjærgaard (46' Luka Sucic), Lucas Gourna-Douath, Noah Okafor, Junior Chikwubuike Adamu (74' Benjamin Sesko). Coach: Matthias Jaissle.
Goals: 33' Andrea Belotti 1-0, 40' Paulo Dybala 2-0.
Referee: Slavko Vincic (SVN)   Attendance: 62,593.

ROUND OF 16

09.03.23   Stadion An der Alten Försterei, Berlin:
Union Berlin – Union Saint-Gilloise 3-3 (1-1)
Union Berlin: Frederik Rønnow, Christopher Trimmel (77' Niko Gießelmann), Robin Knoche, Josip Juranovic, Diogo Leite, Danilho Doekhi, Rani Khedira, Janik Haberer (63' Aïssa Laïdouni), Morten Thorsby (77' Jamie Leweling), Kevin Behrens (64' Jordan Siebatcheu), Sheraldo Becker (77' Sven Michel). Coach: Urs Fischer.
Union Saint-Gilloise: Anthony Moris, Bart Nieuwkoop, Christian Burgess, Siebe Van Der Heyden, Ismaël Kandouss, Senne Lynen, Jean Lazare Amani (86' Cameron Puertas), Oussama El Azzouzi, Loïc Lapoussin, Yorbe Vertessen (80' Simon Adingra), Victor Boniface (86' Gustaf Nilsson). Coach: Karel Geraerts.
Goals: 28' Victor Boniface 0-1, 42' Josip Juranovic 1-1, 58' Yorbe Vertessen 1-2, 69' Robin Knoche 2-2, 72' Victor Boniface 2-3, 89' Sven Michel 3-3.
Referee: Orel Grindfeld (ISR)   Attendance: 21,605.

Robin Knoche missed a penalty kick (69').

09.03.23   BayArena, Leverkusen: Bayer Leverkusen – Ferencvárosi TC 2-0 (1-0)
Bayer Leverkusen: Lukás Hrádecký, Jonathan Tah, Jeremie Frimpong, Edmond Tapsoba, Odilon Kossounou, Piero Hincapié, Kerem Demirbay, Nadiem Amiri, Florian Wirtz (89' Patrik Schick), Sardar Azmoun (60' Amine Adli), Moussa Diaby (71' Adam Hlozek).
Coach: Xabi Alonso.
Ferencvárosi TC: Dénes Dibusz, Endre Botka (87' Henry Wingo), Eldar Civic, Myenty Abena, Mats Knoester, Bálint Vécsei, Anderson Esiti, Kristoffer Zachariassen, Adama Traoré (I) (87' Nikolai Baden Frederiksen), Ryan Mmaee, Marquinhos (78' Amer Gojak).
Coach: Stanislav Cherchesov.
Goals: 10' Kerem Demirbay 1-0, 86' Edmond Tapsoba 2-0.
Referee: Davide Massa (ITA)   Attendance: 25,001.

09.03.23   Estádio José Alvalade, Lisboa: Sporting CP – Arsenal 2-2 (1-1)
Sporting CP: Antonio Adán, Sebastián Coates, Ricardo Esgaio (76' Ousmane Diomande), Matheus Reis, Jerry St.Juste, Gonçalo Inácio, Pedro Gonçalves "Pote", Hidemasa Morita, Paulinho (76' Youssef Chermiti), Marcus Edwards (89' Abdul Issahaku Fatawu), Trincão (71' Nuno Santos). Coach: Rúben Amorim.
Arsenal: Matt Turner, Ben White, Jakub Kiwior (71' Gabriel Magalhães), William Saliba, Granit Xhaka, Jorginho (71' Thomas Partey), Oleksandr Zinchenko (63' Takehiro Tomiyasu), Bukayo Saka, Fábio Vieira, Reiss Nelson (71' Emile Smith Rowe), Gabriel Martinelli. Coach: Mikel Arteta.
Goals: 22' William Saliba 0-1, 34' Gonçalo Inácio 1-1, 55' Paulinho 2-1, 62' Hidemasa Morita 2-2 (og).
Referee: Tobias Stieler (GER)   Attendance: 36,006.

09.03.23   Stadio Olimpico, Roma: AS Roma – Real Sociedad 2-0 (1-0)
AS Roma: Rui Patrício, Chris Smalling, Diego Llorente (46' Marash Kumbulla), Rick Karsdorp, Gianluca Mancini, Nemanja Matic, Bryan Cristante, Lorenzo Pellegrini (60' Georginio Wijnaldum), Stephan El Shaarawy (60' Leonardo Spinazzola), Paulo Dybala (88' Edoardo Bove), Tammy Abraham (61' Andrea Belotti). Coach: José Mourinho.
Real Sociedad: Álex Remiro, Diego Rico, Andoni Gorosabel (83' Álex Sola), Robin Le Normand, David Silva (83' Beñat Turrientes), Illarramendi (75' Brais Méndez), Mikel Merino, Zubeldía, Martín Zubimendi, Takefusa Kubo (75' Mohamed Cho), Alexander Sørloth (67' Mikel Oyarzabal). Coach: Imanol Alguacil.
Goals: 13' Stephan El Shaarawy 1-0, 87' Marash Kumbulla 2-0.
Referee: Sandro Schärer (SUI)   Attendance: 61,608.

09.03.23   Estadio Ramón Sánchez Pizjuán, Sevilla: Sevilla FC – Fenerbahçe 2-0 (0-0)
Sevilla FC: Marko Dmitrovic, Jesús Navas, Alex Telles (46' Joan Jordán), Marcos Acuña (87' Suso), Tanguy Nianzou, Ivan Rakitic, Fernando, Nemanja Gudelj, Óliver Torres (70' Lucas Ocampos), Youssef En-Nesyri (87' Rafa Mir), Bryan Gil (70' Érik Lamela). Coach: Jorge Sampaoli.
Fenerbahçe: Altay Bayindir, Serdar Aziz, Samet Akaydin, Attila Szalai, Willian Arão, Irfan Kahveci (87' Arda Güler), Lincoln (82' Bright Osayi-Samuel), Miguel Crespo (67' Diego Rossi), Ferdi Kadioglu, Joshua King (67' Michy Batshuayi), Enner Valencia (82' João Pedro). Coach: Jorge Jesus.
Goals: 56' Joan Jordán 1-0, 85' Érik Lamela 2-0.
Referee: François Letexier (FRA)   Attendance: 24,480.

09.03.23   Allianz Stadium, Torino: FC Juventus – SC Freiburg 1-0 (0-0)
FC Juventus: Wojciech Szczesny, Danilo, Alex Sandro (23' Leonardo Bonucci), Bremer, Ángel Di María, Juan Cuadrado, Filip Kostic (78' Moise Kean), Adrien Rabiot, Manuel Locatelli, Fabio Miretti (46' Nicolò Fagioli), Dusan Vlahovic (67' Federico Chiesa). Coach: Massimiliano Allegri.
SC Freiburg: Mark Flekken, Lukas Kübler, Matthias Ginter, Christian Günter, Philipp Lienhart (68' Manuel Gulde), Kiliann Sildillia, Nicolas Höfler, Vincenzo Grifo, Maximilian Eggestein (59' Yannik Keitel), Roland Sallai (59' Ritsu Dōan), Lucas Höler (88' Michael Gregoritsch). Coach: Christian Streich.
Goal: 53' Ángel Di María 1-0.
Referee: Anastasios Sidiropoulos (GRE)   Attendance: 37,474.

09.03.23   Old Trafford, Manchester: Manchester United – Real Betis 4-1 (1-1)
Manchester United: David de Gea, Raphaël Varane, Luke Shaw (65' Tyrell Malacia), Diogo Dalot (46' Aaron Wan-Bissaka), Lisandro Martínez, Casemiro, Fred (81' Scott McTominay), Bruno Fernandes, Wout Weghorst, Marcus Rashford (65' Jadon Sancho), Antony (82' Facundo Pellistri). Coach: Erik ten Hag.
Real Betis: Claudio Bravo, Germán Pezzella, Youssouf Sabaly, Luiz Felipe, Abner Vinicius, Joaquín (59' Sergio Canales), William Carvalho, Guido Rodríguez (65' Andrés Guardado), Juanmi (80' Willian José), Ayoze Pérez (65' Borja Iglesias), Luiz Henrique (59' Aitor Ruibal). Coach: Manuel Pellegrini.
Goals: 6' Marcus Rashford 1-0, 32' Ayoze Pérez 1-1, 52' Antony 2-1, 58' Bruno Fernandes 3-1, 82' Wout Weghorst 4-1.
Referee: Daniel Siebert (GER)   Attendance: 72,998.

09.03.23   Stadion Wojska Polskiego, Warszawa (POL):
Shakhtar Donetsk – Feyenoord Rotterdam 1-1 (0-0)
Shakhtar Donetsk: Anatoliy Trubin, Yaroslav Rakitskyi, Mykola Matviyenko, Lucas Taylor, Taras Stepanenko, Dmytro Kryskiv (62' Neven Djurasek), Artem Bondarenko (90' Yegor Nazaryna), Georgiy Sudakov (90' Ivan Petryak), Oleksandr Zubkov (77' Marian Shved), Dmytro Topalov, Lassina Traoré (62' Kevin Kelsy). Coach: Igor Jovicevic.
Feyenoord Rotterdam: Timon Wellenreuther, Dávid Hancko, Lutsharel Geertruida, Marcus Pedersen (57' Gernot Trauner), Quilindschy Hartman, Sebastian Szymanski (72' Javairô Dilrosun), Orkun Kökçü, Mats Wieffer, Alireza Jahanbakhsh (86' Ezequiel Bullaude), Oussama Idrissi (72' Igor Paixão), Danilo. Coach: Arne Slot.
Goals: 79' Yaroslav Rakitskyi 1-0, 88' Ezequiel Bullaude 1-1).
Referee: Ivan Krusliak (SVK)   Attendance: 17,423.

16.03.23   Sükrü Saracoglu Stadium, Istanbul: Fenerbahçe – Sevilla FC 1-0 (1-0)
Fenerbahçe: Altay Bayindir, Serdar Aziz (84' Diego Rossi), Samet Akaydin, Attila Szalai, Jayden Oosterwolde, Miha Zajc (75' Mert Hakan Yandas), Ferdi Kadioglu, Ismail Yüksel, Arda Güler (84' Emre Mor), Enner Valencia (84' João Pedro), Michy Batshuayi (19' Joshua King). Coach: Jorge Jesus.
Sevilla FC: Marko Dmitrovic, Alex Telles, Marcos Acuña, Gonzalo Montiel (83' Jesús Navas), Loïc Badé, Ivan Rakitic (83' Joan Jordán), Fernando, Nemanja Gudelj, Óliver Torres (73' Suso), Rafa Mir (73' Lucas Ocampos), Youssef En-Nesyri (59' Érik Lamela).
Coach: Jorge Sampaoli.
Goal: 41' Enner Valencia 1-0 (p).
Referee: Michael Oliver (ENG)   Attendance: 44,775.

16.03.23   Europa-Park Stadion, Freiburg im Breisgau: SC Freiburg – FC Juventus 0-2 (0-1)
SC Freiburg: Mark Flekken, Manuel Gulde, Lukas Kübler, Matthias Ginter, Christian Günter (74' Npah Weißhaupt), Kiliann Sildillia, Nicolas Höfler, Maximilian Eggestein (46' Kenneth Schmidt), Michael Gregoritsch (74' Nils Petersen), Lucas Höler (62' Vincenzo Grifo), Ritsu Dōan (62' Roland Sallai). Coach: Christian Streich.
FC Juventus: Wojciech Szczesny, Danilo, Bremer, Federico Gatti, Juan Cuadrado (85' Mattia De Sciglio), Filip Kostic (70' Samuel Iling-Junior), Adrien Rabiot, Manuel Locatelli (84' Enzo Barrenechea), Nicolò Fagioli, Moise Kean (90+1' Matías Soulé), Dusan Vlahovic (70' Federico Chiesa). Coach: Massimiliano Allegri.
Goals: 45' Dusan Vlahovic 0-1 (p), 90+5' Federico Chiesa 0-2.
Referee: Serdar Gözübüyük (HOL)   Attendance: 33,420.
Send off: 44' Manuel Gulde.

16.03.23   Estadio Benito Villamarín, Sevilla: Real Betis – Manchester United 0-1 (0-0)
Real Betis: Rui Silva, Germán Pezzella, Youssouf Sabaly, Aitor Ruibal (59' Borja Iglesias), Édgar González, Abner Vinicius (26' Juan Miranda), Joaquín (59' Sergio Canales), William Carvalho, Guido Rodríguez (66' Andrés Guardado), Juanmi, Ayoze Pérez (59' Willian José). Coach: Manuel Pellegrini.
Manchester United: David de Gea, Harry Maguire, Tyrell Malacia, Aaron Wan-Bissaka (75' Diogo Dalot), Lisandro Martínez (75' Victor Lindelöf), Casemiro, Fred (60' Marcel Sabitzer), Bruno Fernandes (68' Anthony Elanga), Facundo Pellistri, Wout Weghorst, Marcus Rashford (60' Jadon Sancho). Coach: Erik ten Hag.
Goal: 56' Marcus Rashford 0-1.
Referee: Srdjan Jovanovic (SRB)   Attendance: 54,643.

16.03.23   De Kuip, Rotterdam: Feyenoord Rotterdam – Shakhtar Donetsk 7-1 (3-0)
Feyenoord Rotterdam: Timon Wellenreuther, Gernot Trauner, Dávid Hancko, Marcos López (57' Jacob Rasmussen), Lutsharel Geertruida, Sebastian Szymanski (58' Ezequiel Bullaude), Orkun Kökçü (68' Mo Taabouni), Santiago Giménez (57' Danilo). Coach: Arne Slot.
Shakhtar Donetsk: Anatoliy Trubin, Mykola Matviyenko, Bogdan Mykhailichenko, Valeriy Bondar, Yukhym Konoplya, Taras Stepanenko (54' Yegor Nazaryna), Dmytro Kryskiv (46' Neven Djurasek), Artem Bondarenko (54' Danylo Sikan), Georgiy Sudakov, Oleksandr Zubkov (63' Ivan Petryak), Lassina Traoré (54' Kevin Kelsy). Coach: Igor Jovicevic.
Goals: 9' Santiago Giménez 1-0, 24', 38' Orkun Kökçü 2-0, 3-0 (p), 49', 60' Oussama Idrissi 4-0, 5-0, 64' Alireza Jahanbakhsh 6-0, 66' Danilo 7-0, 87' Kevin Kelsy 7-1.
Referee: Jesús Gil Manzano (ESP)   Attendance: 37,500.

16.03.23   Lotto Park, Brussels: Union Saint-Gilloise – Union Berlin 3-0 (1-0)
Union Saint-Gilloise: Anthony Moris, Bart Nieuwkoop, Christian Burgess, Siebe Van Der Heyden, Ismaël Kandouss, Teddy Teuma (85' Oussama El Azzouzi), Senne Lynen, Jean Lazare Amani, Loïc Lapoussin, Victor Boniface (90+2' Casper Terho), Simon Adingra (67' Gustaf Nilsson). Coach: Karel Geraerts.
Union Berlin: Frederik Rønnow, Robin Knoche, Jérôme Roussillon (74' Christopher Trimmel), Josip Juranovic (74' Niko Gießelmann), Diogo Leite, Danilho Doekhi, Rani Khedira, Morten Thorsby (67' Jamie Leweling, Aïssa Laïdouni (56' Janik Haberer), Sheraldo Becker, Sven Michel (56' Jordan Siebatcheu). Coach: Urs Fischer.
Goals: 18' Teddy Teuma 1-0, 63' Jean Lazare Amani 2-0, 90+4' Loïc Lapoussin 3-0.
Referee: José María Sánchez Martínez (ESP)   Attendance: 15,681.
Send off: 80' Janik Haberer.

16.03.23   16.03.23   Puskás Aréna, Budapest: Ferencvárosi TC – Bayer Leverkusen 0-2 (0-1)
Ferencvárosi TC: Dénes Dibusz, Eldar Civic, Henry Wingo (14' Marquinhos, 90+1' Krisztián Lisztes), Myenty Abena, Mats Knoester, Bálint Vécsei, Anderson Esiti, Amer Gojak (78' Balász Manner), Kristoffer Zachariassen, Adama Traoré (I), Ryan Mmaee (90+1' Nikolai Baden Frederiksen). Coach: Stanislav Cherchesov.
Bayer Leverkusen: Lukás Hrádecký, Jonathan Tah, Jeremie Frimpong (82' Timothy Fosu-Mensah), Mitchel Bakker, Edmond Tapsoba, Piero Hincapié (82' Odilon Kossounou), Robert Andrich (86' Kerem Demirbay), Exequiel Palacios, Florian Wirtz (71' Amine Adli), Sardar Azmoun (71' Adam Hlozek), Moussa Diaby. Coach: Xabi Alonso.
Goals: 3' Moussa Diaby 0-1, 81' Amine Adli 0-2.
Referee: Artur Soares Dias (POR)   Attendance: 50,675.

16.03.23   Emirates Stadium, London: Arsenal – Sporting CP 1-1 (1-0,1-1) (AET)
Arsenal: Aaron Ramsdale, Takehiro Tomiyasu (9' Ben White), Gabriel Magalhães, William Saliba (21' Rob Holding), Granit Xhaka, Jorginho (65' Thomas Partey), Oleksandr Zinchenko, Fábio Vieira (101' Martin Ødegaard), Gabriel Jesus (46' Leandro Trossard), Reiss Nelson (66' Bukayo Saka), Gabriel Martinelli. Coach: Mikel Arteta.
Sporting CP: Antonio Adán, Ricardo Esgaio, Matheus Reis (94' Nuno Santos), Jerry St.Juste, Gonçalo Inácio, Ousmane Diomande, Manuel Ugarte, Pedro Gonçalves "Pote" (94' Dário Essugo), Paulinho (89' Youssef Chermiti), Marcus Edwards (119' Mateo Tanlongo), Trincão (105' Arthur Gomes). Coach: Rúben Amorim.
Goals: 19' Granit Xhaka 1-0, 62' Pedro Gonçalves "Pote" 1-1.
Referee: Antonio Mateu Lahoz (ESP)   Attendance: 59,929.
Send off: 118' Manuel Ugarte.

Sporting CP won on penalties after extra time (5:3).

Penalties: St. Juste 1-0, Ødegaard 1-1, Ricardo Esgaio 2-1, Saka 2-2, Gonçalo Inácio 3-2, Trossard 3-3, Arthur Gomes 4-3, Gabriel Martinelli missed, Nuno Santos 5-3.

16.03.23   Reale Arena, San Sebastián: Real Sociedad – AS Roma 0-0
Real Sociedad: Álex Remiro, Diego Rico, Andoni Gorosabel (72' Álex Sola), Robin Le Normand, David Silva, Brais Méndez (79' Mohamed Cho), Mikel Merino, Zubeldía, Martín Zubimendi, Alexander Sørloth (62' Carlos Fernández), Mikel Oyarzabal (71' Takefusa Kubo). Coach: Imanol Alguacil.
AS Roma: Rui Patrício, Chris Smalling, Leonardo Spinazzola, Rick Karsdorp (41' Nicola Zalewski), Gianluca Mancini, Ibañez, Georginio Wijnaldum, Bryan Cristante, Lorenzo Pellegrini (87' Edoardo Bove), Paulo Dybala (75' Stephan El Shaarawy), Andrea Belotti (76' Tammy Abraham). Coach: José Mourinho.
Referee: István Kovács (ROM)   Attendance: 35,054.
Send off: 90+9' Carlos Fernández.

QUARTER-FINALS

13.04.23   De Kuip, Rotterdam: Feyenoord Rotterdam – AS Roma 1-0 (0-0)
Feyenoord Rotterdam: Justin Bijlow, Gernot Trauner, Dávid Hancko, Lutsharel Geertruida, Quilindschy Hartman, Sebastian Szymanski, Orkun Kökçü, Mats Wieffer, Alireza Jahanbakhsh (72' Danilo), Oussama Idrissi (64' Igor Paixão), Santiago Giménez (83' Marcos López). Coach: Arne Slot.
AS Roma: Rui Patrício, Chris Smalling, Leonardo Spinazzola (84' Zeki Çelik), Gianluca Mancini, Ibañez, Nemanja Matic, Bryan Cristante, Lorenzo Pellegrini (46' Georginio Wijnaldum), Nicola Zalewski, Paulo Dybala (26' Stephan El Shaarawy), Tammy Abraham (58' Andrea Belotti). Coach: José Mourinho.
Goal: 53' Mats Wieffer 1-0.
Referee: José María Sánchez Martínez (ESP)   Attendance: 42,960.

Lorenzo Pellegrini missed a penalty kick (43').

13.04.23   Old Trafford, Manchester: Manchester United – Sevilla FC 2-2 (2-0)
Manchester United: David de Gea, Raphaël Varane (46' Harry Maguire), Tyrell Malacia, Aaron Wan-Bissaka, Lisandro Martínez, Casemiro, Marcel Sabitzer, Bruno Fernandes (62' Christian Eriksen), Anthony Martial (62' Wout Weghorst), Jadon Sancho (62' Anthony Elanga), Antony (81' Facundo Pellistri). Coach: Erik ten Hag.
Sevilla FC: Yassine Bounou "Bono", Marcos Acuña, Marcão, Gonzalo Montiel (90' Papu Gómez), Tanguy Nianzou (73' Suso), Ivan Rakitic, Fernando, Érik Lamela (66' Youssef En-Nesyri), Nemanja Gudelj, Lucas Ocampos, Óliver Torres (46' Jesús Navas).
Coach: José Luis Mendilíbar.
Goals: 14', 21' Marcel Sabitzer 1-0, 2-0, 84' Tyrell Malacia 2-1 (og), 90+2' Harry Maguire 2-2 (og).
Referee: Felix Zwayer (GER)   Attendance: 72,825.

13.04.23   Allianz Stadium, Torino: FC Juventus – Sporting CP 1-0 (0-0)
FC Juventus: Wojciech Szczesny (44' Mattia Perin), Danilo, Bremer, Federico Gatti, Ángel Di María (85' Paul Pogba), Juan Cuadrado, Filip Kostic (62' Nicolò Fagioli), Adrien Rabiot, Manuel Locatelli (85' Leandro Paredes), Arkadiusz Milik (62' Dusan Vlahovic), Federico Chiesa. Coach: Massimiliano Allegri.
Sporting CP: Antonio Adán, Sebastián Coates, Ricardo Esgaio (77' Héctor Bellerín), Jerry St.Juste (45+4' Ousmane Diomande), Gonçalo Inácio, Nuno Santos (62' Matheus Reis), Pedro Gonçalves "Pote", Hidemasa Morita, Marcus Edwards (77' Dário Essugo), Trincão, Youssef Chermiti (62' Arthur Gomes). Coach: Rúben Amorim.
Goal: 73' Federico Gatti 1-0.
Referee: Halil Umut Meler (TUR)   Attendance: 38,490.

13.04.23   BayArena, Leverkusen: Bayer Leverkusen – Union Saint-Gilloise 1-1 (0-0)
Bayer Leverkusen: Lukáš Hrádecký, Jonathan Tah, Jeremie Frimpong, Mitchel Bakker, Edmond Tapsoba, Piero Hincapié, Robert Andrich, Exequiel Palacios (46' Kerem Demirbay), Florian Wirtz, Moussa Diaby (87' Adam Hlozek), Amine Adli (67' Sardar Azmoun).
Coach: Xabi Alonso.
Union Saint-Gilloise: Anthony Moris, Bart Nieuwkoop, Christian Burgess, Siebe Van Der Heyden, Ismaël Kandouss, Teddy Teuma, Senne Lynen (80' Oussama El Azzouzi), Jean Lazare Amani, Loïc Lapoussin, Yorbe Vertessen (75' Cameron Puertas), Victor Boniface (89' Gustaf Nilsson). Coach: Karel Geraerts.
Goals: 51' Victor Boniface 0-1, 82' Florian Wirtz 1-1.
Referee: Ivan Kruzliak (SVK)   Attendance: 30,210.

20.04.23   Estadio Ramón Sánchez Pizjuán, Sevilla: Sevilla FC – Manchester United 3-0 (1-0)
Sevilla FC: Yassine Bounou "Bono", Jesús Navas, Marcos Acuña (85' Alex Telles), Marcão (29' Suso), Loïc Badé, Ivan Rakitic, Fernando, Érik Lamela (80' Bryan Gil), Nemanja Gudelj, Lucas Ocampos, Youssef En-Nesyri. Coach: José Luis Mendilíbar.
Manchester United: David de Gea, Victor Lindelöf, Harry Maguire, Diogo Dalot, Aaron Wan-Bissaka (46' Luke Shaw), Christian Eriksen (86' Anthony Elanga), Casemiro, Marcel Sabitzer (68' Fred), Anthony Martial (54' Wout Weghorst), Jadon Sancho (46' Marcus Rashford), Antony. Coach: Erik ten Hag.
Goals: Sevilla FC: 8' Youssef En-Nesyri 1-0, 47' Loïc Badé 2-0, 81' Youssef En-Nesyri 3-0.
Referee: Artur Soares Dias (POR)   Attendance: 41,974.

20.04.23   Estádio José Alvalade, Lisboa: Sporting CP – FC Juventus 1-1 (1-1)
Sporting CP: Antonio Adán, Sebastián Coates, Ricardo Esgaio, Gonçalo Inácio (81' Matheus Reis), Ousmane Diomande, Nuno Santos (87' Arthur Gomes), Manuel Ugarte, Pedro Gonçalves "Pote", Hidemasa Morita, Marcus Edwards, Trincão (81' Youssef Chermiti).
Coach: Rúben Amorim.
FC Juventus: Wojciech Szczesny, Danilo, Alex Sandro, Bremer (73' Federico Gatti), Ángel Di María, Juan Cuadrado, Adrien Rabiot, Manuel Locatelli, Fabio Miretti (72' Paul Pogba), Dusan Vlahovic (71' Arkadiusz Milik), Federico Chiesa (78' Filip Kostic).
Coach: Massimiliano Allegri.
Goals: 9' Adrien Rabiot 0-1, 20' Marcus Edwards 1-1 (p).
Referee: François Letexier (FRA)   Attendance: 45,903.

20.04.23   Lotto Park, Brussels: Union Saint-Gilloise – Bayer Leverkusen 1-4 (0-2)
Union Saint-Gilloise: Anthony Moris, Bart Nieuwkoop, Christian Burgess, Koki Machida, Ismaël Kandouss (46' Casper Terho), Teddy Teuma (87' Oussama El Azzouzi), Senne Lynen, Jean Lazare Amani (81' Cameron Puertas), Loïc Lapoussin, Yorbe Vertessen (32 Simon Adingra), Victor Boniface (81' Gustaf Nilsson). Coach: Karel Geraerts.
Bayer Leverkusen: Lukás Hrádecký, Jonathan Tah, Jeremie Frimpong (71' Amine Adli), Mitchel Bakker, Edmond Tapsoba (59' Odilon Kossounou), Piero Hincapié, Robert Andrich, Nadiem Amiri (59' Kerem Demirbay), Florian Wirtz, Moussa Diaby (86' Karim Bellarabi), Adam Hlozek (86' Sardar Azmoun). Coach: Xabi Alonso.
Goals: 2' Moussa Diaby 0-1, 37' Mitchel Bakker 0-2, 60' Jeremie Frimpong 0-3, 64' Casper Terho 1-3, 79' Adam Hlozek 1-4.
Referee: Antonio Mateu Lahoz (ESP)   Attendance: 17,069.

Union Saint-Gilloise played their home match at Lotto Park, Brussels instead of their regular stadium Joseph Marien Stadium, Brussels, which did not meet UEFA requirements.

20.04.23   Stadio Olimpico, Roma: AS Roma – Feyenoord Rotterdam 4-1 (0-0,2-1) (AET)
AS Roma: Rui Patrício, Chris Smalling (78' Zeki Çelik), Leonardo Spinazzola, Diego Llorente (72' Ibañez), Gianluca Mancini, Georginio Wijnaldum (21' Stephan El Shaarawy, 105' Marash Kumbulla), Nemanja Matic, Bryan Cristante, Lorenzo Pellegrini, Nicola Zalewski (73' Paulo Dybala), Andrea Belotti (73' Tammy Abraham). Coach: José Mourinho.
Feyenoord Rotterdam: Justin Bijlow, Gernot Trauner (105' Ezequiel Bullaude), Dávid Hancko, Lutsharel Geertruida, Quilindschy Hartman (105' Marcos López), Sebastian Szymanski (90' Marcus Pedersen), Orkun Kökçü, Mats Wieffer (105' Javairô Dilrosun), Alireza Jahanbakhsh (74' Danilo), Oussama Idrissi (64' Igor Paixão), Santiago Giménez (YC39,RC120).
Coach: Arne Slot.
Goals: 60' Leonardo Spinazzola 1-0, 80' Igor Paixão 1-1, 89' Paulo Dybala 2-1, 101' Stephan El Shaarawy 3-1, 109' Lorenzo Pellegrini 4-1.
Referee: Anthony Taylor (ENG)   Attendance: 66,742.

AS Roma won after extra time.

102

SEMI-FINALS

11.05.23   Allianz Stadium, Torino: FC Juventus – Sevilla FC 1-1 (0-1)
FC Juventus: Wojciech Szczesny, Leonardo Bonucci (61' Federico Gatti), Danilo, Alex Sandro, Ángel Di María (70' Paul Pogba), Juan Cuadrado, Filip Kostic (46' Samuel Iling-Junior), Adrien Rabiot, Manuel Locatelli, Fabio Miretti (46' Federico Chiesa), Dusan Vlahovic (61' Arkadiusz Milik). Coach: Massimiliano Allegri.
Sevilla FC: Yassine Bounou "Bono", Jesús Navas, Marcos Acuña, Loïc Badé, Ivan Rakitic, Fernando, Nemanja Gudelj, Lucas Ocampos (34' Gonzalo Montiel), Óliver Torres (74' Papu Gómez), Youssef En-Nesyri, Bryan Gil (82' Érik Lamela). (Coach: José Luis Mendilíbar).
Goals: 26' Youssef En-Nesyri 0-1, 90+7' Federico Gatti 1-1.
Referee: Daniel Siebert (GER)   Attendance: 34,816.

11.05.23   Stadio Olimpico, Roma: AS Roma – Bayer Leverkusen 1-0 (0-0)
AS Roma: Rui Patrício, Leonardo Spinazzola, Zeki Çelik, Gianluca Mancini, Ibañez, Nemanja Matic, Bryan Cristante, Lorenzo Pellegrini, Edoardo Bove (76' Georginio Wijnaldum), Andrea Belotti (77' Paulo Dybala), Tammy Abraham. Coach: José Mourinho.
Bayer Leverkusen: Lukás Hrádecký, Jonathan Tah, Jeremie Frimpong, Edmond Tapsoba, Odilon Kossounou (36' Mitchel Bakker), Piero Hincapié, Robert Andrich (90+2' Nadiem Amiri), Exequiel Palacios, Florian Wirtz, Moussa Diaby (72' Amine Adli), Adam Hlozek (72' Sardar Azmoun). Coach: Xabi Alonso.
Goal: 63' Edoardo Bove 1-0.
Referee: Michael Oliver (ENG)   Attendance: 63,123.

18.05.23   Estádio Ramón Sánchez Pizjuán, Sevilla:
Sevilla FC – FC Juventus 2-1 (0-0,0-0) (AET)
Sevilla FC: Yassine Bounou "Bono", Jesús Navas (107' Papu Gómez), Marcos Acuña, Loïc Badé, Ivan Rakitic, Fernando, Nemanja Gudelj, Lucas Ocampos (70' Érik Lamela), Óliver Torres (62' Suso, 118' Karim Rekik), Youssef En-Nesyri, Bryan Gil (100' Gonzalo Montiel). Coach: José Luis Mendilíbar.
FC Juventus: Wojciech Szczesny, Danilo, Bremer, Federico Gatti, Ángel Di María (64' Federico Chiesa), Juan Cuadrado (106' Arkadiusz Milik), Adrien Rabiot, Manuel Locatelli (86' Fabio Miretti), Nicolò Fagioli (41' Leandro Paredes), Moise Kean (63' Dusan Vlahovic), Samuel Iling-Junior (86' Filip Kostic). Coach: Massimiliano Allegri.
Goals: 65' Dusan Vlahovic 0-1, 71' Suso 1-1, 95' Érik Lamela 2-1.
Referee: Danny Makkelie (HOL)   Attendance: 42,186.
Send off: 115' Marcos Acuña.

Sevilla FC won after extra time.

18.05.23   BayArena, Leverkusen: Bayer Leverkusen – AS Roma 0-0
Bayer Leverkusen: Lukás Hrádecký, Jonathan Tah (86' Nadiem Amiri), Jeremie Frimpong, Mitchel Bakker (73' Amine Adli), Edmond Tapsoba, Piero Hincapié, Kerem Demirbay, Exequiel Palacios (80' Adam Hlozek), Florian Wirtz, Sardar Azmoun, Moussa Diaby. Coach: Xabi Alonso.
AS Roma: Rui Patrício, Leonardo Spinazzola (34' Nicola Zalewski), Zeki Çelik (78' Chris Smalling), Gianluca Mancini, Ibañez, Nemanja Matic, Bryan Cristante, Lorenzo Pellegrini, Edoardo Bove, Andrea Belotti (46' Georginio Wijnaldum), Tammy Abraham. Coach: José Mourinho.
Referee: Slavko Vincic (SVN)   Attendance: 30,210.

FINAL

31.05.23   Puskas Aréna, Budapest: Sevilla FC – AS Roma 1-1 (0-1,1-1) (AET)
Sevilla FC: Yassine Bounou "Bono", Alex Telles (95' Karim Rekik), Nemanja Gudelj (120+8' Marcão), Loïc Badé, Jesús Navas (95' Gonzalo Montiel), Ivan Rakitic, Fernando (120+9' Joan Jordán), Bryan Gil (46' Érik Lamela), Óliver Torres (46' Suso), Lucas Ocampos, Youssef En-Nesyri. Coach: José Luis Mendilíbar.
AS Roma: Rui Patrício, Gianluca Mancini, Chris Smalling, Ibañez, Zeki Çelik (90' Nicola Zalewski). Bryan Cristante, Nemanja Matic (120' Edoardo Bove), Leonardo Spinazzola (105' Diego Llorente), Paolo Dybala (68' Georginio Wijnaldum), Lorenzo Pellegrini (105' Stephan El Shaarawy),Tammy Abraham (75' Andrea Belotti). Coach: José Mourinho.
Goals: 34' Paolo Dybala 0-1, 55' Gianluca Mancini 1-1 (og).
Referee: Anthony Taylor (ENG)   Attendance: 61,476.

Sevilla FC won on penalties after extra time (4:1).

Penalties: Ocampos 1-0, Cristante 1-1, Lamela 2-1, Mancini missed, Rakitic 3-1, Ibañez missed, Montiel 4-1,

UEFA EUROPA LEAGUE
2023-2024

THIRD QUALIFYING ROUND

The winners of the ties will advance to the **Play-off Round**.

The losers will be transferred to the **UEFA Europa Conference League Play-off Round** of their respective path.

(Champions Path)

08.08.23   Astana Arena, Astana: FK Astana – PFC Ludogorets Razgrad 2-1 (1-1)
FK Astana: Josip Condric, Zarko Tomasevic, Abzal Beysebekov, Yan Vorogovskiy, Aleksandr Marochkin, Kamo Hovhannisyan, Fabien Ourega (61' Timur Dosmagambetov), Stjepan Loncar, Maks Ebong (75' Dusan Jovancic), Abat Aymbetov (61' Marin Tomasov), Dembo Darboe (84' Elkhan Astanov). Coach: Grigoriy Babayan.
PFC Ludogorets Razgrad: Sergio Padt, Marcel Heister (78' Spas Delev), Noah Sonko-Sundberg, Aslak Witry, Olivier Verdon, Franco Russo, Claude Gonçalves (57' Ivan Yordanov), Jakub Piotrowski (78' Pedro Naressi), Kiril Despodov (57' Dominik Yankov), Bernard Tekpetey (66' Caio Vidal), Rwan Cruz. Coach: Ivaylo Petev.
Goals: 34' Noah Sonko-Sundberg 0-1, 40' Zarko Tomasevic 1-1, 53' Aleksandr Marochkin 2-1.
Referee: Horatiu Fesnic (ROM)   Attendance: 23,967.

10.08.23   Vilniaus LFF stadionas, Vilnius: FK Zalgiris – BK Häcken 1-3 (0-1)
FK Zalgiris: Edvinas Gertmonas, Stipe Vucur, Mario Pavelic, Joël Bopesu, Nassim Hnid, Nicolás Gorobsov (71' Liviu Antal), Yuriy Kendysh, Oliver Buff (46' Yukiyoshi Karashima), Marko Milickovic (60' Arvydas Novikovas), Paulius Golubickas, Mathias Oyewusi. Coach: Vladimir Cheburin.
BK Häcken: Peter Abrahamsson, Even Hovland, Simon Sandberg (78' Tomas Totland), Johan Hammar, Kristoffer Lund, Mikkel Rygaard, Samuel Gustafson, Romeo Amané, Amor Layouni (90' Momodou Sonko), Ibrahim Sadiq (78' Tobias Sana), Srdjan Hrstic (77' Filip Trpcevski). Coach: Per-Mathias Høgmo.
Goals: 38', 47' Srdjan Hrstic 0-1, 0-2, 70' Mikkel Rygaard 0-3, 85' Nassim Hnid 1-3.
Referee: Mykola Balakin (UKR)   Attendance: 4,789.

10.08.23 Tofiq Bahramov adina Respublija stadionu, Baku:
  Qarabag FK – HJK Helsinki 2-1 (0-0)
Qarabag FK: Sahrudin Mahammadaliyev, Bahlul Mustafazade (90+2' Badavi Hüseynov), Kevin Medina, Yassine Benzia (71' Hamidou Keyta), Marko Jankovic, Abdellah Zoubir, Toral Bayramov (90+2' Maksim Medvedev), Elvin Cafarquliyev, Leandro Andrade (90+2' Patrick Andrade), Júlio Romão, Redon Xhixha (71' Juninho). Coach: Qurban Qurbanov.
HJK Helsinki: Jesse Öst, Jukka Raitala, Joona Toivio, Pyry Soiri (59' Tuomas Ollila), Miro Tenho, Kevin Kouassivi-Benissan, Atomu Tanaka (72' Filip Rogic), Lucas Lingman, Georgios Kanellopoulos (90+3' Përparim Hetemaj), Bojan Radulovic (72' Anthony Olusanya), Topi Keskinen (72' Santeri Hostikka). Coach: Toni Korkeakunnas.
Goals: 55' Leandro Andrade 1-0, 77' Anthony Olusanya 1-1, 85' Juninho 2-1.
Referee: Roi Reinshreiber (ISR)   Attendance: 24,984.

10.08.23 Bolshaya Sportivnaya Arena, Tiraspol:
  FC Sheriff Tiraspol – BATE Borisov 5-1 (2-0)
FC Sheriff Tiraspol: Maksim Koval, Gaby Kiki, Munashe Garananga, Ricardinho, Kostas Apostolakis (81' Didier Bueno), Alejandro Artunduaga, João Paulo, Cédric Badolo, Peter Ademo, Vinícius Paiva (64' Armel Zohouri), David Ankeye (71' Momo Yansane). Coach: Roberto Bordin.
BATE Borisov: Andrey Kudravets, Ruslan Khadarkevich, Vladislav Malkevich, Danila Nechaev, Sidi Bane, Valeriy Gromyko, Dmitri Podstrelov (46' Dmitri Antilevskiy), Artem Kontsevoy, Sead Islamovic (46' Denis Grechikho), Valeriy Bocherov, Denis Laptev. Coach: Kirill Alshevskiy.
Goals: 12' David Ankeye 1-0, 32' Cédric Badolo 2-0, 47' David Ankeye 3-0, 50' Sidi Bane 3-1, 90+3', 90+8' Momo Yansane 4-1, 5-1.
Referee: Mohammed Al-Hakim (SWE)   Attendance: 5,400.

10.08.23 Stadion pod Bijelim Brijegom, Mostar: Zrinjski Mostar – Breidablik 6-2 (5-0)
Zrinjski Mostar: Marko Maric, Mario Ticinovic, Slobodan Jakovljevic, Hrvoje Barisic (29' Matej Senic), Josip Corluka (85' Kerim Memija), Dario Canadjija, Antonio Ivancic, Mario Cuze (85' Ivan Jukic), Nemanja Bilbija, Tomislav Kis (66' Damir Zlomislic), Matija Malekinusic (66' Petar Misic). Coach: Krunoslav Rendulic.
Breidablik: Anton Ari Einarsson, Damir Muminovic, Höskuldur Gunnlaugsson, Viktor Örn Margeirsson, Andri Yeoman (65' Davíd Ingvarsson), Oliver Sigurjónsson, Gísli Eyjólfsson, Viktor Einarsson, Jason Dadi Svanthórsson (46' Klæmint Olsen), Anton Lúdvíksson, Kristinn Steindórsson (65' Ágúst Hlynsson). Coach: Óskar Hrafn Thorvaldsson.
Goals: 2' Tomislav Kis 1-0, 21' Matija Malekinusic 2-0, 30' Tomislav Kis 3-0, 33' Nemanja Bilbija 4-0, 40' Matija Malekinusic 5-0, 55' Antonio Ivancic 6-0, 64' Anton Lúdvíksson 6-1, 74' Gísli Eyjólfsson 6-2.
Referee: Nicholas Walsh (SCO)   Attendance: 6,200.
Sent off: 31' Viktor Einarsson.

17.08.23   Bolt Arena, Helsinki: HJK Helsinki – Qarabag FK 1-2 (1-1)
HJK Helsinki: Niki Mäenpää, Jukka Raitala, Joona Toivio, Miro Tenho (39' Aapo Halme), Kevin Kouassivi-Benissan, Tuomas Ollila (46' Matti Peltola), Lucas Lingman, Georgios Kanellopoulos (62' Përparim Hetemaj), Santeri Hostikka (46' Anthony Olusanya), Bojan Radulovic (62' Hassane Bandé), Topi Keskinen. Coach: Toni Korkeakunnas.
Qarabag FK: Sahrudin Mahammadaliyev, Bahlul Mustafazade (46' Badavi Hüseynov), Kevin Medina, Yassine Benzia (87' Patrick Andrade), Marko Jankovic, Abdellah Zoubir, Toral Bayramov (87' Maksim Medvedev), Elvin Cafarquliyev, Leandro Andrade (79' Nariman Axundzade), Júlio Romão, Redon Xhixha (73' Juninho). Coach: Qurban Qurbanov.
Goals: 10' Santeri Hostikka 1-0, 45+3' Toral Bayramov 1-1 (p), 55' Yassine Benzia 1-2.
Referee: Willy Delajod (FRA)   Attendance: 7,612.
Sent off: 16' Kevin Kouassivi-Benissan.

17.08.23   Bravida Arena, Göteborg: BK Häcken – FK Zalgiris 5-0 (1-0)
BK Häcken: Peter Abrahamsson, Even Hovland, Simon Sandberg, Johan Hammar, Kristoffer Lund, Mikkel Rygaard (79' Isak Brusberg), Samuel Gustafson, Romeo Amané (65' Pontus Dahbo), Amor Layouni (74' Tobias Sana), Ibrahim Sadiq (74' Momodou Sonko), Srdjan Hrstic (65' Ali Youssef). Coach: Per-Mathias Høgmo.
FK Zalgiris: Edvinas Gertmonas, Stipe Vucur, Mario Pavelic, Joël Bopesu, Nassim Hnid, Nicolás Gorobsov (74' Ovidijus Verbickas), Arvydas Novikovas (60' Romualdas Jansonas), Yuriy Kendysh (60' Yukiyoshi Karashima), Donatas Kazlauskas (74' Liviu Antal), Paulius Golubickas (86' Marko Milickovic), Mathias Oyewusi. Coach: Vladimir Cheburin.
Goals: 28' Srdjan Hrstic 1-0, 56' Samuel Gustafson 2-0, 63', 73' Ibrahim Sadiq 3-0, 4-0 (p), 90+2' Momodou Sonko 5-0.
Referee: António Nobre (POR)   Attendance: 3,926.
Sent off: 84' Mathias Oyewusi.

17.08.23   Kópavogsvöllur, Kópavogur: Breidablik – Zrinjski Mostar 1-0 (0-0)
Breidablik: Brynjar Atli Bragason, Damir Muminovic, Höskuldur Gunnlaugsson, Viktor Örn Margeirsson, Davíd Ingvarsson, Andri Yeoman (46' Klæmint Olsen), Oliver Sigurjónsson (82' Ágúst Thorsteinsson), Gísli Eyjólfsson, Jason Dadi Svanthórsson, Anton Lúdvíksson, Kristinn Steindórsson (64' Ágúst Hlynsson). Coach: Óskar Hrafn Thorvaldsson.
Zrinjski Mostar: Marko Maric, Mario Ticinovic (83' Kerim Memija), Slobodan Jakovljevic (79' Matej Senic), Hrvoje Barisic, Josip Corluka, Dario Canadjija, Antonio Ivancic, Mario Cuze, Nemanja Bilbija, Tomislav Kis (60' Mato Stanic), Matija Malekinusic (79' Franko Sabljic). Coach: Krunoslav Rendulic.
Goal: 55' Slobodan Jakovljevic 1-0 (og).
Referee: Anastasios Papapetrou (GRE)   Attendance: 673.

17.08.23   Városi-Stadion, Mezőkövesd (HUN):
BATE Borisov – FC Sheriff Tiraspol 2-2 (1-2)
BATE Borisov: Vyacheslav Dergachev, Ruslan Khadarkevich (82' Aleksandr Martynov), Danila Nechaev (76' Vladislav Malkevich), Sherif Jimoh, Sidi Bane, Sergey Volkov (65' Valeriy Gromyko), Denis Grechikho, Artem Kontsevoy, Valeriy Bocherov, Ilya Vasilevich (66' Dmitri Podstrelov), Aleksandr Shestyuk (46' Denis Laptev). Coach: Kirill Alshevskiy.
FC Sheriff Tiraspol: Maksim Koval, Gaby Kiki (54' Cristian Tovar), Munashe Garananga, Ricardinho (66' Momo Yansane), Kostas Apostolakis (54' Armel Zohouri), Alejandro Artunduaga, João Paulo, Cédric Badolo, Jerome Mbekeli (85' Dan-Angelo Botan), Peter Ademo, Luvannor (66' David Ankeye). Coach: Roberto Bordin.
Goals: 25' Artem Kontsevoy 1-0, 40' Ricardinho 1-1 (p), 45+2' Luvannor 1-2 (p), 90+4' Denis Laptev 2-2.
Referee: Tamás Bognár (HUN)   Attendance: behind closed doors.

Due to the country's involvement in the Russian invasion of Ukraine, Belarusian teams were required to play their home matches at neutral venues and behind closed doors until further notice.

17.08.23   Huvepharma Arena, Razgrad: PFC Ludogorets Razgrad – FK Astana 5-1 (1-1)
PFC Ludogorets Razgrad: Simon Sluga, Marcel Heister, Noah Sonko-Sundberg, Aslak Witry, Olivier Verdon (46' Igor Plastun), Claude Gonçalves (70' Pedro Naressi), Jakub Piotrowski, Ivan Yordanov, Kiril Despodov (78' Spas Delev), Bernard Tekpetey (78' Caio Vidal), Rwan Cruz (81' Matías Tissera). Coach: Ivaylo Petev.
FK Astana: Josip Condric, Zarko Tomasevic, Yan Vorogovskiy, Aleksandr Marochkin, Kamo Hovhannisyan, Fabien Ourega (80' Mikhail Gabyshev), Dusan Jovancic, Stjepan Loncar (62' Timur Dosmagambetov), Maks Ebong (62' Islambek Kuat), Abat Aymbetov (52' Marin Tomasov), Dembo Darboe (80' Abzal Beysebekov). Coach: Grigoriy Babayan.
Goals: 25' Bernard Tekpetey 1-0, 29' Dembo Darboe 1-1, 47' Jakub Piotrowski 2-1, 50' Bernard Tekpetey 3-1, 58' Jakub Piotrowski 4-1, 67' Kiril Despodov 5-1.
Referee: Anthony Taylor (ENG)   Attendance: 5,469.
Sent off: 77' Dusan Jovancic.

(Main Path)

10.08.23   Fortuna Arena, Praha: Slavia Praha – SK Dnipro-1 3-0 (2-0)
Slavia Praha: Ondrej Kolár, Oscar Dorley, Igoh Ogbu, Tomás Holes, Lukás Masopust, Lukás Provod, Ondrej Lingr (79' Petr Sevcík), Christos Zafeiris (90' Matej Jurásek), Ivan Schranz, Mick van Buren (79' Mojmír Chytil), Václav Jurecka (79' Conrad Wallem).
Coach: Jindrich Trpisovský.
SK Dnipro-1: Yakiv Kinareykin, Volodymyr Adamyuk, Oleksandr Svatok (46' Yevgeniy Pasich), Vasyl Kravets, Ruslan Babenko (61' Oleksandr Pikhalyonok), Maksym Tretyakov (11' Bogdan Lyednyev), Domingo Blanco, Oleksiy Gutsulyak, Valentyn Rubchynskyi (80' Bill), Eduard Sarapii, Oleksandr Filippov (80' Daniel Kiwinda). Coach: Oleksandr Kucher.
Goals: 5', 38' Ivan Schranz 1-0, 2-0, 81' Conrad Wallem 3-0.
Referee: Lawrence Visser (BEL)   Attendance: 19,102.
Sent off: 59' Igoh Ogbu.

10.08.23   Stadio Georgios Karaiskáki, Piraeus: Olympiakos Piraeus – KRC Genk 1-0 (1-0)
Olympiakos Piraeus: Alexandros Paschalakis, Rodinei, Quini, Nicolás Freire, Panagiotis Retsos, Iborra, Kostas Fortounis (76' Andreas Ndoj), João Carvalho (63' Sotirios Alexandropoulos), Georgios Masouras (76' Ayoub El Kaabi), Mady Camara (84' Marios Vrousai), Youssef El-Arabi (63' Pep Biel). Coach: Diego Martínez.
KRC Genk: Maarten Vandevoordt, Joris Kayembe (70' Gerardo Arteaga), Carlos Cuesta, Mark McKenzie, Daniel Muñoz, Patrik Hrosovský, Mike Trésor (80' Christopher Bonsu Baah), Bilal El Khannouss, Matías Galarza (66' Aziz Ouattara), Joseph Paintsil, Toluwalase Arokodare (66' Yira Sor). Coach: Wouter Vrancken.
Goal: 1' Kostas Fortounis 1-0.
Referee: Glenn Nyberg (SWE)   Attendance: 24,123.

17.08.23   Cegeka Arena, Genk: KRC Genk – Olympiakos Piraeus 1-1 (1-0)
KRC Genk: Maarten Vandevoordt, Joris Kayembe, Carlos Cuesta, Mark McKenzie (90+8' Luca Oyen), Daniel Muñoz, Patrik Hrosovský (90+8' Toluwalase Arokodare), Aziz Ouattara, Bilal El Khannouss, Joseph Paintsil, Yira Sor (90' Christopher Bonsu Baah), Alieu Fadera (70' Matías Galarza). Coach: Wouter Vrancken.
Olympiakos Piraeus: Alexandros Paschalakis, Rodinei, Quini, Nicolás Freire, Panagiotis Retsos, Iborra, Kostas Fortounis (90+8' Andreas Ndoj), João Carvalho (46' Sotirios Alexandropoulos), Georgios Masouras (68' Pep Biel), Mady Camara (80' Marios Vrousai), Ayoub El Kaabi (68' Youssef El-Arabi). Coach: Diego Martínez.
Goals: 30' Joseph Paintsil 1-0 (p), 90+5' Sotirios Alexandropoulos 1-1.
Referee: Tobias Stieler (GER)   Attendance: 11,998.
Sent off: 65' Joseph Paintsil, 90+10' Rodinei.

Joseph Paintsil missed a penalty kick (27').

17.08.23   Kosická furbalová aréna, Kosice (SVK): SK Dnipro-1 – Slavia Praha 1-1 (1-0)
SK Dnipro-1: Yakiv Kinareykin, Oleksandr Kaplienko, Vasyl Kravets (73' Oleksandr Svatok), Ruslan Babenko, Oleksandr Pikhalyonok (73' Bogdan Lyednyev), Oleksiy Gutsulyak, Yevgeniy Pasich, Sergiy Gorbunov (64' Daniel Kiwinda), Valentyn Rubchynskyi (77' Volodymyr Tanchyk), Eduard Sarapii, Oleksandr Filippov (64' Bill).
Coach: Oleksandr Kucher.
Slavia Praha: Ondrej Kolár, Oscar Dorley (85' Jakub Hromada), Aiham Ousou, Tomás Holes, Lukás Masopust (70' David Doudera), Petr Sevcík, Lukás Provod, Christos Zafeiris, Ivan Schranz (70' Tomás Vlcek), Mick van Buren (75' Mojmír Chytil), Václav Jurecka (85' Matej Jurásek). Coach: Jindrich Trpisovský.
Goals: 45+1' Valentyn Rubchynskyi 1-0, 52' Václav Jurecka 1-1.
Referee: Jesús Gil Manzano (ESP)   Attendance: 5,855.

Due to the Russian invasion of Ukraine, Ukrainian teams were required to play their home matches at neutral venues until further notice.

PLAY-OFF ROUND

The winners of the ties advanced to the Group Stage.
The losers were transferred to the UEFA Europa Conference League Group Stage.

24.08.23   Fortuna Arena, Praha: Slavia Praha – Zorya Luhansk 2-0 (0-0)
Slavia Praha: Ondrej Kolár, Tomás Vlcek, Tomás Holes, Lukás Masopust, Petr Sevcík, Lukás Provod (68' Bolu Ogungbayi), David Doudera (88' Conrad Wallem), Matej Jurásek (58' Mick van Buren), Christos Zafeiris, Ivan Schranz (57' Václav Jurecka), Mojmír Chytil (68' Muhamed Tijani). Coach: Jindrich Trpisovský.
Zorya Luhansk: Mykyta Turbaevskyi, Igor Kiryukhantsev (86' Danyil Alefirenko), Roman Vantukh, Igor Snurnitsyn, Jordan, Dmytro Myshnyov (46' Petar Micin), Kyrylo Dryshlyuk, Arseniy Batagov, Oleksandr Yatsyk (77' Vyacheslav Churko), Denys Antyukh (82' Igor Gorbach), Eduardo Guerrero (82' Vladyslav Bugay).
Coaches: Nenad Lalatovic & Mladen Bartulovic.
Goals: 81' Muhamed Tijani 1-0, 90+4' Lukás Masopust 2-0.
Referee: Kristo Tohver (EST)   Attendance: 18,522.

24.08.23   Bravida Arena, Göteborg: BK Häcken – Aberdeen FC 2-2 (1-0)
BK Häcken: Peter Abrahamsson, Even Hovland, Simon Sandberg (84' Tomas Totland), Johan Hammar, Valgeir Lunddal Fridriksson (84' Jacob Laursen), Mikkel Rygaard, Samuel Gustafson, Romeo Amané (63' Ishaq Abdulrazak), Amor Layouni (90+1' Franklin Tebo Uchenna), Ibrahim Sadiq, Srdjan Hrstic (63' Ali Youssef). Coach: Per-Mathias Høgmo.
Aberdeen FC: Kelle Roos, Nicky Devlin, Slobodan Rubezic, Jack MacKenzie, Graeme Shinnie, Dante Polvara (70' Jamie McGrath), Leighton Clarkson, Ryan Duncan (70' James McGarry), Bojan Miovski, Duk (80' Ester Sokler), Shayden Morris (63' Angus MacDonald).
Coach: Barry Robson.
Goals: 36' Amor Layouni 1-0, 69' Ibrahim Sadiq 2-0 (p), 75' Bojan Miovski 2-1, 79' Nicky Devlin 2-2.
Referee: Filip Glova (SVK)   Attendance: 4,424.
Sent off: 90' Johan Hammar.

24.08.23   Huvepharma Arena, Razgrad: PFC Ludogorets Razgrad – AFC Ajax 1-4 (0-3)
PFC Ludogorets Razgrad: Sergio Padt, Marcel Heister, Noah Sonko-Sundberg, Aslak Witry, Olivier Verdon, Claude Gonçalves (46' Dominik Yankov), Jakub Piotrowski, Ivan Yordanov (78' Pedro Naressi), Kiril Despodov (57' Spas Delev), Bernard Tekpetey (56' Caio Vidal), Rwan Cruz (65' Rick). Coach: Ivaylo Petev.
AFC Ajax: Jay Gorter, Owen Wijndal (79' Anass Salah-Eddine), Jakov Medic, Devyne Rensch, Jorrel Hato, Kenneth Taylor (73' Branco van den Boomen), Mohammed Kudus (90+1' Mika Godts), Benjamin Tahirovic, Steven Berghuis (72' Davy Klaassen), Steven Bergwijn, Brian Brobbey (46' Carlos Forbs). Coach: Maurice Steijn.
Goals: 16', 18' Mohammed Kudus 0-1, 0-2, 40' Brian Brobbey 0-3, 50' Mohammed Kudus 0-4, 70' Olivier Verdon 1-4 (p).
Referee: Marco Di Bello (ITA)   Attendance: 9,880.

24.08.23   Stadion Stozice, Ljubljana: Olimpija Ljubljana – Qarabag FK 0-2 (0-2)
Olimpija Ljubljana: Matevz Vidovsek, David Sualehe, Jorge Silva (84' Justas Lasickas), Ahmet Muhamedbegovic, Marcel Ratnik, Timi Elsnik, Agustin Doffo, Saar Fadida (59' Diogo Pinto), Svit Seslar (72' Nemanja Motika), Rui Pedro, Pedro Lucas (72' Mustafa Nukic). Coach: João Henriques.
Qarabag FK: Luka Gugeshashvili, Bahlul Mustafazade, Kevin Medina, Toral Bayramov (84' Adama Diakhaby), Elvin Cafarquliyev (88' Maksim Medvedev), Yassine Benzia (75' Matheus Silva), Marko Jankovic, Abdellah Zoubir, Leandro Andrade (75' Juninho), Júlio Romão, Redon Xhixha (84' Hamidou Keyta). Coach: Qurban Qurbanov.
Goals: 32' Kevin Medina 0-1, 44' Leandro Andrade 0-2.
Referee: Georgi Kabakov (BUL)   Attendance: 6,123.
Sent off: 90+5' David Sualehe.

24.08.23   Stadion Maksimir, Zagreb: Dinamo Zagreb – AC Sparta Praha 3-1 (1-1)
Dinamo Zagreb: Ivan Nevistic, Stefan Ristovski, Dino Peric (86' Bosko Sutalo), Sadegh Moharrami, Josip Misic, Luka Ivanusec (87' Bohdan Mykhaylichenko), Marko Bulat (76' Petar Sucic), Robert Ljubicic, Martin Baturina (65' Luka Stojkovic), Bruno Petkovic, Dario Spikic (65' Mahir Emreli). Coach: Sergej Jakirovic.
AC Sparta Praha: Peter Vindahl Jensen, Jaroslav Zelený (82' Matej Rynes), Asger Sørensen, Filip Panák, Tomás Wiesner, Lukás Sadílek (68' Qazim Laçi), Lukás Haraslín (62' Martin Minchev), Kaan Kairinen, Veljko Birmancevic (68' Jakub Pesek), Ladislav Krejcí (II), Victor Olatunji (62' Jan Kuchta). Coach: Brian Priske.
Goals: 39' Ladislav Krejcí 0-1 (p), 44' Dario Spikic 1-1, 59' Dino Peric 2-1, 61' Luka Ivanusec 3-1.
Referee: Marco Guida (ITA)   Attendance: 12,170.

24.08.23   Lotto Park, Brussels: Union Saint-Gilloise – FC Lugano 2-0 (1-0)
Union Saint-Gilloise: Anthony Moris, Christian Burgess, Koki Machida, Kevin Mac Allister, Mathias Rasmussen (66' Noah Sadiki), Jean Lazare Amani, Cameron Puertas, Charles Vanhoutte, Dennis Eckert Ayensa (66' Gustaf Nilsson), Loïc Lapoussin (90+1' Fedde Leysen), Casper Terho. Coach: Alexander Blessin.
FC Lugano: Amir Saipi, Kreshnik Hajrizi, Milton Valenzuela, Allan Arigoni (65' Jhon Espínoza), Albian Hajdari, Jonathan Sabbatini (76' Hadj Mahmoud), Renato Steffen, Anto Grgic, Uran Bislimi (77' Roman Macek), Mattia Bottani (76' Yanis Cimignani), Zan Celar (84' Shkelqim Vladi). Coach: Mattia Croci-Torti.
Goals: 8' Dennis Eckert Ayensa 1-0, 71' Casper Terho 2-0.
Referee: Enea Jorgji (ALB)   Attendance: 7,238.

Union Saint-Gilloise played their home match at the Lotto Park in Brussels, instead of their regular stadium the Joseph Marien Stadium in Brussels, which did not meet the UEFA requirements.

24.08.23   Stadión Tehelné pole, Bratislava: Slovan Bratislava – Aris Limassol 2-1 (1-0)
Slovan Bratislava: Milan Borjan, Kevin Wimmer, Kenan Bajric, Lucas Lovat, César Blackman, Juraj Kucka, Jan Kankava, Marko Tolic (88' Kyriakos Savvadis), Nino Marcelli (78' Sharani Zuberu), Dávid Strelec (67' Tigran Barseghyan), Malik Abubakari (88' Vladimír Weiss). Coach: Vladimir Weiss.
Aris Limassol: Vaná, Steeve Yago, Caju, Eric Boakye, Alex Moucketou-Moussounda (46' Franz Brorsson), Július Szöke (77' Morgan Brown), Leo Bengtsson (63' Mariusz Stepinski), Karol Struski (46' Veljko Nikolic), Shavy Warren Babicka (35' Jaden Montnor), Mihlali Mayambela, Yannick Gomis. Coach: Aleksey Shpilevski.
Goals: 34' Marko Tolic 1-0, 57' Dávid Strelec 2-0, 73' Mihlali Mayambela 2-1.
Referee: William Collum (SCO)   Attendance: 17,564.

24.08.23   Tórsvøllur, Tórshavn: KÍ Klaksvík – FC Sheriff Tiraspol 1-1 (0-0)
KÍ Klaksvík: Jonatan Johansson, Odmar Færø, Vegard Forren, Heini Vatnsdal, Patrick Da Silva, Jóannes Danielsen, Árni Frederiksberg, Luc Kassi (77' Mads Mikkelsen), Deni Pavlovic (81' Latif Isaak Ahmed), Jákup Andreasen, Sivert Gussiås (67' Hallur Hánsson).
Coach: Magne Hoseth.
FC Sheriff Tiraspol: Maksim Koval, Cristian Tovar, Gaby Kiki, Armel Zohouri, Munashe Garananga, Alejandro Artunduaga, João Paulo (63' Ricardinho), Cédric Badolo, Jerome Mbekeli, Peter Ademo, David Ankeye (63' Luvannor). Coach: Roberto Bordin.
Goals: 52' Patrick Da Silva 1-0, 73' Jerome Mbekeli 1-1.
Referee: Rade Obrenovic (SVN)   Attendance: 3,413.

KÍ Klaksvík played their home match at the Tórsvøllor in Tórshavn, instead of their regular stadium the Vid Djúpumý in Klaksvík, which did not meet the UEFA requirements.

24.08.23   Stadio Georgios Karaiskáki, Piraeus:
           Olympiakos Piraeus – FK Cukaricki Stankom 3-1 (3-0)
Olympiakos Piraeus: Alexandros Paschalakis, Quini, Nicolás Freire, Panagiotis Retsos (70' Jackson Porozo), Iborra, Kostas Fortounis, Pep Biel (83' Sotirios Alexandropoulos), Georgios Masouras (59' Gustavo Scarpa), Mady Camara (59' Santiago Hezze), Marios Vrousai, Ayoub El Kaabi (71' Youssef El-Arabi). Coach: Diego Martínez.
FK Cukaricki Stankom: Filip Samurovic, Miladin Stevanovic, Nemanja Tosic, Uros Drezgic, Viktor Rogan (46' Bojica Nikcevic), Luka Subotic, Stefan Kovac (46' Marko Docic), Sambou Sissoko, Nikola Stankovic (69' Igor Miladinovic), Ibrahima N'Diaye (46' Aleksa Jankovic), Djordje Ivanovic (86' Zé Mário Gomes). Coach: Igor Matic.
Goals: 3' Ayoub El Kaabi 1-0, 15' Kostas Fortounis 2-0, 40' Ayoub El Kaabi 3-0, 90+3' Igor Miladinovic 3-1.
Referee: Donatas Rumsas (LTU)   Attendance: 24,332.

24.08.23   Raiffeisen Arena, Linz: LASK Linz – Zrinjski Mostar 2-1 (2-0)
LASK Linz: Tobias Lawal, Philipp Ziereis, René Renner, Felix Luckeneder, Andrés Andrade, Robert Zulj, Branko Jovicic (70' Maksym Talovyerov), Sascha Horvath (80' Ivan Ljubic), Florian Flecker (70' Sanoussy Ba), Ibrahim Mustapha (53' Lenny Pintor), Moses Usor (53' Thomas Goiginger). Coach: Thomas Sageder.
Zrinjski Mostar: Marko Maric, Mario Ticinovic (82' Kerim Memija), Josip Corluka, Matej Senic, Ivica Batarelo, Dario Canadjija, Antonio Ivancic (67' Tomislav Kis), Mario Cuze (53' Ivan Jukic), Tarik Ramic (46' Mato Stanic), Nemanja Bilbija, Matija Malekinusic (67' Franko Sabljic). Coach: Krunoslav Rendulic.
Goals: 4', 12' Robert Zulj 1-0, 2-0, 71' Nemanja Bilbija 2-1.
Referee: Orel Grinfeld (ISR)   Attendance: 8,300.

31.08.23   Tofiq Bahramov adina Respublika stadionu, Baku:
Qarabag FK – Olimpija Ljubljana 1-1 (1-1)
Qarabag FK: Luka Gugeshashvili, Bahlul Mustafazade, Kevin Medina, Toral Bayramov (89' Richard Almeyda), Elvin Cafarquliyev, Yassine Benzia (82' Matheus Silva), Marko Jankovic (90' Hamidou Keyta), Abdellah Zoubir, Leandro Andrade, Júlio Romão, Redon Xhixha (66' Juninho). Coach: Qurban Qurbanov.
Olimpija Ljubljana: Matevz Vidovsek, Aljaz Krefl, Jorge Silva (77' Justas Lasickas), Mateo Karamatic, Marcel Ratnik, Timi Elsnik, Agustin Doffo, Diogo Pinto (77' Admir Bristric), Rui Pedro (66' Saar Fadida), Pedro Lucas (66' Mustafa Nukic), Nemanja Motika (54' Ivan Posavec). Coach: João Henriques.
Goals: 24' Toral Bayramov 1-0 (p), 36' Diogo Pinto 1-1.
Referee: Alejandro Hernández Hernández (ESP)   Attendance: 27,354.

31.08.23   Arena Lublin, Lublin (POL): Zorya Luhansk – Slavia Praha 2-1 (2-0)
Zorya Luhansk: Mykyta Turbaevskyi, Igor Kiryukhantsev, Roman Vantukh, Igor Snurnitsyn, Jordan, Dmytro Myshnyov (80' Vyacheslav Churko), Arseniy Batagov, Oleksandr Yatsyk (46' Kyrylo Dryshlyuk), Denys Antyukh (80' Igor Gorbach), Eduardo Guerrero, Danyil Alefirenko (67' Vikentii Voloshyn). Coach: Mladen Bartulovic.
Slavia Praha: Ondrej Kolár, Oscar Dorley, Tomás Vlcek, Igoh Ogbu (46' Petr Sevcík), Tomás Holes, Lukás Masopust, Lukás Provod (80' Michal Tomic), David Doudera (46' Matej Jurásek), Christos Zafeiris, Ivan Schranz (73' Muhamed Tijani), Mick van Buren (56' Václav Jurecka). Coach: Jindrich Trpisovský.
Goals: 32' Danyil Alefirenko 1-0, 41' Denys Antyukh 2-0, 83' Matej Jurásek 2-1.
Referee: Jérôme Brisard (FRA)   Attendance: 964.

Due to the Russian invasion of Ukraine, Ukrainian teams were required to play their home matches at neutral venues until further notice.

31.08.23   Bolshaya Sportivnaya Arena, Tiraspol: FC Sheriff Tiraspol – KÍ Klaksvík 2-1 (1-1)
FC Sheriff Tiraspol: Maksim Koval, Cristian Tovar, Gaby Kiki, Armel Zohouri, Munashe Garananga, Alejandro Artunduaga (61' Kostas Apostolakis), João Paulo, Cédric Badolo (62' Ricardinho), Jerome Mbekeli (90+4' David Ankeye), Peter Ademo, Luvannor (85' Momo Yansane). Coach: Roberto Bordin.
KÍ Klaksvík: Jonatan Johansson, Odmar Færø, Vegard Forren (21' Børge Petersen), Heini Vatnsdal, Patrick Da Silva, Jóannes Danielsen, Árni Frederiksberg, René Joensen (75' Sivert Gussiâs), Luc Kassi (75' Mads Mikkelsen), Deni Pavlovic (63' Hallur Hánsson), Jákup Andreasen. Coach: Magne Hoseth.
Goals: 16' Luvannor 1-0 (p), 34' Luc Kassi 1-1, 74' Armel Zohouri 2-1.
Referee: Halil Umut Meler (TUR)   Attendance: 5,493.

31.08.23   Alphamega Stadium, Kolossi: Aris Limassol – Slovan Bratislava 6-2 (3-1)
Aris Limassol: Vaná, Steeve Yago, Caju, Franz Brorsson (79' Slobodan Urosevic), Eric Boakye (62' Morgan Brown), Július Szöke, Karol Struski, Mariusz Stepinski (62' Alex Moucketou-Moussounda), Mihlali Mayambela, Yannick Gomis (79' Shavy Warren Babicka), Jaden Montnor (46' Leo Bengtsson). Coach: Aleksey Shpilevski.
Slovan Bratislava: Milan Borjan, Kevin Wimmer, Kenan Bajric, Lucas Lovat (70' Matús Vojtko), César Blackman, Juraj Kucka, Jaba Kankava, Marko Tolic (58' Malik Abubakari), Nino Marcelli (58' Tigran Barseghyan), Dávid Strelec (70' Filip Lichý), Sharani Zuberu (58' Aleksandar Cavric). Coach: Vladimir Weiss.
Goals: 21' Yannick Gomis 1-0, 24' Július Szöke 2-0, 37' Dávid Strelec 2-1,
45+7', 51' Yannick Gomis 3-1, 4-1, 66' Mihlali Mayambela 5-1, 72' Morgan Brown 6-1, 88' Tigran Barseghyan 6-2.
Referee: Erik Lambrechts (BEL)   Attendance: 2,872.

31.08.23   epet ARENA, Praha: AC Sparta Praha – Dinamo Zagreb 4-1 (2-0)
AC Sparta Praha: Peter Vindahl Jensen, Asger Sørensen, Filip Panák, Tomás Wiesner (85' Jakub Pesek), Qazim Laçi (68' Lukás Sadílek), Lukás Haraslín (63' Veljko Birmancevic), Kaan Kairinen, Ladislav Krejcí (II), Matej Rynes (63' Jaroslav Zelený), Jan Kuchta (84' Adam Karabec), Victor Olatunji. Coach: Brian Priske.
Dinamo Zagreb: Ivan Nevistic, Stefan Ristovski, Dino Peric, Sadegh Moharrami (46' Bosko Sutalo), Josip Misic, Marko Bulat (89' Josip Drmic), Robert Ljubicic, Martin Baturina, Bruno Petkovic, Dario Spikic (73' Mahir Emreli), Antonio Marin (46' Bohdan Mykhaylichenko). Coach: Sergej Jakirovic.
Goals: 2' Lukás Haraslín 1-0, 24' Asger Sørensen 2-0, 67' Filip Panák 3-0,
71' Martin Baturina 3-1, 87' Victor Olatunji 4-1.
Referee: Tobias Stieler (GER)   Attendance: 17,953.

31.08.23   Gradski stadion Dubocica, Leskovac:
            FK Cukaricki Stankom – Olympiakos Piraeus 0-3 (0-2)
FK Cukaricki Stankom: Filip Samurovic, Miladin Stevanovic, Nemanja Tosic, Uros Drezgic (81' Vojin Serafimovic), Luka Subotic, Bojica Nikcevic, Sambou Sissoko, Nikola Stankovic (78' Stefan Kovac), Igor Miladinovic (65' Mattéo Ahlinvi), Djordje Ivanovic (78' Samuel Owusu), Aleksa Jankovic (46' Zé Mário Gomes). Coach: Igor Matic.
Olympiakos Piraeus: Alexandros Paschalakis, Rodinei, Nicolás Freire, Panagiotis Retsos (57' Jackson Porozo), Kostas Fortounis (58' Gustavo Scarpa), Pep Biel, Georgios Masouras (68' João Carvalho), Mady Camara (46' Sotirios Alexandropoulos), Santiago Hezze, Marios Vrousai, Ayoub El Kaabi (46' Youssef El-Arabi). Coach: Diego Martínez.
Goals: 34' Georgios Masouras 0-1, 45+1' Pep Biel 0-2, 52' Panagiotis Retsos 0-3.
Referee: Danny Makkelie (HOL)   Attendance: 6,812.

FK Cukaricki Stankom played their home match at the Gradski stadion Dubocica in Leskovac, instead of their regular stadium the Cukaricki Stadium in Beograd, which did not meet the UEFA requirements.

31.08.23   Johan Cruijff Arena, Amsterdam: AFC Ajax – PFC Ludogorets Razgrad 0-1 (0-0)
AFC Ajax: Jay Gorter, Owen Wijndal (81' Anass Salah-Eddine), Jakov Medic, Devyne Rensch, Jorrel Hato, Branco van den Boomen (46' Davy Klaassen), Kenneth Taylor, Benjamin Tahirovic, Steven Bergwijn (72' Mika Godts), Brian Brobbey, Carlos Forbs (59' Steven Berghuis). Coach: Maurice Steijn.
PFC Ludogorets Razgrad: S Sluga, Marcel Heister, Noah Sonko-Sundberg, Aslak Witry, Olivier Verdon, Claude Gonçalves, Jakub Piotrowski (81' Pedro Naressi), Ivan Yordanov (60' Dominik Yankov), Bernard Tekpetey (81' Spas Delev), Caio Vidal (67' Rick), Rwan Cruz (46' Matías Tissera). Coach: Ivaylo Petev.
Goal: 62' Matías Tissera 0-1.
Referee: Ivan Kruzliak (SVK)   Attendance: 50,900.

31.08.23   Stade de Genève, Lancy: FC Lugano – Union Saint-Gilloise 0-1 (0-1)
FC Lugano: Steven Deana, Kreshnik Hajrizi (52' Lukas Mai), Milton Valenzuela, Allan Arigoni (46' Jhon Espínoza), Albian Hajdari, Jonathan Sabbatini, Roman Macek (46' Ignacio Aliseda), Uran Bislimi, Hadj Mahmoud (46' Anto Grgic), Mattia Bottani (74' Yanis Cimignani), Zan Celar. Coach: Mattia Croci-Torti.
Union Saint-Gilloise: Anthony Moris, Christian Burgess, Koki Machida, Kevin Mac Allister, Noah Sadiki (85' Elton Kabangu), Jean Lazare Amani (77' Nathan Huygevelde), Cameron Puertas (65' Mathias Rasmussen), Charles Vanhoutte, Dennis Eckert-Ayensa (65' Gustaf Nilsson), Loïc Lapoussin (77' Henok Teklab), Casper Terho. Coach: Alexander Blessin.
Goal: 6' Dennis Eckert-Ayensa 0-1.
Referee: Harm Osmers (GER)   Attendance: 1,171.
Sent off: 90+3' Albian Hajdari.

FC Lugano played their home match at the Stade de Genève in Lancy, instead of their regular stadium the Cornaredo Stadium in Lugano, which did not meet the UEFA requirements.

31.08.23   Pittodrie Stadium, Aberdeen: Aberdeen FC – BK Häcken 1-3 (0-2)
Aberdeen FC: Kelle Roos, Nicky Devlin, Richard Jensen, James McGarry (73' Ryan Duncan), Slobodan Rubezic, Graeme Shinnie, Jamie McGrath (78' Ester Sokler), Leighton Clarkson, Bojan Miovski, Duk, Shayden Morris (88' Jonny Hayes). Coach: Barry Robson.
BK Häcken: Peter Abrahamsson, Even Hovland, Simon Sandberg (90+6' Tomas Totland), Valgeir Lunddal Fridriksson (61' Jacob Laursen), Franklin Tebo Uchenna, Mikkel Rygaard, Samuel Gustafson, Romeo Amané, Amor Layouni, Ibrahim Sadiq, Srdjan Hrstic. Coach: Per-Mathias Høgmo.
Goals: 14', 41' Ibrahim Sadiq 0-1, 0-2, 55' Bojan Miovski 1-2 (p), 81' Amor Layouni 1-3 (p).
Referee: Daniel Siebert (GER)   Attendance: 19,237.

31.08.23   Stadion pod Bijeli Brijeg, Mostar: Zrinjski Mostar – LASK Linz 1-1 (1-0)
Zrinjski Mostar: Marko Maric, Mario Ticinovic, Hrvoje Barisic, Josip Corluka (87' Kerim Memija), Matej Senic, Dario Canadjija, Ivan Jukic (56' Tomislav Kis), Antonio Ivancic (80' Damir Zlomislic), Mario Cuze (90' Aldin Hrvanovic), Nemanja Bilbija, Matija Malekinusic (56' Franko Sabljic). Coach: Krunoslav Rendulic.
LASK Linz: Tobias Lawal, Philipp Ziereis, René Renner, Felix Luckeneder, Andrés Andrade, Robert Zulj, Branko Jovicic (81' Ivan Ljubic), Sascha Horvath, Florian Flecker, Ibrahim Mustapha (65' Elias Havel), Moses Usor (46' Marin Ljubicic). Coach: Thomas Sageder.
Goals: 38' Nemanja Bilbija 1-0 (p), 52' Branko Jovicic 1-1.
Referee: Tiago Martins (POR)   Attendance: 6,520.

GROUP STAGE

The group winners advanced to the Round of 16
The second-placed team in the group advanced to the Knockout Round Play-offs
The third-placed team in the group transferred to the UEFA Europa Conference League

GROUP A

West Ham United	6	5	0	1	10	-	4	15
SC Freiburg	6	4	0	2	17	-	7	12
Olympiakos Piraeus	6	2	1	3	11	-	14	7
TSC Backa Topola	6	0	1	5	6	-	19	1

GROUP B

Brighton & Hove Albion	6	4	1	1	10	-	5	13
Olympique Marseille	6	3	2	1	14	-	10	11
AFC Ajax	6	1	2	3	10	-	13	5
AEK Athens	6	1	1	4	6	-	12	4

GROUP C

Glasgow Rangers FC	6	3	2	1	8	-	6	11
AC Sparta Praha	6	3	1	2	9	-	7	10
Real Betis	6	3	0	3	9	-	7	9
Aris Limassol	6	1	1	4	7	-	13	4

GROUP D

Atalanta Bergamo	6	4	2	0	12	-	4	14
Sporting CP	6	3	2	1	10	-	6	11
Sturm Graz	6	1	1	4	4	-	9	4
Raków Częstochowa	6	1	1	4	3	-	10	4

GROUP E

Liverpool FC	6	4	0	2	17	-	7	12
Toulouse FC	6	3	2	1	8	-	9	11
Union Saint-Gilloise	6	2	2	2	5	-	8	8
LASK Linz	6	1	0	5	6	-	12	3

GROUP F

Villarreal CF	6	4	1	1	9	-	7	13
Stade Rennais	6	4	0	2	13	-	6	12
Maccabi Haifa	6	1	2	3	3	-	9	5
Panathinaikos	6	1	1	4	7	-	10	4

GROUP G								
Slavia Praha	6	5	0	1	17	-	4	15
AS Roma	6	4	1	1	12	-	4	13
Servette FC	6	1	2	3	4	-	13	5
FC Sheriff Tiraspol	6	0	1	5	5	-	17	1
GROUP H								
Bayer Leverkusen	6	6	0	0	19	-	3	18
Qarabag FK	6	3	1	2	7	-	9	10
Molde FK	6	2	1	3	12	-	12	7
BK Häcken	6	0	0	6	3	-	17	6

GROUP A

21.09.23   London Stadium, London: West Ham United – TSC Backa Topola 3-1 (0-0)
West Ham United: Lukasz Fabianski, Angelo Ogbonna, Aaron Cresswell (46' Emerson), Thilo Kehrer, Konstantinos Mavropanos, James Ward-Prowse, Pablo Fornals (61' Michail Antonio), Lucas Paquetá (86' Maxwel Cornet), Mohammed Kudus, Danny Ings (76' Tomás Soucek), Saïd Benrahma. Coach: David Moyes.
TSC Backa Topola: Nikola Simic, Goran Antonic, Nemanja Petrovic (81' Marko Rakonjac), Milos Cvetkovic, Nemanja Stojic, Mateja Djordjevic (69' Vukasin Krstic), Milán Rádin, Nikola Kuveljic (80' Milos Vulic), Ifet Djakovac (80' Aleksandar Cirkovic), Petar Stanic, Sasa Jovanovic (90+2' Martin Mircevski). Coach: Zarko Lazetic.
Goals: 47' Petar Stanic 0-1, 66', 70' Mohammed Kudus 1-1, 2-1, 82' Tomás Soucek 3-1.
Referee: Filip Glova (SVK)   Attendance: 41,374.

21.09.23   Stadio Georgios Karaiskáki, Piraeus: Olympiakos Piraeus – SC Freiburg 2-3 (1-2)
Olympiakos Piraeus: Alexandros Paschalakis, Rodinei, Nicolás Freire, Panagiotis Retsos, Francisco Ortega (78' Quini), Kostas Fortounis (78' Ola Solbakken), Pep Biel (46' Daniel Podence), Georgios Masouras (61' Stevan Jovetic), Mady Camara, Santiago Hezze (24' Iborra), Ayoub El Kaabi. Coach: Diego Martínez.
SC Freiburg: Noah Atubolu, Lukas Kübler, Matthias Ginter, Philipp Lienhart, Kenneth Schmidt (55' Kiliann Sildillia), Nicolas Höfler, Vincenzo Grifo (76' Noah Weißhaupt), Maximilian Eggestein, Roland Sallai (76' Maximilian Philipp), Ritsu Dōan (90+2' Junior Adamu), Lucas Höler (90+2' Yannik Keitel). Coach: Christian Streich.
Goals: 9' Roland Sallai 0-1, 40' Ayoub El Kaabi 1-1, 45+7' Vincenzo Grifo 1-2 (p), 74' Ayoub El Kaabi 2-2, 86' Maximilian Philipp 2-3.
Referee: Allard Lindhout (HOL)   Attendance: 30,056.

05.10.23   Europa-Park Stadion, Freiburg im Breisgau:
         SC Freiburg – West Ham United 1-2 (0-1)
SC Freiburg: Noah Atubolu, Lukas Kübler (76' Noah Weißhaupt), Matthias Ginter, Philipp Lienhart, Kiliann Sildillia, Nicolas Höfler, Vincenzo Grifo (87' Maximilian Breunig), Maximilian Eggestein (76' Merlin Röhl), Roland Sallai, Lucas Höler (76' Maximilian Philipp), Junior Adamu (46' Ritsu Dōan). Coach: Christian Streich.
West Ham United: Lukasz Fabianski, Vladimír Coufal, Thilo Kehrer (71' Emerson), Nayef Aguerd, Konstantinos Mavropanos, James Ward-Prowse (90' Danny Ings), Pablo Fornals (71' Tomás Soucek), Lucas Paquetá (90' Divin Mubama), Edson Álvarez, Mohammed Kudus (80' Saïd Benrahma), Jarrod Bowen). Coach: David Moyes.
Goals: 8' Lucas Paquetá 0-1, 49' Roland Sallai 1-1, 66' Nayef Aguerd 1-2.
Referee: Mohammed Al-Hakim (SWE)   Attendance: 34,100.

05.10.23   TSC Arena, Backa Topola: TSC Backa Topola – Olympiakos Piraeus 2-2 (0-1)
TSC Backa Topola: Veljko Ilic, Goran Antonic (79' Milos Vulic), Nemanja Petrovic, Milos Cvetkovic, Josip Calusic, Nemanja Stojic, Milán Rádin (88' Martin Mircevski), Ifet Djakovac, Petar Stanic (79' Milos Pantovic), Sasa Jovanovic (87' Bence Sós), Marko Rakonjac (90+3' Jovan Vlalukin). Coach: Zarko Lazetic.
Olympiakos Piraeus: Alexandros Paschalakis, Rodinei, Quini, Panagiotis Retsos, Andreas Ndoj, Kostas Fortounis (74' Sotirios Alexandropoulos), Daniel Podence (62' Stevan Jovetic), Georgios Masouras (63' Ola Solbakken), Mady Camara, Santiago Hezze, Ayoub El Kaabi (74' Jackson Porozo). Coach: Diego Martínez.
Goals: 16' Georgios Masouras 0-1, 57' Daniel Podence 0-2, 63' Ifet Djakovac 1-2, 90' Milos Pantovic 2-2.
Referee: Benoît Bastien (FRA)   Attendance: 3,778.
Sent off: 71' Andreas Ndoj.

26.10.23   Stadio Georgios Karaiskáki, Piraeus:
         Olympiakos Piraeus – West Ham United 2-1 (2-0)
Olympiakos Piraeus: Alexandros Paschalakis, Rodinei (74' Quini), Panagiotis Retsos, Jackson Porozo, Francisco Ortega, Kostas Fortounis (90+5' Stevan Jovetic), Daniel Podence (85' Ola Solbakken), Mady Camara, Sotirios Alexandropoulos (85' Georgios Masouras), Santiago Hezze, Ayoub El Kaabi (90+5' Gustavo Scarpa). Coach: Diego Martínez.
West Ham United: Alphonse Aréola, Angelo Ogbonna, Emerson, Thilo Kehrer, Konstantinos Mavropanos, James Ward-Prowse (72' Edson Álvarez), Tomás Soucek, Pablo Fornals (57' Lucas Paquetá), Mohammed Kudus (72' Maxwel Cornet), Danny Ings (58' Michail Antonio), Saïd Benrahma (58' Jarrod Bowen). Coach: David Moyes.
Goals: 33' Kostas Fortounis 1-0, 45+2' Rodinei 2-0, 87' Lucas Paquetá 2-1.
Referee: Andris Treimanis (LVA)   Attendance: 30,623.

26.10.23   TSC Arena, Backa Topola: TSC Backa Topola – SC Freiburg 1-3 (1-0)
TSC Backa Topola: Veljko Ilic, Goran Antonic, Nemanja Petrovic (79' Bence Sós), Milos Cvetkovic (78' Jovan Vlalukin), Josip Calusic, Nemanja Stojic, Milán Rádin, Milos Vulic (68' Milos Pantovic), Ifet Djakovac (79' Petar Stanic), Sasa Jovanovic (79' Aleksandar Cirkovic), Marko Rakonjac. Coach: Zarko Lazetic.
SC Freiburg: Noah Atubolu, Manuel Gulde, Matthias Ginter, Philipp Lienhart, Nicolas Höfler, Vincenzo Grifo (80' Junior Adamu), Maximilian Eggestein (80' Kiliann Sildillia), Roland Sallai (24' Lucas Höler), Ritsu Dōan (80' Lukas Kübler), Noah Weißhaupt, Maximilian Philipp (45+1' Michael Gregoritsch). Coach: Christian Streich.
Goals: 13' Nemanja Petrovic 1-0, 49', 59', 73' Vincenzo Grifo 1-1 (p), 1-2, 1-3.
Referee: Aliyar Aghayev (AZE)   Attendance: 3,400.

09.11.23   Europa-Park Stadion, Freiburg im Breisgau:
SC Freiburg – TSC Backa Topola 5-0 (1-0)
SC Freiburg: Noah Atubolu, Manuel Gulde, Matthias Ginter, Philipp Lienhart (78' Lukas Kübler), Kiliann Sildillia, Nicolas Höfler, Vincenzo Grifo (78' Junior Adamu), Maximilian Eggestein, Noah Weißhaupt (70' Jordy Makengo), Merlin Röhl (57' Michael Gregoritsch), Lucas Höler (70' Ritsu Dōan). Coach: Christian Streich.
TSC Backa Topola: Veljko Ilic, Goran Antonic (72' Milos Cvetkovic), Nemanja Petrovic, Jovan Vlalukin (46' Josip Calusic), Nemanja Stojic, Mateja Djordjevic, Milos Vulic, Nikola Kuveljic (46' Aleksandar Cirkovic), Ifet Djakovac (67' Milán Rádin), Sasa Jovanovic (67' Milos Pantovic), Uros Milovanovic. Coach: Zarko Lazetic.
Goals: 24' Merlin Röhl 1-0, 56' Maximilian Eggestein 2-0, 69' Noah Weißhaupt 3-0, 80' Junior Adamu 4-0, 90+2' Ritsu Dōan 5-0.
Referee: Rohit Saggi (NOR)   Attendance: 31,700.

09.11.23   London Stadium, London: West Ham United – Olympiakos Piraeus 1-0 (0-0)
West Ham United: Lukasz Fabianski, Vladimír Coufal, Emerson, Nayef Aguerd, Konstantinos Mavropanos, James Ward-Prowse, Lucas Paquetá, Edson Álvarez (80' Tomás Soucek), Mohammed Kudus (89' Divin Mubama), Saïd Benrahma (84' Maxwel Cornet), Jarrod Bowen. Coach: David Moyes.
Olympiakos Piraeus: Alexandros Paschalakis, Rodinei, Panagiotis Retsos, Jackson Porozo, Francisco Ortega, Kostas Fortounis, Daniel Podence (76' Georgios Masouras), Mady Camara, Sotirios Alexandropoulos (76' Gustavo Scarpa), Santiago Hezze (90' Pep Biel), Stevan Jovetic (56' Ayoub El Kaabi). Coach: Diego Martínez.
Goal: 73' Lucas Paquetá 1-0.
Referee: Matej Jug (SVN)   Attendance: 55,811.

30.11.23   Europa-Park Stadion, Freiburg im Breisgau:
SC Freiburg – Olympiakos Piraeus 5-0 (4-0)
SC Freiburg: Noah Atubolu, Matthias Ginter, Philipp Lienhart (66' Manuel Gulde), Kiliann Sildillia, Jordy Makengo, Nicolas Höfler (78' Roland Sallai), Vincenzo Grifo (78' Noah Weißhaupt), Maximilian Eggestein, Ritsu Dōan, Michael Gregoritsch (66' Merlin Röhl), Lucas Höler (67' Junior Adamu). Coach: Christian Streich.
Olympiakos Piraeus: Alexandros Paschalakis, Rodinei (84' Quini), Panagiotis Retsos, Francisco Ortega, Andreas Ndoj, Kostas Fortounis, Daniel Podence (50' Georgios Masouras), Mady Camara, Sotirios Alexandropoulos (46' Iborra), Santiago Hezze (83' João Carvalho), Ayoub El Kaabi (84' Youssef El-Arabi). Coach: Diego Martínez.
Goals: 3', 8', 36' Michael Gregoritsch 1-0, 2-0, 3-0, 42' Kiliann Sildillia 4-0, 77' Ritsu Dōan 5-0.
Referee: Irfan Peljto (BIH)   Attendance: 34,000.

30.11.23   TSC Arena, Backa Topola: TSC Backa Topola – West Ham United 0-1 (0-0)
TSC Backa Topola: Veljko Ilic, Goran Antonic, Nemanja Petrovic, Milos Cvetkovic, Josip Calusic, Nemanja Stojic, Milán Rádin (76' Milos Vulic), Nikola Kuveljic (77' Jovan Vlalukin), Ifet Djakovac, Uros Milovanovic (77' Milos Pantovic), Aleksandar Cirkovic (86' Bence Sós). Coach: Zarko Lazetic.
West Ham United: Lukasz Fabianski, Aaron Cresswell (79' Emerson), Nayef Aguerd, Konstantinos Mavropanos, Ben Johnson (79' Thilo Kehrer), James Ward-Prowse, Tomás Soucek, Pablo Fornals, Lucas Paquetá, Saïd Benrahma (67' Maxwel Cornet), Divin Mubama (67' Danny Ings). Coach: David Moyes.
Goal: 89' Tomás Soucek 0-1.
Referee: Allard Lindhout (HOL)   Attendance: 4,256.

14.12.23   London Stadium, London: West Ham United – SC Freiburg 2-0 (2-0)
West Ham United: Lukasz Fabianski, Vladimír Coufal (88' Thilo Kehrer), Emerson, Nayef Aguerd, Konstantinos Mavropanos, James Ward-Prowse, Tomás Soucek, Lucas Paquetá (72' Divin Mubama), Edson Álvarez (54' Pablo Fornals), Mohammed Kudus (88' Maxwel Cornet), Jarrod Bowen (72' Danny Ings). Coach: David Moyes.
SC Freiburg: Noah Atubolu, Manuel Gulde, Matthias Ginter, Kiliann Sildillia, Jordy Makengo (74' Lukas Kübler), Nicolas Höfler, Vincenzo Grifo (69' Noah Weißhaupt), Maximilian Eggestein (56' Lucas Höler), Roland Sallai (46' Merlin Röhl), Ritsu Dōan, Michael Gregoritsch (56' Junior Adamu). Coach: Christian Streich.
Goals: 14' Mohammed Kudus 1-0, 42' Edson Álvarez 2-0,
Referee: João Pedro Pinheiro (POR)   Attendance: 48,876.

14.12.23   Stadio Georgios Karaiskáki, Piraeus:
Olympiakos Piraeus – TSC Backa Topola 5-2 (3-0)
Olympiakos Piraeus: Alexandros Paschalakis, Rodinei, Panagiotis Retsos, Francisco Ortega, Andreas Ndoj, Kostas Fortounis (72' Sotirios Alexandropoulos), Daniel Podence, Georgios Masouras (64' Pep Biel), Mady Camara (86' Omar Richards), Santiago Hezze (73' João Carvalho), Ayoub El Kaabi (64' Youssef El-Arabi). Coach: Carlos Carvalhal.
TSC Backa Topola: Veljko Ilic, Nemanja Petrovic (56' Bence Sós), Milos Cvetkovic, Josip Calusic (87' Jovan Vlalukin), Nemanja Stojic, Vukasin Krstic, Milán Rádin (55' Milos Vulic), Nikola Kuveljic, Ifet Djakovac, Uros Milovanovic (56' Marko Rakonjac), Aleksandar Cirkovic (72' Petar Stanic). Coach: Zarko Lazetic.
Goals: 21' Ayoub El Kaabi 1-0, 40', 42' Daniel Podence 2-0, 3-0, 46' Veljko Ilic 4-0 (og), 48' Ifet Djakovac 4-1, 61' Aleksandar Cirkovic 4-2, 68' Youssef El-Arabi 5-2.
Referee: Morten Krogh Hansen (DEN)   Attendance: 33,296.
Sent off: 60' Nikola Kuveljic.

GROUP B

21.09.23   John Cruijff Arena, Amsterdam: AFC Ajax – Olympique Marseille 3-3 (2-2)
AFC Ajax: Jay Gorter, Borna Sosa, Josip Sutalo, Anton Gaaei, Jorrel Hato, Kenneth Taylor, Benjamin Tahirovic (46' Silvano Vos), Steven Berghuis (84' Branco van den Boomen), Steven Bergwijn (90+3' Jakov Medic), Brian Brobbey (85' Chuba Akpom), Carlos Forbs (90+3' Gastón Ávila). Coach: Maurice Steijn.
Olympique Marseille: Pau López, Jonathan Clauss, Chancel Mbemba, Samuel Gigot, Renan Lodi (80' Leonardo Balerdi), Geoffrey Kondogbia (65' Vítinha), Valentin Rongier, Amine Harit (79' François Mughe), Azzedine Ounahi, Pierre-Emerick Aubameyang (79' Joaquín Correa), Iliman Ndiaye (65' Jordan Veretout). Coach: Jacques Abardonado.
Goals: 9' Carlos Forbs 1-0, 20' Steven Berghuis 2-0, 23' Jonathan Clauss 2-1,
38' Pierre-Emerick Aubameyang 2-2, 52' Kenneth Taylor 3-2,
78' Pierre-Emerick Aubameyang 3-3.
Referee: Maurizio Mariani (ITA)   Attendance: 53,000.
Sent off: 90+1' Silvano Vos.

21.09.23   American Express Stadium, Falmer:
Brighton & Hove Albion – AEK Athens 2-3 (1-2)
Brighton & Hove Albion: Jason Steele, Pervis Estupiñán, Igor Julio, Jan Paul van Hecke, James Milner (55' Tariq Lamptey), Pascal Groß, Solly March, Billy Gilmour (86' Facundo Buonanotte), Kaoru Mitoma (86' Simon Adingra), Ansu Fati, João Pedro (82' Danny Welbeck). Coach: Roberto De Zerbi.
AEK Athens: Cican Stankovic, Ehsan Hajsafi (60' Milad Mohammadi), Djibril Sidibé, Gerasimos Mitoglou, Jens Jønsson, Mijat Gacinovic (79' Niclas Eliasson), Orbelín Pineda (79' Petros Mantalos), Damian Szymanski, Nordin Amrabat, Serge Araújo (68' Steven Zuber), Levi García (68' Ezequiel Ponce). Coach: Matías Almeyda.
Goals: 11' Djibril Sidibé 0-1, 30' João Pedro 1-1 (p), 40' Mijat Gacinovic 1-2, 67' João Pedro 2-2 (p), 84' Ezequiel Ponce 2-3.
Referee: Kristo Tohver (EST)   Attendance: 30,178.

05.10.23   Orange Vélodrome, Marseille:
Olympique Marseille – Brighton & Hove Albion 2-2 (2-0)
Olympique Marseille: Pau López, Jonathan Clauss, Chancel Mbemba, Michael Murillo, Leonardo Balerdi, Jordan Veretout (51' Azzedine Ounahi), Valentin Rongier, Amine Harit, Pierre-Emerick Aubameyang (62' Vítinha), Joaquín Correa (62' Ismaïla Sarr), Iliman Ndiaye (79' Renan Lodi). Coach: Gennaro Gattuso.
Brighton & Hove Albion: Jason Steele, Joël Veltman, Lewis Dunk, Tariq Lamptey, Jan Paul van Hecke, Pascal Groß, Solly March (76' Simon Adingra), Mahmoud Dahoud (67' Billy Gilmour), Kaoru Mitoma, Danny Welbeck (77' Evan Ferguson), Ansu Fati (66' João Pedro). Coach: Roberto De Zerbi.
Goals: 19' Chancel Mbemba 1-0, 20' Jordan Veretout 2-0, 54' Pascal Groß 2-1, 88' João Pedro 2-2 (p).
Referee: Mykola Balakin (UKR)   Attendance: 63,465.

05.10.23   OPAP Arena, Athens: AEK Athens – AFC Ajax 1-1 (0-1)
AEK Athens: Cican Stankovic, Ehsan Hajsafi (74' Niclas Eliasson), Domagoj Vida, Djibril Sidibé (67' Lazaros Rota), Harold Moukoudi, Mijat Gacinovic (79' Milad Mohammadi), Orbelín Pineda (67' Jens Jønsson), Damian Szymanski, Nordin Amrabat, Serge Araújo, Ezequiel Ponce (67' Petros Mantalos). Coach: Matías Almeyda.
AFC Ajax: Jay Gorter, Josip Sutalo, Gastón Ávila, Devyne Rensch, Jorrel Hato, Kenneth Taylor, Benjamin Tahirovic (84' Branco van den Boomen), Steven Berghuis, Steven Bergwijn, Brian Brobbey (74' Chuba Akpom), Carlos Forbs (84' Amourricho van Axel Dongen). Coach: Maurice Steijn.
Goals: 30' Steven Bergwijn 0-1 (p), 74' Domagoj Vida 1-1.
Referee: Matej Jug (SVN)   Attendance: 29,524.

26.10.23   Orange Vélodrome, Marseille: Olympique Marseille – AEK Athens 3-1 (1-0)
Olympique Marseille: Rubén Blanco, Jonathan Clauss (89' Bilal Nadir), Chancel Mbemba, Renan Lodi, Leonardo Balerdi (89' Bamo Meïté), Geoffrey Kondogbia, Jordan Veretout (88' Michael Murillo), Valentin Rongier, Amine Harit (74' Pierre-Emerick Aubameyang), Iliman Ndiaye, Vítinha (75' Ismaïla Sarr). Coach: Gennaro Gattuso.
AEK Athens: Cican Stankovic, Ehsan Hajsafi (44' Milad Mohammadi), Domagoj Vida, Djibril Sidibé (46' Ezequiel Ponce), Harold Moukoudi, Petros Mantalos (59' Georgios Athanasiadis), Jens Jønsson, Orbelín Pineda, Damian Szymanski (75' Konstantinos Galanopoulos), Nordin Amrabat (75' Niclas Eliasson), Steven Zuber. Coach: Matías Almeyda.
Goals: 27' Vítinha 1-0, 53' Orbelín Pineda 1-1, 60' Amine Harit 2-1 (p), 69' Jordan Veretout 3-1 (p).
Referee: Daniel Stefanski (POL)   Attendance: 65,092.
Sent off: 57' Cican Stankovic.

26.10.23   American Express Stadium, Falmer: Brighton & Hove Albion – AFC Ajax 2-0 (1-0)
Brighton & Hove Albion: Jason Steele, Joël Veltman, Lewis Dunk, Jan Paul van Hecke (85' Adam Webster), James Milner (85' Mahmoud Dahoud), Pascal Groß, Billy Gilmour (64' Carlos Baleba), Kaoru Mitoma, Ansu Fati (64' Facundo Buonanotte), João Pedro (75' Evan Ferguson), Simon Adingra. Coach: Roberto De Zerbi.
AFC Ajax: Diant Ramaj, Borna Sosa, Josip Sutalo, Anton Gaaei, Jorrel Hato, Kenneth Taylor, Benjamin Tahirovic (60' Branco van den Boomen), Steven Berghuis (60' Mika Godts), Steven Bergwijn (76' Chuba Akpom), Brian Brobbey (75' Silvano Vos), Carlos Forbs (46' Kristian Hlynsson). Coach: Hedwiges Maduro.
Goals: 42' João Pedro 1-0, 53' Ansu Fati 2-0.
Referee: Bartosz Frankowski (POL)   Attendance: 30,540.

09.11.23   John Cruijff Arena, Amsterdam: AFC Ajax – Brighton & Hove Albion 0-2 (0-1)
AFC Ajax: Diant Ramaj, Josip Sutalo, Devyne Rensch (78' Georges Mikautadze), Anton Gaaei (57' Borna Sosa), Jorrel Hato, Kenneth Taylor (46' Chuba Akpom), Kristian Hlynsson (57' Carlos Forbs), Silvano Vos (73' Benjamin Tahirovic), Steven Berghuis, Steven Bergwijn, Brian Brobbey. Coach: John van 't Schip.
Brighton & Hove Albion: Bart Verbruggen, Joël Veltman, Lewis Dunk (46' Igor Julio), Jan Paul van Hecke, James Milner (8' Billy Gilmour), Pascal Groß, Mahmoud Dahoud (65' Pervis Estupiñán, 77' Carlos Baleba), Kaoru Mitoma, Ansu Fati (65' Evan Ferguson), João Pedro, Simon Adingra. Coach: Roberto De Zerbi.
Goals: 15' Ansu Fati 0-1, 53' Simon Adingra 0-2.
Referee: Nikola Dabanovic (MNE)   Attendance: 52,095.

09.11.23   OPAP Arena, Athens: AEK Athens – Olympique Marseille 0-2 (0-1)
AEK Athens: Georgios Athanasiadis, Ehsan Hajsafi, Domagoj Vida, Djibril Sidibé, Harold Moukoudi, Petros Mantalos, Mijat Gacinovic (63' Steven Zuber), Orbelín Pineda (63' Sergio Araújo), Damian Szymanski (81' Konstantinos Galanopoulos), Nordin Amrabat (76' Niclas Eliasson), Levi García (63' Ezequiel Ponce). Coach: Matías Almeyda.
Olympique Marseille: Pau López, Jonathan Clauss (90+5' Bilal Nadir), Chancel Mbemba, Renan Lodi, Leonardo Balerdi, Geoffrey Kondogbia, Jordan Veretout (90+6' Samuel Gigot), Amine Harit (90+5' Emran Soglo), Joaquín Correa (59' Ismaïla Sarr), Iliman Ndiaye (86' Michael Murillo), Vítinha. Coach: Gennaro Gattuso.
Goals: 25' Chancel Mbemba 0-1, 90+3' Ismaïla Sarr 0-2.
Referee: Glenn Nyberg (SWE)   Attendance: 30,530.

30.11.23   OPAP Arena, Athens: AEK Athens – Brighton & Hove Albion 0-1 (0-0)
AEK Athens: Cican Stankovic, Ehsan Hajsafi, Domagoj Vida, Harold Moukoudi, Lazaros Rota, Petros Mantalos (72' Sergio Araújo), Mijat Gacinovic, Orbelín Pineda (82' Rodolfo Pizarro), Damian Szymanski, Nordin Amrabat (72' Niclas Eliasson), Steven Zuber (72' Ezequiel Ponce). Coach: Matías Almeyda.
Brighton & Hove Albion: Bart Verbruggen, Joël Veltman, Lewis Dunk, Igor Julio, Pascal Groß, Billy Gilmour (88' Carlos Baleba), Kaoru Mitoma (69' Mahmoud Dahoud), Jack Hinshelwood, João Pedro (77' James Milner), Evan Ferguson (87' Joshua Duffus), Simon Adingra. Coach: Roberto De Zerbi.
Goal: 55' João Pedro 0-1 (p).
Referee: Sandro Schärer (SUI)   Attendance: 30,520.
Sent off: 65' Mijat Gacinovic.

30.11.23   Orange Vélodrome, Marseille: Olympique Marseille – AFC Ajax 4-3 (2-2)
Olympique Marseille: Pau López, Jonathan Clauss, Chancel Mbemba, Samuel Gigot, Renan Lodi (87' Michael Murillo), Geoffrey Kondogbia, Jordan Veretout (87' Vítinha), Amine Harit (87' Azzedine Ounahi), Pierre-Emerick Aubameyang (90+5' Bamo Meïté), Joaquín Correa (66' Iliman Ndiaye), Ismaïla Sarr. Coach: Gennaro Gattuso.
AFC Ajax: Diant Ramaj, Borna Sosa (77' Ar'Jany Martha), Devyne Rensch, Anton Gaaei, Jorrel Hato, Kenneth Taylor (77' Chuba Akpom), Benjamin Tahirovic (90+4' Jaydon Banel), Steven Berghuis, Steven Bergwijn, Brian Brobbey (90+4' Anass Salah-Eddine), Carlos Forbs (46' Kristian Hlynsson). Coach: John van 't Schip.
Goals: 9' Pierre-Emerick Aubameyang 1-0 (p), 10' Brian Brobbey 1-1, 26' Chancel Mbemba 2-1, 30' Brian Brobbey 2-2, 47' Pierre-Emerick Aubameyang 3-2, 79' Chuba Akpom 3-3, 90+3' Pierre-Emerick Aubameyang 4-3 (p).
Referee: Simone Sozza (ITA)   Attendance: 60,638.
Sent off: 63' Steven Berghuis, Michael Valkanis (assistent manager).

14.12.23   John Cruijff Arena, Amsterdam: AFC Ajax – AEK Athens 3-1 (2-1)
AFC Ajax: Diant Ramaj, Borna Sosa, Josip Sutalo, Devyne Rensch (74' Tristan Gooijer), Jorrel Hato, Kenneth Taylor, Kristian Hlynsson (86' Georges Mikautadze), Benjamin Tahirovic, Chuba Akpom, Brian Brobbey (46' Ar'Jany Martha), Carlos Forbs (62' Anton Gaaei). Coach: John van 't Schip.
AEK Athens: Georgios Athanasiadis, Ehsan Hajsafi, Domagoj Vida, Harold Moukoudi (83' Konstantinos Galanopoulos), Lazaros Rota, Petros Mantalos, Niclas Eliasson, Damian Szymanski (90+1' Milad Mohammadi), Nordin Amrabat (61' Rodolfo Pizarro), Steven Zuber, Levi García (83' Jens Jønsson). Coach: Matías Almeyda.
Goals: 5' Chuba Akpom 1-0, 11' Levi García 1-1, 20' Kenneth Taylor 2-1, 56' Chuba Akpom 3-1.
Referee: Craig Pawson (ENG)   Attendance: 53,926.

14.12.23   American Express Stadium, Falmer:
Brighton & Hove Albion – Olympique Marseille 1-0 (0-0)
Brighton & Hove Albion: Jason Steele, Lewis Dunk, Igor Julio, Jan Paul van Hecke, Pascal Groß, Billy Gilmour (90' Carlos Baleba), Kaoru Mitoma, Jack Hinshelwood (74' James Milner), Facundo Buonanotte (74' Adam Lallana), João Pedro (90' Joël Veltman), Simon Adingra (64' Evan Ferguson). Coach: Roberto De Zerbi.
Olympique Marseille: Pau López, Jonathan Clauss, Chancel Mbemba, Renan Lodi (55' Michael Murillo), Leonardo Balerdi, Jordan Veretout (78' Geoffrey Kondogbia), Amine Harit (78' Ismaïla Sarr), Azzedine Ounahi, Bamo Meïté, Pierre-Emerick Aubameyang, Vítinha (52' Iliman Ndiaye). Coach: Gennaro Gattuso.
Goal: 88' João Pedro 1-0.
Referee: José María Sánchez Martínez (ESP)   Attendance: 30,214.

GROUP C

21.09.23   epet ARENA, Praha: AC Sparta Praha – Aris Limassol 3-2 (2-1)
AC Sparta Praha: Peter Vindahl Jensen, Jaroslav Zelený, Asger Sørensen, Ángelo Preciado, Martin Vitík, Qazim Laçi (77' David Pavelka), Lukás Haraslín (65' Veljko Birmancevic), Kaan Kairinen (31' Lukás Sadílek), Ladislav Krejcí (II), Jan Kuchta (65' Adam Karabec), Victor Olatunji (78' Václav Sejk). Coach: Brian Priske.
Aris Limassol: Vaná, Slobodan Urosevic, Caju, Franz Brorsson, Eric Boakye, Július Szöke (66' Morgan Brown), Leo Bengtsson (85' Jaden Montnor), Karol Struski, Aleksandr Kokorin (75' Mariusz Stepinski), Mihlali Mayambela (85' Alex Mouncketou-Moussounda), Yannick Gomis (66' Shavy Warren Babicka). Coach: Aleksey Shpilevski.
Goals: 11' Aleksandr Kokorin 0-1 (p), 20', 25' Ladislav Krejcí (II) 1-1, 2-1, 67' Martin Vitík 3-1, 90' Shavy Warren Babicka 3-2.
Referee: Jérôme Brisard (FRA)   Attendance: 17,371.

21.09.23   Ibrox Stadium, Glasgow: Glasgow Rangers FC – Real Betis 1-0 (0-0)
Glasgow Rangers FC: Jack Butland, James Tavernier, Connor Goldson, Ben Davies, Borna Barisic, John Lundstram, José Cifuentes (81' Ryan Jack), Tom Lawrence (62' Sam Lammers), Kemar Roofe (89' Cyriel Dessers), Rabbi Matondo, Abdallah Sima (89' Dujon Sterling). Coach: Michael Beale.
Real Betis: Claudio Bravo, Marc Bartra, Germán Pezzella, Héctor Bellerín, Abner Vinicius, Isco (88' Assane Diao), Marc Roca, Guido Rodríguez, Borja Iglesias (72' Willian José), Abde Ezzalzouli (72' Rodri), Luiz Henrique (72' Ayoze Pérez). Coach: Manuel Pellegrini.
Goal: 67' Abdallah Sima 1-0.
Referee: Lawrence Visser (BEL)   Attendance: 45,634.

05.10.23   Estadio Benito Villamarín, Sevilla: Real Betis – AC Sparta Praha 2-1 (1-1)
Real Betis: Rui Silva, Germán Pezzella, Aitor Ruibal, Juan Miranda (46' Abner Vinicius), Isco, William Carvalho (60' Andrés Guardado), Marc Roca, Guido Rodríguez, Borja Iglesias (75' Willian José), Abde Ezzalzouli (46' Ayoze Pérez), Assane Diao (85' Héctor Bellerín). Coach: Manuel Pellegrini.
AC Sparta Praha: Peter Vindahl Jensen, Asger Sørensen, Filip Panák, Tomás Wiesner (60' Ángelo Preciado), Qazim Laçi (68' Lukás Sadílek), Lukás Haraslín (80' Adam Karabec), Kaan Kairinen, Veljko Birmancevic (68' Jakub Pesek), Ladislav Krejcí (II), Matej Rynes, Jan Kuchta (80' Victor Olatunji). Coach: Brian Priske.
Goals: 3' Veljko Birmancevic 0-1, 9' Assane Diao 1-1, 79' Isco 2-1.
Referee: Duje Strukan (CRO)   Attenance: 45,037.

05.10.23 Alphamega Stadium, Limassol: Aris Limassol – Glasgow Rangers FC 2-1 (1-0)
Aris Limassol: Vaná, Steeve Yago, Slobodan Urosevic, Eric Boakye (80' Franz Brorsson), Alex Moucketou-Moussounda, Július Szöke, Leo Bengtsson (67' Aleksandr Kokorin), Karol Struski (67' Morgan Brown), Shavy Warren Babicka (89' Matija Spoljaric), Mihlali Mayambela, Yannick Gomis (89' Mariusz Stepinski). Coach: Aleksey Shpilevski.
Glasgow Rangers FC: Jack Butland, James Tavernier, Connor Goldson, Ben Davies, Borna Barisic, John Lundstram, Scott Wright (84' Ross McCausland), Nicolas Raskin (67' José Cifuentes), Cyriel Dessers, Sam Lammers (68' Kemar Roofe), Abdallah Sima.
Coach: Steven Davis.
Goals: 9' Alex Moucketou-Moussounda 1-0, 59' Shavy Warren Babicka 2-0, 70' Abdallah Sima 2-1.
Referee: Horatiu Fesnic (ROM) Attendance: 3,911.

26.10.23 epet ARENA, Praha: AC Sparta Praha – Glasgow Rangers FC 0-0
AC Sparta Praha: Peter Vindahl Jensen, Asger Sørensen, Filip Panák, Ángelo Preciado (27' Tomás Wiesner), Martin Vitík, Qazim Laçi (66' Lukás Sadílek), Kaan Kairinen, Veljko Birmancevic (75' Jakub Pesek), Matej Rynes, Adam Karabec (65' Victor Olatunji), Jan Kuchta. Coach: Brian Priske.
Glasgow Rangers FC: Jack Butland, James Tavernier, Connor Goldson, John Souttar, Ben Davies, John Lundstram, Todd Cantwell (64' Scott Wright), Nicolas Raskin, Cyriel Dessers (74' Danilo), Sam Lammers, Abdallah Sima. Coach: Philippe Clement.
Referee: Sascha Stegemann (GER) Attendance: 18,250.

26.10.23 Alphamega Stadium, Limassol: Aris Limassol – Real Betis 0-1 (0-0)
Aris Limassol: Vaná, Steeve Yago, Slobodan Urosevic, Eric Boakye (26' Caju), Alex Moucketou-Moussounda, Július Szöke, Leo Bengtsson (86' Jaden Montnor), Karol Struski (62' Morgan Brown), Shavy Warren Babicka, Mihlali Mayambela (85' Matija Spoljaric), Yannick Gomis (85' Mariusz Stepinski). Coach: Aleksey Shpilevski.
Real Betis: Rui Silva, Germán Pezzella, Aitor Ruibal, Abner Vinicius, William Carvalho (79' Andrés Guardado), Marc Roca, Guido Rodríguez, Willian José (72' Assane Diao), Ayoze Pérez (79' Borja Iglesias), Abde Ezzalzouli (89' Rodri), Luiz Henrique (72' Isco).
Coach: Manuel Pellegrini.
Goal: 75' Ayoze Pérez 0-1.
Referee: Filip Glova (SVK) Attendance: 3,945.

09.11.23 Estadio Benito Villamarín, Sevilla: Real Betis – Aris Limassol 4-1 (1-0)
Real Betis: Claudio Bravo, Germán Pezzella (84' Quique Fernández), Aitor Ruibal, Abner Vinicius, Andrés Guardado (59' Guido Rodríguez), William Carvalho, Marc Roca, Rodri (59' Isco), Borja Iglesias (59' Ayoze Pérez), Abde Ezzalzouli, Luiz Henrique (75' Nabil Fekir). Coach: Manuel Pellegrini.
Aris Limassol: Vaná, Steeve Yago, Slobodan Urosevic, Caju, Franz Brorsson (46' Alex Moucketou-Moussounda), Július Szöke, Karol Struski (75' Morgan Brown), Shavy Warren Babicka (82' Mariusz Stepinski), Mihlali Mayambela (76' Aleksandr Kokorin), Yannick Gomis, Jaden Montnor (46' Leo Bengtsson). Coach: Aleksey Shpilevski.
Goals: 34' Borja Iglesias 1-0, 64' Aitor Ruibal 2-0, 79' Marc Roca 3-0, 84' Aleksandr Kokorin 3-1, 90+4' Abde Ezzalzouli 4-1.
Referee: Mohammed Al-Hakim (SWE) Attendance: 41,768.

Nabil Fekir missed a penalty kick (76').

09.11.23   Ibrox Stadium, Glasgow: Glasgow Rangers FC – AC Sparta Praha 2-1 (2-0)
Glasgow Rangers FC: Jack Butland, James Tavernier, Connor Goldson, Ben Davies, Borna Barisic, Ryan Jack, John Lundstram, Todd Cantwell (69' Ross McCausland), Sam Lammers (90+5' José Cifuentes), Danilo (85' Cyriel Dessers), Abdallah Sima (85' Tom Lawrence).
Coach: Philippe Clement.
AC Sparta Praha: Peter Vindahl Jensen, Jaroslav Zelený, Asger Sørensen, Ángelo Preciado, Martin Vitík, James Gomez (46' Tomás Wiesner), Lukáš Sadílek (59' Lukáš Haraslín), Kaan Kairinen, Veljko Birmancevic, Jan Kuchta (67' Václav Sejk), Victor Olatunji (46' Qazim Laçi, 85' Patrik Vydra). Coach: Brian Priske.
Goals: 11' Danilo 1-0, 20' Todd Cantwell 2-0, 77' Lukáš Haraslín 2-1.
Referee: Davide Massa (ITA)   Attendance: 48,838.

30.11.23   epet ARENA, Praha: AC Sparta Praha – Real Betis 1-0 (0-0)
AC Sparta Praha: Peter Vindahl Jensen, Jaroslav Zelený, Filip Panák, Ángelo Preciado, Martin Vitík, Qazim Laçi, Lukáš Haraslín (74' Jakub Pesek), Kaan Kairinen (89' David Pavelka), Veljko Birmancevic (82' Lukáš Sadílek), Ladislav Krejcí (II), Jan Kuchta (82' Victor Olatunji). Coach: Brian Priske.
Real Betis: Rui Silva, Germán Pezzella, Aitor Ruibal, Abner Vinicius (84' Juan Miranda), Andrés Guardado (84' Willian José), Marc Roca, Guido Rodríguez, Nabil Fekir (46' Isco), Borja Iglesias, Abde Ezzalzouli (70' Ayoze Pérez), Assane Diao (76' Luiz Henrique).
Coach: Manuel Pellegrini.
Goal: 54' Lukáš Haraslín 1-0.
Referee: Nikola Dabanovic (MNE)   Attendance: 18,095.

30.11.23   Ibrox Stadium, Glasgow: Glasgow Rangers FC – Aris Limassol 1-1 (0-1)
Glasgow Rangers FC: Jack Butland, James Tavernier, John Souttar, Ben Davies, Borna Barisic, John Lundstram, José Cifuentes, Todd Cantwell (36' Ross McCausland), Sam Lammers (58' Tom Lawrence), Danilo, Abdallah Sima (79' Rabbi Matondo).
Coach: Philippe Clement.
Aris Limassol: Vaná, Steeve Yago, Slobodan Urosevic, Caju, Alex Moucketou-Moussounda, Július Szöke, Leo Bengtsson (90' Franz Brorsson), Karol Struski (90' Morgan Brown), Shavy Warren Babicka (63' Mariusz Stepinski), Aleksandr Kokorin, Mihlali Mayambela (74' Jaden Montnor). Coach: Aleksey Shpilevski.
Goals: 28' Shavy Warren Babicka 0-1, 49' Ross McCausland 1-1.
Referee: Rohit Saggi (NOR)   Attendance: 48,890.

14.12.23   Estadio Benito Villamarín, Sevilla: Real Betis – Glasgow Rangers FC 2-3 (2-2)
Real Betis: Rui Silva, Germán Pezzella, Héctor Bellerín (82' Aitor Ruibal), Juan Miranda, Andrés Guardado, Isco, William Carvalho (82' Luiz Henrique), Marc Roca, Ayoze Pérez, Borja Iglesias (70' Willian José), Assane Diao (70' Abde Ezzalzouli).
Coach: Manuel Pellegrini.
Glasgow Rangers FC: Jack Butland, James Tavernier, Connor Goldson, Ben Davies, Borna Barisic, John Lundstram, José Cifuentes (46' Dujon Sterling), Cyriel Dessers (65' Kemar Roofe), Sam Lammers, Ross McCausland (65' Rabbi Matondo), Abdallah Sima.
Coach: Philippe Clement.
Goals: 10' Abdallah Sima 0-1, 14' Juan Miranda 1-1, 20' Cyriel Dessers 1-2, 37' Ayoze Pérez 2-2, 78' Kemar Roofe 2-3.
Referee: Srdjan Jovanovic (SRB)   Attendance: 48,380.

14.12.23 Alphamega Stadium, Limassol: Aris Limassol – AC Sparta Praha 1-3 (0-3)
Aris Limassol: Vaná, Steeve Yago, Slobodan Urosevic, Caju, Alex Moucketou-Moussounda (46' Franz Brorsson), Július Szöke (65' Morgan Brown), Leo Bengtsson, Karol Struski, Aleksandr Kokorin (84' Mariusz Stepinski), Mihlali Mayambela (76' Matija Spoljaric), Yannick Gomis (64' Jaden Montnor). Coach: Aleksey Shpilevski.
AC Sparta Praha: Peter Vindahl Jensen, Jaroslav Zelený, Asger Sørensen (66' Patrik Vydra), Ángelo Preciado (36' Tomás Wiesner), Martin Vitík, Qazim Laçi, Lukás Haraslín (66' Adam Karabec), Kaan Kairinen, Veljko Birmancevic (78' Jakub Pesek), Ladislav Krejcí (II), Jan Kuchta (78' Victor Olatunji). Coach: Brian Priske.
Goals: 4' Jan Kuchta 0-1, 11', 45+1' Veljko Birmancevic 0-, 0-3, 84' Leo Bengtsson 1-3.
Referee: Harm Osmers (GER)   Attendance: 2,859.

GROUP D

21.09.23 Gewiss Stadium, Bergamo: Atalanta Bergamo – Raków Czestochowa 2-0 (0-0)
Atalanta Bergamo: Juan Musso, Rafael Tolói, Berat Djimsiti, Davide Zappacosta (76' Emil Holm), Matteo Ruggeri, Giorgio Scalvini, Marten de Roon (62' Éderson), Teun Koopmeiners, Charles De Ketelaere (90+2' Mitchel Bakker), Luis Muriel (62' Aleksey Miranchuk), Ademola Lookman (76' Mario Pasalic). Coach: Gian Piero Gasperini.
Raków Czestochowa: Vladan Kovacevic, Milan Rundic, Adnan Kovacevic, Bogdan Racovitan, Gustav Berggren (71' Ben Lederman), Srdjan Plavsic (78' Jean Carlos), Vladyslav Kocherhin (61' Marcin Cebula), Deian Sorescu, Giannis Papanikolaou, John Yeboah (61' Sonny Kittel), Lukasz Zwolinski (70' Ante Crnac). Coach: Dawid Szwarga.
Goals: 49' Charles De Ketelaere 1-0, 66' Éderson 2-0.
Referee: Roi Reinshreiber (ISR)   Attendance: 13,698.

21.09.23 Merkur Arena, Graz: Sturm Graz – Sporting CP 1-2 (0-0)
Sturm Graz: Kjell Scherpen, Gregory Wüthrich, Jusuf Gazibegovic (89' Max Johnston), David Affengruber, Amadou Danté, Stefan Hierländer (88' Mohammed Fuseini), Jon Gorenc Stankovic, Otar Kiteishvili (69' Tomi Horvat), Alexander Prass, William Bøving (88' Bryan Teixeira), Manprit Sarkaria (63' Szymon Wlodarczyk). Coach: Christian Ilzer.
Sporting CP: Antonio Adán, Sebastián Coates, Matheus Reis (62' Nuno Santos), Gonçalo Inácio, Ousmane Diomande, Morten Hjulmand (76' Hidemasa Morita), Daniel Bragança (77' Marcus Edwards), Paulinho, Viktor Gyökeres, Trincão (62' Pedro Gonçalves "Pote"), Geny Catamo (77' Iván Fresneda). Coach: Rúben Amorim.
Goals: 58' William Bøving 1-0, 76' Viktor Gyökeres 1-1, 84' Sebastián Coates 1-2.
Referee: Nikola Dabanovic (MNE)   Attendance: 13,517.

05.10.23 Estádio José Alvalade, Lisboa: Sporting CP – Atlanta Bergamo 1-2 (0-2)
Sporting CP: Antonio Adán, Matheus Reis (90+2' Daniel Bragança), Gonçalo Inácio, Iván Fresneda (67' Ricardo Esgaio), Ousmane Diomande, Nuno Santos (46' Marcus Edwards), Morten Hjulmand (46' Sebastián Coates), Pedro Gonçalves "Pote", Hidemasa Morita, Paulinho (46' Geny Catamo), Viktor Gyökeres. Coach: Rúben Amorim.
Atalanta Bergamo: Juan Musso, Berat Djimsiti (54' Rafael Tolói), Davide Zappacosta (66' Emil Holm), Sead Kolasinac, Matteo Ruggeri, Giorgio Scalvini (81' José Palomino), Marten de Roon, Teun Koopmeiners, Éderson (66' Mario Pasalic), Charles De Ketelaere (54' Gianluca Scamacca), Ademola Lookman. Coach: Gian Piero Gasperini.
Goals: 33' Giorgio Scalvini 0-1, 43' Matteo Ruggeri 0-2, 76' Viktor Gyökeres 1-2 (p).
Referee: Alejandro Hernández Hernández (ESP)   Attendance: 42,301.

05.10.23   ArcelorMittal Park, Sosnowiec: Raków Czestochowa – Sturm Graz 0-1 (0-1)
Raków Czestochowa: Vladan Kovacevic, Milan Rundic, Adnan Kovacevic, Bogdan Racovitan, Sonny Kittel (75' Gustav Berggren), Marcin Cebula (59' John Yeboah), Srdjan Plavsic, Vladyslav Kocherhin (75' Ben Lederman), Fran Tudor, Giannis Papanikolaou (85' Bartosz Nowak), Fabian Piasecki (60' Ante Crnac). Coach: Dawid Szwarga.
Sturm Graz: Kjell Scherpen, Gregory Wüthrich, Jusuf Gazibegovic, David Affengruber, Amadou Danté, Stefan Hierländer, Jon Gorenc Stankovic, Otar Kiteishvili (76' Bryan Teixeira), Alexander Prass (88' Javier Serrano), William Bøving (64' Manprit Sarkaria), Szymon Wlodarczyk (76' Seedy Jatta). Coach: Christian Ilzer.
Goal: 23' William Bøving 0-1.
Referee: Aliyar Aghayev (AZE)   Attendance: 8,993.

Raków Czestochowa played their home matches at the ArcelorMittal Park in Sosnowiec, instead of their regular stadium, the Miejski Stadion Pilkarski "Raków" in Czestochowa, which did not meet UEFA requirements.

26.10.23   Merkur Arena, Graz: Sturm Graz – Atalanta Bergamo 2-2 (1-2)
Sturm Graz: Kjell Scherpen, Gregory Wüthrich (62' Dimitri Lavalée), Jusuf Gazibegovic, David Affengruber, Amadou Danté, Stefan Hierländer, Jon Gorenc Stankovic, Otar Kiteishvili (62' Javier Serrano), Alexander Prass (70' William Bøving), Manprit Sarkaria (77' Tomi Horvat), Seedy Jatta (61' Szymon Wlodarczyk). Coach: Christian Ilzer.
Atalanta Bergamo: Juan Musso, Rafael Tolói (81' Giorgio Scalvini), Berat Djimsiti, Davide Zappacosta (77' Mitchel Bakker), Sead Kolasinac, Matteo Ruggeri (63' Hans Hateboer), Marten de Roon, Teun Koopmeiners, Éderson, Luis Muriel (64' Gianluca Scamacca), Ademola Lookman (64' Charles De Ketelaere). Coach: Gian Piero Gasperini.
Goals: 13' Alexander Prass 1-0, 34', 45+7' Luis Muriel 1-1, 1-2 (p), 80' Szymon Wlodarczyk 2-2 (p).
Referee: Duje Strukan (CRO)   Attendance: 14,167.
Sent off: 52' Stefan Hierländer.

26.10.23   ArcelorMittal Park, Sosnowiec: Raków Czestochowa – Sporting CP 1-1 (0-1)
Raków Czestochowa: Vladan Kovacevic, Milan Rundic, Zoran Arsenic (14' Jean Carlos), Bogdan Racovitan, Marcin Cebula (75' Bartosz Nowak), Gustav Berggren, Srdjan Plavsic, Vladyslav Kocherhin (86' Ben Lederman), Fran Tudor, John Yeboah (75' Fabian Piasecki), Ante Crnac. Coach: Dawid Szwarga.
Sporting CP: Franco Israel, Sebastián Coates, Ricardo Esgaio, Matheus Reis (90' Nuno Santos), Gonçalo Inácio, Ousmane Diomande, Morten Hjulmand (90' Daniel Bragança), Pedro Gonçalves "Pote" (58' Geny Catamo), Hidemasa Morita, Marcus Edwards (58' Paulinho), Viktor Gyökeres. Coach: Rúben Amorim.
Goals: 14' Sebastián Coates 0-1, 79' Fabian Piasecki 1-1.
Referee: Anastasios Papapetrou (GRE)   Attendance: 10,518.
Sent off: 8' Viktor Gyökeres.

09.11.23   Gewiss Stadium, Bergamo: Atalanta Bergamo – Sturm Graz 1-0 (0-0)
Atalanta Bergamo: Juan Musso, Rafael Tolói, Berat Djimsiti, Davide Zappacosta (46' Hans Hateboer), Sead Kolasinac, Mitchel Bakker (89' Emil Holm), Marten de Roon, Teun Koopmeiners (86' Aleksey Miranchuk), Éderson, Gianluca Scamacca (62' Luis Muriel), Ademola Lookman (62' Mario Pasalic). Coach: Gian Piero Gasperini.
Sturm Graz: Kjell Scherpen, Gregory Wüthrich, Jusuf Gazibegovic, Dimitri Lavalée, David Affengruber (79' Mohammed Fuseini), David Schnegg (86' Amadou Danté), Jon Gorenc Stankovic, Alexander Prass, William Bøving (59' Tomi Horvat), Manprit Sarkaria, Szymon Wlodarczyk (59' Bryan Teixeira). Coach: Christian Ilzer.
Goal: 50' Berat Djimsiti 1-0.
Referee: Jérôme Brisard (FRA)   Attendance: 14,739.

09.11.23   Estádio José Alvalade, Lisboa: Sporting CP – Raków Czestochowa 2-1 (1-0)
Sporting CP: Antonio Adán, Sebastián Coates, Ricardo Esgaio (56' Iván Fresneda), Jerry St. Juste (70' Ousmane Diomande), Gonçalo Inácio (56' Matheus Reis), Nuno Santos, Daniel Bragança, Pedro Gonçalves "Pote" (56' Morten Hjulmand), Paulinho, Marcus Edwards (70' Tiago Ferreira), Trincão. Coach: Rúben Amorim.
Raków Czestochowa: Vladan Kovacevic, Milan Rundic, Bogdan Racovitan, Bartosz Nowak (18' Adnan Kovacevic), Gustav Berggren (82' Sonny Kittel), Srdjan Plavsic, Jean Carlos, Vladyslav Kocherhin (61' Ben Lederman), Fran Tudor, John Yeboah (62' Marcin Cebula), Ante Crnac (46' Fabian Piasecki). Coach: Dawid Szwarga.
Goals: 14', 52' Pedro Gonçalves "Pote" 1-0 (p), 2-0 (p), 70' Milan Rundic 2-1.
Referee: Enea Jorgji (ALB)   Attendance: 32,940.
Sent off: 12' Bogdan Racovitan.

30.11.23   Gewiss Stadium, Bergamo: Atalanta Bergamo – Sporting CP 1-1 (1-0)
Atalanta Bergamo: Juan Musso, Berat Djimsiti, Sead Kolasinac (86' Emil Holm), Hans Hateboer, Matteo Ruggeri, Giorgio Scalvini (87' Mitchel Bakker), Marten de Roon, Teun Koopmeiners (69' Aleksey Miranchuk), Éderson, Gianluca Scamacca (64' Luis Muriel), Ademola Lookman (64' Mario Pasalic). Coach: Gian Piero Gasperini.
Sporting CP: Antonio Adán, Ricardo Esgaio (46' Geny Catamo), Matheus Reis, Jerry St. Juste (81' Sebastián Coates), Gonçalo Inácio, Ousmane Diomande, Morten Hjulmand (77' Nuno Santos), Pedro Gonçalves "Pote", Hidemasa Morita, Viktor Gyökeres, Trincão (46' Marcus Edwards). Coach: Rúben Amorim.
Goals: 23' Gianluca Scamacca 1-0, 56' Marcus Edwards 1-1.
Referee: Michael Oliver (ENG)   Attendance: 14,865.

30.11.23   Merkur Arena, Graz: Sturm Graz – Raków Czestochowa 0-1 (0-0)
Sturm Graz: Kjell Scherpen, Alexandar Borkovic (72' Stefan Hierländer), Jusuf Gazibegovic (88' Max Johnston), Dimitri Lavalée, David Affengruber, David Schnegg, Jon Gorenc Stankovic, Tomi Horvat (72' Otar Kiteishvili), Alexander Prass (87' Leon Grgic), Manprit Sarkaria, Szymon Wlodarczyk (61' William Bøving). Coach: Christian Ilzer.
Raków Czestochowa: Vladan Kovacevic, Milan Rundic, Adnan Kovacevic (75' Ben Lederman), Marcin Cebula (75' John Yeboah), Bartosz Nowak (75' Sonny Kittel), Gustav Berggren, Jean Carlos, Vladyslav Kocherhin, Fran Tudor, Deian Sorescu (90+1' Srdjan Plavsic), Ante Crnac (75' Fabian Piasecki). Coach: Dawid Szwarga.
Goal: 81' John Yeboah 0-1.
Referee: Filip Glova (SVK)   Attendance: 12,517.

14.12.23   Estádio José Alvalade, Lisboa: Sporting CP – Sturm Graz 3-0 (1-0)
Sporting CP: Franco Israel, Luís Neto, Sebastián Coates, Ricardo Esgaio (56' Dário Essugo), Matheus Reis (46' Gonçalo Inácio), Nuno Santos (75' Pedro Gonçalves "Pote"), Morten Hjulmand (46' Hidemasa Morita), Daniel Bragança, Paulinho, Viktor Gyökeres (46' Marcus Edwards), Trincão. Coach: Rúben Amorim.
Sturm Graz: Kjell Scherpen, Jusuf Gazibegovic, Dimitri Lavalée, David Affengruber, David Schnegg, Jon Gorenc Stankovic, Otar Kiteishvili (75' Javier Serrano), Tomi Horvat (83' Stefan Hierländer), Alexander Prass, Manprit Sarkaria (82' Szymon Wlodarczyk), Seedy Jatta (57' William Bøving). Coach: Christian Ilzer.
Goals: 39' Viktor Gyökeres 1-0, 60', 70' Gonçalo Inácio 2-0, 3-0.
Referee: William Collum (SCO)   Attendance: 24,733.

14.12.23   ArcelorMittal Park, Sosnowiec: Raków Czestochowa – Atalanta Bergamo 0-4 (0-2)
Raków Czestochowa: Vladan Kovacevic, Adnan Kovacevic, Bogdan Racovitan, Bartosz Nowak (81' Sonny Kittel), Gustav Berggren, Srdjan Plavsic, Jean Carlos (78' Deian Sorescu), Vladyslav Kocherhin (62' Marcin Cebula), Fran Tudor, John Yeboah (61' Ante Crnac), Lukasz Zwolinski (81' Fabian Piasecki). Coach: Dawid Szwarga.
Atalanta Bergamo: Marco Carnesecchi (84' Francesco Rossi), Hans Hateboer, Emil Holm (84' Marco Palestra), Nadir Zortea, Tommaso Del Lungo, Giovanni Bonfanti, Mario Pasalic, Aleksey Miranchuk (89' Tommaso De Nipoti), Michel Adopo (90+1' Leonardo Mendicino), Charles De Ketelaere, Luis Muriel (90' Moustapha Cissé). Coach: Gian Piero Gasperini.
Goals: 14' Luis Muriel 0-1, 27' Giovanni Bonfanti 0-2, 72' Luis Muriel 0-3, 90+2' Charles De Ketelaere 0-4.
Referee: Enea Jorgji (ALB)   Attendance: 10,386.

GROUP E

21.09.23   Raiffeisen Arena, Linz: LASK Linz – Liverpool FC 1-3 (1-0)
LASK Linz: Tobias Lawal, Philipp Ziereis, René Renner (88' George Bello), Felix Luckeneder (80' Ebrima Darboe), Andrés Andrade, Robert Zulj, Branko Jovicic, Sascha Horvath, Florian Flecker (89' Sanoussy Ba), Elias Havel (68' Ibrahim Mustapha), Marin Ljubicic (68' Moussa Koné). Coach: Thomas Sageder.
Liverpool FC: Caoimhín Kelleher, Virgil van Dijk, Kostas Tsimikas, Ibrahima Konaté (82' Joel Matip), Wataru Endo (60' Alexis Mac Allister), Ryan Gravenberch (74' Mohamed Salah), Harvey Elliott, Stefan Bajcetic (61' Joe Gomez), Luis Díaz, Darwin Núñez, Ben Doak (60' Dominik Szoboszlai). Coach: Jürgen Klopp.
Goals: 14' Florian Flecker 1-0, 56' Darwin Núñez 1-1 (p), 63' Luis Díaz 1-2, 88' Mohamed Salah 1-3.
Referee: Marco Di Bello (ITA)   Attendance: 18,091.

21.09.23 Lotto Park, Brussels: Union Saint-Gilloise – Toulouse FC 1-1 (0-1)
Union Saint-Gilloise: Anthony Moris, Christian Burgess, Kevin Mac Allister, Fedde Leysen, Noah Sadiki, Alessio Castro-Montes, Jean Lazare Amani, Loïc Lapoussin (87' Casper Terho), Cameron Puertas (84' Mathias Rasmussen), Charles Vanhoutte (62' Mohammed Amoura), Gustaf Nilsson (62' Kevin Rodríguez). Coach: Alexander Blessin.
Toulouse FC: Guillaume Restes, Mikkel Desler, Gabriel Suazo (82' Moussa Diarra), Rasmus Nicolaisen, Logan Costa, Niklas Schmidt, Vincent Sierro, Cristian Cásseres Jr. (60' César Gelabert), Aron Dønnum (61' Warren Kamanzi), Zakaria Aboukhlal (41' Frank Magri), Thijs Dallinga (82' Yanis Begraoui). Coach: Carles Martínez.
Goals: 45+4' Thijs Dallinga 0-1 (p), 69' Mohammed Amoura 1-1.
Referee: Rohit Saggi (NOR)   Attendance: 12,162.
Sent off: 90+5' Logan Costa.

Union Saint-Gilloise played their home matches at the Lotto Park in Brussels, instead of their regular stadium the Joseph Marien Stadium in Brussels, which did not meet the UEFA requirements.

05.10.23 Anfield, Liverpool: Liverpool FC – Union Saint-Gilloise 2-0 (1-0)
Liverpool FC: Alisson Becker, Kostas Tsimikas, Trent Alexander-Arnold (63' Joe Gomez), Ibrahima Konaté, Jarell Quansah, Wataru Endo (46' Alexis Mac Allister), Ryan Gravenberch (79' Dominik Szoboszlai), Harvey Elliott, Mohamed Salah (46' Curtis Jones), Diogo Jota, Darwin Núñez (46' Luis Díaz). Coach: Jürgen Klopp.
Union Saint-Gilloise: Anthony Moris, Christian Burgess, Koki Machida, Kevin Mac Allister (86' Ross Sykes), Alessio Castro-Montes, Jean Lazare Amani (75' Mathias Rasmussen), Cameron Puertas, Charles Vanhoutte (75' Noah Sadiki), Gustaf Nilsson (67' Kevin Rodríguez), Casper Terho (67' Loïc Lapoussin), Mohammed Amoura.
Coach: Alexander Blessin.
Goals: 44' Ryan Gravenberch 1-0, 90+2' Diogo Jota 2-0.
Referee: Morten Krogh Hansen (DEN)   Attendance: 49,513.

05.10.23 Stadium de Toulouse, Toulouse: Toulouse FC – LASK Linz 1-0 (1-0)
Toulouse FC: Guillaume Restes, Mikkel Desler, Gabriel Suazo, Rasmus Nicolaisen, Moussa Diarra, Niklas Schmidt (90+1' Warren Kamanzi), Vincent Sierro, Cristian Cásseres Jr., Aron Dønnum (77' Yanis Begraoui), César Gelabert (61' Frank Magri), Thijs Dallinga (77' Denis Genreau). Coach: Carles Martínez.
LASK Linz: Tobias Lawal, Philipp Ziereis, Andrés Andrade, George Bello (88' Sanoussy Ba), Maksym Talovierov (88' Ibrahim Mustapha), Robert Zulj, Branko Jovicic (69' Ebrima Darboe), Ivan Ljubic, Florian Flecker, Marin Ljubicic (69' Moussa Koné), Moses Usor (59' Elias Havel). Coach: Thomas Sageder.
Goal: 31' Gabriel Suazo 1-0.
Referee: Nicholas Walsh (SCO)   Attendance: 29,233.

26.10.23   Lotto Park, Brussels: Union Saint-Gilloise – LASK Linz 2-1 (0-1)
Union Saint-Gilloise: Anthony Moris, Christian Burgess, Koki Machida, Kevin Mac Allister, Alessio Castro-Montes (64' Casper Terho), Jean Lazare Amani (75' Noah Sadiki), Loïc Lapoussin, Cameron Puertas, Charles Vanhoutte, Mohammed Amoura, Kevin Rodríguez (64' Dennis Eckert-Ayensa). Coach: Alexander Blessin.
LASK Linz: Tobias Lawal, Philipp Ziereis, Filip Stojkovic (72' Florian Flecker), Felix Luckeneder, George Bello (46' Thomas Goiginger), Maksym Talovierov, Robert Zulj, Sascha Horvath, Ivan Ljubic, Marin Ljubicic (67' Ibrahim Mustapha), Moses Usor (76' Andrés Andrade). Coach: Thomas Sageder.
Goals: 24' Moses Usor 0-1, 84' Cameron Puertas 1-1 (p), 90+4' Christian Burgess 2-1.
Referee: Atilla Karaoglan (TUR)   Attendance: 11,426.

26.10.23   Anfield, Liverpool: Liverpool FC – Toulouse FC 5-1 (3-1)
Liverpool FC: Caoimhín Kelleher, Joel Matip, Joe Gomez, Trent Alexander-Arnold (67' Cody Gakpo), Luke Chambers (67' Jarell Quansah), Wataru Endo, Curtis Jones (89' James McConnell), Ryan Gravenberch (70' Mohamed Salah), Harvey Elliott, Diogo Jota, Darwin Núñez (66' Calum Scanlon). Coach: Jürgen Klopp.
Toulouse FC: Guillaume Restes, Mikkel Desler (72' Warren Kamanzi), Gabriel Suazo (67' Frank Magri), Rasmus Nicolaisen, Logan Costa, Moussa Diarra, Niklas Schmidt, Vincent Sierro, Cristian Cásseres Jr. (67' César Gelabert), Aron Dønnum (67' Denis Genreau), Thijs Dallinga (80' Yanis Begraoui). Coach: Carles Martínez.
Goals: 9' Diogo Jota 1-0, 16' Thijs Dallinga 1-1, 30' Wataru Endo 2-1, 34' Darwin Núñez 3-1, 65' Ryan Gravenberch 4-1, 90+3' Mohamed Salah 5-1.
Referee: Rade Obrenovic (SVN)   Attendance: 49,338.

09.11.23   Raiffeisen Arena, Linz: LASK Linz – Union Saint-Gilloise 3-0 (2-0)
LASK Linz: Tobias Lawal, Philipp Ziereis, Filip Stojkovic (75' Florian Flecker), Andrés Andrade, George Bello (75' René Renner), Maksym Talovierov, Robert Zulj, Sascha Horvath, Ivan Ljubic (87' Branko Jovicic), Ibrahim Mustapha (75' Marin Ljubicic), Moses Usor (83' Husein Balic). Coach: Thomas Sageder.
Union Saint-Gilloise: Anthony Moris, Christian Burgess, Koki Machida, Kevin Mac Allister, Alessio Castro-Montes (57' Casper Terho), Jean Lazare Amani, Loïc Lapoussin, Cameron Puertas (75' Henok Teklab), Charles Vanhoutte (57' Noah Sadiki), Dennis Eckert-Ayensa (46' Kevin Rodríguez), Mohammed Amoura (57' Mathias Rasmussen). Coach: Alexander Blessin.
Goals: 25' Sascha Horvath 1-0 (p), 45+4' Maksym Talovierov 2-0, 77' Robert Zulj 3-0.
Referee: Simone Sozza (ITA)   Attendance: 15,900.

09.11.23   Stadium de Toulouse, Toulouse: Toulouse FC – Liverpool FC 3-2 (1-0)
Toulouse FC: Guillaume Restes, Mikkel Desler, Gabriel Suazo, Rasmus Nicolaisen, Logan Costa, Moussa Diarra, Niklas Schmidt (69' Frank Magri), Vincent Sierro, Cristian Cásseres Jr., Aron Dønnum (81' Warren Kamanzi), Thijs Dallinga (88' César Gelabert).
Coach: Carles Martínez.
Liverpool FC: Caoimhín Kelleher, Joel Matip, Joe Gomez, Kostas Tsimikas (46' Dominik Szoboszlai), Jarell Quansah, Wataru Endo (46' Trent Alexander-Arnold), Alexis Mac Allister, Harvey Elliott, Cody Gakpo (73' Darwin Núñez), Luis Díaz (81' Diogo Jota), Ben Doak (46' Mohamed Salah). Coach: Jürgen Klopp.
Goals: 36' Aron Dønnum 1-0, 58' Thijs Dallinga 2-0, 74' Cristian Cásseres Jr. 2-1 (og), 76' Frank Magri 3-1, 89' Diogo Jota 3-2.
Referee: Georgi Kabakov (BUL)   Attendance: 32,026.

30.11.23   Anfield, Liverpool: Liverpool FC – LASK Linz 4-0 (2-0)
Liverpool FC: Caoimhín Kelleher, Joe Gomez, Kostas Tsimikas (82' Luke Chambers), Ibrahima Konaté (56' Trent Alexander-Arnold), Jarell Quansah, Wataru Endo, Ryan Gravenberch (82' Conor Bradley), Harvey Elliott, Mohamed Salah (55' Curtis Jones), Cody Gakpo, Luis Díaz (56' Darwin Núñez). Coach: Jürgen Klopp.
LASK Linz: Tobias Lawal, Philipp Ziereis, Filip Stojkovic (61' Florian Flecker), Andrés Andrade, George Bello (61' René Renner), Maksym Talovierov (61' Elias Havel), Robert Zulj, Sascha Horvath, Ivan Ljubic, Marin Ljubicic (61' Ibrahim Mustapha, 74' Moussa Koné), Moses Usor. Coach: Thomas Sageder.
Goals: 12' Luis Díaz 1-0, 15' Cody Gakpo 2-0, 51' Mohamed Salah 3-0 (p), 90+2' Cody Gakpo 4-0.
Referee: Urs Schnyder (SUI)   Attendance: 49,666.

30.11.23   Stadium de Toulouse, Toulouse: Toulouse FC – Union Saint-Gilloise 0-0
Toulouse FC: Guillaume Restes, Mikkel Desler, Gabriel Suazo (66' Frank Magri), Rasmus Nicolaisen, Logan Costa, Moussa Diarra, Niklas Schmidt (78' César Gelabert), Vincent Sierro, Cristian Cásseres Jr., Aron Dønnum (90+3' Denis Genreau), Thijs Dallinga (90+3' Warren Kamanzi). Coach: Carles Martínez.
Union Saint-Gilloise: Anthony Moris, Christian Burgess, Koki Machida, Kevin Mac Allister (89' Dennis Eckert-Ayensa), Mathias Rasmussen (66' Jean Lazare Amani), Alessio Castro-Montes (77' Casper Terho), Loïc Lapoussin, Cameron Puertas, Charles Vanhoutte (77' Noah Sadiki), Mohammed Amoura, Kevin Rodríguez (66' Gustaf Nilsson).
Coach: Alexander Blessin.
Referee: Matej Jug (SVN)   Attendance: 31,205.

14.12.23   Lotto Park, Brussels: Union Saint-Gilloise – Liverpool FC 2-1 (2-1)
Union Saint-Gilloise: Anthony Moris, Christian Burgess, Koki Machida, Kevin Mac Allister, Noah Sadiki, Alessio Castro-Montes, Jean Lazare Amani (88' Dennis Eckert-Ayensa), Loïc Lapoussin, Cameron Puertas, Gustaf Nilsson (78' Kevin Rodríguez), Mohammed Amoura (84' Mathias Rasmussen). Coach: Alexander Blessin.
Liverpool FC: Caoimhín Kelleher, Ibrahima Konaté (46' Joe Gomez), Luke Chambers (63' Calum Scanlon), Jarell Quansah, Conor Bradley, Wataru Endo (46' Ryan Gravenberch), Curtis Jones, Harvey Elliott, Cody Gakpo, Kaide Gordon (75' James McConnell), Ben Doak (63' Darwin Núñez). Coach: Jürgen Klopp.
Goals: 32' Mohammed Amoura 1-0, 39' Jarell Quansah 1-1, 43' Cameron Puertas 2-1.
Referee: Orel Grinfeld (ISR)   Attendance: 16,959.

14.12.23   Raiffeisen Arena, Linz: LASK Linz – Toulouse FC 1-2 (0-0)
LASK Linz: Tobias Lawal, Philipp Ziereis, Filip Stojkovic (71' Florian Flecker), Andrés Andrade, George Bello, Maksym Talovierov (79' Thomas Goiginger), Robert Zulj, Sascha Horvath, Ivan Ljubic, Marin Ljubicic (88' Moussa Koné), Moses Usor (89' Elias Havel).
Coach: Thomas Sageder.
Toulouse FC: Guillaume Restes, Rasmus Nicolaisen, Logan Costa, Moussa Diarra, Christian Mawissa (90+3' Kévin Keben), Vincent Sierro, Cristian Cásseres Jr. (76' Naatan Skyttä), Aron Dønnum, César Gelabert (67' Denis Genreau), Thijs Dallinga (76' Gabriel Suazo), Ibrahim Cissoko (67' Frank Magri). Coach: Carles Martínez.
Goals: 54' Thijs Dallinga 0-1, 61' Marin Ljubicic 1-1, 83' Gabriel Suazo 1-2.
Referee: Fabio Maresca (ITA)   Attendance: 16,100.

GROUP F

21.09.23 Roazhon Park, Rennes: Stade Rennais – Maccabi Haifa 3-0 (2-0)
Stade Rennais: Steve Mandanda, Warmed Omari, Arthur Theate, Adrien Truffert, Lorenz Assignon, Nemanja Matic (69' Baptiste Santamaría), Benjamin Bourigeaud (73' Enzo Le Fée), Ludovic Blas (83' Mathis Lambourde), Désiré Doué, Bertug Yildirim (70' Amine Gouiri), Ibrahim Salah (73' Fabian Rieder). Coach: Bruno Génésio.
Maccabi Haifa: Itamar Nizan, Daniel Sundgren, Shon Goldberg (72' Lorenco Simic), Pierre Cornud, Abdoulaye Seck, Tjaronn Chery (81' Erik Shuranov), Mahmoud Jaber, Show (62' Ali Muhammad), Dean David (46' Dia Saba), Frantzdy Pierrot (62' Maor Kandil), Anan Khalaili. Coach: Mesay Dego.
Goals: 1' Ludovic Blas 1-0, 31' Adrien Truffert 2-0, 55' Bertug Yildirim 3-0.
Referee: Harm Osmers (GER)   Attendance: 26,838.

21.09.23   Olympiako Stadio Spyros Louis, Athens: Panathinaikos – Villarreal CF 2-0 (1-0)
Panathinaikos: Alberto Brignoli, Hörður Magnússon, Bart Schenkeveld, Filip Mladenovic, Giannis Kotsiras, Rubén Pérez (77' Willian Arão), Bernard (77' Filip Djuricic), Daniel Mancini (68' Tonny Vilhena), Adam Gnezda Cerin, Sebastián Palacios (88' Aitor Cantalapiedra), Fotis Ioannidis (69' Andraz Sporar). Coach: Ivan Jovanovic.
Villarreal CF: Pepe Reina, Kiko Femenía, Aïssa Mandi, Matteo Gabbia, Étienne Capoue, Denis Suárez (29' Yéremy Pino), Manu Trigueros (61' Gerard Moreno), Alfonso Pedraza, Santi Comesaña (61' Dani Parejo), José Luis Morales (77' Álex Baena), Ben Brereton (61' Alexander Sørloth). Coaches: Miguel Tena & Pacheta.
Goals: 38' Fotis Ioannidis 1-0, 78' Andraz Sporar 2-0.
Referee: Craig Pawson (ENG)   Attendance: 57,003.

Panathinaikos played their home matches at the Olympiako Stadio Spyros Louis in Athens, instead of their regular stadium the Leoforos Alexandras Stadium in Athens.

05.10.23   Estadio de la Cerámica, Villarreal: Villarreal CF – Stade Rennais 1-0 (1-0)
Villarreal CF: Pepe Reina, Kiko Femenía, Aïssa Mandi, Alberto Moreno (85' Raúl Albiol), Matteo Gabbia, Étienne Capoue, Dani Parejo, Manu Trigueros (74' Santi Comesaña), Álex Baena (57' Alfonso Pedraza), Yéremy Pino (57' José Luis Morales), Alexander Sørloth (85' Ramón Terrats). Coaches: Miguel Tena & Pacheta.
Stade Rennais: Steve Mandanda, Warmed Omari, Arthur Theate, Adrien Truffert, Guela Doué, Benjamin Bourigeaud (73' Enzo Le Fée), Baptiste Santamaría (73' Nemanja Matic), Ludovic Blas, Désiré Doué (81' Martin Terrier), Bertug Yildirim (64' Arnaud Kalimuendo), Ibrahim Salah (64' Amine Gouiri). Coach: Bruno Génésio.
Goal: 36' Alexander Sørloth 1-0.
Referee: Harald Lechner (AUT)   Attendance: 17,458.

Martin Terrier missed a penalty kick (90+2').

05.10.23 Sammy Ofer Stadium, Haifa: Maccabi Haifa – Panathinaikos 0-0
Maccabi Haifa: Shareef Keouf, Daniel Sundgren, Pierre Cornud, Abdoulaye Seck, Lorenco Simic, Dia Saba (68' Frantzdy Pierrot), Mahmoud Jaber, Show (68' Ali Muhammad), Dean David (76' Lior Refaelov), Erik Shuranov (46' Tjaronn Chery), Anan Khalaili (84' Hamza Shibli). Coach: Mesay Dego.
Panathinaikos: Alberto Brignoli, Bart Schenkeveld, Juankar (88' Filip Mladenovic), Tin Jedvaj, Giannis Kotsiras (78' Georgios Vagiannidis), Tonny Vilhena, Bernard, Willian Arão, Daniel Mancini (78' Sebastián Palacios), Adam Gnezda Cerin (67' Filip Djuricic), Fotis Ioannidis (67' Andraz Sporar). Coach: Ivan Jovanovic.
Referee: António Nobre (POR)   Attendance: 29,465.

26.10.23 Olympiako Stadio Spyros Louis, Athens: Panathinaikos – Stade Rennais 1-2 (0-1)
Panathinaikos: Alberto Brignoli, Bart Schenkeveld, Filip Mladenovic, Tin Jedvaj, Georgios Vagiannidis (79' Giannis Kotsiras), Filip Djuricic (74' Andraz Sporar), Bernard (61' Aitor Cantalapiedra), Willian Arão, Adam Gnezda Cerin (62' Tonny Vilhena), Sebastián Palacios (61' Daniel Mancini), Fotis Ioannidis. Coach: Ivan Jovanovic.
Stade Rennais: Steve Mandanda, Warmed Omari, Adrien Truffert (80' Arthur Theate), Lorenz Assignon, Jeanuël Belocian, Nemanja Matic, Benjamin Bourigeaud (30' Baptiste Santamaría), Ludovic Blas, Enzo Le Fée (46' Fabian Rieder), Amine Gouiri (90+2' Martin Terrier), Arnaud Kalimuendo (80' Désiré Doué). Coach: Bruno Génésio.
Goals: 7' Amine Gouiri 0-1, 49' Arnaud Kalimuendo 0-2, 61' Fotis Ioannidis 1-2 (p).
Referee: João Pedro Pinheiro (POR)   Attendance: 13,459.

09.11.23 Roazhon Park, Rennes: Stade Rennais – Panathinaikos 3-1 (1-1)
Stade Rennais: Gauthier Gallon, Christopher Wooh, Arthur Theate, Guela Doué, Jeanuël Belocian, Nemanja Matic (90+3' Lorenz Assignon), Benjamin Bourigeaud (63' Ludovic Blas), Enzo Le Fée, Fabian Rieder (62' Baptiste Santamaría), Martin Terrier (62' Ibrahim Salah), Arnaud Kalimuendo (35' Adrien Truffert). Coach: Bruno Génésio.
Panathinaikos: Alberto Brignoli, Bart Schenkeveld, Filip Mladenovic, Tin Jedvaj, Georgios Vagiannidis (78' Andraz Sporar), Rubén Pérez (79' Willian Arão), Tonny Vilhena, Bernard (71' Aitor Cantalapiedra), Adam Gnezda Cerin (46' Filip Djuricic), Sebastián Palacios (72' Daniel Mancini), Fotis Ioannidis. Coach: Ivan Jovanovic.
Goals: 9' Fabian Rieder 1-0, 34' Fotis Ioannidis 1-1 (p), 65' Ibrahim Salah 2-1, 70' Ludovic Blas 3-1 (p).
Referee: William Collum (SCO)   Attendance: 28,004.
Sent off: 33' Jeanuël Belocian.

09.11.23   AEK Arena – George Karapatakis, Larnaca (CYP):
Maccabi Haifa – Villarreal CF 1-2 (1-0)
Maccabi Haifa: Shareef Keouf, Daniel Sundgren, Pierre Cornud, Abdoulaye Seck, Lorenco Simic, Lior Refaelov (76' Mahmoud Jaber), Ali Muhammad, Show (87' Goni Naor), Ilay Hagag (76' Suf Podgoreanu), Frantzdy Pierrot (66' Dean David), Anan Khalaili (87' Hamza Shibli). Coach: Mesay Dego.
Villarreal CF: Pepe Reina, Aïssa Mandi, Alberto Moreno, Matteo Gabbia, Adrià Altimira, Manu Trigueros (79' Étienne Capoue), Santi Comesaña (46' Jorge Pascual), Ramón Terrats (66' Dani Parejo), Alexander Sørloth, Ben Brereton (66' Álex Baena), Ilias Akhomach (65' Yéremy Pino). Coaches: Miguel Tena & Pacheta.
Goals: 29' Abdoulaye Seck 1-0, 82' Álex Baena 1-1, 86' Alexander Sørloth 1-2.
Referee: Mykola Balakin (UKR)   Attendance: 0.

Manu Trigueros missed a penalty kick (38').

Due to the Israel-Hamas war, Maccabi Haifa played their remaining home matches at a neutral venue and behind closed doors.

30.11.23   Puskás Aréna, Budapest (HUN): Maccabi Haifa – Stade Rennais 0-3 (0-1)
Maccabi Haifa: Shareef Keouf, Rami Gershon, Abdoulaye Seck, Maor Kandil, Lorenco Simic (61' Pierre Cornud), Tjaronn Chery (61' Lior Refaelov), Mahmoud Jaber, Show (32' Goni Naor), Dean David, Frantzdy Pierrot (72' Ilay Hagag), Suf Podgoreanu (46' Anan Khalaili). Coach: Mesay Dego.
Stade Rennais: Steve Mandanda, Warmed Omari, Christopher Wooh, Arthur Theate, Adrien Truffert (62' Mahamadou Nagida), Lorenz Assignon, Nemanja Matic (81' Ludovic Blas), Enzo Le Fée (62' Baptiste Santamaría), Martin Terrier, Amine Gouiri (62' Fabian Rieder), Bertug Yildirim (71' Désiré Doué). Coach: Julien Stéphan.
Goals: 29' Martin Terrier 0-1, 47' Amine Gouiri 0-2, 90+3' Fabian Rieder 0-3.
Referee: Horatiu Fesnic (ROM)   Attendance: 0.

30.11.23   Estadio de la Cerámica, Villarreal: Villarreal CF – Panathinaikos 3-2 (2-0)
Villarreal CF: Pepe Reina, Raúl Albiol (46' Matteo Gabbia), Alberto Moreno, Juan Foyth (78' Adrià Altimira), Jorge Cuenca, Dani Parejo, Manu Trigueros (77' Alfonso Pedraza), Santi Comesaña, Álex Baena (68' Gerard Moreno), José Luis Morales (68' Ben Brereton), Ilias Akhomach. Coach: Marcelino.
Panathinaikos: Alberto Brignoli, Bart Schenkeveld, Filip Mladenovic (87' Juankar), Georgios Vagiannidis, Rubén Pérez, Bernard (60' Filip Djuricic), Willian Arão, Adam Gnezda Cerin (75' Tonny Vilhena), Andraz Sporar (60' Fotis Ioannidis), Sebastián Palacios (88' Daniel Mancini), Aitor Cantalapiedra. Coach: Ivan Jovanovic.
Goals: 29' Álex Baena 1-0, 34' Santi Comesaña 2-0, 47' José Luis Morales 3-0, 66' Sebastián Palacios 3-1, 81' Fotis Ioannidis 3-2.
Referee: Ivan Kruzliak (SVK)   Attendance: 16,993.

Fotis Ioannidis missed a penalty kick (66').

06.12.23   Estadio de la Cerámica, Villarreal: Villarreal CF – Maccabi Haifa 0-0
Villarreal CF: Pepe Reina, Matteo Gabbia, Juan Foyth (57' Alfonso Pedraza), Jorge Cuenca, Adrià Altimira, Étienne Capoue, Manu Trigueros (84' Jorge Pascual), Santi Comesaña (57' Francis Coquelin), Álex Baena (46' José Luis Morales), Ben Brereton (66' Gerard Moreno), Ilias Akhomach. Coach: Marcelino.
Maccabi Haifa: Shareef Keouf, Daniel Sundgren (61' Illay Feingold), Rami Gershon, Maor Kandil, Lorenco Simic, Lior Refaelov, Ali Muhammad (43' Mahmoud Jaber), Show (78' Goni Naor), Ilay Hagag (61' Suf Podgoreanu), Dean David, Anan Khalaili (46' Frantzdy Pierrot). Coach: Mesay Dego.
Referee: Nicholas Walsh (SCO)   Attendance: 9,365.

The match was originally due to be played on 26th October 2023, but was rescheduled to 6th December 2023.

14.12.23   Roazhon Park, Rennes: Stade Rennais – Villarreal CF 2-3 (1-1)
Stade Rennais: Steve Mandanda, Christopher Wooh, Arthur Theate, Lorenz Assignon, Jeanuël Belocian (69' Adrien Truffert), Mahamadou Nagida (69' Ibrahim Salah), Nemanja Matic, Benjamin Bourigeaud (54' Ludovic Blas), Enzo Le Fée, Martin Terrier (84' Arnaud Kalimuendo), Bertug Yildirim (69' Amine Gouiri). Coach: Julien Stéphan.
Villarreal CF: Pepe Reina, Raúl Albiol, Matteo Gabbia, Juan Foyth (48' Ramón Terrats), Adrià Altimira, Étienne Capoue (85' Jorge Cuenca), Dani Parejo, Álex Baena, Gerard Moreno (86' Ben Brereton), Alexander Sørloth (73' José Luis Morales), Ilias Akhomach (72' Francis Coquelin). Coach: Marcelino.
Goals: 36' Gerard Moreno 0-1 (p), 37' Lorenz Assignon 1-1, 62' Ilias Akhomach 1-2, 79' Ludovic Blas 2-2, 80' Dani Parejo 2-3.
Referee: Atilla Karaoglan (TUR)   Attendance: 27,761.

14.12.23   Olympiako Stadio Spyros Louis, Athens: Panathinaikos – Maccabi Haifa 1-2 (0-1)
Panathinaikos: Yuriy Lodygin, Bart Schenkeveld, Juankar (81' Filip Mladenovic), Tin Jedvaj, Georgios Vagiannidis, Tonny Vilhena (69' Adam Gnezda Cerin), Bernard, Willian Arão, Sebastián Palacios (69' Daniel Mancini), Aitor Cantalapiedra (89' Andraz Sporar), Fotis Ioannidis. Coach: Ivan Jovanovic.
Maccabi Haifa: Shareef Keouf, Daniel Sundgren (46' Illay Feingold), Rami Gershon, Pierre Cornud (80' Suf Podgoreanu), Abdoulaye Seck, Tjaronn Chery (80' Anan Khalaili), Ali Muhammad (32' Mahmoud Jaber), Show, Ilay Hagag, Dean David (67' Lior Refaelov), Frantzdy Pierrot. Coach: Mesay Dego.
Goals: 20' Dean David 0-1, 74' Tjaronn Chery 0-2, 89' Fotis Ioannidis 1-2.
Referee: Georgi Kabakov (BUL)   Attendance: 13,121.

GROUP G

21.09.23   Stade de Genève, Lancy: Servette FC – Slavia Praha 0-2 (0-1)
Servette FC: Jérémy Frick, Steve Rouiller, Yoan Severin, Bradley Mazikou (84' Ronny Rodelin), Bendegúz Bolla, Miroslav Stevanovic, David Douline (67' Gaël Ondoua), Dereck Kutesa (67' Jérémy Guillemenot), Timothé Cognat, Alexis Antunes (81' Hussayn Touati), Chris Bedia (67' Enzo Crivelli). Coach: René Weiler.
Slavia Praha: Ales Mandous, Oscar Dorley, Michal Tomic (72' Matej Jurásek), Andres Dumitrescu (87' Václav Jurecka), Igoh Ogbu, Tomás Holes, Lukás Masopust, Petr Sevcík (52' Christos Zafeiris), David Doudera (72' Lukás Provod), Conrad Wallem, Mick van Buren (52' Muhamed Tijani). Coach: Jindrich Trpisovský.
Goals: 32' Lukás Masopust 0-1, 58' Igoh Ogbu 0-2.
Referee: Giorgi Kruashvili (GEO)   Attendance: 19,783.

21.09.23   Bolshaya Sportivnaya Arena, Tiraspol: FC Sheriff Tiraspol – AS Roma 1-2 (0-1)
FC Sheriff Tiraspol: Maksim Koval, Cristian Tovar (88' Luvannor), Gaby Kiki, Armel Zohouri, Munashe Garananga, Alejandro Artunduaga (88' Kostas Apostolakis), Amine Talal (90+6' Dan-Angelo Botan), João Paulo, Jerome Mbekeli, Peter Ademo, David Ankeye (71' Ricardinho). Coach: Roberto Bordin.
AS Roma: Mile Svilar, Diego Llorente, Rick Karsdorp, Gianluca Mancini, Evan Ndicka, Bryan Cristante, Renato Sanches (28' Leandro Paredes), Houssem Aouar (62' Edoardo Bove), Nicola Zalewski (61' Leonardo Spinazzola), Stephan El Shaarawy (61' Paulo Dybala), Romelu Lukaku (80' Andrea Belotti). Coach: José Mourinho.
Goals: 45+4' Gaby Kiki 0-1 (og), 57' Cristian Tovar 1-1, 65' Romelu Lukaku 1-2.
Referee: Andris Treimanis (LVA)   Attendance: 10,711.
Sent off: 90+7' João Paulo.

05.10.23   Stadio Olimpico, Roma: AS Roma – Servette FC 4-0 (1-0)
AS Roma: Mile Svilar, Zeki Çelik, Gianluca Mancini (64' Rick Karsdorp), Evan Ndicka, Leandro Paredes, Bryan Cristante, Houssem Aouar (46' Lorenzo Pellegrini, 57' Riccardo Pagano), Edoardo Bove (76' Francesco D'Alessio), Stephan El Shaarawy, Romelu Lukaku (64' Nicola Zalewski), Andrea Belotti. Coach: José Mourinho.
Servette FC: Jérémy Frick, Yoan Severin, Bradley Mazikou, Keigo Tsunemoto, Nicolas Vouilloz, Miroslav Stevanovic (88' Hussayn Touati), Dereck Kutesa (64' Bendegúz Bolla), Gaël Ondoua, Alexis Antunes (64' Timothé Cognat), Enzo Crivelli (63' Jérémy Guillemenot), Chris Bedia (74' David Douline). Coach: René Weiler.
Goals: 21' Romelu Lukaku 1-0, 46' Andrea Belotti 2-0, 52' Lorenzo Pellegrini 3-0, 59' Andrea Belotti 4-0.
Referee: Igor Pajac (CRO)   Attendance: 55,764.

05.10.23   Fortuna Arena, Praha: Slavia Praha – FC Sheriff Tiraspol 6-0 (3-0)
Slavia Praha: Ales Mandous, Oscar Dorley, Andres Dumitrescu, Igoh Ogbu, Tomás Holes, Lukás Masopust (78' Jan Boril), David Doudera (66' Michal Tomic), Conrad Wallem (66' Bolu Ogungbayi), Christos Zafeiris (66' Lukás Provod), Ivan Schranz (66' Mick van Buren), Mojmír Chytil. Coach: Jindrich Trpisovský.
FC Sheriff Tiraspol: Maksim Koval, Cristian Tovar (46' Cédric Badolo), Gaby Kiki, Armel Zohouri, Munashe Garananga, Ricardinho (56' David Ankeye), Alejandro Artunduaga (56' Kostas Apostolakis), Amine Talal, Jerome Mbekeli, Peter Ademo (46' Berkay Vardar), Luvannor. Coach: Roberto Bordin.
Goals: 4' Mojmír Chytil 1-0, 7' Igoh Ogbu 1-0, 39' Munashe Garananga 3-0 (og), 47' Ivan Schranz 4-0, 58' David Doudera 5-0, 71' Mojmír Chytil 6-0.
Referee: Willy Delajod (FRA)   Attendance: 17,844.

26.10.23   Stadio Olimpico, Roma: AS Roma – Slavia Praha 2-0 (2-0)
AS Roma: Mile Svilar, Diego Llorente, Zeki Çelik, Gianluca Mancini, Evan Ndicka, Bryan Cristante, Houssem Aouar (88' Luigi Cherubini), Nicola Zalewski (70' Rick Karsdorp), Edoardo Bove (46' Leandro Paredes), Stephan El Shaarawy (70' Andrea Belotti), Romelu Lukaku (83' Riccardo Pagano). Coach: José Mourinho.
Slavia Praha: Ales Mandous, Oscar Dorley, Tomás Vlcek, Andres Dumitrescu (65' Lukás Provod), Igoh Ogbu, Tomás Holes, Lukás Masopust (46' Matej Jurásek), David Doudera, Christos Zafeiris (82' Václav Jurecka), Ivan Schranz (46' Conrad Wallem), Mick van Buren (71' Mojmír Chytil). Coach: Jindrich Trpisovský.
Goals: 1' Edoardo Bove 1-0, 17' Romelu Lukaku 2-0.
Referee: Espen Eskås (NOR)   Attendance: 64,934.

26.10.23   Bolshaya Sportivnaya Arena, Tiraspol: FC Sheriff Tiraspol – Servette FC 1-1 (0-1)
FC Sheriff Tiraspol: Maksim Koval, Cristian Tovar, Gaby Kiki, Armel Zohouri, Ricardinho, Alejandro Artunduaga (85' Munashe Garananga), Amine Talal, João Paulo (38' Jerome Mbekeli), Cédric Badolo, Luvannor (76' Kostas Apostolakis), David Ankeye.
Coach: Roman Pylypchuk.
Servette FC: Jérémy Frick, Yoan Severin, Bradley Mazikou, Bendegúz Bolla (76' Keigo Tsunemoto), Nicolas Vouilloz, Miroslav Stevanovic, David Douline, Gaël Ondoua, Alexis Antunes (64' Dereck Kutesa), Enzo Crivelli (64' Timothé Cognat), Jérémy Guillemenot (64' Chris Bedia). Coach: René Weiler.
Goals: 41' Enzo Crivelli 0-1, 80' David Ankeye 1-1.
Referee: John Brooks (ENG)   Attendance: 2,834.

09.11.23   Stade de Genève, Lancy: Servette FC – FC Sheriff Tiraspol 2-1 (0-1)
Servette FC: Jérémy Frick, Steve Rouiller, Yoan Severin, Bradley Mazikou (81' Anthony Baron), Bendegúz Bolla, Théo Magnin (54' Enzo Crivelli), Miroslav Stevanovic, Dereck Kutesa, Gaël Ondoua (76' Jérémy Guillemenot), Timothé Cognat (81' Samba Diba), Chris Bedia. Coach: René Weiler.
FC Sheriff Tiraspol: Maksim Koval, Cristian Tovar, Gaby Kiki, Armel Zohouri, Ricardinho (58' Munashe Garananga), Alejandro Artunduaga, Amine Talal, João Paulo, Cédric Badolo, Jerome Mbekeli (72' Kostas Apostolakis), David Ankeye. Coach: Roman Pylypchuk.
Goals: 12' Yoan Severin 0-1 (og), 84' Steve Rouiller 1-1, 90+3' Chris Bedia 2-1 (p).
Referee: Manfredas Lukjancukas (LTU)   Attendance: 15,822.
Sent off: 90' Armel Zohouri, 90+8' Gaby Kiki.

09.11.23   Fortuna Arena, Praha: Slavia Praha – AS Roma 2-0 (0-0)
Slavia Praha: Ales Mandous, Jan Boril, Oscar Dorley (89' Mick van Buren), Igoh Ogbu, Tomás Holes, Lukás Masopust (78' Tomás Vlcek), Lukás Provod, David Doudera, Christos Zafeiris (78' Petr Sevcík), Václav Jurecka (87' Conrad Wallem), Mojmír Chytil (90+5' Jakub Hromada). Coach: Jindrich Trpisovský.
AS Roma: Mile Svilar, Diego Llorente, Oscar Dorley (77' Renato Sanches), Zeki Çelik, Gianluca Mancini, Evan Ndicka, Leandro Paredes (84' João Costa), Houssem Aouar (46' Bryan Cristante), Edoardo Bove, Stephan El Shaarawy (46' Rick Karsdorp), Romelu Lukaku, Andrea Belotti (68' Paulo Dybala). Coach: José Mourinho.
Goals: 50' Václav Jurecka 1-0, 74' Lukás Masopust 2-0.
Referee: François Letexier (FRA)   Attendance: 19,265.

30.11.23   Stade de Genève, Lancy: Servette FC – AS Roma 1-1 (0-1)
Servette FC: Jérémy Frick, Anthony Baron (90+6' Nicolas Vouilloz), Steve Rouiller, Yoan Severin, Keigo Tsunemoto, Bendegúz Bolla (68' Alexis Antunes), Miroslav Stevanovic, Dereck Kutesa (68' Jérémy Guillemenot), Gaël Ondoua, Timothé Cognat (81' Samba Diba), Chris Bedia (81' Hussayn Touati). Coach: René Weiler.
AS Roma: Mile Svilar, Diego Llorente, Zeki Çelik, Evan Ndicka, Leandro Paredes, Bryan Cristante, Houssem Aouar (55' Lorenzo Pellegrini), Edoardo Bove (81' Andrea Belotti), Stephan El Shaarawy (74' Leonardo Spinazzola), Romelu Lukaku, Paulo Dybala (81' Renato Sanches). Coach: José Mourinho.
Goals: 21' Romelu Lukaku 0-1, 50' Chris Bedia 1-1.
Referee: Daniel Stefanski (POL)   Attendance: 28,534.

30.11.23 Bolshaya Sportivnaya Arena, Tiraspol: FC Sheriff Tiraspol – Slavia Praha 2-3 (1-1)
FC Sheriff Tiraspol: Maksim Koval, Cristian Tovar, Munashe Garananga, Ricardinho (74'
Vinícius Paiva, 90+1' Berkay Vardar), Kostas Apostolakis, Alejandro Artunduaga, Amine
Talal, João Paulo, Cédric Badolo, Jerome Mbekeli, Luvannor (46' David Ankeye).
Coach: Roman Pylypchuk.
Slavia Praha: Ales Mandous, Jan Boril, Oscar Dorley, Andres Dumitrescu (61' Conrad
Wallem), Igoh Ogbu, Lukás Masopust, Lukás Provod, David Doudera, Christos Zafeiris, Mick
van Buren (70' Mojmír Chytil), Václav Jurecka (70' Muhamed Tijani).
Coach: Jindrich Trpisovský.
Goals: 19' Václav Jurecka 0-1, 45+3' Cristian Tovar 1-1, 56' Jerome Mbekeli 2-1,
78' Christos Zafeiris 2-2, 90+5' Muhamed Tijani 2-3 (p).
Referee: Christian-Petru Ciochirca (AUT)   Attendance: 1,520.

14.12.23 Stadio Olimpico, Roma: AS Roma – FC Sheriff Tiraspol 3-0 (2-0)
AS Roma: Mile Svilar, Diego Llorente (60' Leandro Paredes), Rick Karsdorp, Zeki Çelik,
Bryan Cristante, Renato Sanches (61' Riccardo Pagano), Houssem Aouar (46' Stephan El
Shaarawy), Nicola Zalewski (86' Mattia Mannini), Edoardo Bove, Romelu Lukaku, Andrea
Belotti (73' Niccolò Pisilli). Coach: José Mourinho.
FC Sheriff Tiraspol: Maksim Koval, Cristian Tovar, Munashe Garananga, Ricardinho, Kostas
Apostolakis (36' Armel Zohouri), Alejandro Artunduaga, Amine Talal, João Paulo, Cédric
Badolo (86' Berkay Vardar), Jerome Mbekeli, David Ankeye (72' Luvannor).
Coach: Roman Pylypchuk.
Goals: 11' Romelu Lukaku 1-0, 32' Andrea Belotti 2-0, 90+3' Niccolò Pisilli 3-0.
Referee: Jérôme Brisard (FRA)   Attendance: 47,803.

14.12.23 Fortuna Arena, Praha: Slavia Praha – Servette FC 4-0 (4-0)
Slavia Praha: Ales Mandous, Oscar Dorley (35' Jakub Hromada), Tomás Vlcek, Igoh Ogbu,
Tomás Holes, David Doudera (82' Samuel Pikolon), Conrad Wallem (61' Andres Dumitrescu),
Christos Zafeiris, Ivan Schranz, Václav Jurecka (61' Michal Tomic), Mojmír Chytil (60'
Muhamed Tijani). Coach: Jindrich Trpisovský.
Servette FC: Jérémy Frick, Yoan Severin, Bradley Mazikou, Bendegúz Bolla (79' Hussayn
Touati), Nicolas Vouilloz, Théo Magnin, Miroslav Stevanovic (62' Keigo Tsunemoto), Gaël
Ondoua, Alexis Antunes (62' Anthony Baron), Samba Diba (62' Timothé Cognat), Chris Bedia
(62' Dereck Kutesa). Coach: René Weiler.
Goals: 15' David Doudera 1-0, 25' Ivan Schranz 2-0, 30', 45+1' Mojmír Chytil 3-0, 4-0.
Referee: Nicholas Walsh (SCO)   Attendance: 18,380.

GROUP H

21.09.23 BayArena, Leverkusen: Bayer Leverkusen – BK Häcken 4-0 (2-0)
Bayer Leverkusen: Matej Kovár, Álex Grimaldo, Jonathan Tah, Edmond Tapsoba (72' Piero
Hincapié), Josip Stanisic, Granit Xhaka (77' Robert Andrich), Nathan Tella (60' Jonas
Hofmann), Exequiel Palacios, Florian Wirtz (72' Jeremie Frimpong), Amine Adli, Victor
Boniface (71' Adam Hlozek). Coach: Xabi Alonso.
BK Häcken: Peter Abrahamsson, Even Hovland, Simon Sandberg (74' Tomas Totland),
Valgeir Lunddal Fridriksson, Aiham Ousou (75' Johan Hammar), Mikkel Rygaard, Samuel
Gustafson, Simon Gustafson (71' Srdjan Hrstic), Romeo Amané (74' Pontus Dahbo), Amor
Layouni, Edward Chilufya (71' Momodou Sonko). Coach: Per-Mathias Høgmo.
Goals: 10' Florian Wirtz 1-0, 16' Amine Adli 2-0, 66' Victor Boniface 3-0,
70' Jonas Hofmann 4-0.
Referee: Manfredas Lukjancukas (LTU)   Attendance: 25,402.

21.09.23   Tofiq Bahramov adina Respublika stadionu, Baku:
Qarabag FK – Molde FK 1-0 (0-0)
Qarabag FK: Andrey Lunev, Maksim Medvedev (87' Badavi Hüseynov), Kevin Medina, Matheus Silva (88' Nariman Axundzade), Elvin Cafarquliyev, Yassine Benzia (81' Toral Bayramov), Marko Jankovic, Abdellah Zoubir, Leandro Andrade (81' Hamidou Keyta), Júlio Romão, Juninho (90+3' Patrick Andrade). Coach: Qurban Qurbanov.
Molde FK: Jacob Karlstrøm, Kristoffer Haugen (70' Martin Linnes), Martin Bjørnbak, Anders Hagelskjær, Casper Øyvann, Mathias Løvik, Magnus Eikrem (70' Fredrik Gulbrandsen), Martin Ellingsen (70' Eirik Hestad), Markus Kaasa (74' Kristian Eriksen), Emil Breivik, Veton Berisha (87' Magnus Grødem). Coach: Erling Moe.
Goal: 55' Leandro Andrade 1-0.
Referee: John Beaton (SCO)   Attendance: 26,500.

05.10.23   Aker Stadion, Molde: Molde FK – Bayer Leverkusen 1-2 (0-2)
Molde FK: Jacob Karlstrøm (41' Oliver Petersen), Kristoffer Haugen (80' Christian Cappis), Anders Hagelskjær, Casper Øyvann, Mathias Løvik, Magnus Eikrem (67' Fredrik Gulbrandsen), Eirik Hestad (68' Eric Bugale Kitolano), Martin Ellingsen, Kristian Eriksen, Markus Kaasa (80' Magnus Grødem), Emil Breivik. Coach: Erling Moe.
Bayer Leverkusen: Matej Kovár, Jonathan Tah, Jeremie Frimpong (90+1' Odilon Kossounou), Edmond Tapsoba (70' Álex Grimaldo), Josip Stanisic, Piero Hincapié, Granit Xhaka, Robert Andrich, Nathan Tella (70' Jonas Hofmann), Adam Hlozek (83' Victor Boniface), Amine Adli (83' Florian Wirtz). Coach: Xabi Alonso.
Goals: 14' Jeremie Frimpong 0-1, 18' Nathan Tella 0-2, 87' Emil Breivik 1-2.
Referee: Anastasios Papapetrou (GRE)   Attendance: 8,190.

05.10.23   Nya Ullevi, Göteborg: BK Häcken – Qarabag FK 0-1 (0-0)
BK Häcken: Peter Abrahamsson, Simon Sandberg (78' Ishaq Abdulrazak), Johan Hammar, Tomas Totland, Aiham Ousou, Mikkel Rygaard, Samuel Gustafson, Simon Gustafson, Amor Layouni, Edward Chilufya (77' Ali Youssef), Momodou Sonko (56' Romeo Amané).
Coach: Per-Mathias Høgmo.
Qarabag FK: Andrey Lunev, Badavi Hüseynov (67' Maksim Medvedev), Kevin Medina, Matheus Silva, Elvin Cafarquliyev, Yassine Benzia (77' Patrick Andrade), Marko Jankovic, Abdellah Zoubir, Leandro Andrade (82' Toral Bayramov), Júlio Romão, Juninho (77' Hamidou Keyta). Coach: Qurban Qurbanov.
Goal: 70' Juninho 0-1.
Referee: Sebastian Gishamer (AUT)   Attendance: 8,124.

BK Häcken played their home matches at the Ullevi in Göteborg, instead of their regular stadium the Bravida Arena in Göteborg, which did not meet UEFA requirements.

26.10.23   Aker Stadion, Molde: Molde FK – BK Häcken 5-1 (3-1)
Molde FK: Oliver Petersen, Kristoffer Haugen, Martin Bjørnbak, Anders Hagelskjær, Casper Øyvann, Mathias Løvik, Magnus Eikrem (63' Eric Bugale Kitolano), Martin Ellingsen (89' Eirik Hestad), Markus Kaasa (75' Christian Cappis), Emil Breivik, Fredrik Gulbrandsen (74' Veton Berisha). Coach: Erling Moe.
BK Häcken: Peter Abrahamsson, Even Hovland, Simon Sandberg (46' Ishaq Abdulrazak), Tomas Totland, Aiham Ousou, Mikkel Rygaard (71' Pontus Dahbo), Samuel Gustafson (81' Isak Brusberg), Simon Gustafson (42' Romeo Amané), Amor Layouni, Edward Chilufya (71' Srdjan Hrstic), Momodou Sonko. Coach: Per-Mathias Høgmo.
Goals: 6' Fredrik Gulbrandsen 1-0, 21' Momodou Sonko 1-1, 27' Magnus Eikrem 2-1, 30' Emil Breivik 3-1, 55' Magnus Eikrem 4-1, 90+3' Martin Bjørnbak 5-1.
Referee: Urs Schnyder (SUI)   Attendance: 5,870.
26.10.23   BayArena, Leverkusen: Bayer Leverkusen – Qarabag FK 5-1 (3-1)

Bayer Leverkusen: Matej Kovár, Álex Grimaldo (80' Gustavo Puerta), Edmond Tapsoba (71' Josip Stanisic), Odilon Kossounou, Piero Hincapié, Granit Xhaka (62' Exequiel Palacios), Robert Andrich, Nathan Tella, Florian Wirtz (70' Adam Hlozek), Amine Adli, Victor Boniface (62' Patrik Schick). Coach: Xabi Alonso.
Qarabag FK: Andrey Lunev, Bahlul Mustafazade, Kevin Medina, Matheus Silva (46' Yassine Benzia), Toral Bayramov, Elvin Cafarquliyev, Marko Jankovic (63' Patrick Andrade), Abdellah Zoubir (87' Hamidou Keyta), Leandro Andrade (71' Nariman Axundzade), Júlio Romão, Juninho (71' Redon Xhixha). Coach: Qurban Qurbanov.
Goals: 4' Florian Wirtz 1-0, 16' Toral Bayramov 1-1 (p), 29' Álex Grimaldo 2-1, 35' Victor Boniface 3-1, 54' Álex Grimaldo 4-1, 57' Edmond Tapsoba 5-1.
Referee: Horatiu Fesnic (ROM)   Attendance: 29,039.

09.11.23   Tofiq Bahramov adina Respublika stadionu, Baku:
Qarabag FK – Bayer Leverkusen 0-1 (0-0)
Qarabag FK: Andrey Lunev (85' Luka Gugeshashvili), Marko Vesovic (83' Maksim Medvedev), Bahlul Mustafazade, Kevin Medina, Elvin Cafarquliyev (89' Badavi Hüseynov), Yassine Benzia (83' Toral Bayramov), Marko Jankovic, Abdellah Zoubir, Leandro Andrade (83' Patrick Andrade), Júlio Romão, Juninho. Coach: Qurban Qurbanov.
Bayer Leverkusen: Matej Kovár, Álex Grimaldo, Jonathan Tah, Josip Stanisic, Piero Hincapié, Granit Xhaka, Robert Andrich, Nathan Tella (61' Jeremie Frimpong), Florian Wirtz (90+7' Adam Hlozek), Amine Adli (61' Jonas Hofmann), Victor Boniface. Coach: Xabi Alonso.
Goal: 90+4' Victor Boniface 0-1 (p).
Referee: Craig Pawson (ENG)   Attendance: 30,055.

09.11.23   Nya Ullevi, Göteborg: BK Häcken – Molde FK 1-3 (0-2)
BK Häcken: Peter Abrahamsson, Even Hovland, Simon Sandberg, Johan Hammar (46' Ishaq Abdulrazak), Tomas Totland, Mikkel Rygaard, Samuel Gustafson, Romeo Amané (62' Pontus Dahbo), Amor Layouni (62' Srdjan Hrstic), Edward Chilufya (87' John Dembe), Momodou Sonko. Coach: Per-Mathias Høgmo.
Molde FK: Oliver Petersen, Kristoffer Haugen (46' Eirik Hestad), Eirik Haugan, Casper Øyvann, Mathias Løvik, Magnus Eikrem (67' Veton Berisha), Martin Ellingsen, Kristian Eriksen, Markus Kaasa (89' Magnus Grødem), Emil Breivik, Fredrik Gulbrandsen (83' Eric Bugale Kitolano). Coach: Erling Moe.
Goals: 16' Fredrik Gulbrandsen 0-1, 24' Kristian Eriksen 0-2, 65' Srdjan Hrstic 1-2, 86' Kristian Eriksen 1-3.
Referee: Donald Robertson (SCO)   Attendance: 5,106.

30.11.23   Aker Stadion, Molde: Molde FK – Qarabag FK 2-2 (0-1)
Molde FK: Oliver Petersen, Kristoffer Haugen, Eirik Haugan, Casper Øyvann, Mathias Løvik, Magnus Eikrem, Martin Ellingsen, Kristian Eriksen, Magnus Grødem (58' Niklas Ødegård), Emil Breivik, Veton Berisha (69' Eric Bugale Kitolano). Coach: Erling Moe.
Qarabag FK: Andrey Lunev, Marko Vesovic, Bahlul Mustafazade, Kevin Medina (78' Badavi Hüseynov), Elvin Cafarquliyev, Yassine Benzia (77' Toral Bayramov), Marko Jankovic, Abdellah Zoubir, Patrick Andrade, Leandro Andrade (89' Hamidou Keyta), Juninho (60' Redon Xhixha). Coach: Qurban Qurbanov.
Goals: 12' Juninho 0-1, 82', 87' Kristian Eriksen 1-1, 2-1, 90+5' Bahlul Mustafazade 2-2.
Referee: Erik Lambrechts (BEL)   Attendance: 5,291.

30.11.23   Nya Ullevi, Göteborg: BK Häcken – Bayer Leverkusen 0-2 (0-1)
BK Häcken: Peter Abrahamsson, Even Hovland, Tomas Totland, Aiham Ousou, Mikkel Rygaard, Samuel Gustafson, Ishaq Abdulrazak, Romeo Amané (68' Pontus Dahbo), Amor Layouni, Edward Chilufya (68' Momodou Sonko), Srdjan Hrstic (81' Ali Youssef).
Coach: Per-Mathias Høgmo.
Bayer Leverkusen: Matej Kovár, Jonathan Tah (80' Odilon Kossounou), Edmond Tapsoba, Josip Stanisic, Piero Hincapié, Robert Andrich, Nathan Tella (63' Patrik Schick), Gustavo Puerta (88' Ayman Aourir), Adam Hlozek (80' Jonas Hofmann), Amine Adli, Victor Boniface (46' Noah Mbamba). Coach: Xabi Alonso.
Goals: 14' Victor Boniface 0-1, 74' Patrik Schick 0-2.
Referee: Julian Weinberger (AUT)   Attendance: 11,234.

14.12.23   BayArena, Leverkusen: Bayer Leverkusen – Molde FK 5-1 (3-0)
Bayer Leverkusen: Niklas Lomb, Jonathan Tah (59' Álex Grimaldo), Edmond Tapsoba (77' Ken Izekor), Josip Stanisic, Piero Hincapié, Jonas Hofmann (59' Amine Adli), Robert Andrich, Nathan Tella, Gustavo Puerta, Patrik Schick (59' Noah Mbamba), Adam Hlozek.
Coach: Xabi Alonso.
Molde FK: Oliver Petersen, Kristoffer Haugen, Eirik Haugan, Anders Hagelskjær, Mathias Løvik, Martin Ellingsen, Kristian Eriksen, Magnus Grødem (71' Niklas Ødegård), Eric Bugale Kitolano (85' Leon-Robin Juberg-Hovland), Markus Kaasa (46' Martin Bjørnbak), Fredrik Gulbrandsen (71' Gustav Nyheim). Coach: Erling Moe.
Goals: 6' Patrik Schick 1-0, 22' Edmond Tapsoba 2-0, 25' Martin Ellingsen 3-0 (og), 60,' 70' Adam Hlozek 4-0, 5-0, 75' Eric Bugale Kitolano 5-1.
Referee: Robert Jones (ENG)   Attendance: 28,504.

14.12.23   Tofiq Bahramov adina Respublika stadionu, Baku:
Qarabag FK – BK Häcken 2-1 (2-0)
Qarabag FK: Andrey Lunev, Marko Vesovic, Badavi Hüseynov, Bahlul Mustafazade, Elvin Cafarquliyev, Yassine Benzia (60' Matheus Silva), Marko Jankovic (89' Patrick Andrade), Abdellah Zoubir (89' Redon Xhixha), Leandro Andrade (85' Nariman Axundzade), Júlio Romão, Juninho (85' Toral Bayramov). Coach: Qurban Qurbanov.
BK Häcken: Peter Abrahamsson, Even Hovland, Simon Sandberg (63' Ishaq Abdulrazak), Tomas Totland, Aiham Ousou, Mikkel Rygaard (46' Pontus Dahbo), Samuel Gustafson, Ali Youssef (70' John Dembe), Romeo Amané, Edward Chilufya, Momodou Sonko (82' Ola Kamara). Coach: Per-Mathias Høgmo.
Goals: 1' Leandro Andrade 1-0, 45+4' Yassine Benzia 2-0, 90+4' Badavi Hüseynov 2-1 (og).
Referee: Juxhin Xhaja (ALB)   Attendance: 28,515.
Sent off: 56' Marko Vesovic.

KNOCKOUT ROUND PLAY-OFFS

15.02.24   De Kuip, Rotterdam: Feyenoord Rotterdam – AS Roma 1-1 (1-0)
Feyenoord Rotterdam: Timon Wellenreuther, Bart Nieuwkoop (78' Givairo Read), Dávid Hancko, Quilindschy Hartman, Thomas Beelen, Calvin Stengs (71' Luka Ivanusec), Mats Wieffer, Ramiz Zerrouki, Ayase Ueda (63' Santiago Giménez), Igor Paixão (79' Antoni Milambo), Yankuba Minteh (63' Ondrej Lingr). Coach: Arne Slot.
AS Roma: Mile Svilar, Leonardo Spinazzola, Diego Llorente, Rick Karsdorp (81' Zeki Çelik), Gianluca Mancini, Leandro Paredes, Lorenzo Pellegrini, Nicola Zalewski (63' Stephan El Shaarawy), Edoardo Bove (87' Bryan Cristante), Romelu Lukaku, Paulo Dybala (87' Tommaso Baldanzi). Coach: Daniele De Rossi.
Goals: 45+1' Igor Paixão 1-0, 67' Romelu Lukaku 1-1.
Referee: Radu Petrescu (ROM)   Attendance: 43,235.

15.02.24   Stadion Wankdorf, Bern: BSG Young Boys – Sporting CP 1-3 (1-2)
BSC Young Boys: David von Ballmoos, Mohamed Camara, Lewin Blum, Aurèle Amenda, Jaouen Hadjam, Sandro Lauper, Filip Ugrinic (46' Cheikh Niasse), Lukasz Lakomy (80' Darian Males), Cedric Itten (61' Silvère Ganvoula), Ebrima Colley (61' Joël Monteiro), Joel Mvuka (61' Meschack Elia). Coach: Raphaël Wicky.
Sporting CP: Antonio Adán, Ricardo Esgaio, Matheus Reis, Eduardo Quaresma, Gonçalo Inácio, Nuno Santos (85' Rafael Nel), Morten Hjulmand (60' Hidemasa Morita), Daniel Bragança (84' Koba Koindredi), Pedro Gonçalves "Pote" (74' Trincão), Marcus Edwards, Viktor Gyökeres (74' Geny Catamo). Coach: Rúben Amorim.
Goals: 31' Aurèle Amenda 0-1 (og), 41' Viktor Gyökeres 0-2 (p), 42' Filip Ugrinic 1-2, 48' Gonçalo Inácio 1-3.
Referee: Benoît Bastien (FRA)   Attendance: 31,500.
Sent off: 88' Mohamed Camara.

15.02.24   Rams Park, Istanbul: Galatasaray – AC Sparta Praha 3-2 (1-0)
Galatasaray: Fernando Muslera, Kaan Ayhan (55' Abdülkerim Bardakçi), Davinson Sánchez, Victor Nelsson, Kerem Demirbay (83' Wilfried Zaha), Lucas Torreira (90' Tanguy Ndombèlé), Berkan Kutlu, Dries Mertens (90+1' Carlos Vinícius), Mauro Icardi, Kerem Aktürkoglu (84' Tetê), Baris Yilmaz. Coach: Okan Buruk.
AC Sparta Praha: Peter Vindahl Jensen, Asger Sørensen, Ángelo Preciado (74' Tomás Wiesner), Martin Vitík, Qazim Laçi (74' Markus Solbakken), Kaan Kairinen, Veljko Birmancevic (84' Lukás Sadílek), Ladislav Krejcí (II), Matej Rynes, Adam Karabec (65' Lukás Haraslín), Jan Kuchta (84' Victor Olatunji). Coach: Brian Priske.
Goals: 19' Kerem Demirbay 1-0, 47' Ángelo Preciado 1-1, 61' Dries Mertens 2-1, 65' Jan Kuchta 2-2, 90+1' Mauro Icardi 3-2.
Referee: Alejandro Hernández Hernández (ESP)   Attendance: 46,583.
Sent off: 62' Victor Nelsson, 80' Matej Rynes.

15.02.24 Volksparkstadion, Hamburg (GER):
Shakhtar Donetsk – Olympique Marseille 2-2 (0-0)
Shakhtar Donetsk: Dmytro Riznyk, Mykola Matvienko, Valeriy Bondar, Yukhym Konoplya (76' Giorgi Gocholeishvili), Irakli Azarovi, Taras Stepanenko (72' Yegor Nazaryna), Oleksandr Zubkov, Artem Bondarenko (90+2' Lassina Traoré), Georgiy Sudakov, Danylo Sikan (77' Kevin), Eguinaldo. Coach: Marino Pusic.
Olympique Marseille: Pau López, Jonathan Clauss, Samuel Gigot, Leonardo Balerdi, Geoffrey Kondogbia, Amine Harit, Azzedine Ounahi, Quentin Merlin, Pierre-Emerick Aubameyang (90+2' Joaquín Correa), Faris Moumbagna (90+2' Bamo Meïté), Luis Henrique (72' Iliman Ndiaye). Coach: Gennaro Gattuso.
Goals: 64' Pierre-Emerick Aubameyang 0-1, 68' Mykola Matvienko 1-1, 90' Iliman Ndiaye 1-2, 90+3' Eguinaldo 2-2.
Referee: Erik Lambrechts (BEL)   Attendance: 28,790.

Due to the Russian invasion of Ukraine, Ukrainian teams were required to play their home matches at neutral venues until further notice.

15.02.24 Stadio Giuseppe Meazza, Milano: AC Milan – Stade Rennais 3-0 (1-0)
AC Milan: Mike Maignan, Simon Kjær (62' Malick Thiaw), Alessandro Florenzi (75' Filippo Terracciano), Theo Hernández, Matteo Gabbia, Ruben Loftus-Cheek (75' Ismaël Bennacer), Christian Pilisic (81' Yacine Adli), Tijjani Reijnders, Yunus Musah, Olivier Giroud, Rafael Leão (62 Noah Okafor). Coach: Stefano Pioli.
Stade Rennais: Steve Mandanda, Warmed Omari, Arthur Theate, Adrien Truffert (75' Mahamadou Nagida), Guela Doué (67' Alidu Seidu), Benjamin Bourigeaud, Baptista Santamaría, Azor Matusiwa (75' Ludovic Blas), Désiré Doué (76' Ibrahim Salah), Martin Terrier, Arnaud Kalimuendo (67' Amine Gouiri). Coach: Julien Stéphan.
Goals: 32', 47' Ruben Loftus-Cheek 1-0, 2-0, 53' Rafael Leão 3-0.
Referee: Nikola Dabanovic (MNE)   Attendance: 69,021.

15.02.24 Stade Bollaert-Delelis, Lens: RC Lens – SC Freiburg 0-0
RC Lens: Brice Samba, Massadio Haïdara (89' Abduqodir Khusanov), Ruben Aguilar (63' Jhoanner Chávez), Jonathan Gradit, Kevin Danso, Przemyslaw Frankowski, Neil El Aynaoui, David Pereira da Costa (72' Angelo Fulgini), Andy Diouf (63' Salis Abdul Samed), Florian Sotoca, Elye Wahi (72' Wesley Saïd). Coach: Franck Haise.
SC Freiburg: Noah Atubolu, Manuel Gulde, Lukas Kübler, Jordy Makengo, Nicolas Höfler, Maximilian Eggestein, Roland Sallai (86' Maximilian Philipp), Ritsu Dōan, Yannik Keitel, Merlin Röhl (79' Vincenzo Grifo), Lucas Höler (86' Michael Gregoritsch).
Coach: Christian Streich.
Referee: Bartosz Frankowski (POL)   Attendance: 38,194.

15.02.24 Estádio do Sport Lisboa e Benfica, Lisboa: SL Benfica – Toulouse FC 2-1 (0-0)
SL Benfica: Anatoliy Trubin, Nicolás Otamendi, António Silva, Álvaro Fernández (59' Alexander Bah), Ángel Di María, João Mário (59' David Neres), Fredrik Aursnes, Rafa Silva, Orkun Kökçü, João Neves, Arthur Cabral (87' Marcos Leonardo). Coach: Roger Schmidt.
Toulouse FC: Guillaume Restes, Mikkel Desler, Gabriel Suazo, Rasmus Nicolaisen, Logan Costa, Moussa Diarra (70' Christian Mawissa), Stijn Spierings (77' Cristian Cásseres Jr.), Vincent Sierro, Aron Dønnum (69' Shavy Warren Babicka), Thijs Dallinga (77' Frank Magri), Yann Gboho (86' Naatan Skyttä). Coach: Carles Martínez.
Goals: 68' Ángel Di María 1-0 (p), 75' Mikkel Desler 1-1, 90+8' Ángel Di María 2-1 (p).
Referee: Donatas Rumsas (LTU)   Attendance: 56,553.
Sent off: 90+6' Christian Mawissa.

15.02.24   Estádio Municipal de Braga, Braga: Sporting Braga – Qarabag FK 2-4 (1-1)
Sporting Braga: Matheus Magalhães, Paulo Oliveira, Cristián Borja, Víctor Gómez (76' Joe Mendes), Sikou Niakaté, João Moutinho, Vítor Carvalho (76' Cher Ndour), Rodrigo Zalazar (68' Pizzi), Simon Banza, Abel Ruiz, Álvaro Djaló (56' Roger Fernandes). Coach: Artur Jorge.
Qarabag FK: Andrey Lunev, Badavi Hüseynov, Bahlul Mustafazade, Matheus Silva, Elvin Cafarquliyev, Yassine Benzia (86' Hamidou Keyta), Marko Jankovic, Abdellah Zoubir (90+7' Redon Xhixha), Leandro Andrade (68' Toral Bayramov), Júlio Romão (86' Aleksey Isaev), Juninho (87' Nariman Axundzade). Coach: Qurban Qurbanov.
Goals: 21' Marko Jankovic 0-1 (p), 44' Simon Banza 1-1, 54' Abdellah Zoubir 1-2, 65' Juninho 1-3, 69' Abdellah Zoubir 1-4, 90+1' João Moutinho 2-4 (p).
Referee: Morten Krogh Hansen (DEN)   Attendance: 12,122.

22.02.24   Roazhon Park, Rennes: Stade Rennais – AC Milan 3-2 (1-1)
Stade Rennais: Steve Mandanda, Warmed Omari, Arthur Theate, Adrien Truffert, Guela Doué (57' Alidu Seidu), Benjamin Bourigeaud, Baptista Santamaría (57' Azor Matusiwa), Désiré Doué (71' Ludovic Blas), Martin Terrier (71' Ibrahim Salah), Amine Gouiri (84' Bertug Yildirim), Arnaud Kalimuendo. Coach: Julien Stéphan.
AC Milan: Mike Maignan, Simon Kjær, Alessandro Florenzi (84' Filippo Terracciano), Theo Hernández, Matteo Gabbia, Ismaël Bennacer (62' Ruben Loftus-Cheek), Christian Pulisic (62' Samuel Chukwueze), Tijjani Reijnders, Yunus Musah (80' Malick Thiaw), Luka Jovic, Rafael Leão (62' Noah Okafor). Coach: Stefano Pioli.
Goals: 11' Benjamin Bourigeaud 1-0, 22' Luka Jovic 1-1, 54' Benjamin Bourigeaud 2-1 (p), 58' Rafael Leão 2-2, 68' Benjamin Bourigeaud 3-2 (p).
Referee: João Pedro Pinheiro (POR)   Attendance: 28,320.

22.02.24   Europa-Park Stadion, Freiburg im Breisgau:
            SC Freiburg – RC Lens 3-2 (0-2,2-2) (AET)
SC Freiburg: Noah Atubolu, Manuel Gulde (86' Matthias Ginter), Lukas Kübler (101' Christian Günter), Kiliann Sildillia (46' Noah Weißhaupt), Jordy Makengo (46' Michael Gregoritsch), Nicolas Höfler, Maximilian Eggestein, Roland Sallai (106' Florent Muslija), Ritsu Dōan, Merlin Röhl (86' Vincenzo Grifo), Lucas Höler. Coach: Christian Streich.
RC Lens: Brice Samba, Jonathan Gradit (103' Andy Diouf), Facundo Medina, Jhoanner Chávez (80' Massadio Haïdara), Abduqodir Khusanov, Przemyslaw Frankowski (73' Ruben Aguilar), Neil El Aynaoui, Salis Abdul Samed (103' Wesley Saïd), David Pereira da Costa (81' Angelo Fulgini), Florian Sotoca, Elye Wahi (74' Morgan Guilavogui).
Coach: Franck Haise.
Goals: 28' David Pereira da Costa 0-1, 45+2' Elye Wahi 0-2, 67', 90+2' Roland Sallai 1-2, 2-2, 99' Michael Gregoritsch 3-2.
Referee: Rade Obrenovic (SVN)   Attendance: 33,911.
Sent off: 120' Lilian Nalis (Ass. Manager).

SC Freiburg won after extra time.

22.02.24 Stadium de Toulouse, Toulouse: Toulouse FC – SL Benfica 0-0
Toulouse FC: Guillaume Restes, Mikkel Desler (30' Warren Kamanzi), Gabriel Suazo (80' Shavy Warren Babicka), Rasmus Nicolaisen, Logan Costa, Moussa Diarra (23' Kévin Keben), Stijn Spierings, Vincent Sierro, Aron Dønnum, Thijs Dallinga, Yann Gboho (80' Frank Magri). Coach: Carles Martínez.
SL Benfica: Anatoliy Trubin, Nicolás Otamendi, Alexander Bah, Morato (46' Álvaro Fernández), António Silva, Ángel Di María (85' Orkun Kökçü), João Mário, Rafa Silva, João Neves, David Neres (68' Fredrik Aursnes), Casper Tengstedt (46' Arthur Cabral). Coach: Roger Schmidt.
Referee: Maurizio Mariani (ITA)   Attendance: 31,810.

22.02.24 Tofiq Bahramov adina Respublika stadionu, Baku:
Qarabag FK – Sporting Braga 2-3 (0-0,0-2) (AET)
Qarabag FK: Andrey Lunev, Marko Vesovic (108' Nariman Axundzade), Badavi Hüseynov, Bahlul Mustafazade, Elvin Cafarquliyev, Yassine Benzia (60' Toral Bayramov), Marko Jankovic, Abdellah Zoubir (117' Redon Xhixha), Leandro Andrade (74' Matheus Silva), Júlio Romão (108' Patrick Andrade), Juninho (74' Hamidou Keyta). Coach: Qurban Qurbanov.
Sporting Braga: Matheus Magalhães, Paulo Oliveira (90' Serdar Saatçi), Cristián Borja (68' Rony Lopes), Víctor Gómez (63' Bruma), Sikou Niakaté, João Moutinho (68' Vítor Carvalho), Pizzi (46' Álvaro Djaló), Rodrigo Zalazar (54' Cher Ndour), Simon Banza, Abel Ruiz, Roger Fernandes. Coach: Artur Jorge.
Goals: 70' Roger Fernandes 0-1, 83' Álvaro Djaló 0-2, 102' Matheus Silva 1-2, 115' Simon Banza 1-3 (p), 120+2' Nariman Axundzade 2-3.
Referee: Georgi Kabakov (BUL)   Attendance: 31,200.
Sent off: 57' Elvin Cafarquliyev.

Qarabag FK won after extra time.

22.02.24 Stadio Olimpico, Roma: AS Roma – Feyenoord Rotterdam 1-1 (1-1,1-1) (AET)
AS Roma: Mile Svilar, Leonardo Spinazzola (105' Angeliño), Diego Llorente (85' Evan Ndicka), Rick Karsdorp (67' Zeki Çelik), Gianluca Mancini, Leandro Paredes, Bryan Cristante, Lorenzo Pellegrini (71' Houssem Aouar), Stephan El Shaarawy (90' Nicola Zalewski), Romelu Lukaku, Paulo Dybala (102' Tommaso Baldanzi). Coach: Daniele De Rossi.
Feyenoord Rotterdam: Timon Wellenreuther, Bart Nieuwkoop (71' Yankuba Minteh), Dávid Hancko, Lutsharel Geertruida, Quilindschy Hartman, Thomas Beelen, Calvin Stengs (59' Ramiz Zerrouki), Quinten Timber, Mats Wieffer (120' Alireza Jahanbakhsh), Santiago Giménez (78' Ayase Ueda), Igor Paixão (59' Luka Ivanusec). Coach: Arne Slot.
Goals: 5' Santiago Giménez 0-1, 16' Lorenzo Pellegrini 1-1.
Referee: Jesús Gil Manzano (ESP)   Attendance: 67,293.

AS Roma won on penalties (4:2).

Penalties: Paredes 1-0), Ueda 1-1, Lukaku (missed), Hancko (missed), Cristante 2-1, Jahanbakhsh (missed), Aouar 3-1, Hartman 3-2, Zalewski 4-2.

22.02.24   Estádio José Alvalade, Lisboa: Sporting CP – BSC Young Boys 1-1 (1-0)
Sporting CP: Antonio Adán, Ricardo Esgaio (85' Iván Fresneda), Matheus Reis, Eduardo Quaresma (80' Luís Neto), Gonçalo Inácio (46' Nuno Santos), Ousmane Diomande, Morten Hjulmand (63' Koba Koindredi), Daniel Bragança, Marcus Edwards, Viktor Gyökeres, Trincão (63' Pedro Gonçalves "Pote"). Coach: Rúben Amorim.
BSC Young Boys: David von Ballmoos, Fabian Lustenberger, Saidy Janko (61' Lewin Blum), Aurèle Amenda, Jaouen Hadjam (61' Noah Persson), Sandro Lauper (78' Lukasz Lakomy), Cheikh Niasse, Darian Males, Cedric Itten (61' Silvère Ganvoula), Meschack Elia (67' Joel Mvuka), Joël Monteiro. Coach: Raphaël Wicky.
Goals: 13' Viktor Gyökeres 1-0, 84' Silvère Ganvoula 1-1 (p).
Referee: Ivan Kruzliak (SVK)   Attendance: 29,393.

Viktor Gyökeres missed a penalty kick (57').

22.02.24   epet ARENA, Praha: AC Sparta Praha – Galatasaray 4-1 (1-1)
AC Sparta Praha: Peter Vindahl Jensen, Asger Sørensen, Filip Panák, Tomás Wiesner (72' Jaroslav Zelený), Ángelo Preciado, Martin Vitík, Qazim Laçi, Lukás Haraslín (87' Lukás Sadílek), Kaan Kairinen, Jan Kuchta, Victor Olatunji (66' Indrit Tuci). Coach: Brian Priske.
Galatasaray: Fernando Muslera, Kaan Ayhan, Abdülkerim Bardakçi, Davinson Sánchez, Kerem Demirbay (75' Tetê), Lucas Torreira (83' Carlos Vinícius), Berkan Kutlu, Dries Mertens (62' Sérgio Oliveira), Mauro Icardi, Kerem Aktürkoglu (62' Wilfried Zaha), Baris Yilmaz. Coach: Okan Buruk.
Goals: 8' Ángelo Preciado 1-0, 16' Abdülkerim Bardakçi 1-1, 74' Indrit Tuci 2-1, 80' Lukás Haraslín 3-1, 90+6' Jan Kuchta 4-1.
Referee: Anthony Taylor (ENG)   Attendance: 18,205.
Sent off: 68' Kaan Ayhan, 90' Okan Buruk (coach).

22.02.24   Orange Vélodrome, Marseille: Olympique Marseille – Shakhtar Donetsk 3-1 (1-1)
Olympique Marseille: Pau López, Jonathan Clauss, Chancel Mbemba, Samuel Gigot, Geoffrey Kondogbia, Amine Harit (90+4' Emran Soglo), Azzedine Ounahi (64' Jordan Veretout), Bamo Meïté, Quentin Merlin, Pierre-Emerick Aubameyang (85' Iliman Ndiaye), Faris Moumbagna (64' Ismaïla Sarr). Coach: Jean-Louis Gasset.
Shakhtar Donetsk: Dmytro Riznyk, Yaroslav Rakitskyi, Mykola Matvienko, Yukhym Konoplya, Irakli Azarovi (84' Pedrinho), Taras Stepanenko (83' Newerton), Oleksandr Zubkov (82' Marian Shved), Artem Bondarenko (84' Dmytro Kryskiv), Georgiy Sudakov, Danylo Sikan (82' Lassina Traoré), Eguinaldo. Coach: Marino Pusic.
Goals: 12' Georgiy Sudakov 0-1 (p), 23' Pierre-Emerick Aubameyang 1-1, 74' Ismaïla Sarr 2-1, 81' Geoffrey Kondogbia 3-1.
Referee: Tobias Stieler (GER)   Attendance: 63,182.

ROUND OF 16

06.03.24   Estádio José Alvalade, Lisboa: Sporting CP – Atalanta Bergamo 1-1 (1-1)
Sporting CP: Franco Israel, Sebastián Coates, Matheus Reis, Eduardo Quaresma, Ousmane Diomande (46' Jerry St. Juste), Hidemasa Morita (84' Daniel Bragança), Koba Koindredi (46' Morten Hjulmand), Paulinho (68' Ricardo Esgaio), Marcus Edwards (46' Viktor Gyökeres), Trincão, Geny Catamo. Coach: Rúben Amorim.
Atalanta Bergamo: Juan Musso, Berat Djimsiti, Sead Kolasinac, Isak Hien (46' Giorgio Scalvini), Matteo Ruggeri, Emil Holm (90' Davide Zappacosta), Marten de Roon, Aleksey Miranchuk (72' Teun Koopmeiners), Éderson, Gianluca Scamacca (82' El Bilal Touré), Ademola Lookman (72' Charles De Ketelaere). Coach: Gian Piero Gasperini.
Goals: 17' Paulinho 1-0, 39' Gianluca Scamacca 1-1.
Referee: Daniel Siebert (GER)   Attendance: 28,528.

07.03.24   epet ARENA, Praha: AC Sparta Praha – Liverpool FC 1-5 (0-3)
AC Sparta Praha: Peter Vindahl Jensen, Jaroslav Zelený, Asger Sørensen (43' Matej Rynes), Ángelo Preciado, Martin Vitík, Lukás Haraslín (65' Qazim Laçi), Kaan Kairinen (74' Adam Karabec), Veljko Birmancevic (74' Indrit Tuci), Ladislav Krejcí, Markus Solbakken, Jan Kuchta (74' Victor Olatunji). Coach: Brian Priske.
Liverpool FC: Caoimhín Kelleher, Andy Robertson, Joe Gomez (46' Conor Bradley), Ibrahima Konaté (50' Virgil van Dijk), Jarell Quansah, Wataru Endo, Alexis Mac Allister (65' Bobby Clark), Harvey Elliott, Cody Gakpo, Luis Díaz (74' Mohamed Salah), Darwin Núñez (51' Dominik Szoboszlai). Coach: Jürgen Klopp.
Goals: 6' Alexis Mac Allister 0-1 (p), 25', 45+3' Darwin Núñez 0-2, 0-3, 46' Conor Bradley 1-3 (og), 53' Luis Díaz 1-4, 90+4' Dominik Szoboszlai 1-5.
Referee: José María Sánchez Martínez (ESP)   Attendance: 18,349.

07.03.24   Stadio Olimpico, Roma: AS Roma – Brighton & Hove Albion 4-0 (2-0)
AS Roma: Mile Svilar, Leonardo Spinazzola (82' Diego Llorente), Zeki Çelik, Gianluca Mancini, Evan Ndicka, Leandro Paredes (72' Edoardo Bove), Bryan Cristante, Lorenzo Pellegrini, Stephan El Shaarawy (88' Nicola Zalewski), Romelu Lukaku (88' Sardar Azmoun), Paulo Dybala (72' Tommaso Baldanzi). Coach: Daniele De Rossi.
Brighton & Hove Albion: Jason Steele, Lewis Dunk, Igor Julio (75' Pervis Estupiñán), Tariq Lamptey, Jan Paul van Hecke, Pascal Groß, Billy Gilmour (81' Carlos Baleba), Facundo Buonanotte (75' Joël Veltman), Danny Welbeck (81' Evan Ferguson), Julio Enciso (46' Ansu Fati), Simon Adingra. Coach: Roberto De Zerbi.
Goals: 13' Paulo Dybala 1-0, 43' Romelu Lukaku 2-0, 64' Gianluca Mancini 3-0,
68' Bryan Cristante 4-0.
Referee: François Letexier (FRA)   Attendance: 64,877.

07.03.24   Tofiq Bahramov adina Respublika stadionu, Baku:
Qarabağ FK – Bayer Leverkusen 2-2 (2-0)
Qarabağ FK: Andrey Lunev, Marko Vesovic, Badavi Hüseynov, Bahlul Mustafazade, Toral Bayramov, Yassine Benzia (90+1' Aleksey Isaev), Marko Jankovic, Abdellah Zoubir (90+1' Redon Xhixha), Patrick Andrade, Leandro Andrade (80' Matheus Silva), Juninho (84' Nariman Axundzade). Coach: Qurban Qurbanov.
Bayer Leverkusen: Matej Kovár, Álex Grimaldo, Jonathan Tah, Edmond Tapsoba, Odilon Koussounou (80' Josip Stanisic), Robert Andrich, Nathan Tella (46' Jeremie Frimpong), Exequiel Palacios (58' Granit Xhaka), Borja Iglesias (80' Patrik Schick), Adam Hlozek (58' Florian Wirtz), Amine Adli. Coach: Xabi Alonso.
Goals: 26' Yassine Benzia 1-0, 45+2' Juninho 2-0, 70' Florian Wirtz 2-1, 90+2' Patrik Schick 2-2.
Referee: Benoît Bastien (FRA)   Attendance: 30,423.

07.03.24   Orange Vélodrome, Marseille: Olympique Marseille – Villarreal CF 4-0 (3-0)
Olympique Marseille: Pau López, Jonathan Clauss (60' Bamo Meïté), Chancel Mbemba, Leonardo Balerdi, Geoffrey Kondogbia, Jordan Veretout (73' Luis Henrique), Amine Harit, Quentin Merlin (85' Emran Soglo), Pierre-Emerick Aubameyang (85' Faris Moumbagna), Ismaïla Sarr, Iliman Ndiaye (60' Azzedine Ounahi). Coach: Jean-Louis Gasset.
Villarreal CF: Pepe Reina, Aïssa Mandi (46' Alberto Moreno), Eric Bailly, Jorge Cuenca, Yerson Mosquera, Francis Coquelin (69' Étienne Capoue), Santi Comesaña (46' Dani Parejo), Álex Baena (46' Alexander Sørloth), Gerard Moreno (65' Kiko Femenía), Gonçalo Guedes, Ilias Akhomach. Coach: Marcelino.
Goals: 23' Jordan Veretout 1-0, 28' Yerson Mosquera 2-0 (og), 42', 59' Pierre-Emerick Aubameyang 3-0 (p), 4-0.
Referee: Serdar Gözübüyük (HOL)   Attendance: 53,396.
Sent off: 62' Alberto Moreno.

07.03.24   Estádio do Sport Lisboa e Benfica, Lisboa:
SL Benfica – Glasgow Rangers FC 2-2 (1-2)
SL Benfica: Anatoliy Trubin, Nicolás Otamendi, Alexander Bah (84' Álvaro Fernández), António Silva, Ángel Di María, Fredrik Aursnes, Rafa Silva, Florentino, João Neves, Arthur Cabral (65' Marcos Leonardo), David Neres (84' Tiago Gouveia). Coach: Roger Schmidt.
Glasgow Rangers FC: Jack Butland, James Tavernier, Connor Goldson, John Souttar, Dujon Sterling (77' Cole McKinnon), Ridvan Yilmaz, John Lundstram, Mohammed Diomandé (84' Nicolas Raskin), Tom Lawrence (77' Ryan Jack), Cyriel Dessers (76' Kemar Roofe), Fábio Silva (90+1' Ross McCausland). Coach: Philippe Clement.
Goals: 7' Tom Lawrence 0-1, 45+2' Ángel Di María 1-1 (p), 45+5 Dujon Sterling 1-2, 67' Connor Goldson 2-2 (og).
Referee: Tobias Stieler (GER)   Attendance: 48,579.

07.03.24 Europa-Park Stadion, Freiburg im Breisgau:
SC Freiburg – West Ham United 1-0 (0-0)
SC Freiburg: Noah Atubolu, Manuel Gulde, Matthias Ginter, Christian Günter, Kiliann Sildillia (82' Lukas Kübler), Nicolas Höfler, Vincenzo Grifo (70' Noah Weißhaupt), Maximilian Eggestein, Roland Sallai (88' Merlin Röhl), Ritsu Dōan (82' Florent Muslija), Lucas Höler (70' Michael Gregoritsch). Coach: Christian Streich.
West Ham United: Lukasz Fabianski, Vladimír Coufal, Kurt Zouma, Emerson (68' Aaron Cresswell), Konstantinos Mavropanos, James Ward-Prowse (81' Kalvin Phillips), Tomás Soucek, Lucas Paquetá (90+1' Michail Antonio), Edson Álvarez, Mohammed Kudus, Jarrod Bowen. Coach: David Moyes.
Goal: 81' Michael Gregoritsch 1-0.
Referee: Alejandro Hernández Hernández (ESP)   Attendance: 34,700.

07.03.24 Stadio Giuseppe Meazza, Milano: AC Milan – Slavia Praha 4-2 (3-1)
AC Milan: Mike Maignan, Simon Kjær, Alessandro Florenzi (46' Davide Calabria), Theo Hernández, Matteo Gabbia (46' Fikayo Tomori), Ruben Loftus-Cheek (66' Luka Jovic), Christian Pulisic, Yacine Adli, Tijjani Reijnders (80' Ismaël Bennacer), Olivier Giroud (80' Noah Okafor), Rafael Leão. Coach: Stefano Pioli.
Slavia Praha: Jindrich Stanek, Oscar Dorley, Tomás Vlcek, Ondrej Zmrzlý (83' Jan Boril), David Zima, El Hadji Diouf, Tomás Holes, Lukás Masopust (87' Conrad Wallem), Lukás Provod (83' Václav Jurecka), David Doudera (86' Michal Tomic), Mojmír Chytil (61' Ivan Schranz). Coach: Jindrich Trpisovský.
Goals: 34' Olivier Giroud 1-0, 36' David Doudera 1-1, 44' Tijjani Reijnders 2-1, 45+1' Ruben Loftus-Cheek 3-1, 65' Ivan Schranz 3-2, 85' Christian Pulisic 4-2.
Referee: Halil Umut Meler (TUR)   Attendance: 59,325.
Sent off: 26' El Hadji Diouf.

14.03.24 Estadio de la Cerámica, Villarreal: Villarreal CF – Olympique Marseille 3-1 (1-0)
Villarreal CF: Filip Jørgensen, Kiko Femenía (84' José Luis Morales), Aïssa Mandi, Eric Bailly (50' Yerson Mosquera), Jorge Cuenca, Étienne Capoue (84' Santi Comesaña), Dani Parejo, Francis Coquelin (66' Álex Baena), Gerard Moreno, Alexander Sørloth, Gonçalo Guedes. Coach: Marcelino.
Olympique Marseille: Pau López, Jonathan Clauss, Chancel Mbemba, Leonardo Balerdi, Geoffrey Kondogbia, Jordan Veretout, Azzedine Ounahi (79' Luis Henrique), Bamo Meïté, Quentin Merlin, Ismaïla Sarr (46' Pierre-Emerick Aubameyang), Iliman Ndiaye (46' Amine Harit). Coach: Jean-Louis Gasset.
Goals: 32' Étienne Capoue 1-0, 54' Alexander Sørloth 2-0, 86' Yerson Mosquera 3-0, 90+4' Jonathan Clauss 3-1.
Referee: István Kovács (ROM)   Attendance: 15,378.

14.03.24 Ibrox Stadium, Glasgow: Glasgow Rangers FC – SL Benfica 0-1 (0-0)
Glasgow Rangers FC: Jack Butland, James Tavernier, Connor Goldson, John Souttar, Ridvan Yilmaz, John Lundstram, Scott Wright (73' Rabbi Matondo), Mohammed Diomandé (85' Nicolas Raskin), Tom Lawrence (73' Todd Cantwell), Cyriel Dessers (77' Kemar Roofe), Fábio Silva. Coach: Philippe Clement.
SL Benfica: Anatoliy Trubin, Nicolás Otamendi, Alexander Bah, António Silva, Ángel Di María (90' João Mário), Fredrik Aursnes, Rafa Silva (90+2' Tiago Gouveia), Florentino, João Neves, David Neres (65' Orkun Kökçü), Marcos Leonardo (46' Casper Tengstedt).
Coach: Roger Schmidt.
Goal: 66' Rafa Silva 0-1.
Referee: Ivan Kruzliak (SVK)   Attendance: 49,943.

14.03.24   London Stadium, London: West Ham United – SC Freiburg 5-0 (2-0)
West Ham United: Lukasz Fabianski, Aaron Cresswell, Vladimír Coufal, Kurt Zouma, Konstantinos Mavropanos, Tomás Soucek, Lucas Paquetá (62' James Ward-Prowse), Edson Álvarez (86' Kalvin Phillips), Mohammed Kudus (86' Danny Ings), Michail Antonio (79' Ben Johnson), Jarrod Bowen (86' George Earthy). Coach: David Moyes.
SC Freiburg: Noah Atubolu, Manuel Gulde (62' Lukas Kübler), Matthias Ginter, Christian Günter, Kiliann Sildillia (68' Merlin Röhl), Nicolas Höfler (62' Florent Muslija), Vincenzo Grifo (46' Michael Gregoritsch), Maximilian Eggestein, Roland Sallai, Ritsu Dōan, Lucas Höler (68' Maximilian Philipp). Coach: Christian Streich.
Goals: 9' Lucas Paquetá 1-0, 32' Jarrod Bowen 2-0, 52' Aaron Cresswell 3-0, 77', 85' Mohammed Kudus 4-0, 5-0.
Referee: Marco Guida (ITA)   Attendance: 51,014.

14.03.24   Fortuna Arena, Praha: Slavia Praha – AC Milan 1-3 (0-3)
Slavia Praha: Jindrich Stanek, Oscar Dorley, Tomás Vlcek (46' Michal Tomic), Igoh Ogbu, Ondrej Zmrzlý, David Zima, Tomás Holes, Lukás Provod (82' Matej Jurásek), David Doudera (82' Ivan Schranz), Conrad Wallem (70' Christos Zafeiris), Mojmír Chytil (59' Václav Jurecka). Coach: Jindrich Trpisovský.
AC Milan: Mike Maignan (21' Marco Sportiello), Davide Calabria (46' Pierre Kalulu), Fikayo Tomori (46' Malick Thiaw), Theo Hernández, Matteo Gabbia, Ruben Loftus-Cheek (76' Tijjani Reijnders), Christian Pulisic (63' Samuel Chukwueze), Yacine Adli, Yunus Musah, Olivier Giroud, Rafael Leão. Coach: Stefano Pioli.
Goals: 33 Christian Pulisic 0-1, 36' Ruben Loftus-Cheek 0-2, 45+6' Rafael Leão 0-3, 84' Matej Jurásek 1-3.
Referee: Glenn Nyberg (SWE)   Attendance: 19,334.
Sent off: 20' Tomás Holes.

14.03.24   Anfield, Liverpool: Liverpool FC – AC Sparta Praha 6-1 (4-1)
Liverpool FC: Caoimhín Kelleher, Andy Robertson, Joe Gomez (46' Kostas Tsimikas), Jarell Quansah (66' Virgil van Dijk), Conor Bradley, Wataru Endo (46' James McConnell), Dominik Szoboszlai, Bobby Clark (73' Mateusz Musialowski), Mohamed Salah, Cody Gakpo, Darwin Núñez (46' Harvey Elliott). Coach: Jürgen Klopp.
AC Sparta Praha: Peter Vindahl Jensen, Jaroslav Zelený, Ángelo Preciado, Martin Vitík, Qazim Laçi (58' Lukás Sadílek), Kaan Kairinen, Veljko Birmancevic (66' Indrit Tuci), Ladislav Krejcí, Matej Rynes (46' Filip Panák), Markus Solbakken (74' Patrik Vydra), Jan Kuchta (58' Lukás Haraslín). Coach: Brian Priske.
Goals: 7' Darwin Núñez 1-0, 8' Bobby Clark 2-0, 10' Mohamed Salah 3-0, 14' Cody Gakpo 4-0, 42' Veljko Birmancevic 4-1, 48' Dominik Szoboszlai 5-1, 55' Cody Gakpo 6-1.
Referee: Artur Soares Dias (POR)   Attendance: 59,581.

14.03.24   American Express Stadium, Falmer: Brighton & Hove Albion – AS Roma 1-0 (1-0)
Brighton & Hove Albion: Bart Verbruggen, Lewis Dunk, Pervis Estupiñán (61' Igor Julio), Tariq Lamptey (61' Evan Ferguson), Jan Paul van Hecke, Adam Lallana (53' Facundo Buonanotte), Pascal Groß, Billy Gilmour (85' Carlos Baleba), Danny Welbeck, Julio Enciso (53' Ansu Fati), Simon Adingra. Coach: Roberto De Zerbi.
AS Roma: Mile Svilar, Leonardo Spinazzola, Zeki Çelik, Gianluca Mancini, Evan Ndicka, Bryan Cristante, Lorenzo Pellegrini, Nicola Zalewski (73' Diego Llorente), Tommaso Baldanzi (83' Houssem Aouar), Edoardo Bove, Sardar Azmoun (90+1' João Costa).
Coach: Daniele De Rossi.
Goal: 37' Danny Welbeck 1-0.
Referee: Felix Zwayer (GER)   Attendance: 30,380.

14.03.24   Gewiss Stadium, Bergamo: Atalanta Bergamo – Sporting CP 2-1 (0-1)
Atalanta Bergamo: Juan Musso, Berat Djimsiti, Sead Kolasinac, Mitchel Bakker (46' Davide Zappacosta), Isak Hien, Emil Holm, Marten de Roon, Aleksey Miranchuk (76' Mario Pasalic), Éderson (64' Teun Koopmeiners), Gianluca Scamacca (64' Charles De Ketelaere), Ademola Lookman (85' El Bilal Touré). Coach: Gian Piero Gasperini.
Sporting CP: Franco Israel, Ricardo Esgaio (61' Geny Catamo), Matheus Reis (62' Nuno Santos), Jerry St. Juste (75' Eduardo Quaresma), Gonçalo Inácio, Ousmane Diomande, Morten Hjulmand, Pedro Gonçalves "Pote" (36' Daniel Bragança), Marcus Edwards, Viktor Gyökeres, Trincão (75' Paulinho). Coach: Rúben Amorim.
Goals: 33' Pedro Gonçalves "Pote" 0-1, 46' Ademola Lookman 1-1, 59' Gianluca Scamacca 2-1.
Referee: Sandro Schärer (SUI)   Attendance: 14,649.

14.03.24   BayArena, Leverkusen: Bayer Leverkusen – Qarabag FK 3-2 (0-0)
Bayer Leverkusen: Matej Kovár, Jeremie Frimpong, Edmond Tapsoba, Odilon Koussounou (79' Josip Stanisic), Piero Hincapié (60' Álex Grimaldo), Granit Xhaka, Jonas Hofmann (28' Exequiel Palacios), Robert Andrich, Florian Wirtz, Borja Iglesias (59' Patrik Schick), Amine Adli. Coach: Xabi Alonso.
Qarabag FK: Andrey Lunev, Marko Vesovic (87' Kevin Medina), Badavi Hüseynov, Bahlul Mustafazade, Elvin Cafarquliyev, Yassine Benzia (66' Toral Bayramov), Marko Jankovic, Abdellah Zoubir (86' Patrick Andrade), Leandro Andrade (78' Matheus Silva), Júlio Romão, Juninho (78' Nariman Axundzade). Coach: Qurban Qurbanov.
Goals: 58' Abdellah Zoubir 0-1, 67' Juninho 0-2, 72' Jeremie Frimpong 1-2, 90+3', 90+7' Patrik Schick 2-2, 3-2.
Referee: Anthony Taylor (ENG)   Attendance: 30,210.
Sent off: 62' Elvin Cafarquliyev.

QUARTER-FINALS

11.04.24   Stadio Giuseppe Meazza, Milano: AC Milan – AS Roma 0-1 (0-1)
AC Milan: Mike Maignan, Davide Calabria, Theo Hernández, Matteo Gabbia, Malick Thiaw, Ruben Loftus-Cheek, Ismaël Bennacer (59' Yacine Adli), Christian Pulisic (78' Samuel Chukwueze), Tijjani Reijnders, Olivier Giroud, Rafael Leão (78' Noah Okafor).
Coach: Stefano Pioli.
AS Roma: Mile Svilar, Chris Smalling, Leonardo Spinazzola, Zeki Çelik, Gianluca Mancini, Leandro Paredes (89' Edoardo Bove), Bryan Cristante, Lorenzo Pellegrini (89' Houssem Aouar), Stephan El Shaarawy, Romelu Lukaku (90+2' Diego Llorente), Paulo Dybala (81' Tammy Abraham). Coach: Daniele De Rossi.
Goal: 17' Gianluca Mancini 0-1.
Referee: Clément Turpin (FRA)   Attendance: 75,023.

11.04.24   Anfield, Liverpool: Liverpool FC – Atalanta Bergamo 0-3 (0-1)
Liverpool FC: Caoimhín Kelleher, Virgil van Dijk, Joe Gomez, Kostas Tsimikas (46' Andy Robertson), Ibrahima Konaté, Wataru Endo (76' Diogo Jota), Curtis Jones (46' Dominik Szoboszlai), Alexis Mac Allister, Harvey Elliott (46' Mohamed Salah), Cody Gakpo, Darwin Núñez (60' Luis Díaz). Coach: Jürgen Klopp.
Atalanta Bergamo: Juan Musso, Berat Djimsiti, Davide Zappacosta, Isak Hien, Matteo Ruggeri, Marten de Roon, Mario Pasalic, Teun Koopmeiners, Éderson, Charles De Ketelaere (89' Aleksey Miranchuk), Gianluca Scamacca. Coach: Gian Piero Gasperini.
Goals: 38', 60' Gianluca Scamacca 0-1, 0-2, 83' Mario Pasalic 0-3.
Referee: Halil Umut Meler (TUR)   Attendance: 59,004.

11.04.24   BayArena, Leverkusen: Bayer Leverkusen – West Ham United 2-0 (0-0)
Bayer Leverkusen: Matej Kovár, Álex Grimaldo, Jonathan Tah, Jeremie Frimpong (67' Nathan Tella), Edmond Tapsoba, Josip Stanisic (66' Piero Hincapié), Granit Xhaka, Exequiel Palacios, Florian Wirtz, Patrik Schick (76' Victor Boniface), Amine Adli (76' Jonas Hofmann). Coach: Xabi Alonso.
West Ham United: Lukasz Fabianski, Aaron Cresswell, Vladimír Coufal, Kurt Zouma, Emerson, Konstantinos Mavropanos (86' Nayef Aguerd), James Ward-Prowse, Tomás Soucek, Lucas Paquetá, Mohammed Kudus (86' Ben Johnson), Michail Antonio. Coach: David Moyes.
Goals: 83' Jonas Hofmann 1-0, 90+1' Victor Boniface 2-0.
Referee: Artur Soares Dias (POR)   Attendance: 30,210.

11.04.24   Estádio do Sport Lisboa e Benfica, Lisboa:
           SL Benfica – Olympique Marseille 2-1 (1-0)
SL Benfica: Anatoliy Trubin, Nicolás Otamendi, Alexander Bah, António Silva, Ángel Di María, Fredrik Aursnes, Rafa Silva, Florentino, João Neves, David Neres (71' João Mário), Casper Tengstedt (71' Marcos Leonardo). Coach: Roger Schmidt.
Olympique Marseille: Pau López, Chancel Mbemba (67' Emran Soglo), Samuel Gigot, Leonardo Balerdi, Geoffrey Kondogbia, Jordan Veretout, Amine Harit, Quentin Merlin (45+2' Iliman Ndiaye), Pierre-Emerick Aubameyang, Faris Moumbagna (53' Azzedine Ounahi), Luis Henrique. Coach: Jean-Louis Gasset.
Goals: 16' Rafa Silva 1-0, 52' Ángel Di María 2-0, 67' Pierre-Emerick Aubameyang 2-1.
Referee: Michael Oliver (ENG)   Attendance: 53,845.

18.04.24   Stadio Olimpico, Roma: AS Roma – AC Milan 2-1 (2-0)
AS Roma: Mile Svilar, Chris Smalling, Leonardo Spinazzola, Zeki Çelik, Gianluca Mancini, Leandro Paredes, Lorenzo Pellegrini (82' Angeliño), Edoardo Bove (82' Renato Sanches), Stephan El Shaarawy, Romelu Lukaku (29' Tammy Abraham), Paulo Dybala (43' Diego Llorente). Coach: Daniele De Rossi.
AC Milan: Mike Maignan, Davide Calabria (46' Tijjani Reijnders), Fikayo Tomori, Theo Hernández, Matteo Gabbia, Ruben Loftus-Cheek (46' Samuel Chukwueze), Ismaël Bennacer (40' Luka Jovic), Christian Pulisic (69' Noah Okafor), Yunus Musah (69' Alessandro Florenzi), Olivier Giroud, Rafael Leão. Coach: Stefano Pioli.
Goals: 12' Gianluca Mancini 1-0, 22' Paulo Dybala 2-0, 85' Matteo Gabbia 2-1.
Referee: Szymon Marciniak (POL)   Attendance: 66,025.
Sent off: 31' Zeki Çelik.

18.04.24 Gewiss Stadium, Bergamo: Atalanta Bergamo – Liverpool FC 0-1 (0-1)
Atalanta Bergamo: Juan Musso, Berat Djimsiti, Davide Zappacosta, Sead Kolasinac, Isak Hien, Matteo Ruggeri, Marten de Roon, Aleksey Miranchuk (79' Ademola Lookman), Teun Koopmeiners, Éderson (75' Mario Pasalic), Gianluca Scamacca (75' Charles De Ketelaere).
Coach: Gian Piero Gasperini.
Liverpool FC: Alisson Becker, Virgil van Dijk, Andy Robertson (79' Jayden Danns), Trent Alexander-Arnold (72' Joe Gomez), Ibrahima Konaté, Curtis Jones, Dominik Szoboszlai (67' Harvey Elliott), Alexis Mac Allister, Mohamed Salah (67' Darwin Núñez), Cody Gakpo, Luis Díaz (66' Diogo Jota). Coach: Jürgen Klopp.
Goal: 7' Mohamed Salah 0-1 (p).
Referee: François Letexier (FRA)   Attendance: 14,994.

18.04.24 London Stadium, London: West Ham United – Bayer Leverkusen 1-1 (1-0)
West Ham United: Lukasz Fabianski, Aaron Cresswell, Vladimír Coufal (84' Ben Johnson), Kurt Zouma, Nayef Aguerd (45+2' Angelo Ogbonna), James Ward-Prowse, Tomás Soucek, Edson Álvarez (84' Maxwel Cornet), Mohammed Kudus, Michail Antonio, Jarrod Bowen.
Coach: David Moyes.
Bayer Leverkusen: Matej Kovár, Álex Grimaldo (68' Amine Adli), Jonathan Tah, Josip Stanisic, Odilon Kossounou (29' Edmond Tapsoba), Piero Hincapié, Granit Xhaka, Nathan Tella (46' Jeremie Frimpong), Exequiel Palacios, Florian Wirtz (87' Robert Andrich), Patrik Schick (46' Victor Boniface). Coach: Xabi Alonso.
Goals: 13' Michail Antonio 1-0, 89' Jeremie Frimpong 1-1.
Referee: José María Sánchez Martínez (ESP)   Attendance: 62,473.
Sent off: 30' Billy McKinlay (ass. coach), 30' Sebastián Parilla (ass. coach).

18.04.24 Orange Vélodrome, Marseille:
            Olympique Marseille – SL Benfica 1-0 (0-0,1-0) (AET)
Olympique Marseille: Pau López, Chancel Mbemba (46' Michael Murillo), Samuel Gigot (100' Raimane Daou), Leonardo Balerdi, Geoffrey Kondogbia, Jordan Veretout, Amine Harit (110' Gaël Lafont), Azzedine Ounahi (59' Luis Henrique), Emran Soglo (58' Faris Moumbagna), Pierre-Emerick Aubameyang, Iliman Ndiaye (75' Joaquín Correa).
Coach: Jean-Louis Gasset.
SL Benfica: Anatoliy Trubin, Nicolás Otamendi, Alexander Bah, António Silva, Ángel Di María, Fredrik Aursnes, Rafa Silva (102' Arthur Cabral), Florentino, João Neves, David Neres (61' João Mário), Casper Tengstedt (61' Orkun Kökçü). Coach: Roger Schmidt.
Goal: 79' Faris Moumbagna 1-0.
Referee: Felix Zwayer (GER)   Attendance: 59,645.

Olympique Marseille won on penalties (4:2).

Penalties: Di María (missed), Correa 0-1, Kökçü 1-1, Kondogbia 1-2, Otamendi 2-2, Balerdi 2-3, António Silva (missed), Luis Henrique 2-4.

SEMI-FINALS

02.05.24 Orange Vélodrome, Marseille: Olympique Marseille – Atalanta Bergamo 1-1 (1-1)
Olympique Marseille: Pau López, Jonathan Clauss (65' Quentin Merlin), Chancel Mbemba, Michael Murillo (72' Azzedine Ounahi), Leonardo Balerdi, Geoffrey Kondogbia, Jordan Veretout, Amine Harit (72' Iliman Ndiaye), Pierre-Emerick Aubameyang, Ismaïli Sarr (65' Faris Moumbagna), Luis Henrique. Coach: Jean-Louis Gasset.
Atalanta Bergamo: Juan Musso, Berat Djimsiti, Davide Zappacosta (84' Hans Hateboer), Sead Kolasinac (17' Mario Pasalic), Matteo Ruggeri, Giorgio Scalvini, Marten de Roon, Teun Koopmeiners, Éderson, Charles De Ketelaere (84' Aleksey Miranchuk), Gianluca Scamacca (59' Ademola Lookman). Coach: Gian Piero Gasperini.
Goals: 11' Gianluca Scamacca 0-1, 20' Chancel Mbemba 1-1.
Referee: Daniel Siebert (GER)   Attendance: 64,475.

02.05.24 Stadio Olimpico, Roma: AS Roma – Bayer Leverkusen 0-2 (0-1)
AS Roma: Mile Svilar, Chris Smalling, Leonardo Spinazzola, Rick Karsdorp (62' Angeliño), Gianluca Mancini, Leandro Paredes (79' Tommaso Baldanzi), Bryan Cristante, Lorenzo Pellegrini, Stephan El Shaarawy, Romelu Lukaku (79' Sardar Azmoun), Paulo Dybala (90+1' Tammy Abraham). Coach: Daniele De Rossi.
Bayer Leverkusen: Matej Kovár, Álex Grimaldo (90+3' Odilon Kossounou), Jonathan Tah, Jeremie Frimpong (88' Exequiel Palacios), Edmond Tapsoba, Josip Stanisic, Piero Hincapié, Granit Xhaka, Robert Andrich, Florian Wirtz (77' Jonas Hofmann), Amine Adli (77' Nathan Tella). Coach: Xabi Alonso.
Goals: 28' Florian Wirtz 0-1, 73' Robert Andrich 0-2.
Referee: François Letexier (FRA)   Attendance: 64,073.

09.05.24 Gewiss Stadium, Bergamo: Atalanta Bergamo – Olympique Marseille 3-0 (1-0)
Atalanta Bergamo: Juan Musso, Berat Djimsiti, Davide Zappacosta (76' Hans Hateboer), Isak Hien, Matteo Ruggeri, Marten de Roon, Teun Koopmeiners, Éderson (56' Giorgio Scalvini), Charles De Ketelaere (61' Mario Pasalic), Gianluca Scamacca (56' Aleksey Miranchuk), Ademola Lookman (77' El Bilal Touré). Coach: Gian Piero Gasperini.
Olympique Marseille: Pau López, Jonathan Clauss (72' Faris Moumbagna), Chancel Mbemba (59' Azzedine Ounahi), Samuel Gigot, Leonardo Balerdi, Geoffrey Kondogbia, Jordan Veretout, Amine Harit (84' Joaquín Correa), Quentin Merlin (72' Luis Henrique), Pierre-Emerick Aubameyang, Iliman Ndiaye (59' Ismaïli Sarr). Coach: Jean-Louis Gasset.
Goals: 30' Ademola Lookman 1-0, 52' Matteo Ruggeri 2-0, 90+4' El Bilal Touré 3-0.
Referee: Jesús Gil Manzano (ESP)   Attendance: 14,994.

09.05.24 BayArena, Leverkusen: Bayer Leverkusen – AS Roma 2-2 (0-1)
Bayer Leverkusen: Matej Kovár, Álex Grimaldo (90' Odilon Kossounou), Jonathan Tah, Jeremie Frimpong (90' Josip Stanisic), Edmond Tapsoba, Piero Hincapié, Granit Xhaka, Jonas Hofmann (81' Florian Wirtz), Exequiel Palacios, Adam Hlozek (74' Patrik Schick), Amine Adli. Coach: Xabi Alonso.
AS Roma: Mile Svilar, Leonardo Spinazzola (21' Nicola Zalewski), Angeliño (81' Chris Smalling), Gianluca Mancini, Evan Ndicka, Leandro Paredes, Bryan Cristante, Lorenzo Pellegrini (81' Tammy Abraham), Stephan El Shaarawy, Romelu Lukaku, Sardar Azmoun (72' Edoardo Bove). Coach: Daniele De Rossi.
Goals: 43', 66' Leandro Paredes 0-1 (p), 0-2 (p), 82' Gianluca Mancini 1-2 (og), 90+7' Josip Stanisic 2-2.
Referee: Danny Makkelie (HOL)   Attendance: 30,210.

FINAL

22.05.24   Aviva Stadium, Dublin: Atalanta Bergamo – Bayer Leverkusen 3-0 (2-0)
Atalanta Bergamo: Juan Musso, Berat Djimsiti, Isak Hien, Sead Kolasinac (46' Giorgio Scalvini), Davide Zappacosta (84' Hans Hateboer), Éderson, Teun Koopmeiners, Matteo Ruggeri (90+1' Rafael Tolói), Charles De Ketelaere (57' Mario Pasalic), Gianluca Scamacca (84' El Bilal Touré), Ademola Lookman. Coach: Gian Piero Gasperini.
Bayer Leverkusen: Matej Kovár, Josip Stanisic (46' Victor Boniface), Jonathan Tah, Edmond Tapsoba, Jeremie Frimpong (81' Nathan Tella), Granit Xhaka, Exequiel Palacios (68' Robert Andrich), Piero Hincapié, Florian Wirtz (81' Patrik Schick), Álex Grimaldo (68' Adam Hlozek), Amine Adli. Coach: Xabi Alonso.
Goals: 12', 26' 75' Ademola Lookman 1-0, 2-0, 3-0.
Referee: István Kovács (ROM)   Attendance: 47,135.

FAIRS CUP/UEFA CUP/EUROPA LEAGUE WINNERS

Fairs Cup (1958-1971), UEFA-Cup (1972-2009), Europa League (2010-2024).

1958	FC Barcelona	Spain
1960	FC Barcelona	Spain
1961	AS Roma	Italy
1962	Valencia CF	Spain
1963	Valencia CF	Spain
1964	Real Zaragoza	Spain
1965	Ferencvárosi TC	Hungary
1966	FC Barcelona	Spain
1967	Dinamo Zagreb	Croatia
1968	Leeds United	England
1969	Newcastle United	England
1970	Arsenal FC	England
1971	Leeds United	England
1972	Tottenham Hotspur	England
1973	Liverpool FC	England
1974	Feyenoord	Netherlands
1975	Borussia Mönchengladbach	Germany
1976	Liverpool FC	England
1977	Juventus	Italy
1978	PSV	Netherlands
1979	Borussia Mönchengladbach	Germany
1980	Eintracht Frankfurt	Germany
1981	Ipswich Town	England
1982	IFK Göteborg	Sweden
1983	RSC Anderlecht	Belgium
1984	Tottenham Hotspur	England
1985	Real Madrid	Spain
1986	Real Madrid	Spain
1987	IFK Göteborg	Sweden
1988	Bayer Leverkusen	Germany
1989	SSC Napoli	Italy
1990	Juventus	Italy
1991	Internazionale	Italy
1992	AFC Ajax	Netherlands
1993	Juventus	Italy
1994	Internazionale	Italy
1995	Parma AC	Italy
1996	Bayern München	Germany
1997	FC Schalke 04	Germany
1998	Internazionale	Italy
1999	Parma AC	Italy
2000	Galatasaray	Turkey
2001	Liverpool FC	England
2002	Feyenoord	Netherlands
2003	FC Porto	Portugal
2004	Valencia CF	Spain
2005	CSKA Moskva	Russia
2006	Sevilla FC	Spain
2007	Sevilla FC	Spain
2008	Zenith St. Petersburg	Russia

Year	Club	Country
2009	Shakhtar Donetsk	Ukraine
2010	Atlético Madrid	Spain
2011	FC Porto	Portugal
2012	Atlético Madrid	Spain
2013	Chelsea FC	England
2014	Sevilla FC	Spain
2015	Sevilla FC	Spain
2016	Sevilla FC	Spain
2017	Manchester United	England
2018	Atlético Madrid	Spain
2019	Chelsea FC	England
2020	Sevilla FC	Spain
2021	Villarreal CF	Spain
2022	Eintracht Frankfurt	Germany
2023	Sevilla FC	Spain
2024	Atalanta	Italy

ALL-TIME WINNERS – COUNTRY

Spain	20
England	13
Italy	11
Germany	7
Netherlands	4
Sweden	2
Portugal	2
Russia	2
Hungary	1
Croatia	1
Belgium	1
Turkey	1
Ukraine	1

ALL-TIME WINNERS – CLUB

Club	Wins
Sevilla FC	7
Atlético Madrid	3
FC Barcelona	3
Juventus	3
Internazionale	3
Liverpool FC	3
Valencia CF	3
Leeds United	2
Borussia Mönchengladbach	2
Eintracht Frankfurt	2
IFK Göteborg	2
Tottenham Hotspur	2
Real Madrid	2
Parma AC	2
Feyenoord	2
FC Porto	2
AS Roma	1
Real Zaragoza	1
Ferencvárosi TC	1
Dinamo Zagreb	1
Newcastle United	1
Arsenal FC	1
PSV	1
Ipswich Town	1
RSC Anderlecht	1
Bayer Leverkusen	1
SSC Napoli	1
AFC Ajax	1
Bayern München	1
FC Schalke 04	1
Galatasaray	1
CSKA Moskva	1
Zenith St. Petersburg	1
Shakhtar Donetsk	1
Chelsea FC	2
Manchester United	1
Villarreal CF	1
Atalanta	1